international
AIR POWER
REVIEW

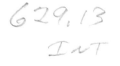
AIRtime Publishing
United States of America • United Kingdom

international AIR POWER REVIEW

Published quarterly by AIRtime Publishing Inc.
US office: 120 East Avenue, Norwalk, CT 06851
UK office: CAB International Centre, Nosworthy Way,
Wallingford, Oxfordshire, OX10 8DE

© 2001, 2002 AIRtime Publishing Inc.
Fw 190 cutaway © Aerospace Publishing Ltd
F-14 cutaway © Mike Badrocke/Aviagraphica
Photos and other illustrations are the copyright
of their respective owners

Softbound Edition ISSN 1473-9917 / ISBN 1-880588-36-6
Hardcover Deluxe Casebound Edition ISBN 1-880588-37-4

Publisher
Mel Williams

Editor
David Donald
e-mail: airpower@btinternet.com

Assistant Editors
John Heathcott, Daniel J. March

Sub Editor
Karen Leverington

US Desk
Tom Kaminski

Russia/CIS Desk
Piotr Butowski, Zaur Eylanbekov
e-mail: zaur@airtimepublishing.com

Europe and Rest of World Desk
John Fricker, Jon Lake

Correspondents
Argentina: Jorge Felix Nuñez Padin
Australia: Nigel Pittaway
Belgium: Dirk Lamarque
Brazil: Claudio Lucchesi
Bulgaria: Alexander Mladenov
Canada: Jeff Rankin-Lowe
France: Henri-Pierre Grolleau
India: Pushpindar Singh
Israel: Shlomo Aloni
Italy: Luigino Caliaro
Japan: Yoshitomo Aoki
Netherlands: Tieme Festner
Romania: Danut Vlad
Spain: Salvador Mafé Huertas
USA: Rick Burgess, Brad Elward, Peter Mersky, Bill Sweetman

Artists
Chris Davey, Zaur Eylanbekov, Mark Rolfe, John Weal, Iain Wyllie

Designer
Zaur Eylanbekov

Controller
Linda DeAngelis

Origination by Universal Graphics, Singapore
Printed in Singapore by KHL Printing

International Air Power Review is published quarterly in two editions (Softbound and Deluxe Casebound) and is available by subscription or as single volumes. Please see details opposite.

Acknowledgments
We wish to thank the following for their kind help with the preparation of this issue:

Pascal Jover
The authors of the *Senior Bowl* article would like to thank Glenn Chapman, Jerry Miller, Jim Walborn, Bill Fox and the many others who asked to remain behind the scenes.
The author of the *IAR-93/Orao* article wishes to thank to Dipl.Eng. Simion Tǎtaru from INCAS, Alex Trandafir, Vladimir Jovanovic from Belgrade, and Marko Malec from Kranj, Slovenia, for their kind support.

The following credits should have appeared in Volume 2
B-58 Hustler cutaway © Aerospace Publishing Ltd, Tu-160 cutaway © Mike Badrocke, Tu-160 line drawings © Aviatsiya i Vremya
Artists: Piotr Butowski, Zaur Eylanbekov, Keith Fretwell, Oleg Podkladov, Mark Rolfe, John Weal, Vasiliy Zolotov
Acknowledgments: Gordon Bartley/BAE SYSTEMS, Peter J. Cooper, Tony Eccles/BAE SYSTEMS, John Heathcott, Eric Hehs/LMTAS, Aleksandr Larionov, Jonathan Lee/BAE SYSTEMS, Peter R. March, Terry Panopalis, Derek Percival/MRF, Dylan Roberts/BAE SYSTEMS, Julia Sevin/BAE SYSTEMS, Richard L. Ward

The editors welcome photographs for possible publication but can accept no responsibility for loss or damage to unsolicited material.

Subscriptions & Back Volumes

Readers in the USA, Canada, Central/South America and the rest of the world (except UK and Europe) please write to:
AIRtime Publishing, P.O. Box 5074, Westport, CT 06881, USA
Tel (203) 838-7979 • Fax (203) 838-7344
Toll free 1 800 359-3003
e-mail: airpower@airtimepublishing.com

Readers in the UK & Europe please write to:
AIRtime Publishing, RAFBFE, P.O. Box 1940,
RAF Fairford, Gloucestershire GL7 4NA, England
Tel +44 (0)1285 713456 • Fax +44 (0)1285 713999

One-year subscription rates (4 quarterly volumes),
inclusive of shipping & handling/postage and packing:
Softbound Edition
USA $59.95, UK £48, Europe £56/EUR 89, Canada Cdn $93,
Rest of World US $79 (surface) or US $99 (air)
Deluxe Casebound Edition
USA $79.95, UK £68, Europe £76/EUR 121, Canada Cdn $122,
Rest of World US $99 (surface) or US $119 (air)

Two-year subscription rates (8 quarterly volumes),
inclusive of shipping & handling/postage and packing:
Softbound Edition
USA $112, UK £92, Europe £105/EUR 168, Canada Cdn $174,
Rest of World US $148 (surface) or US $188 (air)
Deluxe Casebound Edition
USA $149, UK £130, Europe £146/EUR 233, Canada Cdn $229,
Rest of World US $187 (surface) or US $227 (air)

Single-volume/Back Volume Rates by Mail:
Softbound Edition
US $16, UK £12, Europe £12/EUR 19, Cdn $25 (plus s&h/p&p)
Deluxe Casebound Edition
US $20, UK £17, Europe £17/EUR 27, Cdn $31 (plus s&h/p&p)

All prices are subject to change without notice.
Canadian residents please add GST. Connecticut residents please add sales tax.

Shipping and handling (postage and packing) rates
for back volume/non-subscription orders are as follows:

	USA	UK	Europe	Canada	ROW (surf.)	ROW (air)
1 item	$4.50	£3	£4/EUR 6.40	Cdn $7.50	US $8	US $16
2 items	$6.50	£5	£6/EUR 9.60	Cdn $11	US $12	US $27
3 items	$8.50	£7	£8/EUR 12.80	Cdn $14	US $16	US $36
4 items	$10	£9	£10/EUR 16	Cdn $16.50	US $19	US $46
5 items	$11.50	£11	£12/EUR 19.20	Cdn $19	US $23	US $52
6 or more	$13	£12	£13/EUR 20.80	Cdn $21.50	US $25	US $59

Volume Three
Winter 2001/2002

CONTENTS

MAJOR FEATURES PLANNED FOR VOLUME FOUR
Focus Aircraft: Dassault Rafale, **Warplane Classic:** Consolidated B-24 Liberator: Part 1, **News Report:** Operation Enduring Freedom, **Air Combat:** Gunships in Vietnam: Part 1, **Variant File:** Beriev Be-12, **Air Power Analysis:** Air Combat Command **Special Feature:** 160th SOAR – US Army Special Forces, **Pioneers and Prototypes:** Myasishchev M-50 'Bounder'

PROGRAMME UPDATE

Lockheed Martin F-35 JSF

On 26 October 2001 the US Under Secretary of Defense for Acquisition, Technology and Logistics, Edward C. 'Pete' Aldridge Jr, ended months of speculation by announcing that the Lockheed Martin Joint Strike Fighter submission had been adjudged the winner of the competition – potentially the largest defence programme ever undertaken – and had been awarded a contract to proceed to the System Development and Demonstration (SDD) phase. The contract, administered by the Naval Air Systems Command, is worth $18,981,928,201 to the Lockheed Martin team, which includes Northrop Grumman (20 per cent) and BAE Systems (14 per cent). Development work is scheduled to run until April 2012.

At the same time, engine manufacturer Pratt & Whitney was awarded a $4,803,460,088 contract to develop the F135 engine (previously designated F119-611). Rolls-Royce has an 11 per cent stake in the F135 programme. A General Electric/Rolls-Royce team has also been given the go-ahead to develop the F136 engine (a version of the F120 developed for the F-22/F-23) as an alternative to the F135 for production aircraft.

Despite Boeing's perceived advantages in areas such as project management, the

outcome of the decision was influenced considerably by the performance of the Concept Demonstrator Aircraft. Boeing admits that its X-32 was out-performed in many areas by Lockheed Martin's X-35, especially in the critical STOVL tests. Following the decision, Boeing and Lockheed Martin opened informal discussions which may result in the loser being offered some work on the project.

Instead of adopting the in-sequence F-24 designation, the Lockheed Martin JSF is now known as the F-35. Versions will be the F-35A CTOL for the USAF, F-35B CV for the US Navy and F-35C STOVL for the USMC. The UK remains undecided as to which version it will procure. The two full-partner nations have a stated requirement for 3,002 aircraft. Canada,

Lockheed Martin's X-35 was a clear winner in the air, especially in the STOVL version. The X-35B's lift fan nearly doubles the thrust available for hovering, allowing it to hover well within the power limits and in hot-and-high conditions. However, to get the clutch/driveshaft assembly to work reliably was a herculean engineering task. On the other hand, Boeing's X-32B, with its simple direct-lift system, was operating at its thrust limits, with no growth potential.

Denmark, Italy, the Netherlands and Norway have joined the programme as co-operative partners, while Israel, Singapore and Turkey have also joined as FMS participants.

Under the SDD contract 14 flying aircraft will be built, comprising five CTOL, four CV and five STOVL machines. All will make their first flights from Lockheed Martin's Fort Worth,

PROJECT DEVELOPMENT

International

Boeing 767 tanker agreement
Development of a tanker/transport version of the Boeing 767-200R was launched in mid-year from an Italian air force (AMI) requirement for four aircraft of this type, plus options for two more. Boeing and Alenia reached agreement on the $720 million joint development and production programme, for planned deliveries from 2004. Apart from three-point hose and drogue air refuelling systems, the AMI 767s would have provision for an alternative refuelling boom, to operate with its 30 leased ex-USAF F100-PW-220E-powered Block 15ADF F-16As and four Block 10OCU F-16Bs, plus another four F-16Bs for spares. These will replace Italy's leased Tornado ADVs from 2003.

BVRAAM progress
Three of the partner countries in MBDA's UK-led beyond-visual-range air-to-air missile (BVRAAM) programme, including France and Sweden, have signed an MoU confirming their joint commitment to this project. Italian agreement followed in October, leaving Germany and Spain expected to

follow suit by the year-end, together with signature of a UK Smart Procurement development contract for BVRAAM with MBDA.

Portugal joins NH-90 group
Portugal have formalised their entry as an industrial partner in NATO's multi-national NH-90 transport/ASW/SAR helicopter programme, joining France, Germany, Italy and the Netherlands. Budget cuts delays have also been accompanied by reductions in original overall requirements for 726 NH-90s, to 595 (464 TTH tactical transport versions, and 131 navalised NFHs).

India

LCA flight-test progress
First-phase testing of India's Light Combat Aircraft (LCA) was successfully completed by Wing Cmdr Raghunath Nambiar on 2 June, with the 12th flight of the TD-1 technology demonstrator prototype at the National Flight Test Centre (NFTC) in Bangalore. Wing Cmdr Nambiar had flown the last six sorties, following the first six from 4 January this year by Wing Cmdr Rajiv Kothiyal. In these "flawless" sorties, totalling about

Following the first flight of the Super Lynx 300, the programme received a boost with the finalisation of a £26.9 million order by the Thai navy for two new Super Lynx 300s on 1 August. The deal includes integrated logistic support and services, with AgustaWestland agreeing to accept counter-trade of Thai products totalling half the programme price.

seven hours, the LCA was restricted in short-endurance flights to a maximum 610 km/h (329 kt) or Mach 0.71 at altitudes up to 8000m (26,247 ft).

More internal fuel will be carried for the next series of 35-40 flights, to achieve the first supersonic sorties, higher angles of attack, and fly-by-wire deployment of leading-edge slats and air brakes. First flight of the second prototype LCA TD-2 was due in December, and of TD-3, with the indigenous Kaveri turbofan instead of the current GE F404, by the year-end. This is now not expected until 2004, however.

Some 1,200 flying hours or about 1,500 flights will be required for IAF acceptance. Safe release of drop tanks and missile trials will follow, for planned initial IAF service entry and operational clearance in 2005-2006. Reduction was planned of the current $17 million estimated LCA unit cost to $15 million, while increasing its 70% indigenous content to 80%.

United Kingdom

FSTA competition hots up
Contestants for the UK MoD's £13 billion Future Strategic Tanker

The first low-rate initial production (LRIP) F-22A Raptor will be delivered to the 325th Fighter Wing at Tyndall AFB, Florida in early 2003.

Texas, plant, but flight testing will be divided between the AFFTC at Edwards AFB and the Navy's test centre at Patuxent River (seven aircraft at each facility). In addition, there will be eight non-flying airframes built, comprising a static and fatigue test airframe for each variant, a radar cross section model and a carrier suitability CV airframe which will be used for drop tests to assess the integrity of the airframe and undercarriage under repeated heavy landings.

A preliminary design review is scheduled for March 2003, followed by the critical design review a year later. The first SDD aircraft, an F-35A, is scheduled to fly for the first time in October 2005. Low-rate initial production (LRIP) approval is scheduled for 2006, with an expected five lots of aircraft totalling 465 in the LRIP batch, after which full-rate production will commence. Delivery to the USAF and USMC is scheduled for 2008.

Lockheed Martin F-22 Raptor

On 15 August the Defense Acquisition Board agreed that the Lockheed Martin F-22A had met all its exit criteria and approved low-rate initial production (LRIP) for the fighter. The approval authorises Lockheed Martin to begin production of 10 F-22As using FY01 funds, and another 13 with FY02 money. LRIP will run through fiscal 2005, when production increases to 30 aircraft. The programme will shift into full-rate production in 2006. The DAB's deci-

sion will require the Department of Defense and the USAF obtain a budget increase in excess of the programme's current $37.6 billion cap. The board also reduced the number of F-22As that would be procured from 331 to 295, however the production costs will rise to $45 billion. The research, development and testing of the new fighter has already cost approximately $18 billion, meaning the total cost for the programme is about $63 billion. Assembly of the first operational F-22 Raptor, serial 01-4018 began at Lockheed Martin's Fort Worth, Texas, facility in March 2001 and eight of the fighters have already been used in the test programme.

Boeing-Sikorsky RAH-66

The RAH-66 Comanche Engineering Manufacturing Development (EMD) phase is accelerating and the Boeing Sikorsky team has begun designing and fabricating tools for the production of 13 additional helicopters. Aircraft three, the first EMD aircraft, will be delivered to Sikorsky's West Palm Beach,

Florida, flight test facility in early 2004 and it will be followed by aircraft 4, 5, 6 and 8 through 14. The number 7 and 15 aircraft will go directly to the Army for Initial Operating and Test and Evaluation (IOTE). The final aircraft will be delivered in early 2005. Two RAH-66 prototypes, undergoing flight tests in Florida, have completed more than 400 hours of flight to date and have met all test goals. The number 2 prototype is being equipped with an EMD core Mission Equipment Package (MEP) and will return to flight test status in December 2001. The Night Vision Pilotage System (NVPS) will be tested beginning in the second quarter of 2002, followed by the Target Acquisition System (TAS) in the fourth quarter of 2002. The Number 1 prototype flew for the first time with uprated LHTEC T800-LHT-801 engines on 1 June 2001. Rated at 1,563 shp (1165.5 kW), the engines provide a 17 per cent power increase over earlier T800-LHT-800 engines. During the 1.2-hour test flight demonstrated a variety of manoeuvres and airspeeds up to 120 kt (222 km/h). This performance level assures full capability for the Army's Objective Force reconnaissance and attack system over 95 percent of the world's potential battlefields. LHTEC (Light Helicopter Turbine Engine Company) is a consortium composed of Rolls-Royce and Honeywell. Besides the uprated powerplant, the aircraft is currently being equipped with an alternative pylon design, radar dome and the latest rotor and tail configuration that features anhedral blade tips.

Aircraft (FSTA) programme, to acquire 10-15 replacements for the RAF's current 20 air-refuelling BAe VC10s and nine Lockheed TriStars, were narrowed to only two consortia in July. As the MoD's largest Private Finance Initiative (PFI) programme proposed to date, FSTA will provide RAF air-to-air refuelling (AAR) services, operated from RAF Brize Norton with service pilots, over 30 years from 2007-09.

Four short-listed consortia were originally invited to provide fully-costed submissions, from six late-1999 outline proposals. These comprised Air Reach, led by Rolls-Royce; BAE Systems; Eurotanker, including FR Aviation and Thales; and Serco's Strategic Support Management (SSM) group.

In mid-January, however, Air Reach and Eurotanker joined forces with other major European companies, to form the AirTanker group. This now includes the European Aeronautic, Defence and Space Company (EADS), Rolls-Royce, Cobham's FR Aviation, Halliburton Brown & Root Services and Thales Defence. AirTanker's submission is based on the Airbus A330-200 with Rolls-Royce Trent turbofans, for its FSTA proposals.

Last summer, BAE Systems joined the Serco-led SSM group in negotiations with Boeing to form the Tanker and Transport Service

Company (TTSC), for a combined FSTA proposal. This is based on using current British Airways Boeing 767-300s, and linked with Boeing's March establishment of a B.767 Tanker Programmes Office within its Military Aerospace Sector, to market air-refuelling applications.

A final decision on an FSTA PFI programme go-ahead is planned in mid-2002, followed by contracts in 2003 to the preferred bidder, for 2007 service entry.

Super Lynx 300 flies

Flight development of the Rolls-Royce/Honeywell CTS800-4N-powered Super Lynx 300, which also features an all-new integrated glass cockpit, started on 12 June at AgustaWestland's Yeovil airfield. Its 33% extra power will facilitate tropical operations, starting in Malaysia, with its launch order for six, for delivery from 2003. More export sales are already being sought, including a potential contract for 30 in Oman.

United States

MH-60R completes first flight

The first test article MH-60R aircraft made its initial flight at Sikorsky's Stratford, Connecticut, test facility

on 19 July 2001. During the 1.7-hour test flight basic flight acceptance test procedures, including engine power checks, auto rotation and vibration checks, were performed.

Following Navy acceptance the aircraft underwent additional testing in Stratford prior to its first stop at the Naval Air Warfare Center Aircraft Division (NAWCAD) at NAS Patuxent River, Maryland, where flight test instrumentation is being installed. Once this task has been completed the aircraft will be flown to Lockheed Martin's systems integration facility in Owego, New York where the new mission

General Atomic's Altus I remotely operated aircraft (ROA) recently carried out signals intelligence (SIGINT) and surveillance missions at Camp Pendleton, California, in support of the US Navy and Marine Corps. The ROA carried a new payload comprising an ESM component and digital data link designed to identify signals on the ground such as threat emitters.

The prototype MH-60R was remanufactured by Sikorsky from an SH-60B, receiving a number of structural improvements including a strengthened floor. The SH-60B tailcone and dynamic components were removed and underwent standard depot level maintenance (SDLM). Additionally, a new Lockheed Martin-developed glass cockpit is incorporated. Originally known as the SH-60R, the designation MH-60R was approved on 25 May 2001 to better reflect the MH-60R's multi-mission role.

Airbus A400M

Progress was made in June with Europe's potential $20 billion seven-nation programme for the four-turboprop A400M tactical-strategic airlift transport at the Paris air show, where defence ministers from six of the countries signed a Memorandum of Understanding for development and acquisition of an initial 193 aircraft. A400M commitments, for which Turboprop International's new TP400 was selected last November as powerplant, were then reaffirmed from Belgium (7), France (50), Germany (73), Luxembourg (1), Spain (27), Turkey (26, then budget-cut to 20, and finally 10), and Britain (25). Italy originally planned to buy 16 A400Ms, but failed to gain parliamentary approval ·in June. Having bought 22 Lockheed Martin C-130Js and 12 Alenia/LM C-27Js, it then withdrew its A400M requirement and planned 7.5% programme participation. Portugal rejoined, however, to order three A400Ms, increasing planned launch orders to 196 aircraft. Agreement was also reached on maximum A400 purchase price through commercial contracts, with firm mid/late-2007 initial deliveries. Initial A400M contracts were expected to be signed on 16 November with Airbus Military Company, through Europe's OCCAR (Organisation Conjoint de Co-operation en Matiere d'Armament) procurement agency as contracting authority.

Further A400M procurement cuts were possible, however, notably from Germany, which originally earmarked some DM10 billion ($4.36 billion) to acquire 73 aircraft. But Bonn estimates of DM205.8 million ($89.7 million) programme unit costs for this number would require some DM15.6 billion, possibly reducing German A400M procurement to around 55 aircraft. Even higher cost estimates, comprising "about FFr50 billion ($6.5 billion)" for AdA's 50 A400Ms, or $130 million programme unit cost, were officially quoted last summer in France.

Global Express ASTOR

The first Global Express aircraft equipped with aerodynamic modifications associated with the airborne stand-off radar (ASTOR) made its initial flight from Bombardier's Flight Test Center (BFTC) at Mid-Continent Airport in Wichita, Kansas on 3 August 2001. Registered C-FBGX, the Global Express development aircraft (c/n 9001) was fitted with modifications that include a canoe-shaped radome under the forward fuselage that will house the ASTOR's dual-mode radar antenna, a SATCOM antenna radome on the upper fuselage, a "bullet-fairing extension" on the vertical stabiliser and delta fins under the aft fuselage. During the 3-hour, 18-minute flight the development aircraft conducted a series of tests at altitudes up to 25,000 ft (7620 m) and speeds up to 250 kt (288 mph; 463 km/h) that were designed to verify the configuration. The flight trials will continue into second quarter 2002.

Under development by Raytheon Systems for the UK Ministry of Defence, ASTOR is a long-range airborne surveillance system, which will be carried on board Bombardier Global Express aircraft. The first production aircraft will be delivered in 2002 to Raytheon's Greenville, Texas, facility where the airframe modifications and systems integration will be carried out. Four subsequent aircraft will be modified and equipped by Raytheon Systems Limited in the UK. The system is scheduled to enter service with the Royal Air Force in 2005.

---

systems, including sonar, radar, Electronic Support Measures (ESM), Integrated Self Defense Suite and Displays will be installed and tested. Two prototype MH-60Rs have been undergoing testing with NAWCAD's Rotary Wing Aircraft Test Squadron. Sikorsky and Lockheed are currently under contract to remanufacture nine SH-60B aircraft to MH-60R configuration. These include four test articles and five low-rate initial production aircraft that will be delivered in 2001 and 2002 respectively. The Navy recently restructured the MH-60R program and rather than remanufacturing SH-60B and SH-60F airframes, as had earlier been planned, the remainder of the 243 aircraft will be newly built.

The prototype of Boeing's CH-47F heavy-lift helicopter, the sixth Chinook type, completed its first flight at the company's Philadelphia manufacturing facility on 25 June 2001. The 5-minute flight, which followed a series of comprehensive system checks, involved hover and basic manoeuvres was used to validate aircraft handling qualities. The CH-47F modernisation programme will update the US Army's CH-47D Chinook fleet through remanufacturing and vibration reduction and the installation of more powerful Honeywell T55-GA-14A-714 engines. Improved avionics will include an integrated digital mission management systems and a digital map.

X-47A Pegasus UAV roll out

Northrop Grumman has completed production of the company-funded X-47A Pegasus unmanned air vehicle (UAV) and rolled out the vehicle at Mojave, California on 31 July 2001. The UAV will be used to demonstrate aerodynamic qualities suitable for autonomous operation from an aircraft-carrier. The UAV was built by Scaled Composites at Mojave Airport but will be moved to the company's facility in El Segundo, California, where a series of systems checkout tests will be performed in preparation for its first flight, expected by the end of 2001. The results of the Pegasus demonstration effort will support the contractor's work on a naval unmanned combat air vehicle (UCAV-N).

Hawkeye 2000 system flies

The E-2C Hawkeye 2000 production system test aircraft flew for the first time at Northrop Grumman's facility in St Augustine, Florida on 28 June 2001. Originally built as a Group I aircraft, E-2C A-130 (BuNo. 163849) was later flown to NAS Patuxent River, Maryland, where additional testing will be conducted. The first production Hawkeye 2000 (A-179) is currently undergoing system testing in St Augustine and will be flown for the first time in October 2001.

New radar for AH-1Z Cobra

Longbow International, a joint venture between Lockheed Martin and Northrop Grumman, has teamed with Bell Helicopter to develop the Cobra Radar System (CRS) for Bell's AH-1Z Cobra helicopter. The system will consist of a pod-based millimetre-wave radar (MWR) that will be mounted on a wingtip or stores position of the AH-1Z helicopter. It will be integrated with the AGM-114L RF Hellfire fire-and-forget missile and existing M299 launcher. The system, which automatically searches, detects, classifies, and prioritises multiple moving and stationary targets on land and in the air, will provide the Cobra with capabilities similar to those of the US Army's AH-64D.

Schweizer VTUAV prototype

On 2 July 2001 Schweizer Aircraft Company delivered the second prototype of the Fire Scout Vertical take-off and landing tactical unmanned aerial vehicle (VTUAV) to Northrop Grumman's Integrated Systems Sector (ISS). The company-procured vehicle will be used in Fire Scout VTUAV system risk-reduction testing. Dubbed P-3, the vehicle, which includes a dual-redundant avionics system similar to the one designed for the production Fire Scout system, will be used in system risk-reduction testing. It will begin flight tests at the end of the year and operate alongside a manned VTUAV system as part of the company-funded, two-vehicle test fleet. The first engineering and manufacturing development (EMD) vehicle, E-1, is expected to be delivered in July, and the EMD flight test programme is scheduled to begin in February 2002. The system, which recently entered low-rate initial production (LRIP), is designed to autonomously take-off from and land on any aviation-capable ship. The first LRIP system will be deployed by the US Marine Corps' VTUAV Fleet Introduction Team, which is part of Marine Air Control Group (MACG)-38 at MCAS Miramar, California, and will include three air vehicles, two ground control stations, a datalink suite, remote data terminals and modular mission payloads.

Boeing targets USCG contract

Boeing has teamed with three European contractors as part of its pursuit of the second phase of the US Coast Guard's $20 billion Integrated Deepwater System programme. The team includes European Aeronautic, Defense and Space (EADS), Eurocopter, an EADS Company and Spain's Construcciones Aeronauticas (CASA) which will be responsible for the aviation portion of programme. The programme, which integrates all of the coast guard's resources, will modernise and replace the service's existing fleet of ships, aircraft and sensors that operate in the deepwater mission environment that typically includes areas that are more than 50 miles (80 km) offshore. It also includes a communications and information network that will integrate all systems, significantly increasing operational effectiveness. Boeing will have responsibility for the system integration, information and communications systems and logistics. CASA's role will primarily be limited to fixed-wing aircraft while Eurocopter will concentrate on rotary-wing types. A contract award is expected in April 2002.

Sensors for ABL delivered

Lockheed Martin recently delivered the first of six shipsets of airborne laser infra-red search and track (IRST) sensors to Boeing for installation in the YAL-1A airborne laser (ABL) aircraft. The sensors were developed from the IRST that equips the F-14D Tomcat. Four of the sensors were sent to Wichita, Kansas, where Boeing is modifying a 747-400 Freighter to become the YAL-1A weapon-system platform.

Two sensors were delivered to Boeing's Seattle facility where integrated testing with missile-tracking software will be carried out in the BMC4I 'Virtual Lab'.

When installed, the IRST sensors comprise the ABL's wide-area surveillance subsystem that will maintain 360° surveillance over hundreds of miles from the aircraft during a mission. After detecting a boosting theatre ballistic missile, the information is sent to the battle management command, control, communication, computers and intelligence (BMC4I) tracker, which will use that information to track the missile's trajectory, and send commands to another surveillance component, the active ranging system (ARS). ARS provides mission personnel with a highly accurate three-dimensional track of its missile target. Flight testing of the ABL systems will begin next spring. Initially, each system will be tested separately, then with the system as a whole. The ABL beam control system and lasers are to be installed aboard the aircraft beginning next spring at Edwards AFB, California. ABL is designed to operate hundreds of miles away from an adversary's location and will lock onto an enemy missile shortly after launch. The system's chemical oxygen iodine laser system will direct an intense beam of heat that causes the missile's skin to rupture, its fuel to explode and its warhead will fall onto or near enemy territory.

USAF C-130J-30 airdrop tests

Lockheed Martin recently completed USAF airdrop testing of the stretched version of the USAF's C-130J Hercules at the Air Force Flight Test Center at Edwards AFB, California. Using three C-130J-30 aircraft destined for the Rhode Island Air National Guard, the contractor demonstrated the aircraft's ability to deploy parachute-assisted pallet loads up to 42,000 lb (19051 kg) and paratroop drops from altitudes as high as 25,000 ft (7620 m). Subsequent testing will be conducted at Pope AFB, North Carolina, where paratroop testing will be conducted with the assistance of the US Army's 82nd Airborne Division. Once that phase of testing has been completed, the aircraft will be delivered to the 143nd Airlift Wing at Quonset State Airport, Providence, Rhode Island, in November 2001.

Enhanced Apache Longbow

The first enhanced US Army AH-64D Apache Longbow attack helicopter completed its maiden flight on 12 July 2001 at Boeing's Mesa, Arizona, facility. The pre-production Apache Longbow incorporates a number of commercial off-the-shelf (COTS) enhancements that will reduce costs and allow for future growth and extend the system's operational life. The 23-minute flight also marked the start of the second multi-year production batch that includes 269 aircraft for the US Army. The sixth lot of Army Longbows will begin coming off the production line in early 2002 and by 2006, the service's fleet of AH-64Ds will grow to 501 helicopters.

Tiger Meet 2001

Marking the 40th anniversary of this annual event, Tiger Meet 2001 took place at Kleine Brogel air base in Belgium during June. Participants included (from top to bottom), Luftwaffe Tornado ECR 96+44 from JBG 32; F-15E Strike Eagle 91-0601 from the USAF's 494th FS/ 48th FW; F-16BM J-657 from 313 Sqn, KLu; Mirage 2000C '12-YG' from EC 1/12 'Cambrésis', Armée de l'Air and Mirage F1B '330-AD' from test unit CEAM 330, Armée de l'Air.

UPGRADES AND MODIFICATIONS

Algeria

Russia to update 'Fencer'
Russia's Chkalov aircraft works has signed a US$120 million contract with the al-Quwwat al Jawwiya al-Jaza'eriya (Algerian Air Force) to modernise 22 Su-24MK 'Fencers'.

Argentina

Pampa relaunched
A major relaunch of the original FMA IA-63 Pampa single-turbofan low-cost jet-trainer project, announced last summer by Lockheed Martin Aircraft Argentina (LMAASA), will involve extensive upgrades, costing $15 million, of 12 of the 18 aircraft originally built for the FAA. Options are included for another 24, and budget allocations made by Argentine Naval Aviation for eight from a new construction programme. Designated AT-63s, the redesigned Pampas will retain their 3,500-lb (15.57-kN) Honeywell TFE731-2CN turbofan powerplants, with full-authority digital engine control (FADEC) and improved MTBF specifications. They will gain additional light ground-attack capabilities, however, from new Elbit 1553B digital mission-system avionics, and five external stores pylon attachments. These and other changes are being retrofitted into two IA-63s as AT-63 prototypes, for roll-out later this year, and initial production at about one aircraft per month from 2002. Given the required funding, new AT-63s could follow in early 2003.

Potential orders for up to 40 AT-63 are already under discussion, within possible markets (including Israel) of 300 or more from world requirements for 1,200 jet-trainers by 2010. Further AT-63 development plans from 2007 include installation of an uprated 4,150-lb (18.46-kN) TFE731-40R engine; a redesigned and strengthened 7-g wing and

nosewheel unit; defensive EW systems; and a nose-mounted laser-rangefinder.

China

Russian radar upgrade for J-8
Following last year's revelation of a switch by the Chinese armed forces from defensive to offensive military strategies, planned increases in defence spending of no less than 17.7 per cent were announced by the Beijing government in March, to modernise its arms and equipment. Funding allocations have included an initial $5 million AF/PLA contract for long-awaited fire-control radar upgrades of China's Shenyang J-8-IIM 'Finback' fighter.

China's plans to procure and produce of up to 100 of the N010 Zhuk-8-2 X-band advanced multi-mode development of the MiG-29's original Phazotron N019 radar, for J-8 installations. Zhuk air-to-air capabilities include track-while-scan of 10 targets up to 80 km (43 nm), and simultaneous attack of up to four. Zhuk flight development began in the J-8 as far back as 1997, for improved performance and Russian AAM/ASM capabilities.

Egypt

Hawkeye fleet expanded
A late 1999 US$138 million Egyptian air force contract to upgrade its five Group 0 Northrop Grumman E-2C airborne early warning and control (AEW&C) aircraft to Hawkeye 2000 standard, was augmented on 19 June by a further ex-USN aircraft. Operated by the EAF since 1986, all six Hawkeyes will be modified in St Augustine, Fla, and Bethpage, NY, by Northrop Grumman's Airborne Early Warning and Electronic Warfare (AEW&EW) Systems. Egypt will receive its first modified Hawkeye in October 2002.

Greece's first upgraded F-4E (01523, named **Princess of Andravida**)*, reworked by DASA at Manching, Germany, was completed in July and flew sorties over a weapons range at Meppen. Production upgrades will be undertaken in Greece.*

Below: Pictured during July, this Transall C.160D of Luftwaffe test unit WTD 61 was noted at Manching sporting a pylon and unidentified store under its starboard wing.

NATO

E-3 upgrades
The European Aeronautic Defence and Space Company (EADS) has teamed with Northrop Grumman as part of a competition to re-engine NATO's fleet of airborne warning and control systems (AWACS) and trainer cargo aircraft (TCA). Under terms of the agreement, EADS would be the prime contractor and would perform aircraft modifications required to install the Pratt & Whitney JT8D-219 engine on the modified Boeing 707 airframes. Northrop Grumman's Integrated Systems Sector (ISS) would provide engineering support and conduct the military qualification of the re-engined AWACS aircraft.

Meanwhile, the USAF's Electronic Systems Center at Hanscom AFB, Massachusetts has issued a $24 million long-lead production contract to Boeing covering the modernisation of the 17 E-3As in NATO's AWACS fleet. The programme will provide the aircraft with upgrades to computers, displays, communications, navigation and target identification systems. One aircraft, modified as part of an engineering, manufacturing and development (EMD) contract, is currently undergoing flight testing.

Poland

IAI 'Fitter' upgrades
Poland plans to upgrade 20 WLOP Sukhoi Su-22M4 'Fitter-K' ground-attack fighters, the work to be carried out by the Lahav Division of Israel Aircraft Industries. Some 80 Su-22M4s and 18 two-seat

Su-22UM3K 'Fitter-Gs' have been operated by two WLOP fighter-bomber and one bomber-reconnaissance Air Regiments.

United States

C-130 modernisation
The USAF Aeronautical Systems Center has selected Boeing to develop the US$4 billion C-130 Avionics Modernization Program (AMP), which has a total potential value of approximately $4 billion. Under the programme, Boeing will develop a common cockpit avionics system for the USAF's C-130 tactical airlift fleet, which includes around 500 aircraft. The new avionics system will feature six digital displays and the flight management system installed in the company's 737 commercial airliner, allowing the aircraft to meet Global Air Traffic Management requirements. Aircraft modification will be conducted at the company's Aerospace Support Center in San Antonio, Texas, and by the USAF's Warner Robins Air Logistics Center at Robins AFB, Georgia, and the Ogden Air Logistics Center, at Hill AFB, Utah. The installation of modification kits will begin in 2004 and continue through 2014.

C-5 RERP contract awarded
The USAF has awarded Lockheed Martin a $21 million contract to conduct risk reduction studies associated with C-5 Galaxy RERP. The C-5 RERP is the second phase of the comprehensive modernisation plan for the Galaxy and is aimed at increasing fleet availability and reducing operational costs by up to 30 per cent. The

---

Indonesian Hawks adapted for Indian training

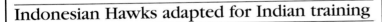

This Hawk Mk 63, which has languished at Hurn airport for some while in the wake of the UK arms embargo against Indonesia, has re-emerged in a new company scheme to be used for preliminary training of Indian Air Force instructors prior to receipt of the IAF order. BAE Systems conducts a sizeable overseas training programme at Warton for the Hawk and PC-9 aircraft.

Su-25 Scorpion and Su 39 Strike Shield

The first flight of a prototype upgraded Sukhoi Su-25K 'Frogfoot' ground-attack aircraft was made at the Tbilisi Aerospace Manufacturing (TAM) factory airfield on 18 April, in a joint modernisation programme launched with Israel's Elbit Systems. Renamed Scorpion, the programme is aimed at Georgia's 50 or so Su-25Ks, and many countries still operating some of 800 'Frogfoots' originally built at Tbilisi and Ulan Ude.

Apart from new dual Mil Std 1553B digitised mission system avionics developed by Elbit for many combat aircraft installations, structural upgrades also feature in the Scorpion project, to operate with eastern and western weapons and targeting equipment. Most 'Frogfoot' production has been undertaken in Tbilisi, which has built the single-seat version since 1978. The first two Su-25UB two-seat combat trainers were also built at Tbilisi, before production was transferred to the Ulan Ude Aircraft Plant in 1985.

Production in Tbilisi for Russia ended in 1991, with an experimental batch of 12 upgraded single-seat Su-25Ts, equipped with a new PrNK-56 Voskhod navigation/targeting system, to launch laser-guided KBP/Tula 9M120 Vikhr anti-tank/attack missiles. They were not delivered to Russia until 1998, however, when eight were transferred to the VVS. Another 18 Su-25Ts were built for Georgia, apparently without some of the new Russian mission systems.

From 1995, UUAZ began producing single-seat 'Frogfoot' versions for the Russian VVS, with an initial batch of seven or eight Su-25TMs. Converted from two-seat trainer airframes, these were further upgraded in Russia with additional advanced systems. VVS production is still unfunded, but the Su-25TM is also being offered for export with new Russian avionics as the Su-39 Strike Shield. Late 1980s Ulan Ude 'Frogfoot' production further included 10 navalised two-seat Su-25UTG versions, with an arrester gear and reinforced landing-gear, for aircraft-carrier deck-operation training.

The cockpit of the Scorpion upgrade features two large MFDs either side of a new HUD and UFC (upfront controller). The first prototype (below) was publicly revealed at the 2001 Paris air show, in full Georgian air force colours.

Upgraded Sentry reaches IOC

VH-3As that support Atlantic Fleet headquarters.

The USAF recently accepted the seventh E-3 Sentry modified under the radar system improvement programme (RSIP) and declared that the newest version of the airborne warning platform had reached initial operational capability (IOC). The RSIP modifications increased the sensitivity of the AN/APY-1/2 pulse Doppler radar, and allows it to detect and track smaller targets as well as increasing the system reliability. Modifications include a new radar computer, radar control maintenance panel, electrical and mechanical hardware and software changes. The kits were installed by the Oklahoma Air Logistics Center at Tinker AFB and the centre will modify the remainder of the USAF's 25 aircraft by February 2005.

F-16 CCIP kits delivered

Lockheed Martin recently delivered the first eight modification kits for the USAF's F-16 common configuration implementation programme (CCIP). The CCIP involves major changes to the aircraft avionics and cockpit displays; initial kits will only be incorporated in Block 50/52 aircraft and include the modular mission computer and colour cockpit. The first aircraft is scheduled for completion in January 2002. Beginning in March 2002, the Block 50/52 kits will also include the combined interrogator transponder, which will provide the aircraft with an autonomous BVR air-intercept capability. These aircraft will also be capable of alternately carrying the advanced FLIR targeting pod or the HARM targeting pod. In 2003 the Link 16 multi-functional information distribution system (MIDS), the Joint Helmet-Mounted Cueing System (JHMCS), and an electronic horizontal situation indicator will be added. Modifications to the Block 40/42 aircraft will begin in 2005. Around 650 Block 40/50 aircraft will upgraded under the CCIP.

programme will focus on upgrading the aircraft with modern commercial engines and systems along with minor structural enhancements that will ensure the aircraft is operationally viable through 2040. The USAF anticipates that it will issue System Development and Demonstration (SDD) contract in December 2001. The $800 million SDD phase, which will last five years, will result in flight qualification of four updated C-5 aircraft. Upon the successful completion of SDD, the programme will move into a production phase that will initially see the retrofit of the C-5B fleet. The total programme cost is estimated to be approximately $6 billion. Lockheed Martin has selected the General Electric CF6-80-C2 turbofan to power the Galaxy along with Goodrich engine pylons, a Hamilton Sunstrand auxiliary power unit (APU), and various other components.

Viking fatigue tests begin

Lockheed Martin Aeronautics recently began full-scale fatigue testing (FSFT) of a US Navy S-3B Viking at its Marietta, Georgia, facility under a $40 million contract. The testing will be used to determine whether the lifetime of the S-3B airframe, which is currently certified for a structural life of 13,000 hours, can be extended. Once the fatigue tests have been completed in late 2002 the Navy hopes to certify the airframe for 17,750 flight hours.

UH-3H(ET) delivered

The first of four modified UH-3H executive transports was handed over to HC-2 at Chambers Field, on Norfolk Naval Base on 27 July 2001. The aircraft will replace the

Above: Work on testing a new defensive avionics suite for the USAF's B-1B Lancer fleet began in October 2001, engineers from the Electronic Warfare Directorate at Edwards AFB working with the 419th Flight Test Squadron to complete the work. Here a modified aircraft is backed into the Benefield Anechoic Facility at Edwards.

Right: Northrop Grumman delivered the first Block 20 E-8C Joint Surveillance Target Attack Radar System (JSTARS) production aircraft to the 93d Air Control Wing at Robins AFB, Georgia on 6 August 2001. The aircraft is the 11th production aircraft and is equipped with commercial-off-the-shelf (COTS) computers rather than those designed specifically to a military specification. The contractor is currently producing four more E-8Cs, and has received long-lead funding for one additional aircraft.

PROCUREMENT AND DELIVERIES

Algeria

Combat aircraft from CIS
As a follow-on to reported Soviet arms supplies of $11 billion between 1962-89, reported orders for or deliveries of CIS arms and equipment in 1999-2000 have included the supply to the Algerian air force (QJA) of additional combat aircraft. In addition to 25 more Su-24MK/MR 'Fencers', upgraded and refurbished by the Novosibirsk Aviation Production Association (NAPO), these have included 28 surplus MiG-29S 'Fulcrum-Cs' received from a $700 million contract with Belarus, to which Russia also contributed eight two-seat MiG-29UB trainers.

These are reportedly being armed with Vympel R-23 (AA-7 'Apex') and Vympel R-73 (AA-10 'Archer') medium-and close-range AAMs, of which up to 276 are being supplied by Russia and 289 from Ukraine. This is the first mention of possible use of the elderly AA-7, produced with semi-active radar or IR homing heads, by the MiG-29. Other Russian missile deliveries to Algeria have included 48 Zvezda-Strela 3M-60 Uran anti-ship systems, with Kh-35 (SS-N-25) 'Switchblade' missiles.

Ukraine is also reported to have supplied 28 Mil Mi-24V 'Hind-D' attack helicopters to Algeria by the end of last year, supplementing a similar number of Mi-24s delivered earlier, together with 40 Mil Mi-8/17s. Jointly with Ukraine, the Mi-24s are being upgraded by South Africa's Advanced Technologies & Engineering (ATE), using its Mk III package of mainly indigenous components, using similar systems and weapons to those developed for Denel's AH-2A Rooivalk attack helicopter, now being produced for the SAAF.

Australia

UAV plans announced
Northrop Grumman's RQ-4A Global Hawk unmanned air vehicle and a tactical UAV had been included in the future defence planning of the Australian Government, and will be procured as part of the Defence Capability Plan 2001-2010. The plan calls for purchasing the initial versions of both UAVs in 2004/5 with the first deliveries in 2007.

Austria

Gripen leads RFI responses
Responses for Requests for Information issued last December by the Austrian air force (OeLk) to five industry contenders for 24 new combat aircraft, with options for another six, to replace its 23 SAAB J 35 Drakens and 27 SAAB 105Oes, resulted in an almost immediate return from SAAB/BAE Systems for the JAS 39C Gripen. Requests for Proposals, expected to follow this summer, were also being contested

Agreement was reported in July for the transfer of 19 of the 27 SIAI-Marchetti SF.260MS/W piston-engine basic trainers, operated by the Republic of Singapore air force since 1984, to the Indonesian armed forces. Other recent recipients of new examples have included Venezuela (above) and Mauretania (below), both countries taking delivery of F.260EUs during 2000/01.

by the Boeing F/A-18E/F, Dassault Mirage 2000-5 Mk 2, Eurofighter Typhoon and Lockheed Martin Block 50/52 F-16C/D.

Brazil

Cougars ordered
The Brazilian Army (AVEX) has purchased eight Eurocopter AS 532UE Cougar transport helicopters that will equip its first logistic transport helicopter battalion. The Cougars will be equipped with a hoist, sling, side-mounted machine-gun, and ferry fuel tanks. The Army is also studying a midlife upgrade programme that would equip its Panthers with night vision capabilities, a new engine and armament.

Brazil buys ALX
Embraer has announced that it has been awarded a contract by the Fuerza Aeréa Brasil (FAB) for the purchase of 76 ALX light attack aircraft – a derivative of Embraer's Super Tucano trainer. The first delivery is planned for 2003 and the contract includes options for 23 additional aircraft.

Bulgaria

F-16 procurement rejected
Bulgarian government requests to the US earlier this year for quotations for the transfer of 12-22 refurbished surplus ex-USAF F-16A/Bs or new F-16C/Ds, plus supporting equipment, to replace its obsolete Soviet-supplied MiG-21s and MiG-23s, were cancelled in August, through lack of funding. Instead, a decision was announced to refurbish Bulgaria's 17 MiG-29s and four MiG-29UBs, most of which were grounded because of spares and technical support deficiencies. A contract was expected to be placed with EADS/RSK MiG Product Support (MAPS), in Germany, later this year to return all Bulgaria's MiG-29s to service, and equip them with new communications and IFF equipment for basic NATO interoperability.

Chile

Fighters and tankers for FAC
The US Department of Defense has formally notified the US Congress of its plan to sell 10 Block 50+ F-16C/Ds and two KC-135A tankers to Chile in a deal worth more than $700 million. The F-16s will be powered by either the P&W F100-PW-229 or GE F110-GE-129 engine and equipped with the AN/APG-68(v)XM radar and night vision goggle-compatible cockpits. Also included are four Litening II laser designation/targeting pods,

40 LAU-129 launchers, six AN/ALQ-131 and six AN/ALQ-184 electronic countermeasures pods. Although the contract includes a variety of munitions the AIM-120 AMRAAM missile is not included. The KC-135As will be reworked to KC-135R configuration prior to delivery. The total value of the contracts is estimated to be $636 million for the F-16 and $78 million for the KC-135.

China

More Su-30 deliveries
Delivery of the first 10 of 38 multi-role Su-30MKKs ordered from a $1.5 billion 1999 contract with AVPK Sukhoi OKB and KnAAPO, and serialled from 501 onwards, began in December 2000, to the AF/PLA's 3rd Fighter Division at the PRC's Wuhu air base, in Anhui province. KnAAPO started delivering the next batch of nine to Wuhu in August this year, with new digital avionics suites incorporating colour liquid-crystal multi-function cockpit displays. Delivery of the remaining 19 Su-30MKKs to Cangzhou air base, in Hubei province, is scheduled by the year-end, by which time negotiations for a further 40 are expected to be finalised by China.

Czech Republic

Gripen interest hardens
Stringent conditions, including payment in local currency, 150 per cent offset contracts, and Czech language documentation, resulted in mid-year withdrawal of all western industry submissions for the Czech Republic's 24-36 new combat aircraft requirement, apart from SAAB/BAE's JAS 39 Gripen. Former bids had included new or surplus Boeing F/A-18s and Lockheed Martin F-16s, Mirage 2000-5s from Dassault, and Eurofighter Typhoons via EADS.

Funding assistance for the CKr75 billion ($1.86 billion) new fighter budget limit was proposed by the Czech government from proposed export of about half the 72 new Aero L-159A light fighters being built for the air force. SAAB/BAE is reportedly offering commercial loan facilities for 15 per cent of the Gripen contract value, and payment credits over 15 years.

Dominica

Super Tucano contract signed
The Fuerza Aerea Dominicana became the first export customer for the EMBRAER EMB-314 Super Tucano in August, from a contract for 10 of these turboprop light ground-attack and advanced train-

ers. These will supplement some four remaining Cessna A-37Bs on drug interdiction, patrol and training missions.

Hungary

Gripen beats F-16 lease deal
Defence department recommendations earlier this year for leases over two five-year periods of 20 ex-Turkish Block 30 GD F-16Cs and four F-16Ds costing Fts160 billion ($557 million), for Hungary's new combat aircraft requirements, were countered by rival proposals from SAAB/BAE for the Gripen. As accepted in September, their offer comprised a 12-year lease at a lower cost of Fts130-140 billion ($452.56-487.4 million), with 100 per cent offsets, of 14 later-generation JAS 39 Gripens transferred from the Swedish air force. These would be available for delivery within 24 months of contract signature, after upgrades to current Batch 3 NATO-interoperable standards, and could be followed by new-build JAS 39C Gripens.

Indonesia

Russian orders revived
Mil Moscow Helicopter Plant (MVZ) announced receipt of a $12-14 million contract from the Indonesian navy (TNI-AL) in May for 10 rotary-wing aircraft. A 1997 agreement to acquire 12 Su-30KI single-seat multi-role fighters and eight Mil Mi-171-1V helicopters was cancelled after Indonesia's currency collapse, although a prototype TNI-AU Su-30KI had been built and flown. Funding for this requirement is now being revived, following a contract placed last year for four Mi-17s.

In addition to two Ulan Ude-built Mi-171 'Hip' transport helicopters, the new order includes eight Mi-2 light twin-turboshaft eight-seat utility helicopters, for delivery by the year-end. Mi-2s have been built only in Poland by WSK-Swidnik since 1964, although many have been supplied to Soviet, Russian and eastern bloc

customers. Indonesia's Mi-2s will come from Rostvertol, although some surplus Mi-2s have recently been refurbished or overhauled for resale to military and commercial operators.

More CN-235MPAs ordered
Six Airtech IPTN (now Indonesian Aerospace/IAe) CN-235MPA maritime patrol aircraft operated by Indonesian Naval Aviation (DPAL) from a June 1996 $151 million joint order with the TNI-AU, are to be supplemented by a further three from a $42.3 million mid-2001 contract. Three new CN-235-220s to be built by IAe will be equipped with Thales Airborne Maritime Situation Control System (AMASCOS), integrating the French company's Ocean Master surveillance radar, Chlio thermal imaging camera, Gemini navigation computer, and an ESM suite, for the new contract. The Indonesian navy has already received nine of these systems, and has a requirement for another six CN-235s.

Israel

Israel orders more F-16Is
Israel's Defense Ministry has announced plans to exercise an option to buy more than 50 additional two-seat F-16I fighters from the Lockheed Martin in a deal worth between $1-2 billion. The aircraft will be powered by Pratt & Whitney F100-PW-229 engines and deliveries will begin in 2006 when Lockheed Martin completes the 50 aircraft that were ordered in 1999.

Italy

Italy buys Predators
The Aeronautica Militare Italiana (AMI) or Italian air force has placed a $60 million order with General Atomics Aeronautical Systems for an RQ-1A Predator system. The contract includes options for additional aircraft and an unspecified number of General Atomics Lynx synthetic aperture radars (SAR). First deliveries are expected within 7-9 months.

Recent hardware deliveries in Canada have included CT-155 155218 (above), the last of 18 aircraft for the NATO Flying Training in Canada (NFTC) establishment at CFB Moose Jaw, on 4 September 2001. Two additional aircraft will be delivered in 2002. Also added to the Canadian Forces inventory is the first (149901, below) of 15 AW 320 Cormorant (EH Industries EH 101 SAR) helicopters intended to replace aging CH-113 Labradors.

Japan

JGSDF selects AH-64D
Selection was announced in August by the Japanese Ground Self-Defence Force (JGSDF) of the Boeing AH-64D Longbow Apache, to meet its long-standing AH-X attack helicopter programme, to replace 88 Fuji/Bell AH-1S HueyCobras. Negotiations then began for initial procurement of 10 Boeing-built AH-64Ds, from total JGSDF requirements for 60, for service entry from about 2005. Fuji Heavy Industries will undertake component manufacture and assembly of the remaining 50 AH-64s.

Myanmar

MiG-29 purchase agreed
Long-term negotiations with Russia for the acquisition of advanced combat aircraft, which began in 1996, were finally concluded in June, with a $130 million contract from the Myanmar government with RSK MiG for 10 MiG-29s. These are believed to comprise eight refurbished single-seat 'Fulcrums' and two MiG-29UB combat trainers, from about 70 built for the VVS but undelivered through lack of funding. With accompanying AAMs and equipment, their delivery from long-term storage over the past decade at MiG's Lukhovitsy facility, near Moscow, may start later this year.

New Zealand

Seasprites delivered
The pair of new SH-2G(NZ) Seasprite helicopters arrived in

New Zealand by ship recently. Destined for service with the Royal New Zealand Navy, the aircraft were flown to Auckland International Airport where Kaman Aerospace and the New Zealand company Safe Air completed further checks prior to delivering the helicopters to the Ministry of Defence in late July.

Peru

FAP gets BVRAAM capability
Recent photographs of Peruvian air force MiG-29SEs with Vympel R-77 (AA-12 'Adder') active radar-guided AAMs, indicated a new level of beyond-visual-range air combat capabilities in Latin America. The AA-12s were part of a $385 million FAP package, based on 18 surplus "Fulcrums", including two two-seat MiG-29UB combat trainers, and 14 ground-attack Sukhoi Su-25K/UBKs, bought from Belarus in 1996. Three newly-built MiG-29UBs, plus spares and support equipment, acquired from MiG MAPO from a $117 million September 1998 contract, then ensured continuing Russian technical support.

Poland

C-295 for transport roles
Negotiations began last spring with EADS/CASA, following selection of eight C-295M stretched twin-turboprop tactical transports costing $212 million to replace the WLOP's 10 ageing Antonov An-26s in 2003-05, although PZL and Antonov offered 10 upgraded An-32Ms, with PW150A turboprops and western avionics for only $150 million, as

As part of an apparent sales initiative, CASA applied Austrian air force markings and bogus '6T-AA' codes to this CN 235-300 demonstrator, photographed in June 2001. Austria's air arm lacks a significant fixed-wing transport capability.

alternatives. In July, Polish Chief of Staff Lt Gen Czeslaw Piatas said in Washington that medium-lift helicopters and four Lockheed Martin C-130 transports were also needed to support Polish peacekeeping forces in Kosovo.

Portugal

EC635s for new army branch
Formation of a new army aviation element of the Portuguese armed forces was announced earlier this year, with an initial order for nine Eurocopter EC635 light single-turboshaft armed utility helicopters. These will be equipped with single 20-mm (0.787-in) GiAT NC621 cannon or 12.7-mm (0.5-in) FN Herstal HMP 400 machine-gun pods, plus 12-round 70-mm (2.75-in) rocket-pods, for delivery later this year.

South Africa

BBJs delivered to SAAF
On 26 June 2001 Boeing delivered a Boeing Business Jet (BBJ) to the Armaments Corporation of South Africa Ltd. (ARMSCOR), which purchased the aircraft on behalf of the South African Air Force (SAAF). The SAAF will use the BBJ as an intercontinental VIP transport in the South African Air Force fleet and it will be based at Waterkloof AFB, Pretoria.

Singapore

More Apaches ordered
Singapore air force orders for eight Boeing/MDH AH-64D all-weather attack helicopters, due for delivery from 2002, included an option for a further 12 Longbow Apaches, taken up in August this year. Costing some $617 million, the new contract will include spare GE T700 engines, Boeing/Rockwell AGM-114L Hellfire ATMs, plus spares, support equipment and training.

Sweden

Light helicopter contract
A SKr1.2 billion ($110.36 million) contract was announced by AgustaWestland in June to supply 20 Agusta A109M military helicopters, designated Hkp 15s, for Swedish military use. Following delivery between October 2002 and 2007, 12 will be used for basic training, and eight for corvette-based naval utility and training.

Taiwan

Seahawks enter service
On 9 July 2001 the Republic of China Navy commissioned its second squadron equipped with Sikorsky S-70C(M)-2 Seahawk helicopters. Based at Hualien, in eastern Taiwan, the 702d Helicopter Antisubmarine Squadron is assigned 11 aircraft and the first of these was delivered in September 2000. The Navy previously received ten S-70C(M)-1 helicopters and nine of these are operated by the 701st Helicopter Antisubmarine Squadron, also based at Hualien.

United States

Second C-40A ordered
The USAF has exercised an option it has with Boeing for six C-40s and ordered a second aircraft that will be assigned to the District of Columbia Air National Guard's 201st Airlift Squadron at Andrews AFB, Maryland. The squadron currently operates four elderly Boeing C-22Bs (former 727-100 series airliners). The new C-40 will normally be configured to carry 26 passengers but can be reconfigured to carry up to 60 passengers, and its 5,000-nm (9260-km) range is more than double the range of the C-22B.

GV delivered to MacDill
The 6th Air Mobility Wing at MacDill AFB, Florida, received the first (01-0028) of three new C-37A Gulfstream Vs on 25 July 2001. The aircraft will be operated by the 310th Airlift Squadron, replacing the wing's EC-135N and CT-43 that are used to support the CINCs of US Central Command (USCENTCOM) and US Southern Command (USSOUTHCOM). The wing's EC-135N is scheduled for retirement in September 2001. The next Gulfstream V was scheduled to arrive in August and the third will follow in March 2002.

Formal B-2A offer made
On 15 May 2001 Northrop Grumman submitted a formal 'letter of offer' to the USAF in which it proposed building 40 additional Spirit bombers at a cost of $29.4 billion. The aircraft would be delivered at a rate of four per year over 10 years at an average cost of $735 million each.

Yemen

New fighters and trainers
In addition to at least six Chengdu F-7M Airguard fighters from China, the Republic of Yemen air force (RYAF) has reportedly received a dozen L-39C advanced trainers from Aero Vodochody in the Czech Republic, over the past few months. The L-39s will provide lead-in training for the 50 or so MiG-21MF/bis/UM, 25 MiG-23ML/UB and 18 Sukhoi Su-22M2/UM3 fighters operated by the mainly Russian-supplied RYAF.

RSK MiG was reported in September to have sold 10-12 MiG-29s, plus two two-seat MiG-29UB combat trainers, costing some $200 million, to the RYAF. Options worth another $100 million were also reportedly included for six MiG-29s and four MiG-29UBs. Before unification, North Yemen acquired eight MiG-29s and two MiG-29UBs from Moldova in 1994; several were lost in combat and the remainder withdrawn.

AIR ARM REVIEW

Germany

GAF ready for Eurofighter

Preparations have reached an advanced stage at Laage air base, near Rostock, in north-east Germany, for reception of the first of 180 required Luftwaffe Eurofighters, due for delivery from next summer. Germany's initial 44 Eurofighters will then begin replacing the MDC F-4Fs and MiG-29s of JG 73 'Steinhoff' at Laage.

Training of JG 73 instructor pilots will begin on Eurofighter at the Manching factory next September, and continue at Laage from April 2003. Parallel ground engineer training will proceed at the Luftwaffe's Technical College at Kaufbeuren. JG 73 will become operational with its Eurofighters in mainly air-defence roles from March 2005, when JG 74 will begin similar conversion from F-4Fs at Neuberg. JG 71 will then replace its F-4Fs from 2007 at Wittmund, while JG 72 will similarly re-equip at Rheine from 2009.

From 2012, the Luftwaffe will begin receiving 40 more Eurofighters, including five two-seat versions. Equipped for both air-defence and ground-attack missions, in swing-role configurations, these will replace Tornados in six strike/reconnaissance/SEAD wings.

New Zealand

RNZAF loses combat element

Having cancelled previous NZ government plans to replace the RNZAF's 17 MDC A-4K/TA-4K Skyhawks with the lease/purchase of 13 ex-Pakistani Block 15OCU F-16As and 15 two-seat F-16Bs, the current Labour administration announced its decision in May to withdraw and dispose of both the Skyhawks and the RNZAF's 17 Aermacchi MB-339CB lead-in fighter trainers by the year-end. Government defence studies claimed that their continued operation over the next decade would have cost NZ$1.2 billion ($484.5 million), although their withdrawal will save only NZ$870 million ($351.26 million).

Skyhawk training operations with live weapons ended on 1 July, and with the MB-339s, they were to be grounded and offered for disposal in December.

Although the Labour government cancelled the Project Sirius avionics upgrade of the RNZAF's six Lockheed P-3K Orion maritime patrol aircraft, it plans to continue their operation, alongside five C-130H transports, which will be upgraded or replaced by up to six C-130Js now on option. The last of the RNZAF's P-3Ks to undergo major structural upgrades by Australian Aerospace through NZ's NZ$98 million ($41 million) Project Kestrel programme was returned to service on 30 August. Replacements will also be sought for two RNZAF Boeing 727-2QCs for government transport.

Sri Lanka

Heavy aircraft losses

Eight Sri Lankan air force aircraft worth $350 million, plus three

Appropriately named Ciao BELLa and adorned with an impressive sharkmouth, the last AB 204B in service with Austria's air arm was retired on 29 June 2001. Delivered in the mid-1960s (as the first turbine-powered helicopter in the Austrian inventory), the AB 204s were almost certainly the last UH-1B-series 'Hueys' in military use anywhere.

Airbus A330/A340s of the national airlines, were destroyed in an attack on Colombo's Katunayake International Airport by Tamil guerrilla forces on 24 July. Identified SLAF losses included two of 12 IAI Kfir C-2/7s and a TC-2 on strength, one of four MiG-27 'Floggers' recently delivered from Ukraine, and several of a dozen Mil Mi-24/35 'Hind' attack helicopters.

Taiwan

US weapons proposals

In the first significant policy move in relation to China since the Lockheed EP-3/Chengdu J-8 collision incident in April, President Bush announced a new and major US arms package offer to Taiwan on 24 April. If accepted, this could be the biggest US arms sale to Taiwan since the $6 billion supply of 150 Lockheed Martin F-16s and associated weapons in 1992.

Its emphasis is strongly towards maritime systems, notably including 12 Lockheed Martin P-3C Orion ASW aircraft; four ex-USN 'Kidd'-class air defence/ASW destroyers, armed with Raytheon Standard 2 ShAMs; and Sikorsky MH-53E mine-sweeping helicopters. Also

on offer were army vehicles, artillery, and more Boeing Avenger truck-mounted short-range air defence Stinger launchers.

Taiwan has been seeking an ABM capability, to counter current deployment of some 260 M-9 and M-11 ballistic missiles only 160 km (86 nm) or so away on mainland China. These are expected to increase to around 600 by 2005.

Turkey

Procurement plans curtailed

Currency problems have resulted in a review, deferments and cutbacks of 32 military equipment programmes, worth in all nearly $20 billion. Apart from cuts in planned THK Airbus A400M procurement from 26 to only 10 aircraft, $1 billion follow-on licensed production of another 32 F-16s to the 232 already completed was also suspended, together with $400 million requirements for 37 short, medium and long-range UAVs. Deferral was further expected of Turkish navy contracts for up to 14 more Penguin AShM-armed Sikorsky S-70B Seahawk ASW/ASuW helicopters, from eight approved last year, which would almost treble its

---

Singaporean fighters

Right: Singapore's single-seat Tiger IIs have all been upgraded to F-5S standard, with Grifo-F radar, modernised cockpit and other improvements. This aircraft serves with No. 149 Squadron at Paya Lebar.

Below: The RSAF has formed a second F-16 squadron at Tengah, in the shape of No. 143 'Phoenix' Squadron. It operates both F-16Cs and F-16Ds, the latter being F100-powered Block 52s with enlarged spines. As well as the traditional squadron emblem on the fin, the aircraft also have yellow/black checkerboard fin stripes to help distinguish them from No. 140's machines.

Singapore's long-time Tengah-based F-16 operator – No. 140 'Osprey' Squadron – also operates the new Block 52 aircraft, including this 'big-spine' F-16D.

Luftwaffe fighter units Jagdgeschwaderen 72 and 73 marked their 40th anniversaries in August with these strikingly-painted F-4F ICE Phantoms. JG 72's aircraft (38+37, above) sported national colours, while the JG 73 F-4F (38+31, below) was blue overall with a large crane motif (the unit's emblem) in yellow over the aircraft's spine and tail fin. As JG 73 also operates MiG-29s, an example of the latter was also decorated.

Below: Flygvapnet (the Swedish air force) celebrated the 75th anniversary of its foundation in 2001. This Saab JA 37 Viggen of 2./F16 'Petter Blå' at Uppsala was finished in an overall blue/yellow scheme to mark the occasion.

initial $200 million 1998 order. Similar deferment is likely of the planned THK purchase of six Sikorsky HH-60D Night Hawk special operations helicopters.

Budget cuts from $4.5 billion to $1.5 billion for TFLC requirements for 145 Bell Helicopter Textron AH-1Z King Cobras, will allow co-production procurement of only about 50 of these helicopters.

Contract negotiations for the THK's $2 billion AEW&C requirement, for which six Boeing 737-700 Improved Gross Weight AEW&C aircraft, plus options on a seventh, were selected last November, were deferred in May, although US industry sources were optimistic concerning their early resumption.

United Kingdom

EH 101 prospects

Further UK EH101 prospects are presented by the MoD's Future Organic Airborne Early-Warning (FOAEW) programme, to supplement new RN AgustaWestland Sea King AEW.Mk 7 helicopters on Britain's two new CVF carriers from 2012, among possible tilt-rotor and fixed-wing alternatives. Another sales target is the MoD's emerging $7 billion Support Amphibious Battlefield Rotorcraft (SABR) requirement, for 50 or more 32-seat support and SAR helicopters, to replace RN/RAF Sea Kings, Commandos and RAF Pumas, from about 2008.

RAF closes last overseas base

After nearly 50 years, formal closure took place on 15 June of RAF Bruggen, Germany, as the RAF's last operating base in mainland Europe and further afield. Bruggen officially shut down in October, however, after the Tornado GR.Mk 1/4s of Nos 9 and 31 Sqns had flown back to Marham in the UK. Last ground units will withdraw by next March, although the RAF will maintain some presence in Germany until spring 2002. Bruggen was built from scratch in North Rhein Westphalia, during 1952-53, and has played a key part in recent Serbian operations.

United States

Sea Stallions retired

The USAF retired its last four TH-53A Sea Stallions on 27 July 2001 at Kirtland AFB. Assigned to the 58th Special Operations Squadron (SOS), the aircraft had been used to support training for MH-53J/M crews but have been replaced by five MH-53J Pave Low III helicopters transferred from the inactivated 31st SOS at Osan, Korea.

USAF to reduce B-52 fleet

Just days after announcing plans to reduce the size of its B-1B bomber force, the USAF has disclosed that it will retire 18 B-52H bombers by 2003. A total of 94 bombers is currently assigned to just two wings within Air Combat Command, however only 76 are operational at any given time and the remainder are maintained as an attrition reserve at a cost of $65-75 million/year. The B-52s are currently rotated so that no single aircraft remains in storage for a prolonged period. The US Congress has continually provided funding to maintain the attrition reserve over the past six years.

'Night Stalkers' arrive in Korea

The first three MH-47Es assigned to the US Army's newly activated E Company 160th Aviation (E/160th AVN) recently arrived at K-2 Air Base at Taegu Airport, Republic of Korea, aboard USAF C-17A Globemaster IIIs. Equipped to fly long-distance special operations missions, the unit will begin operations with a complement of six Chinooks during August. A total of 100 personnel will be assigned to the unit, which replaces a USAF helicopter squadron at Osan Air Base in Korea.

USS *Iwo Jima* commissioned

The USS *Iwo Jima* (LHD 7), was commissioned on 30 June as the Navy's newest amphibious assault ship during ceremonies held at NAS Pensacola, Florida. The ship is the seventh vessel of the 'Wasp'-class and the second ship to be named after the Pacific island battle. Decommissioned in 1993, the first *Iwo Jima* (LPH 2) was the lead ship in a class of helicopter carriers built in the 1960s.

AETC Starlifters retired

On 28 July the 57th Airlift Squadron was inactivated in ceremonies held at Altus AFB, Oklahoma, bringing an end to the C-141B training mission at the Air Education & Training Command base. The honour of being the final aircraft to depart was bestowed upon serial 66-0206, which has logged more than 40,000 hours flying time and was the final C-141 winner in the 2000 Air Mobility Command Rodeo. The retirement of the AETC Starlifters leaves just 35 C-141Bs assigned to Air Mobility Command and 16 C-141Cs operating with ANG units in Mississippi and Tennessee, and another 40 assigned to five Air Force Reserve Command squadrons in California, Maryland and Ohio.

The first of three EH 101 versions, the ASW/ASUW aircraft, has entered service with the Marina Militare Italiana at Luni. Following will be an AEW version, and the UTH version for utility/assault transport.

Above: Pictured at NAWS Point Mugu during August 2001, this all-grey USAF NC-130H is believed to be on loan to the US Navy. Serialled 65-0979, the Hercules was built as an HC-130H SAR aircraft and was later converted as a DC-130H drone director. During the 1980s it became an NC-130H and has supported a number of classified programmes.

Operation Enduring Freedom

After days of growing tension, the United States and United Kingdom unleashed Operation Enduring Freedom on the night of 7 October 2001. The opening assault was spearheaded by Northrop Grumman B-2s flying directly from their home base at Whiteman AFB, Missouri, supported by Rockwell B-1Bs and Boeing B-52Hs flying from the British Indian Ocean Territories island of Diego Garcia. Tomahawk missiles were launched by US Navy surface vessels and Royal Navy submarines, while carrier aircraft flying from *Enterprise* and *Carl Vinson* dropped precision-guided weapons.

Initial assaults were mounted against air defence, and command and control centres within Afghanistan, as well as against known terrorist training camps of the Al-Qaeda network. With air supremacy achieved quickly against the Taliban's virtually non-existent air

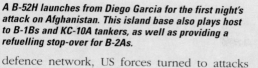

A B-52H launches from Diego Garcia for the first night's attack on Afghanistan. This island base also plays host to B-1Bs and KC-10A tankers, as well as providing a refuelling stop-over for B-2As.

defence network, US forces turned to attacks against military infrastructure targets. By late October the Taliban front lines in the war with the opposition Northern Alliance were under increasing attack, and US Special Forces had increased the scope of their operations within Afghanistan, having mounted one major set-piece attack on an airfield and a command and control centre near Kandahar, which involved a paradrop from MC-130s.

B-1s and B-52s have accounted for the greatest amount of tonnage dropped, but in terms of sortie numbers the US Navy's carrier aircraft have borne the brunt. *Theodore Roosevelt* arrived to relieve *Enterprise* in mid-October, and for a period all three carriers were launching strikes. *Kitty Hawk* is also on-station, but

with only a partial air wing aboard to allow the vessel to act as a floating Special Forces base. However, some F/A-18 combat sorties have been launched. USAF F-15Es have also been involved, flying from land bases in the region, as have AC-130 gunships.

With the exception of the submarine-launched Tomahawk attacks, British involvement has been restricted to support, with VC10s refuelling US Navy aircraft. A Nimrod R.Mk 1 and two Canberra PR.Mk 9s have provided reconnaissance and surveillance support.

All the while that bombing has been ongoing, the US has also been fighting a 'hearts and minds' battle, involving the use of C-17s dropping food rations to the many Afghans who face starvation as a result of the country's worst drought for many years. EC-130 Commando Solo psywar aircraft have also been highly active on radio broadcast missions.

The full story of the opening weeks of Enduring Freedom, and continuing developments in the campaign, will be featured in the next volume of *International Air Power Review*.

Above: With up to four carriers launching strikes from the northern Arabian Sea, the F/A-18 Hornet has been the backbone of the tactical forces employed against Taliban targets. Above is VFA-94's 'CAG-bird', clutching a GBU-31 JDAM to its wing pylon and adorned with 20 mission markings on the nose. Hornets have also delivered LGBs, often designated by F-14 'Fast-FACs'.

Right: UK support for Enduring Freedom, known as Operation Veritas, has involved tanker and reconnaissance missions. Here a VC10 of No. 101 Sqn refuels F/A-18s of VFA-22 after a strike.

OPERATIONS AND DEPLOYMENTS

United States

Vipers to Slovakia
F-16Cs and personnel assigned to the 31st Fighter Wing's 555th Fighter Squadron deployed from Aviano AB Italy, to Malacky AB, Slovakia in June 2001. The unit conducted weapons training on a range in Kuchnya near Bratislava.

Eagles to Poland
F-15s and personnel from the Oregon ANG's 173rd FW/114th FS deployed to Minsk-Mazowiecki AB in late May 2001. While in Poland the unit trained against MiG-29s operated by the Polish Air Force's 1st Fighter Squadron and participated in Sentry White Eagle, a two-week training exercise.

EP-3E returned
The US Navy's disassembled EP-3E departed Hainan Island, China aboard a chartered Russian An-124 cargo aircraft on 3 July 2001 and arrived at Lockheed Martin's facility at Dobbins AFB in Marietta,

The Virginia Air National Guard's 192rd Fighter Wing/149th Fighter Squadron recently began equipping its F-16Cs with the Litening 2 targeting pod. The unit has received four of the $1.5 million targeting pods which allow the pilot to detect ground targets as far away as 40 miles (64 km), deliver laser-guided munitions and fly low-level missions at night. In addition to the pod the aircraft are being fitted with the situational awareness data link (SADL) that allows the aircraft to transmit and receive target and mission data between aircraft and ground forces.

Georgia, on 4 July. The Navy would have preferred to repair the aircraft and fly it home, however the Chinese government denied the request and forced the costly disassembly. In order to move the aircraft off the Chinese island a 12-person Lockheed Martin recovery team began disassembling it on 13 June in an operation that cost

approximately $5.8 million. The Navy and Lockheed Martin hope to return the aircraft to service, however before repairs can be conducted engineers will determine whether this is cost-effective. Should the EP-3E not be deemed repairable the Navy has set aside $45 million for the conversion of a P-3C to the ARIES II configuration.

Macedonia
Operations Eagle and Essential Harvest

In 2001 trouble in the war-torn Balkans flared up once more into open conflict. NATO forces in the region sought to keep the situation under control, in turn requiring a major surveillance effort, which was mostly performed by UAVs. After a political breakthough in August, NATO then faced the hazardous task of collecting weapons from rebel forces.

Above: British paratroops deplane from an RAF TriStar at Skopje. 2 PARA was the lead unit in the NATO effort to collect weapons from the National Liberation Army following the political accord which ended the fighting in Macedonia.

Left: Petrovec (Skopje) became the focus of NATO operations in Macedonia. Here a German army CH-53G shares the ramp with a USAF C-130, while in the busy skies are another C-130 and a Lynx AH.Mk 9. The airfield is also Macedonia's principal airport, and military operations are integrated with civilian movements.

Above: With VVARM (Macedonian air force) 'Hips' in the background, two Hunter UAVs are prepared for a mission from Petrovec.

Left: The General Atomics RQ-1 Predator is flown by the USAF's 11th Reconnaissance Squadron, home-based at Indian Springs AFAF, Nevada. The Predator has a multi-sensor suite, including EO/IR sensors in the Skyball turret under the nose. Another key sensor is the TESAR imaging radar.

Operation Eagle

Heavy fighting along the tense border between Macedonia and Kosovo in March 2001 prompted NATO to launch a major effort to enhance its surveillance capabilities in the Balkans. Alliance commanders were demanding increased surveillance in an effort to boost their campaign, codenamed Operation Eagle, to stop ethnic Albanian insurgents conducting cross-border operations into Macedonia from Kosovo.

In past Balkan crises, NATO commanders were able to draw on high-tech manned surveillance assets such as the USAF U-2 and RC-135 Rivet Joint, US Navy EP-3 Aries II, British Canberra PR.Mk 9 and scores of 'fast-mover' tactical reconnaissance aircraft from a number of NATO countries. However, the high cost and huge manpower requirements of supporting these systems at Italian bases meant allied governments were loath to commit them to the latest Balkan crisis. The reduction in tactical fighters has been particularly dramatic: only 22 NATO aircraft, including reconnaissance types, were assigned to the Balkan theatre on any given day in 2001, compared to 41 in the previous year. Further cutbacks are proposed for 2002. In the words of one NATO surveillance officer, the Balkans are no longer "the crisis of the day". The 'heavy metal' surveillance systems were needed elsewhere, particularly in Iraq and the Far East.

The high-tech aircraft continue to be available in the Balkan theatre but on a much reduced basis, sharing their precious flight hours with the Middle Eastern theatre. NATO peacekeeping units in the Balkans were required to take up the strain with less expensive systems, which were more closely integrated with land forces brigade and divisional formations. The 'normalisation' of airspace over Bosnia also had an impact on the type of surveillance aircraft that could function over that country, making UAV (unmanned air vehicle) operations more complicated. In 2001, NATO commanders had to confront the latest Balkan crisis with a very new surveillance force mix.

UAVs take up the strain

In March 2001 the only UAVs supporting NATO peacekeepers in the Balkans were short-range German Army EMT Ingenieurgesellschaft LUNA X-2000 UAVs operating near Prizren, inside Kosovo. They bore the brunt of the surveillance effort in support of the German-led Multi-National Brigade (South) during the height of the March fighting between Macedonian security forces and Albanian insurgents. Operating from field locations, they provided limited surveillance of key sections of the border where German troops were trying to stop small groups of insurgents crossing back and forth into Kosovo. The LUNA unit had been in Kosovo when the current crisis

erupted. When it was due to rotate home in May, the French, in order to retain the surveillance capability, offered to replace it with a CL-289 UAV of the 61st Artillery Regiment.

For the first three months of 2001, NATO commanders in the Balkans had to rely for their real-time video imagery requirements on the US Army C-12 MARS (Cessna 337) owned by Florida-based AirScan and contracted by the US Army, plus a single US Navy or Dutch P-3C Orion based in Italy.

In late March, Britain and the US announced that they were to deploy, respectively, their BAE Systems Phoenix and General Atomics RQ-1B Predator systems to the Kosovo-Macedonia region. At the end of March, a 55-strong detachment of the USAF's 11th Reconnaissance Squadron was in the process of standing up its unit at Macedonia's Petrovec airport, and on 3 April it launched its first air vehicle for a test flight. The Phoenix of the Royal Artillery's 57 Battery, 39 Regiment, became operational in Kosovo in June.

NATO surveillance experts were particularly keen to gain the services of the Predator because it can operate close to sensitive border regions with Yugoslavia, in the Presevo Valley region, where US force protection restrictions prevented manned surveillance aircraft operating within 5 km (3 miles) of the border. "The lack of UAVs really hurt us," said a senior NATO surveillance expert based in Italy. "The 5-km restriction on US manned aircraft meant we could not fly right up to the Presevo Valley and get real-time imagery from the aircraft's electro-optical system. With the UAV, we can do that."

Predator

The 11th Reconnaissance Squadron is one of two active-duty Predator squadrons, normally based at Indian Springs Air Force Auxiliary Field, Nevada. Although the squadron had been scheduled for rotation to the Balkans this summer, the recent crisis in Macedonia meant the unit had to make a rapid deployment to the small Balkan country, say USAF officers.

"Our mission is to support NATO's Kosovo Force (KFOR) and Stabilisation Force (SFOR) [in Bosnia] as needed with real-time motion

Flying from Sigonella, US Navy and Dutch P-3 Orions have made occasional surveillance missions in support of operations in the Balkans, but the reduced numbers on deployment mean that they cannot provide the extent of coverage which was available during Allied Force.

video, including infra-red," said Lieutenant Colonel Chuck Acree, commander of the detachment. "We provide video day and night to KFOR. We bring live video, in colour, of what is happening, right now. That makes a difference to how troops on the ground do their job."

Predators have been in and out of the Balkan theatre since the summer of 1995 when they supported NATO's Operation Deliberate Force bombing campaign, and played a prominent part in the 1999 Kosovo war. Wing icing problems have meant the Predators were usually withdrawn from the Balkans during winter months. The region's high mountain ranges are also a challenge to the air vehicle, prompting the USAF to order the first upgraded RQ-1B from General Atomics in 1999. The B version of the proven Predator features a turbo-charged engine, wings equipped for de-icing, ARC-210 radios and mode 4 identification friend or foe (IFF) equipment. "We have the RQ-1B variant of the Predator, which has the wet wing or weeping wing capability for de-icing," said Acree. "It has a turbo-charged engine with 40 per cent greater power, which has a big effect on our climb capability."

Acree described the Predator's imagery product as "very much in demand by our customers", prompting regular requests for its return to the Balkans in times of crisis. "The challenge this year compared to last autumn has been due to the normalisation of Balkan airspace, particularly over Bosnia," said Acree. "This has made life more challenging." NATO surveillance officers based in Italy say the return of upper airspace control to Bosnia's

The US Army's Task Force Hunter deployed six IAI/TRW RQ-5s to Petrovec in May. At least four of the UAVs wear nose art, these two being Wing Nuts *(foreground) and* Witch Hunter.

An RQ-1B Predator sets out on a surveillance flight along the Kosovo-Macedonia border. The 11th RS was the main in-theatre reconnaissance asset from March to May, after which Hunters assumed the task.

civilian authorities allows commercial flights to take place between 29,000 and 39,000 ft (8840 and 9144 m), but it means that restrictions are now in place on alliance air operations and operational flexibility has been reduced.

According to officers of the 11th Squadron, all analysis of 'product' collected by the units is carried out by other agencies. The video is transmitted via the US satellite Joint Broadcast System to US and NATO headquarters in Belgium, Germany, Bosnia, Kosovo and Italy, as well as the US European Command Joint Analysis Centre at RAF Molesworth in Britain and to various locations in the continental US.

"We collect imagery of targets. I steer the sensor ball, make sure the sensor's properly focussed and zoomed and is pointing in the right place," an 11th Squadron sensor operator and imagery analyst told *Jane's Defence Weekly*. "Once we have done a target we go to another

The BAE Systems Phoenix UAV has been used by the British Army for short-range reconnaissance missions in Kosovo. The high mountains along the Kosovo-Macedonia border prevented it from being used in support of Operation Eagle.

one. We have the capability to dynamically retask to new targets.

"The sensor fit in our Predators is standard. We have four sensors – day TV, spotter, synthetic aperture radar (SAR), forward-looking infra-red (FLIR) – which we use selectively. What the customers ask for depends on the nature of the target. Video imagery is a whole lot easier to use than still imagery, you can close in on what you want to look at."

The Kosovo-Macedonia border interdiction mission poses a number of new challenges to NATO UAV units now deployed to the Balkans. Particularly important is safe airspace separation in the crowded skies above Skopje and up the Kacanik Gorge region into Kosovo. A civilian air traffic control regime exists in Macedonia, while in Kosovo NATO has jurisdiction.

The Kacanik Gorge is a major scene of insurgent activity and a key target for NATO UAVs, but it is also the main route into and out of Kosovo for alliance helicopters carrying people and cargo from logistic bases in Macedonia. NATO ground units have deployed artillery units along the border to fire illumination rounds over suspected infiltration routes. This all contributes to an airspace deconfliction nightmare, and a strict regime of 'time blocks' or 'windows' is in place, co-ordinated by KFOR air operations centre in Pristina and the Balkan Combined Air Operations Centre (CAOC) in Vicenza, Italy. They issue a daily airspace co-ordination order to allocate airspace.

"We treat the Predator like any other aircraft," said Acree. "That includes deconfliction with other air traffic. We talk on the radio with the civilian control tower at Petrovec to get clearance for take-off, just like any other aircraft. When we did our local orientation sortie we were flying around the pattern – mixing up with airliners was no problem. Once in Kosovo and Bosnia, our flights are regulated by the NATO airspace co-ordination order. That is our tool for deconfliction, just like anyone else flying around here."

An AirScan Cessna 337 sits outside its base at Petrovec. Under the wing can be seen the datalink pod which transmits FLIR imagery to a ground station. The Cessnas were used to cover a shortfall in surveillance cover until Predator UAVs could be deployed.

Ensuring dynamic exploitation of intelligence gained by NATO's UAVs will be the true test of their worth. Previous imagery from the Predator has been made available via the Joint Broadcast System to US commanders at the huge Camp Bondsteel base in southeastern Kosovo and KFOR Main Headquarters in Pristina.

AirScan's Cessna

Florida-based airborne surveillance company AirScan operates a Cessna 337 in Macedonia in support of US Army attempts to monitor the tense Kosovo-Macedonia border. The private company works under a contract awarded in autumn 2000 to provide surveillance support to US peacekeeping missions in Bosnia, Macedonia and Kosovo. This includes up to 100 hours of flying per month.

Initially one, but now two, of the company's Cessna aircraft, which wear US civilian registrations, are based at Petrovec airport to the east of Macedonia's capital, Skopje. They are equipped with a Wescam FLIR pod under the port wing and datalink under the starboard wing.

It is understood that the aircraft have flown daily missions along the border as part of the NATO effort to interdict the movement of ethnic Albanian insurgents into Macedonia from Kosovo. The aircraft were active in Macedonia at the height of the fighting in Tetovo in mid-March, two weeks before USAF General Atomics RQ-1B Predators arrived at Petrovec to assume the mission of providing real-time imagery support for US forces. The AirScan aircraft operate solely on behalf of US forces and do not share their imagery with NATO forces.

AirScan has airborne surveillance contracts with a number of US government agencies and has recently worked for oil companies in Angola, and the Colombian government.

Arrival of the Hunter

US Army surveillance capability was boosted in May by the arrival of IAI/TRW RQ-5/BQM-155A Hunter unmanned aerial vehi-

A German soldier displays a LUNA X-2000 drone. This light UAV was widely used for scouting ahead of NATO patrols and for border surveillance.

cles at Petrovec. This deployment was the third to Macedonia by Alpha Company, 15th Military Intelligence Battalion (Aerial Exploitation) since it first served in the Balkans during the 1999 Kosovo war. "We are the US Army's only deployable UAV unit," said company commander Captain Dan Dittenber.

The ongoing conflict in Macedonia and the prospect of NATO peacekeepers deploying to the country to disarm rebel fighters led the US Army to decide to keep the 65-strong task force and its six Hunter air vehicles in Macedonia beyond their originally scheduled end-of-tour date of mid-August. In the event, Task Force Hunter did not begin deploying back to its home base until October.

After taking over the interdiction mission from the Predators, Task Force Hunter began flying nightly surveillance missions along the mountainous and heavily wooded Kosovo-Macedonia border, looking for activity by rebel fighters of the National Liberation Army (NLA). The information is used to alert US and NATO ground troops to conduct intercept operations.

In June the task force was closely involved in operations to escort NLA fighters from Aracinovo, providing continuous surveillance of a US Army convoy as it moved through rebel and government positions. Hunters were in the air throughout the operation and were instrumental in finding the convoy a safe route back to the US base at Camp Able Sentry (CAS) at Petrovec, after Macedonian civilians blocked its route with burning barricades and started to stone the American HUMVEEs and buses.

"We looked down routes to see if there were obstructions and if the vehicles could make it down the route," said Hunter mission commander Sergeant Donald Pezzatta. "We had two aircraft up, each one holding off on the sides of the convoy, we were switching pictures between them. This was real-time to CAS Tactical Operations Centre, where Brigadier General William David [commander of US forces in Kosovo and Macedonia] was watching the video."

According to Dittenber, the General was very enthusiastic about the support provided by the UAV. "The General said the Hunter was 'priceless – worth its weight in gold'," said Dittenber. "Our guys had a real sense of accomplishment because US soldiers, our friends from CAS, were out there on the ground."

In the 31 missions flown by the task force since it conducted its first mission on 19 May, it had logged 367 flight hours for the loss of only one air vehicle. This went down in western Kosovo near the border with Albania, after a suspected failure of the air vehicle's main computer. According the Dittenber, the air vehicle's parachute deployed to cushion its

C-130s figured prominently in the airlift of equipment into Macedonia. This scene at Skopje shows a line of three RAF Hercules, led by the green 'special forces' aircraft. At the rear is a Hercules C.Mk 4 (C-130J).

landing. "It was in real good shape, only a damaged vertical stabiliser, wing and nose wheel," he said. "It will fly again after TRW repairs it and recertifies it."

Dittenber led a recovery team in two helicopters to retrieve the downed Hunter. "We took the wing, tail and antenna off and carried back it back to a CH-47D helicopter – it was a tight fit, but we got it in. From us hitting ground to taking off was 45 minutes."

Operation Eagle was at its height between June and early August 2001 as the war raged out of control in Macedonia. During this period, NATO troops were able to carry out almost daily intercepts of rebel supply columns entering Macedonia from Kosovo. NATO troops seized some 155 assault rifles, 60 machineguns, 65 anti-tank weapons, over 100,000 rounds of 7.62-mm ammunition and 50,000 rounds of 12.7-mm ammunition, as well as hundreds of mines, hand grenades and mortar rounds. Almost 500 suspected rebel fighters were captured.

In mid-August NATO launched Operation Essential Harvest, to support the Macedonian peace deal between rebels and the Skopje government. Some 4,600 NATO troops established weapon collection points. Operation Eagle continued its activities to prevent more weapons being smuggled into Macedonia, requiring NATO's surveillance assets to continue their mission.

Essential Harvest

As the giant Chinook helicopter approached the small field next to the rebel assault course, local ethnic Albanian villagers, rebel fighters and British paratroopers tried to ignore the dust cloud. Minutes later the helicopter was airborne leaving a party of Macedonian members of parliament and journalists on the ground. They had come to see the rebel fighters of the National Liberation Army (NLA) hand over their

France and Germany have been heavily involved in peacekeeping operations in Macedonia, and Transalls from both countries are regular visitors to Skopje. Following the success of Essential Harvest, a new NATO stabilising force was established in Macedonia, known as Task Force Fox. The German army leads this multinational force.

arms to the Paras and looked very nervous being so far behind enemy lines. The flight up to the weapon collection site had taken them over shell-damaged villages from the eight-month long war, but the arrival of NATO troops had at last calmed the situation. NATO helicopters were now flying freely over the front-lines, where only a few weeks before rebel and government forces had been confronting each other in the latest Balkan ethnic war zone.

As the weapon collection operation gathered momentum, NATO diplomats had to convince Macedonia's parliament to begin voting through the constitutional changes required under the US and European Union peace plan, which had brought a pause in the conflict. This was a new type of operation for NATO. Its military power was not being used to force the peace, but rather as an enabling component in a complex peace plan.

NATO officially launched Operation Essential Harvest on 22 August 2001, opening the way for more than 4,500 NATO troops from 13 allied countries to move into Macedonia to establish weapons collection points where rebel fighters could voluntarily surrender their arms.

Airlift was central to the conduct of the operation, with most contributing nations relying on aircraft to move their contingents to the land-locked Balkan country. Once the operation was under way, NATO commanders relied on helicopters to move their troops to the weapon collection points and remove war material handed in by rebel fighters.

Planning and deployment

Plans for the operation began in earnest in late June, when 16 Brigade was nominated as the tactical headquarters by NATO. Its commander, Brigadier Barney White-Spunner, and his planning staff, conducted four reconnaissance missions to Macedonia during July to get the lie of the land and work out how they would conduct their mission. During these visits they made use of a British Army Air Corps Westland

The RAF's newest transport, the C-17A, was used operationally for the first time, transporting equipment for the British detachment to Skopje. Here an aircraft is loaded at RAF Brize Norton.

Gazelle AH.Mk 1 of 654 Squadron, detached south to Macedonia from its normal base at Pristina Airport in Kosovo.

NATO peace negotiators were hard at work during July and into August trying to bring the two sides together as the war seemed to be escalating out of control. They were able to drag the parties to sign the so-called Framework Agreement for Peace on 13 August. To capitalise on the momentum of the peace deal, Britain pushed NATO into agreeing to deploy 16 Brigade headquarters ahead of a durable ceasefire being in place, which had previously been a NATO condition for launching Essential Harvest.

A small element of 16 Brigade's command team flew to Naples to confer with NATO's southern regional commander, US Navy Admiral James Ellis, on 16 August, before flying into Skopje's Petrovec airport the following day in a blaze of publicity.

Handling the arrival of the aircraft carrying 16 Brigade's equipment, vehicles and personnel was a small French air force team that ran NATO's Airport of Disembarcation (APOD) at Petrovec, Macedonia's principal civil and military airport.

The first task of Brigadier White-Spunner and his troops was to set up a system of liaison between the rebel and government forces to cement the tenuous ceasefire. In the first ever operational sortie by the new Boeing C-17A Globemaster III of the RAF's No. 99 Squadron on 18 August, three Army Air Corps Westland Lynx AH.Mk 7s of 657 Squadron were delivered to Petrovec. They were needed to carry British special forces teams deep into rebel territory to establish contact with the commanders of the NLA. They were soon joined by two 654 Squadron Gazelles and two Westland Puma HC.Mk 1s of No. 33 Squadron, detached from Pristina to assist 16 Brigade.

Border blockade

Hardline Macedonian nationalists were far from happy with the arrival of NATO troops in their country and they set about making life as difficult as possible for Task Force Harvest, as the NATO force was now code-named. A group of protestors blocked the main road from Kosovo into Macedonia, preventing NATO Kosovo Force (KFOR) troops in the UN-administered Yugoslav province from providing logistic support for the new task force, or receiving supplies from the huge NATO logistics base at Petrovec. Allied troop contingents now began to set up a fixed-wing and heli-copter airlift to overfly the protestors. Central to this effort were the four Boeing CH-47D Chinooks of the US Army's 101st Airborne Division based at Camp Bondsteel in southern Kosovo. Bravo Company of the 101st Division's

7th Battalion were soon flying an hourly shut-tle with underslung loads back and forth between Camp Able Sentry at Petrovec to Bondsteel and other locations in Kosovo. German KFOR troops also began a shuttle between their main Kosovo base at Prizren and their supply base in Macedonia at Erebino, west of Skopje, using VFW-Fokker/Sikorsky CH-53G Stallions and Bell/Dornier UH-1D Hueys. Two Italian Army Aviation Agusta-Bell AB 412s also flew into Petrovec Airport to help the Italian contingent of Task Force Harvest.

The first four days of the operation saw just over two dozen sorties by RAF Lockheed Hercules of the Lyneham Transport Wing and six RAF C-17A sorties. With the help of Brize Norton-based VC10s, the Hercules and C-17 force moved almost 400 British personnel to Macedonia to allow 16 Brigade's commander to get his headquarters fully operational. Dozens of allied aircraft were also soon heading for Petrovec. First to arrive were two Czech Antonov An-26s carrying a company of para-troopers. A French Air Force CASA CN235 followed soon after with a small group of staff officers heading for 16 Brigade's headquarters.

On 20 August, NATO's Supreme Allied Commander Europe, USAF General Joe Ralston, made a brief visit to Skopje in a USAF 86th Wing C-20 executive jet to meet allied comman-ders and diplomats to assess if conditions were right to give the go ahead to formally launch Operation Essential Harvest. Despite almost nightly breaches of the ceasefire and political in-fighting within the ranks of the Macedonian

government, the NAC accepted General Ralston's recommendation to begin the opera-tion. A formal activation order was issued and the first troop contingents began moving late on 22 August.

First to arrive was a contingent of French Foreign Legion infantrymen, which was flown to Petrovec on French Air Force Douglas DC-8s and C.160 Transalls. An RAF VC10 of No. 101 Squadron brought the first elements of the British Army's 2nd Battalion, the Parachute Regiment (2 PARA) into Macedonia in the early hours of the following day. More British troops followed during the day on eight flights as Lockheed TriStars of No. 216 Squadron joined the airlift. Dutch Fokker 60s and McDonnell Douglas KDC-10s, German C.160s, Canadian and Belgian Hercules were much in evidence moving their contingents. Canada hired giant Antonov An-124 airlifters to help move the LAV armoured vehicles of its contingent from Bosnia to Petrovec. Chartered Lynden Air Cargo L-100 Hercules also joined the airlift effort.

RAF Hercules were sent to Pristina on 26 August to pick-up the Scimitar armoured vehicles of the Scots Dragoon Guards, which had been stopped from joining 16 Brigade because of the border blockade. They were then flown southwards to Petrovec.

An aviation element of the Task Force Harvest Multi-National Brigade grew as the NATO mission gathered pace. The US Army offered to make Bravo Company's Chinooks available for troop and cargo movement tasks. A further four Chinooks, from F Company, 159th Aviation Battalion, were deployed to Camp Able Sentry from Germany to take over the border re-supply tasks, freeing Bravo Company to fully support Task Force Harvest. In total, some 230 hours were flown by the Chinooks until the border was re-opened in mid-September. A USAF Lockheed C-130E Hercules was sent to shuttle people and cargo between Pristina Airport and Petrovec. Two UH-60s were also placed on alert at Camp Able Sentry to fly casualty evacuation missions for the new NATO force. They were called into action sooner than expected on 26 August when a British soldier was fatally injured by a mob of Macedonian nationalists, flying the soldier first to the US Army medical facility at Bondsteel and then back to Skopje's main civil-ian hospital for neurosurgery.

Surveillance support for Task Force Harvest was provided by six IAI/TRW BQM-155A Hunter unmanned aerial vehicles (UAVs) of Alpha Company, 15th Military Intelligence Battalion (Aerial Exploitation), already based at Petrovec Airport.

Weapon collection operations

With ceasefire violations threatening to unravel the peace deal, the commander of Task Force Harvest, Danish Major General Gunnar Lange, and Brigadier White-Spunner, were

NLA weapons are laid out at a collection point (above) while a CH-47D slings in an ISO container. Once troops have loaded the guns into the container, it is removed by Chinook and taken away (right). The CH-47's ability to lift heavy loads and large numbers of troops enabled Task Force Harvest to rapidly establish collection points.

keen to get the 30-day weapon collection operation under way as fast as possible.

Reconnaissance and planning went into high gear on 25 and 26 August to prepare for the first weapons collection operation. Hunter UAVs were sent to scour around the target areas in the village Otlja, northeast of Skopje. At the same time, 657 Squadron Lynxes were moving British Army liaison teams from the 7th Parachute Regiment, Royal Horse Artillery, and the Special Forces to meet rebel and government military commanders to ensure they were ready for what was about to happen.

During 26 August the first elements of the Foreign Legion and 2 PARA were flown in by Chinook to secure the collection site. The operation proper got under way the following morning, when the bulk of the force was delivered by Chinook to establish a wide perimeter to allow the rebels to hand over their arms unmolested. A Royal Air Force Mobile Air Operations Team (MAOT) team was on hand to control the helicopters as they flew in and out of landing zones near the collection site. A brief firefight nearby delayed the opening of the site, but by early afternoon US Army Chinooks, British Gazelles and Pumas, and a French Army Aviation Eurocopter Puma (of the 5ème RHC),

The four CH-47Ds from B Company, 7th Battalion, 101st Airborne were the main transport element of Essential Harvest. While they were diverted to this new task, their routine work in Kosovo was handled by four Chinooks flown in from the Germany-based F Co/159 AVN.

flew in a VIP and media party to view the proceedings.

Even as that operation was continuing, a far more ambitious mission was under way to set up a collection point in the village of Brodec, high in the mountains of western Macedonia. Unlike the Otlja operation, where vehicle-borne troops were also involved, the operation set for 28 August would be undertaken completely by helicopter. As before, Hunter UAVs were sent to scout the lie of the land for 2 PARA, and during 27 August an advanced guard of British paratroopers and Dutch airmobile troops was inserted by two Chinooks. In the early hours of the following morning, eight Chinooks lifts delivered the main body of 2 PARA to establish the collection site. Night vision goggles were used to ensure the helicopters delivered their cargo under the cover of

darkness. Later in the morning the Chinooks then delivered ISO containers for the rebel weapons to be loaded into.

Phase one of the weapon collection mission was completed the following morning, when a company-sized group of 2 PARA was airlifted to southwest Macedonia at Tamuse. These three operations netted more than 1,200 weapons and set the stage for NATO's diplomats to apply pressure on the Macedonia parliament to begin implementing the constitutional changes, as required under the peace plan. This took longer than expected and it was not until 5 September that the parliament passed the vital vote.

Rising tension

In the run up to the key parliamentary vote, Macedonia hardliners continued to stage inci-

Macedonia's air force

The Protiv Vozdusna Odbrana i Voeno Vozduhoplovstvo na Armijata na Republika Makedonija (PVO i VVARM – Macedonian air defence and air force) was formed on 10 June 1992 within the army structure, initially operating a handful of UTVA-75 lightplanes. In March 2001, as Mi-8s and Mi-24s arrived from the Ukraine, the air force (VVARM) became a separate service.

Above: An overview of the VVARM complex at Petrovec shows four Mi-24s and a line of four Su-25 'Frogfoot' attackers (including one Su-25UB two-seater) which were received from the Ukraine. The Su-25s are assigned to the 101 Avijaciska Eskadrila. Il-76 transports were regular visitors in 2001, bringing in equipment for the growing air force.

Left: The 301 Transporta Helikopterska Eskadrila operates 11 Mi-8MTV/Mi-17s in the assault and attack roles. One of the original four Mi-17s was lost in a crash.

Right: The first four Mi-17s were delivered in 1994, originally in a white medevac scheme. From 1996 they adopted camouflage after the arms embargo against Macedonia was dropped. In 2001 they were augmented by eight Ukrainian Mi-8MTVs.

Left: Greece supplied two UH-1Hs to the VVARM, serialled VAM-321 and VAM-322. They operate primarily on casevac duties.

dents in the flashpoint town of Tetovo to destabilise the peace plan. No. 657 Squadron Lynxes were much in evidence, flying surveillance missions over Tetovo to support the 16 Brigade Pathfinder Platoon patrols monitoring the ceasefire line. US Army Blackhawks also ferried NATO negotiators to the main rebel base at Sipkovica, high above Tetovo, to ensure rebel compliance.

During the pause in the fighting the Macedonia air force was hastening its effort to retrain and re-equip. A daily airlift was mounted by chartered Russian and Ukrainian aircraft to bring in material for the Skopje government's hard pressed army and paramilitary police. Small arms and mortar ammunition were among the items unloaded from Ilyushin Il-76 'Candids', Antonov An-124 'Condors' and smaller Antonov An-26/32-class aircraft that were seen arriving at the military section of Petrovec airport, east of the civilian Skopje airport terminal area.

This major arms importation operation also went hand-in-hand with a considerable effort by the Macedonian armed forces to reduce their dependence on Ukrainian air crew and specialists to operate the Macedonian Army Air Force's (VVARM) fleet of Mil Mi-8MTV 'Hip' and Mi-24V 'Hind' helicopters, and Sukhoi Su-25 'Frogfoot' fighter-bombers.

Macedonian aircrews underwent intensive flight training from Petrovec, with fixed-wing pilots undergoing basic training in the Zlin 242L aircraft before transitioning to the Sukhois. The helicopter force was flying more than 10 hours of training daily, with all the Ukrainian-supplied types and Greek-supplied Bell UH-1H Hueys involved in conducting circuit practice around the airport, formation flying and practising attack tactics.

Weapons collection second phase

Within hours of the parliamentary vote on 6 September, 2 PARA began its operation to set up a new weapons collection point at Radusa, northwest of Skopje, inserting reconnaissance teams during the evening. The main helicopter-borne operation went smoothly, with some 150 weapons handed in by the NLA's 115th Brigade on 7 September.

It was the turn of the French to run the next collection site, between 8 and 10 September, at Brodec in Operation Tapanar. US Chinooks again played a key role, flying in the main body of the force into location.

The Italian and Turkish battle group opened its collection site at Otlja on 12 September, moving mainly by vehicle from its bases at nearby Petrovec airport. Gurkha paratroopers attached to 2 PARA got the opportunity to open the final collection site of the second phase of Operation Essential Harvest, when they flew to open a site at Tamuse in western Macedonia on 11 September. This phase of the operation netted more than 1,000 weapons.

Mission accomplished?

The final round of weapons collection began on 20 September with French troops moving by road to Radusa. The Gurkhas were airlifted high into the mountains at Tamuse in Bravo Company's Chinooks and Italian AB 412s the following day in a surprise operation. A day later, the Italian battle group opened the Otlja collection site in a ground operation. It was

Above and right: Arguably the most useful aircraft in the VVARM inventory in the fighting with NLA rebels were the eight Mi-24 'Hinds' (VAM-201 to VAM-208) supplied and initially operated by the Ukraine. They serve with the 201 Protivoklopna Helikopterska Eskadrila (POHE – attack helicopter squadron).

Right: For basic training the VVARM received four Zlin-242Ls from the Czech Republic in 1995. Although they wear civilian registrations, they also carry VVARM serials (VAM-101 to VAM-104) and they serve with the 101 Avijaciska Eskadrila. One aircraft (VAM-102) was lost in an accident on 7 April 1999.

down to 2 PARA to conduct the final collection operation at Brodec, after moving by road to a forward staging area to reduce the flying time to the objective and time between lifts.

On 25 September, NATO Secretary General George Robertson was flown by Chinook to the large German base at Erebino for a ceremony to mark the end of Operation Essential Harvest. As he was announcing that NATO had received more than the projected 3,300 weapons, a constant stream of Chinooks could be heard flying overhead, ferrying 2 PARA back from Brodec to Petrovec Airport.

In a concentrated 30-day period Bravo Company's Chinooks had flown 204 hours in 182 sorties, carrying 3,988 passengers, 26 containers of weapons and 29 vehicles. The A Company, 15th MIB Hunter UAVs had flown 26 missions totalling 196.2 hours in support of Task Force Harvest.

Providing a a rescue/medevac detachment for Task Force Harvest were two US Army UH-60s deployed from Camp Bondsteel (Kosovo) to Camp Able Sentry (Petrovec). Note the 'KFOR' titles.

By the end of September NATO had activated Task Force Fox in Macedonia, with the task of providing protection for unarmed civilian monitors who are to patrol the country's still tense ethnic conflict zones. This predominately German force was to have a quick reaction capability and Bravo Company's Chinooks have the mission of supporting this on-going NATO operation.

Tim Ripley

Force Aérienne du Djibouti

Djibouti air force review

Little unknown Djibouti, a city state in the Horn of Africa, became an administrative capital of the French territory in 1896. On 8 May 1977 the population of the so-called French Somaliland voted for independence and the name changed to the Republic of Djibouti. Djibouti is situated on the eastern coast of Africa between the Red Sea and the Gulf of Aden and covers 23000 km² (8,881 sq miles).

The Djibouti air force (Force Aérienne du Djibouti) was formed after the independence of 27 June 1977 as part of the Djibouti Army. First aircraft were three Nord N.2501 Noratlas transport aircraft and an Alouette II helicopter presented by France. The primary task of the Djibouti air force is to support the Army with transport and liaison duties. Although Djibouti had become independent, France remained responsible for its air defence and this task was initially performed by Escadron de Chasse 3/10 from Creil with Mirage IIIC fighters.

In 1982 the Air Force was augmented by two Aérospatiale AS 355F Ecureuil 2 helicopters and a Cessna U206G Stationair. These were followed in 1985 by a Cessna 402C Utiliner. In 1985 the Alouette II was withdrawn from use and put on display at Ambouli Air Base, as Djibouti's main airport is called. Two years later the three N.2501 Noratlases were also put aside and later given back to France.

New equipment came in 1991 in the form of a Cessna 208 Caravan, followed by several Russian types in the early 1990s. They included four Mi-2s, six Mi-8s and two Mi-17s and a single Antonov An-28 light transport aircraft.

Pilot training, when neccesary, is conducted in France, although the need for new pilots is not large in the approximately 250 men of the Djibouti air force. The FAD has no units of its own and forms as a whole a part of the Army. Ambouli is its only base. The serial system employed by the Djibouti air force forms part of the civilian register, utilising the J2-MAA to - MAW range. For most of the time only the last two letters are carried.

French garrison

France still plays an important role in this small country, with more than 3,000 personnel located in Djibouti. Air defence is nowadays carried out by Armée de l'Air Mirage F1C fighters of Escadron de Chasse 4/33 'Vexin', parented by the base at Reims, supported by SA 330 Pumas of the Escuadron de Transport d'Outre Mer 88 'Larzac', while the Armée de Terre uses SA 330 Pumas of det. 188 in various transport roles for the Foreign Legion.

Losses have been very high among the Russian helicopters and, by May 2001, only one Mi-17 was operational and one Mi-8 had been dispatched for maintenance in Ethiopia. All the others have been crashed or wrecked, as evidenced by the four Mi-8s and Mi-2 on the dump at Ambouli.

One of the Ecureuils (J2-MAF) came back from France in March 2001 after maintenance. The other AS 355F is stored and awaiting maintenance, like the Cessna 402C. The Cessna 208 was in South Africa for overhaul. From this country Djibouti would like to purchase three Bell 412 helicopters by the end of 2001. Further on the shopping list will be transport aircraft of which two types, are favourite – the Antonov An-32 or the PZL M-28, the latter regarded for its PT6 engines.

The large influx of aircraft from the former Warsaw Pact in the early 1990s included three PZL-built Mi-2 'Hoplites' and a PZL-built An-28 'Cash' from Poland. Only one Mi-2 remains (below), dumped alongside four Mi-8s, the others having crashed. The An-28 (above) is one of four FAD aircraft currently operational.

Dick Lobuis

Djibouti received six Mi-8s and a pair of Mi-17s, but none of the Mi-8s is flying. In May 2001 the FAD's only operational helicopters were a single Mi-17 (left) and an Ecureuil (below). An Mi-8 is away on overhaul and should return to bolster the fleet. The Mi-8s were worked hard during the 1993/94 Affar rebellion, utilised for troop transport and attack missions.

In 1982 Djibouti received a handful of light aircraft, including a Cessna U206G (above right), which remains operational on light transport/liaison work. A Cessna 402C (above left) arrived three years later, but this aircraft is now withdrawn from use and stored, albeit in good condition. Other FAD light aircraft include a single Rallye, which crashed, and a Cessna 208 Caravan.

Djibouti Air Force aircraft – May 2001

Serial	Type	c/n	remark
J2-MAA	N.2501F	147	withdrawn from use
J2-MAB	Alouette II	1141	Ambouli, preserved
J2-MAC	N.2501F	183	withdrawn from use
J2-MAD	N.2501F	153	withdrawn from use
J2-MAE	**C. U206G**	**05433**	**operational**
J2-MAF	**AS 355F**	**5269**	**operational**
J2-MAG	AS 355F	5270	Ambouli, stored
J2-MAH	C. 402C	1010	Ambouli, stored
J2-MAI	C. 208		maintenance in S. Africa
J2-MAJ	Mi-8		Ambouli dump
J2-MAK	Mi-2		crashed
J2-MAL	Mi-8		Ambouli dump
J2-MAM	Mi-8	13133	Ambouli dump
J2-MAN	Rallye 235GT	13021	crashed
J2-MAO	Mi-2		Ambouli dump
J2-MAP	Mi-2		crashed
J2-MAQ	Mi-2		crashed
J2-MAR	Mi-8		crashed
J2-MAS	Mi-8		maintenance in Ethiopia
J2-MAT	**An-28**		**operational**
J2-MAU	Mi-8	4541	Ambouli dump
J2-MAV	Mi-17		crashed
J2-MAW	**Mi-17**	**341M14**	**operational**

Upgraded Japanese Seahawk unveiled

Mitsubishi/Sikorsky SH-60K

Initially designated SH-60J Kai, the first prototype of the SH-60K (8401) was rolled-out at Mitsubishi Heavy Industries' (MHI) Komaki Minami Factory on 8 August 2001. Begun in FY 1992, the SH-60K is a development programme of the SH-60J, which is produced by MHI under licence from Sikorsky for the Kaijo Jiei-tai (JMSDF – Japan Maritime Self Defence Force). Production of the first of two prototypes began in FY 1997, under contract to the Boei-cho (JDA – Japan Defence Agency). These two prototypes are not modified from SH-60Js but are built from new.

The SH-60K introduces state-of-the-art ASW equipment with an improved tactical data processing system, which includes a tactical decision aid function and an air-to-air datalink. Radar is also upgraded and adds a target classification mode. FLIR is installed under the aircraft's nose, while new dipping sonar has been developed. The SH-60K will not only be able to carry torpedoes, but also the Type 97 anti-ship missile and anti-submarine depth charges (the SH-60J was only armed with torpedoes). For self-defence the SH-60K has a missile approach warning system and chaff/flare dispensers.

Externally, there are many changes, including the addition of stub wings. The new main rotor blades have a revised tip layout to improve their efficiency. As a result, the SH-60K increases its MTOW to 23,200 lb (10524 kg) from the SH-60J's 21,844 lb (9908 kg) without uprating the engines. The main cabin has been stretched by 13 in (33 cm) just aft of the cockpit and height has increased by 6 in (15 cm). The cockpit is also modernised, with six colour LCD multi-function integrated displays. The auto-flight control system has been improved. In addition to the SH-60J's rotor folding system, the Kai's tail pylon and right stub wing can also be folded.

The first SH-60K flew at Komaki on 9 August 2001, followed by the second on 28 September. The two prototypes will be delivered to the JDA by the end of June 2002, following the completion of MHI tests. Technical and operational tests will be conducted by the Gijutu Kenkyu Honbu (TRDI – Technical Research and Development Institute) and Dai 51 Koku-tai (VX-51 – the JMSDF's evaluation unit) until the middle of 2004. Under the current Chuki Boeiryoku Seibi Keikaku (Mid-term Defence Build-up Plan, FY2001 to FY 2005), the production version of the SH-60K will be ordered in FY 2004 if development encounters no major hurdles. It has not yet been established if production SH-60Ks will be newly built or remanufactured from existing SH-60Js.

Yoshitomo Aoki

The SH-60K is a major reworking of the Seahawk, with a lengthened cabin, stub wings and a totally revised sensor suite. This is the second prototype, finished in standard JMSDF colours with TRDI markings.

The complex blade tip design has allowed Mitsubishi to extract a significant increase in maximum take-off weight without having to adopt increased performance engines.

Tiger wins Australian Air 87 competition

Eurocopter Tiger for AAAC

The Australian Government announced on 10 August 2001 that the Eurocopter Tiger has been selected to fill the Army's Armed Reconnaissance Helicopter requirement. Dubbed the 'Aussie Tiger', the helicopter will be based on the French Tigre Hélicoptère d'Appui Protection (HAP), and a contract for 22 aircraft is scheduled to be signed by December 2001.

The deal is worth an estimated $A1.3 billion, and the Australian Army machines will be assembled in Australia, most likely at a former Hawker Pacific facility in Brisbane (or at Oakey) by Eurocopter International Pacific. Assuming a normal progression to the signing of the contract, Australian production is anticipated to run between 2002 and 2006.

Australian industry involvement, as part of the deal, will see EIP producing tail booms and wiring harnesses for all production Tigers, and Eurocopter have additionally agreed to set up an Australian assembly line for the EC 120 Colibri light helicopter.

The announcement of the Tiger as the preferred option comes after a long selection process which had initially begun in the 1980s as a study to replace the unarmed CAC-built Bell 206-1 in the battlefield reconnaissance role, and later expanded to encompass the replacement of the aerial fire support Iroquois. Following a project definition study undertaken in the mid-1990s, a formal Request for Proposal (RfP) was submitted to industry in May 1998, with Agusta (A 129 Scorpion), Bell Helicopter Textron (AH-1Z), Boeing-Mesa (AH-64D Apache), Denel (Rooivalk), Eurocopter (Aussie Tiger), and Sikorsky (Battlehawk – an armed version of the UH-60L) all submitting bids in response. Such was the importance attached to the Australian order that all of the companies, with the exception of Agusta, brought their aircraft out to Australia for demonstration to the Army, usually coinciding with the biennial Australian International Airshow at Avalon.

A shortlist of the Agusta, Boeing and Eurocopter proposals was drawn up and announced in April 1999. However, the tender process was reopened after complaints from Bell that the Defence Acquisition Organisation (DAO) had not followed correct procedure, and that the original requirements were too

Eurocopter's Tigre HAP demonstrator was much in evidence at the 2001 Avalon show. It was demonstrated with Mistral AAM launch tubes, a potential weapon for the AAAC 'Aussie Tigers'.

vague to enable accurate bidding to occur.

After due reconsideration, the Requests for Tender closed for the final time on 30 April 2001, with the three previously successful companies, and Bell, submitting their final bids. Of these, Agusta was eliminated from the race shortly thereafter (the Scorpion being reportedly too small to meet the Australian Army's needs), and both Bell and Boeing's bids were affected to some degree by the value of the Australian dollar against the US currency.

At the media conference to announce the selection of the Tiger, Defence Minister Peter Reith explained that the European helicopter was chosen "because it was good value for money, and we think it's got a lot of good capabilities. And in terms of getting value for money, that's very important to the customer, for the taxpayer, but it's also important in the sense that this helicopter has a lot of capability, which will be very good for the Army."

Assuming no delays in the contract signing and production, the first Tiger should be handed over to the Australian Army Aviation Corps at the end of 2004, and will re-equip Nos 161 and 162 Reconnaissance Squadrons of No. 1 Aviation Regiment, as well as serving with the School of Army Aviation at Oakey for crew training. At this point in time the aircraft does not have an official name, or designation, but will most likely be known as 'Tiger ARH'.

Two reconnaissance squadrons currently operate the Kiowa from Darwin (161 Sqn) and Townsville (162 Sqn), with both units deploying on a regular basis to East Timor. It will be the timing of these future deployments (and the aircraft and training system delivery schedules) that will decide which of the two will begin receiving the first Tigers. Also, it has yet to be decided if the squadrons will remain at their current locations, or be co-located at either Darwin or Townsville, to provide some synergy of operation. The number being acquired is deemed sufficient to ensure that each squadron will have an on-line availability of six helicopters, with three aircraft allocated for training and enough reserves to cover maintenance and attrition.

Although the Iroquois gunships are currently being operated by the Oakey-based No. 171 Squadron, this unit will not re-equip with the Tiger, and will either disband, or reform within 5 Aviation Regiment when the mooted additional troop-lift helicopters are purchased. The Kiowas may be retained in the basic training role (pending replacement by a commercial type), while the Iroquois are currently planned

Project Air 87 was aggressively pursued by the West's attack helicopter manufacturers, their campaigns including a high-profile presence at Australia's biennial airshow at Avalon. Here the Rooivalk (above, marketed to Australia as the Red Hawk) and AH-1W (below, representing Bell's ARH-1Z Taipan bid) are put through their paces at the 1999 show.

to remain in operation until the introduction of the aforementioned troop-lift helicopters. The strains placed on the Army Aviation Corps' infrastructure during the introduction of the Tiger, however, may well influence these plans.

In Australian service, the Tigers will be armed with the 30-mm GIAT AM-30781 cannon, and will be capable of carrying Folding-Fin Aerial Rockets (FFARs) and air-to-ground missiles. It has yet to be decided if the Euromissile HOT-3 or the American AGM-114K Hellfire will be purchased, though this is anticipated to have been decided by the time of contract signing in late 2001. French Army Tigers are also capable of carrying air-to-air missiles, such as the Matra-BAe Dynamics Mistral or Raytheon FIM-92 Stinger, and (subject to contract negotiations) such a capability is also a possibility for the Australian machines.

Other changes to the basic French model are relatively minor, encompassing uprated MTR-390 engines, a dedicated communications suite, and an Electronic Warfare Self Protection (EWSP) and Identification Friend or Foe (IFF) fit. Should the Hellfire be selected, however, a laser designator will need to be integrated into the roof-mounted sight, replacing the laser rangefinder in the basic HAP model.

The armed reconnaissance helicopter capability is sorely needed by the Australian Defence Force, and is arguably overdue. However, the Army can be confident that the relatively minor changes to an aircraft that is already in initial production should not delay the type's entry into service any longer. Should Australian forces be required to embark on operations (be they of a peacekeeping nature, or something more hostile), they can look forward to a new level of support for troops on the ground.

Nigel Pittaway

New 'Fulcrum' family

MiG-29K, KUB, M1, M2 and OVT

During MAKS'2001 at Zhukovskiy, the Russian Aircraft Corporation MiG presented its new family of MiG-29 variants, based on work performed for the imminent contract for about 50 shipborne MiG-29K fighters for India. This builds on earlier development of the MiG-29M (type 9-15, six prototypes) and MiG-29K (type 9-31, two prototypes).

MiG intends to manufacture at the same time four variants of the same universal multi-role fighter aircraft: the carrierborne MiG-29K (single-seater) and MiG-29KUB (two-seater), as well as the land-based MiG-29M1 (single-seater) and MiG-29M2 (two-seater). They feature maximum commonality between airframes, as well as the same fire-control systems and avionics. According to Nikolay Buntin, manager of the MiG-29K/M development programme, the reduction of differences between the four versions is the key to cheaper production and operation.

Both MiG-29K aircraft on display at MAKS were the prototypes originating from the 1980s. The 9-41 aircraft now being prepared for India will be very similar, but will be equipped with a digital fly-by-wire flight control system, extended wing flaps and with refined local aerodynamics (for example, a slotted flap). The aluminium-lithium alloy 0420, used previously for structural parts of the MiG-29K and MiG-29M (almost 10 per cent of the airframe weight) and saving about 80 kg (176 lb) of the total weight, turned out to be a difficult material from an engineering point of view, and will be replaced by traditional materials.

New avionics made by the Ramenskoye PKB, based on those developed for the Su-30MKK,

The almost finalised Indian order has revitalised the MiG-29K programme, this being one of the two original prototypes. MiG has identified China as a potential customer for the future if its stated plans to acquire a carrier capability proceed.

will be arranged around a Mil Std 1553 databus with a Ts90 central computer. The fire-control system will include the Phazotron Zhuk-M radar, an electro-optical unit, helmet target indication system, as well as a radar homing and warning receiver system. The preceding N010 Zhuk radar undertook about 700 test flights in MiG-29M/K aircraft; the new Zhuk-M has a new processor, but other hardware is left almost unchanged. Specific versions of the installed equipment may differ depending on customer requirements. Indian aircraft, in particular, will be equipped with a French INS (as in the upgraded Indian MiG-21bis); also IFF, electronic warfare and RWR systems will be of non-Russian origin. Thanks to new (smaller and lighter) avionics, the new MiG-29K/Ms will be capable of holding 5100 kg (11,243 lb) of internal fuel, compared with 4500 kg (9,920 lb) in the 1980s MiG-29M/K and 3400 kg (7,495 lb) in the basic MiG-29.

Power for the new MiG-29s will come from the Klimov RD-33 series 3 turbofan (already installed in Malaysian aircraft). At 2,000 hours, these engines have the longest service life of any Russian fighter engines. The RD-33 series 3M 'maritimised' version will have an additional anti-corrosive coating of the internal duct, smokeless burning and extra afterburner range with the thrust increased from 81.4 kN (18,292 lb) to 86.3 kN (19,393 lb). At the same time, the aircraft will have larger air intakes to cater for future thrust increases. At MAKS'2001

the engine design bureau Klimov from St Petersburg presented the RD-33-10M, a major upgrade of the RD-33 with thrust increased to 103 kN (23,146 lb) and with a vectoring nozzle. This engine may be installed in the MiG-29, and will be the prototype for the 117.7-kN (26,450-lb) VK-10M engine intended for the next-generation MiG fighter.

Currently under development from the MiG-29K (type 9-41) is the two-seat MiG-29KUB (type 9-47). The external geometry of the aircraft, as well as its internal structure, will remain essentially unchanged apart from the rear cockpit section. Moreover, the fire-control system is unchanged. Thus, the MiG-29KUB will be a full-value combat aircraft.

The land-based MiG-29M1 single-seater and MiG-29M2 two-seater will be similar to the K and KUB. They feature lighter landing gear, front wheel brakes and a braking parachute instead of an arrester hook. Other structure remains unchanged, including the folding wing, which may be useful for customers with small hangars. The wing-fold mechanism can easily be locked shut if not required.

Development of the two-seat MiG-29M2 is considered pressing. The prototype, having been presented at MAKS'2001 for only a few days, was returned quickly to the hangar to be prepared for its maiden flight on 26 September. The haste is a result of an imminent tender request by Malaysia for a two-seat multi-role fighter. MiG expects to continue its successes from 1995, when 18 MiG-29s were sold to Malaysia. This time, however, it will have a strong rival – Sukhoi's Su-30MKM.

Also at Zhukovskiy was the MiG-29OVT (*otklanyaemyi vektor tyagi*, deflected thrust vector) with movable engine nozzles. The Klimov-made nozzles can be deflected to 15° in any direction (up/down and left/right) and at any range of engine operation, including full afterburning. For now, the MiG-29OVT demonstrator (156) is equipped with mock-up nozzles. Working nozzles will be fitted for a first flight in late 2001/early 2002. The same aircraft will be used for tests of new attachments for air-to-air missiles at the wing tips. The vectoring nozzles will be installed in MiG-29M1 and M2 aircraft, but not in the MiG-29K and KUB – the requirements for reliability during carrier operations are too strict.

Piotr Butowski

Above and right: The MiG-29OVT is a demonstrator for Klimov's 15° thrust-vectoring RD-33 engine, although only dummy nozzles were fitted for display at MAKS. It also introduces wingtip launch rails for light AAMs.

Above: Displayed at MAKS before its first flight on 26 September, the MiG-29M2 is being marketed as a Multi-Role Combat Aircraft. The MiG-29KUB under development for India will look generally similar.

Turkish Fast-jet Training

Konya and Çiğli air bases photographed by Luigino Caliaro

Konya (3ncü Ana Jet Üs - 3rd Main Jet Base) is home to the F-4E (illustrated) conversion units and the weapons training squadron. It also houses a standards and tactics evaluation unit operating both types of aircraft. Students passing through the courses here mostly come from the Türk Hava Kuvvetleri's principal basic/advanced training base at Çiğli. Konya, in common with most THK bases, has a base flight (Irtibat Kita) equipped with Bell UH-1Hs for local rescue duties.

After graduating from Çiğli, prospective Phantom crews join 131nci Filo at Konya, which acts as the type OCU (it also has front-line duties and is a regular participant in NATO exercises). Simulator training precedes Phantom conversion, which covers all aspects of F-4 operations.

As befits its operational status, Konya's aircraft are for the most part housed in hardened shelters (above). 131nci Filo turns out F-4 crews for the THK's four operational F-4E and two front-line RF-4E squadrons. For air-to-air gunnery, 131nci Filo Phantoms use towed targets (right).

Most fast-jet pilots graduating from Çiğli are assigned to 133nci Filo 'Pençe' at Konya, which provides combat readiness transition training. The squadron operates a mixed bag of F/NF-5A/Bs, which have been acquired from a variety of sources, including the Netherlands, Norway, Taiwan and the United States. All types of tactical flying and weapons employment are practised, including formation and night flying, air interceptions and air-to-surface work. Forty-eight of the F-5s are being modified by an IAI/Elbit/Singapore Technologies consortium with 'glass' cockpits to make them more useful in the F-16 fighter lead-in role. The F-5 itself has been retired from the THK front line, but a large number is concentrated at Konya to provide weapons training and various trials functions. Successful graduates of the 133nci Filo course usually progress to the F-16C/D OCU – the Öncel Filo at Akinci.

Drawing aircraft from both 131nci Filo (F-4E) and 133nci Filo (F-5A/B), the 132nci Silah Taktileri ve Standardize Filo 'Hançer' was established in 1989 as a weapons and tactics unit, and has performed the standards role for both F-4E and F-5 since 1996. Its main role is to offer a three-month weapons and tactics course for F-4 and F-5 pilots, graduates then returning to their units as qualified weapons instructors. A five-week air combat course is also undertaken twice each year. The squadron also provides courses in fighter tactics (for radar controllers) and flight management (for newly-assigned squadron commanders). In the standards role it checks out instructors and flight leaders, and checks instrument ratings. The unit also has a research and evaluation function, and it makes use of the Ramon EW training range in Israel. Another commitment is TLP participation.

Below: Based at Konya is 134ncü Akrotim Filo Komutanliği (134th aerobatic team squadron command), better known as the 'Türk Yildizlari' ('Turkish Stars'). The team was formed in 1992, flying modified NF-5As, and it performed its first show that year at Diyarbakir. The team is unique in flying seven supersonic jets.

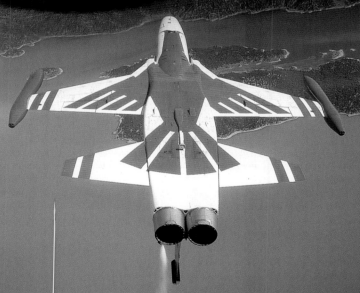

Twelve pilots are assigned to the 'Turkish Stars' squadron. New pilots undergo around six months of training before they are declared ready to fly a display, although this period varies due to seasonal display commitments and aircraft maintenance factors. Initial training begins with formation orientation work, before they fly as no. 7 in the full formation. The display routine typically lasts for 22 minutes and includes 20 separate figures.

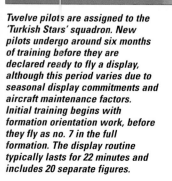

121nci Filo 'Ari' (Tekamül Jet Eğitim Filosu – advanced jet training squadron) at Çiğli flies the Northrop T-38 Talon in the advanced training role. The course lasts for six months, during which the student flies 104 hours in 81 sorties, as well as regular simulator time. Included in the course are four or five long-range navigation sorties. At the end of this course the students move to F-4, F-5 or F-16 units for type conversion and weapons training. Two batches of T-38s, acquired in 1979 and 1993, totalled 67 aircraft. As well as the SF.260s, T-37s and T-38s, Çiğli is also home to the UH-1Hs, and locally-assembled CN-235s and AS 532 Cougars of 125nci Filo (Ulaştirma ve Helikopter Eğitim Filosu – transport and helicopter training squadron), which provides rotary-wing and multi-engine training. 124nci Filo (Standardize Filo Komutanliği – standardisation squadron command) produces instructors and examiners, and provides flight and instrument check courses. It uses all five types of aircraft based at Çiğli.

Left: *The Cessna T-41D is used for both initial screening and primary training. The aircraft are assigned to the Hava Harp Okulu (air force academy) and operate from Istanbul-Ataturk International Airport. Students receive around 55 hours on the T-41 during their four-year course, and also fly gliders.*

Right: *Having graduated from the Air Force Academy, most student pilots go to the 2nci Ana Jet Üs (2nd Main Jet Base) at Çiğli-Izmir, the THK's principal training location. Additionally, between six and 10 students go to Sheppard AFB, Texas, for instruction under the JNJPTS scheme. At Çiğli, initial basic training is provided by 123ncü Filo 'Palaz' (Başlangiç Uçuş Eğitim Filosu – refresher flight training squadron) using SIAI-Marchetti SF.260Ds. The 123nci Filo course encompasses 25 hours in 22 sorties over four months. Although the squadron is based at Çiğli, the flying is usually undertaken at nearby Kaklic to relieve congestion at the main base.*

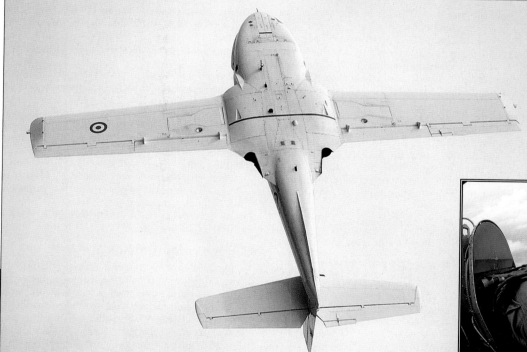

Basic training is performed on the Cessna T-37B/C, which is operated from Çiğli by 122nci Filo 'Akrep' (Temel Jet Uçuş Eğitim Filosu – basic jet flight training squadron). The course lasts for six months and incorporates 112 hours in 90 sorties, plus simulator time. At the end of the course the students are streamed into fast-jet (moving to 121nci Filo), rotary-wing or multi-engine (both to 125nci Filo). The THK acquired around 80 T-37B/Cs in two batches. Non-flying units at Çiğli include the Pilot Adayi Subaylar Filo (undergraduate pilot squadron) which has an administrative function, and the Akademik Filo (academic squadron) which handles ground-based training.

Belgium

In the post-Cold War era, Belgium strives to maintain its defence commitments with ever-shrinking budgets. It is among the nations leading a drive for greater military 'Europeanisation'.

From a personnel strength of around 87,000 some 10 years ago, only 44,500 men and women, including civilian employees, remain in the Belgian armed forces today. The government has no intention of increasing the defence budget, which for several years has been frozen at +/- BFr100 billion ($US2.2 billion); as a result, a further decrease in personnel strength is inevitable, planned to reach 39,500 by 2015. In past years, the average age of personnel has increased significantly. Efforts are being made to counter this, but enticing young people to join the armed forces is proving difficult for all services.

To compensate for the decrease in numbers, the smaller services are to receive new and better equipment. With an eye to future major re-equipment needs, politicians have concentrated on an air force specialised in transport only, foregoing the expensive Joint Strike Fighter. Others, including the Chief of Staff of the FAB/BLu, argued that the replacement of the F-16 is mandatory to retain a valuable air force, and to comply with NATO requirements.

Not only the air force is being targeted in the drive to economise. Upcoming expensive projects are the replacement of the Army's armoured scout vehicles, armoured personnel carriers, trucks and Alouette II helicopters, as well as the Navy's frigates.

Moves have been made to consolidate defence efforts with European partners in an attempt to reduce spending. In view of the current situation, it can be assumed that the future of Belgium's defences may lie in an integrated European defence system.

Dirk Lamarque

Belgische Luchtmacht – Force Aérienne Belge (Belgian air force)

A founding member of NATO, Belgium's current air force traces its roots to the establishment of the Ecole d'Aviation Militaire (Military Aviation School) at Brasschaat on 1 May 1911, followed in April 1913 by the Compagnie d'Aviateurs (Aviators Company).

On 4 August 1914, German forces entered Belgium. Eight months into the war, the Compagnie d'Aviateurs was renamed Aviation Militaire (Military Aviation). At the end of the war, it consisted of 12 operational squadrons equipped with almost 200 aircraft, mainly SPAD VII, XI and XIII, Bréguet XIV and Farman MF.11 types. Losses numbered 62 pilots killed and 160 aircraft destroyed.

Between World Wars I and II, several reorganisations took place. The service changed its name to Aéronautique Militaire (Military Aviation) in March 1920 and was composed of seven groups. Further changes in January 1926 saw the groups of the Aéronautique Militaire reorganised into three regiments. By 1939, a total of 16 squadrons was operational.

The German *Blitzkrieg* of May 1940 virtually obliterated the entire aircraft inventory, which consisted mainly of Fairey Foxes, Fairey Battles, Fiat CR.42s, Gloster Gladiators and a handful of Hawker Hurricanes. The three Belgian regiments could undertake only a few operations against the overwhelming German forces, and military operations lasted for just 18 days.

Some pilots managed to reach Britain during the war and joined the Royal Air Force in a number of operational units. The nucleus of the current Belgian Air Force was formed and integrated into the RAF during those war years. Two operational squadrons (349ste Smaldeel and 350ème Escadrille) still carry the number plate from when they operated as RAF (Belgian) Squadrons.

Post-World War II

The Army-type structure of the Aéronautique Militaire was changed on 1 October 1946 into an independent air force along the lines of the RAF, with a wing/squadron organisation as basis. The designation Air Force came into use in January 1949. Belgian air and ground crew received their training in Britain prior to the establishment in January 1946 of the Elementaire Vliegschool – Ecole de Pilotage Elémentaire (EVS/EPE, Elementary Pilot School) with ex-RAF Tiger Moths, and the technical school in 1946.

Of primary concern to the service was the establishment of an in-country integral training capability, and additional schools were created accordingly. The Ecole de Pilotage Avancée – Gevorderde Vliegschool (Advanced Pilot School) and the Jachtschool – Ecole de Chasse (Fighter School) were established in May 1947 at Brustem and January 1948 at Koksijde, respectively.

Reorganisation of the Military Aviation led to the renumbering of its wings and squadrons in February 1948, accompanied by an increase in the number of attached units:

■ The 160th Wing at Beauvechain became the 1st Wing (Nos 349 and 350 Sqns with Meteor F.Mk 4s, supplemented later with No. 4 Sqn with Spitfires and Nos 10 and 11 Sqns with Mosquitos, plus an Auxiliary Squadron)
■ The 161st Wing at Florennes was renumbered as the 2nd Wing (Nos 1 and 2 Sqns, and No. 3 Sqn with Spitfires)
■ The 169th Wing at Evere changed to the 15th Wing (later moving to Melsbroek, and comprising Nos 20 and 21 Sqns and No. 40 Sqn, with transport and liaison types).

With the arrival of the jet age, the obsolete Spitfires and Mosquitos were replaced between 1948 and 1952 by a total of 355 Gloster Meteor F.Mk 4, F.Mk 8, T.Mk 7 and NF.Mk 11 aircraft, and in 1951 the first of 234 Republic F-84E/G Thunderjets arrived. These aircraft served to expand the air force even further:

■ The 7th Wing at Chièvres (Nos 7, 8 and 9 Sqns with Meteor F.Mk 8s) on 1 December 1950
■ The 10th Wing at Kleine Brogel (Nos 23, 27 and 31 Sqns with F-84Gs) on 29 November 1951
■ The 83rd Instrument Flight Group at Florennes (T-33As) in March 1952
■ The 9th Wing at Bierset (Nos 22, 26 and 30 Sqns with F-84Gs) on 17 September 1953
■ The 13th Wing at Brustem (Nos 25, 29 and 33 Sqns with Meteor F.Mk 8s) on 28 December 1953
■ The 5th Wing at Koksijde (No. 24 Sqn with Meteor F.Mk 8s) on 18 February 1954
■ No. 42 Sqn at Wahn (FRG), initially with F-84Gs, on 15 September 1954

These early jets remained in service for only a few years, being replaced between 1955 and 1957 by some 197 F-84F Thunderjets and 256 Hawker Hunter F.Mk 4s and F.Mk 6s. Beauvechain's Meteor NF.Mk 11s were replaced in 1958 by 53 Avro Canada CF-100 Canuck all-weather interceptors. In the process, a number of squadrons were disestablished, while others changed bases.

The 38 Lockheed T-33A advanced trainers delivered from 1952 were initially operated in one unit at Florennes. Two years later, some were distributed to other fighter bases as well as the fighter school at Koksijde, before being used at Brustem to create the Flight Vol Sans Visibilité – Vliegen Zonder Zicht, VSV/VZZ (Blind Flying Flight).

The transport force was reinforced with two DC-4/C-54As in 1950 (principally for flights to the Belgian Congo), 56 C-119F/Gs delivered from 1952, 12 Percival Pembrokes in 1954 and four DC-6A/Bs in 1958.

Congo commitments

Apart from a few bases in post-war Germany (after both world wars), and the French base of Solenzara, the only out-of-country location used as a permanent base by Belgian military aircraft was the Belgian Congo. In the late 1940s, it was decided to transfer advanced flying training to this African colony. For this purpose, and also for strategic reasons, a large air base was built at Kamina. In September 1953, the first North American Harvard of the Ecole de Pilotage Avancée (EPA – advanced pilot school) arrived, and in January 1960 the first brand-new CM.170 Fouga Magisters were delivered by C-119. The base also housed three Bristol Sycamore Mk 4s, C-47s, Alouette IIs and Piper Cubs, as well as aircraft of the Force Publique du Congo (Public Force of Congo).

Shortly after the declared autonomy of the Belgian Congo, a rebellion broke out in the south of the country. Belgian Harvards and Magisters equipped with machine-guns and rockets were used against the rebels, but the Kamina base had to be evacuated and was ceded in August 1960 to UN forces deployed to the region. The flying school was re-established at Brustem in November with the repatriated CM.170s, but many Harvards were left behind. Close ties with the former colony later required

Belgium relies totally on the F-16 for its tactical needs, its fleet including both MLU-upgraded F-16AM/BMs (foreground) and unmodified aircraft (background). Unit identifiers, including the 'BL' (Kleine Brogel) and 'FS' (Florennes) wing tailcodes, are now rarely worn.

Most FAB/BLu training is undertaken within 1 Wing at Beauvechain, which has two squadrons of Alpha Jets for advanced (7 Smd/Esc) and weapons/tactical (11 Smd/Esc) training. These aircraft are equipped for the latter role, with underfuselage cannon pod and practice bomb carriers under the wings.

Belgium retains around 10 airworthy Magisters from a once large fleet. Their task is to provide a vehicle for staff officers to maintain their flying currency, also making welcome appearances at airshows throughout Europe. They are operated from Beauvechain by 1 Wing's Fouga Flight.

In the precision attack role Belgian F-16s employ the AGM-65 Maverick missile (illustrated) and Paveway II laser-guided bombs. The latter are designated using the Sharpshooter pod, a slightly downgraded export version of the LANTIRN.

Having been restricted for many years to AIM-9 Sidewinder armament for the air defence role, Belgium's F-16AMs now field the AIM-120 AMRAAM. ALQ-131 ECM pods are usually carried on the centreline for EW protection.

Having earlier used the Orpheus camera pod, the Per Udsen/Terma MRP (Modular Reconnaissance Pod) is now available for the F-16's reconnaissance tasks. This pod mounts electro-optical and infra-red sensors which record digitally on to tape.

a few military-backed evacuations of Belgian and other citizens from Zaïre (as the Belgian Congo became known), due to rebellions in that country.

The late 1950s and early 1960s witnessed the first major downsizing of the air force. In all, 14 squadrons were disestablished, and the 9th and 13th Wings were re-equipped with air defence missiles and ultimately relocated to Germany. The 7th Wing disbanded altogether when the last Hawker Hunters retired in 1963, after only seven years of service.

In 1961 the air force received 10 Sikorsky S.58/HSS-1 helicopters for the newly established Heli Flight at Koksijde, charged with SAR. Two years later, the first Lockheed F-104Gs entered service and ushered the BAF into the Mach 2 club. The aircraft were

acquired to replace the obsolete Canucks and part of the F-84F fleet (10th Wing only). The remaining Thunderjets (and Thunderflashes of No. 42 Sqn) were retired in favour of 106 Dassault Mirage 5BA/BD/BRs delivered to the 2nd and 3rd Wings from 1970.

The equipment of the EVS/EPE was rejuvenated with the arrival of 36 SIAI-Marchetti SF.260Ms from 1969 to replace the tired SV-4bis. The Magisters and the T-Birds were replaced by 33 Alpha Jets delivered from October 1978. Some 20 CM.170s were retained in the Fouga Flight, some being detached to fighter bases to allow staff officers to retain their currency on jet aircraft. In 1987 all remaining Fougas were regrouped at Brustem within the newly established No. 33 Sqn.

The early 1970s saw a complete renewal of

the aircraft of the 15th Transport Wing. Twelve Lockheed C-130H Hercules replaced the faithful C-119s. The Percival Pembrokes, Dakotas, DC-4s and DC-6s gave way to six Fairchild-Swearingen Merlin IIIs, three HS.748s and two Dassault Mystère 20s. Two ex-Sabena Boeing 727QCs, equipped with an upper-deck cargo door, were acquired for VIP and long-range transport missions. In the process, No. 40 Sqn (C-119) was disbanded, but the unit was later re-established with five Westland Sea Kings that had replaced the Sikorsky helicopters of the Heli Flight in 1976.

In 1979 the arrival of the General Dynamics (now Lockheed Martin) F-16 announced the definitive end of the '104' era in Belgium. The initial batch of 116 aircraft replaced the Starfighters of the Beauvechain- and Kleine

Brogel-based Nos 349, 350, 23 and 31 Sqns, and No. 349 Sqn became the first operational European F-16 unit in May 1980. Although it was initially planned to replace the Mirages with additional Fighting Falcons, the second and final order accounted for 44 aircraft only. They were used to re-equip the Florennes-based No. 2 Sqn and No. 1 Sqn, the latter having left its Mirage 5BA/BDs at Bierset when it relocated to Florennes. In the opposite direction, No. 42 Sqn joined the Mirage OCU (No. 8 Sqn) of the 3rd Wing. A plan to modernise the Mirage 5 was launched in 1989, and 20 aircraft were placed in storage at Koksijde awaiting their modification. However, the fall of the Iron Curtain and subsequent collapse of the Warsaw Pact made the air force decide not to put these MirSIP (Mirage Safety Improvement Program) Mirages in service, and they were sold to Chile.

The last two Mirage squadrons were disbanded, No. 8 Sqn on 13 September 1991 and No. 42 Sqn on 22 December 1993. All remaining aircraft were flown into storage at Weelde, a reserve base in the north of the country, and have now been disposed of.

Current organisation

Of the 25 squadrons and six training/support units equipped with aircraft that were operational in the 1950s and 1960s, only 11 remain today, operating some 180 aircraft. All units come under a new command structure that was implemented late in 2000. The previous Commando van de Taktische Luchtmacht – Commandement de la Force Aérienne Tactique (Tactical Air Force Command, known as Comdo TAF), and the Commando Training en Steun van de Luchtmacht – Commandement Entraînement et Support de la Force Aérienne (Air Force Training and Support Command, known as Comdo Training & Support), have been merged into a single command named COMOPSAIR (Commandement Opérations Air – Air Operations Command).

This single command comprises the following units from the former Comdo TAF:

■ The 2nd and 10th Tactical Wings, based at Florennes and Kleine Brogel, respectively
■ The 15th Air Transport Wing at Melsbroek
■ The independent 40th SAR Sqn at Koksijde
■ The ATCC (Air Traffic Control Centre) at Semmerzake and the CRC (Control and Reporting Centre) at Glons
■ The units of operational support, which are the Meteorological Wing at Beauvechain, the ATC School/Ecole ATC (Air Traffic Control School) at Koksijde, and base ATC centres

and from the former Comdo Training and Support:

■ The 1st Training Wing at Beauvechain
■ The Koninklijke Technische School van de Luchtmacht – Ecole Royale Technique de la Force Aérienne (Royal Technical School of the Air Force) at Saffraanberg
■ The 20th Wing Support (Support Wing), and the 21st and 22nd Logistieke Wings – Wings Logistique (Logistics Wings) with specialised repair workshops and stores, all at Evere

The BAF aircraft serial system is based on the disused USAF buzz system. All aircraft wear a two-letter code, followed by a sequential serial number. The letters refer to the role and, in some way, to the type of the aircraft. F-16s are serialled in the FA and FB range (F for Fighter): FA for F-16A, FB for F-16B. Transport aircraft are serialled in the C sequence (for Cargo): CA (Airbus), CD (Dassault Falcon 900), CE

(EMBRAER), CH (C-130 Hercules) and CM (Mystère 20). The Westland Sea Kings carry the RS prefix (Rescue Sea King). Training aircraft have the letter order reversed: AT for Alpha Jet Trainer, ST for SIAI-Marchetti Trainer, and MT for Magister Trainer. The air cadets' L-21Bs carry the letters of their type designator (LB), and the gliders carry PL for Planeur (glider).

Combat aircraft

Since the retirement of the Mirage 5 in 1993, the air force has relied on the Lockheed Martin F-16 as its sole combat aircraft type. Reductions in manpower from 18,000 to 10,000, and the closure of three air bases in recent years, have resulted in an air force that has been pared to its bones.

Initial plans for restructuring in the early 1990s would have retained only 72 F-16s in four squadrons, and Nos 349 and 350 Sqns would have disbanded. The BAF managed to keep these two traditionally significant 'RAF' squadrons active by reducing the unit allocation from 18 to 12 aircraft, thereby retaining all six squadrons and an OCU. However, lessons learned from the 1999 operations over Kosovo have driven the air force to implement the so-called Falcon 2000 reorganisation, and return to the initial plan of four squadrons and an OCU. As a result, No. 2 Sqn was disbanded on 20 April 2001, No. 23 Sqn will be disbanded some time in 2001, and the OCU will follow suit in 2002. Its conversion training role will be taken over by a yet to be named squadron, which will also carry on the traditions of No. 23 Sqn. Aircraft allocations for the remaining units will return to 18.

Funds have always been a major problem for the BAF. When the F-16 MLU (Mid-Life Update) was instituted, budget restrictions prohibited the air force from engaging in a total fleet update from the start. The first contract in 1993 provided for not more than 48 upgrades, and the rest of the fleet was to remain unmodified. It was later realised that keeping two different aircraft types in the inventory would mean increased long-term expenses, so finances were allocated for two more MLU batches, of 24 and 18 aircraft. This provided ultimately for a fleet of 90 aircraft, of which some will be put in storage as attrition replacements. All F-16s should be updated to MLU standard by 2002. The remaining non-modified F-16A/Bs are to be put in storage, or sold if a buyer can be found.

Although this upgrade brings the F-16A virtually to F-16C Block 50 standard, the full potential of the aircraft can only be reached with modern weapons and sensors that, until very recently, were not in the BAF inventory. To correct this, orders have been placed for laser guidance kits (GBU-24 and GBU-10E/B), AGM-65 Mavericks and AIM-120 AMRAAMs. A cadre of instructor pilots has recently received training by USAF pilots in the use of night vision goggles (NVG). This will allow the training of all operational F-16 pilots in the use of this equipment by the end of 2001, a qualification process that requires seven sorties and a number of simulator sessions. In 2000, a contract was signed for Lockheed Martin LANTIRN Sharpshooter targeting sensor pods.

With the retirement of its last reconnaissance-configured Mirage 5BRs in 1993, the BAF lost its tactical reconnaissance capability. This was restored with the 1995 loan from the Dutch air

force of two Orpheus recce pods, as used on its F-16A(R), to the newly established Belgian reconnaissance flight of the 1ère Esc at Florennes. This arrangement was only a stop-gap measure until eight Danish Per Udsen (now Terma A/S) Modular Reconnaissance Pods (MRP) were delivered in 1997/99. These pods are now being modified with electro-optical (EO) sensors, and an IRLS (Infra-Red Line Scanner) will soon replace the panoramic wet-film camera. A datalink is currently under study. These features will provide the BAF with an all-weather night/day full EO-IR platform that will be the most advanced recce pod currently available to the F-16 community. Initially, 16 F-16s received the necessary modifications to operate the new pod, but ultimately all MLU F-16s will be capable of operating the system.

The traditionally close ties between the Belgian and Dutch air forces were fortified with the signature of the DATF (Deployable Air Task Force) agreement shortly before the crisis in Kosovo began. Soon after, the force was activated for NATO's Operation Allied Force. Joint Falcon, as the combined detachment was known, was established in October 1996 at Villafranca, Italy, and four BAF F-16s joined the Dutch detachment that had been operating from this location since 1993. At the peak of operations, 12 BAF F-16s were stationed at Amendola, to where the Task Force moved. During the 78 days of the NATO air campaign, the BAF flew 679 sorties on escort, CAP and bombing missions, without experiencing a single loss or mishap.

The Kosovo crisis was significant in that it marked the first time Belgian aircraft had engaged in offensive war operations since the end of World War II. Squadrons of the Florennes-based 2 Wing and Kleine Brogel-based 10 Wing are also assigned to NATO's Rapid Reaction Forces and Immediate Reaction Forces.

In recent years, the BAF has undertaken deployments far from Belgium. Regular low-level training detachments have been made to the Moroccan base of Meknes for more than a decade. Besides regularly participating in Red Flag at Nellis AFB, the BAF has also taken up slots in the Maple Flag exercises at Cold Lake, Alberta. If possible, each fighter-bomber pilot attends one of the 'Flag' exercises at least every two years; pilots specialised in air defence are sent less often.

As a test of capability, in Operation Noordvalk the BAF sent three F-16s to Waterkloof AB in South Africa. They participated in the Africa Aerospace and Defence exhibition in September 2000 and, afterwards, flew operational missions with the SAAF from Louis Trichardt AB for a week with the based Cheetah Cs of No. 2 Sqn. Refuelling support was provided by a USAF KC-135R. Logistic support for this mission was provided 'in-house' by an Airbus A310 and three C-130Hs, one of which acted as a SAR platform during the mostly overwater flights of the F-16s.

Transport

The fleet of 11 Lockheed C-130H Hercules, which has been in service with No. 20 Sqn at Melsbroek since 1972, remains the backbone of the BAF transport force, concentrated within the 15th Wing. All Hercules have now under-

5 Smd/Esc at Beauvechain provides basic training using the SF.260M (right) and instrument training on the SF.260D (above). All of the fleet is being repainted from camouflage to high-conspicuity yellow.

Left: The Belgian C-130 fleet is heavily involved in multinational peacekeeping and humanitarian operations. This 20 Smd/Esc C-130H is seen in Benin while operating on a B-FAST mission.

Below: The Hawker Siddeley HS.748 remained in service in 2001 pending delivery of further ERJ-135/145 aircraft. This 21 Smd/Esc machine has been fitted with a rear-fuselage cargo door.

Left: Greatly enhancing the deployability of Belgium's armed forces are the two Airbus A310s which were taken into service by 21 Smd/Esc in 1997 to replace two Boeing 727s. The two Airbuses, which previously flew with Singapore Airlines, now have more hours on them than the aircraft they replaced.

Below: Belgium's latest aqcuisition is the EMBRAER ERJ-135 (illustrated) and similar, but stretched, ERJ-145. A pair of each variant was purchased to replace the remaining 748s and Merlin IIIs. The latter type retired from service with 21 Smd/Esc as soon as the first ERJ-135 was delivered to the Melsbroek base.

gone an upgrade in which avionics and engine instruments were replaced and an APU (auxiliary power unit) was installed. The loss of one aircraft in a fatal crash at Eindhoven in 1996 was partly offset by the arrival of two Airbus A310s in 1997, but the C-130 fleet was hard-pressed during the Kosovo campaign to maintain the flow of supplies for the F-16s.

Renowned for their humanitarian missions, this expertise of Belgian C-130s has been less required in the recent past. However, the 15th Wing is preparing to be ready to re-engage in these operations. In conjunction with other government ministries, the Defence Department has established a task force known as B-FAST (Belgian First Aid and Support Team), which is designed to respond more quickly to disaster relief operations worldwide. The BAF is responsible mainly for air transport, and has developed a new approach of dropping food supplies in difficult-to-reach areas. Snow Drop, as the method is called, can drop thousands of individually packed food rations with no safety hazard to the receivers. B-FAST and Snow Drop were put to the test in May 2001 in Benin.

In the aftermath of the 1996 crash, additional safety equipment has been installed in these transports and an onboard oxygen generator will replace the original liquid oxygen system. Tests are also in hand for the installation of a cockpit voice recorder and flight data recorder. The search for a replacement for the lost Hercules was pursued seriously for a time, but has now been shelved indefinitely.

Political discussions were launched in 2000 into moving the 15th Wing to a new location,

ostensibly to reduce noise pollution, especially at night. Such a move would simultaneously release the currently occupied corner of the Brussels international airport for further development of civilian air traffic. However, the costs for this move were estimated at BFr4.6 billion ($US100 million) for the cheapest solution (Beauvechain), and considered unbearable by the defence budget. The decision on whether the 15th Wing will relocate has been postponed until 2010.

Staff transport and liaison

As for the liaison fleet of No. 21 Sqn, plans had been made in the past to update the avionics of the Merlin IIIs and HS.748s, and to refurbish the Falcon 20s. The 'on-again, off-again' studies were not fully pursued due to the uncertainty regarding the future of these aircraft. The HS.748s did receive some limited avionics upgrading, but are now being retired. A long-awaited decision on their replacement was taken in April 2000, when the Defence

Minister was authorised to make a request for offers for an order for up to four regional transport aircraft. Candidates for the contract were the ERJ-135/145, the Fairchild-Dornier 328JET and the Canadair CRJ 200. Later that year, EMBRAER was awarded a BFr3.5 billion ($US76 million) contract for the delivery of two ERJ-135s and two longer ERJ-145s. The first, an ERJ-135, was delivered in late 2001. These aircraft replace the HS.748 and Merlin III, operations of the latter having ceased with the delivery of the first ERJ.

The single Falcon 900, received in 1995, was almost supplemented by a second example in late 1999, when a suitable aircraft became available in Morocco. The deal was near to being closed when Dassault objected. The conviction in Belgium of Serge Dassault, found guilty during a legal suit in 1998 of having influenced with bribes the decision to acquire the Dassault Electronique Carapace ECM system for the F-16 fleet, has been alleged to be the cause for the cancellation of this deal. A decision on the fate of the two Falcon 20s was long in coming, but they are almost certain to be upgraded to current standards to keep them in use.

In a surprise move, two A310s were acquired second-hand from Singapore Airlines in 1997 and the first aircraft was delivered within six months of contract signature. They have limited transatlantic capability and do not possess an upper deck cargo door but, nonetheless, they greatly increase the transport capacity of the 15th Wing. Their value lies in their payload/range performance, as well as being more economical to operate on long-distance flights. Most appreciated is their passenger-carrying capability: a single aircraft is able to move up to 200 troops and their equipment, a number that would require at least three or four C-130s. These characteristics have proved valuable in the government's efforts to increase commitments abroad, in line with NATO's policy to engage in out-of-area operations, support of UN peacekeeping tasks, and Europe's own defence policy in the WEU (West European Union). Recent examples are the SFOR and KFOR operations, and regular training deployments in the US, Canada and Africa.

At Koksijde AB in the far west of the country, No. 40 Sqn's five Westland Sea King Mk 48s still provide sterling service in the coastal SAR role after 25 years. They have been upgraded with new rotor blades, search radar, navigational equipment and the long-awaited FLIR turret. An additional Sea King was on the short-term 'wants' list for some time. The helicopter would have been used mainly for training and transport duties, but its acquisition has been cancelled. Plans are being made to find a replacement for the Sea Kings, and as the navy and army are looking for similar-sized helicopters, a bulk buy for the three services may prove to be the most economical solution. Two apparent candidates are the Eurocopter NH 90 and the Sikorsky Seahawk/Black Hawk.

Training

Although budget restrictions are having a serious impact, the Belgian Air Force persists in maintaining its ability to perform full-scale pilot training in-country, at least for the time being. Since 1996, the relevant units have been concentrated at Beauvechain within the 1st Training Wing.

Around 40 new trainee pilots from all armed forces branches and the federal police commence flying training each year on the SF.260s of No. 5 Sqn. After basic training, six to eight months are spent on advanced flying training with the Alpha Jet-equipped No. 7 Sqn. The Alpha Jet is also used for initial operational training, under the auspices of the instructors of No. 11 Sqn. The squadron prepares the young pilots for tactical operations during 85 flying hours. Pilots who have passed these stages successfully, but are not destined for an F-16 unit, return to No. 5 Sqn and undergo an IFR (Instrument Flight Rules) course on SF.260Ds, then go on to fly the C-130 or Sea King.

The equipment is getting old, though. The Alpha Jets will reach their quarter-century milestone in 2003. The SF.260Ms are more than 30 years old and were supplemented with an unannounced order for nine new-build, fully IFR-equipped SF.260Ds in 1992. The replacement of the Marchettis has been under study (at least for the SF.260Ms), but a decision will depend on the available funding and the future training policy that will be adopted. Some manufacturers have presented their aircraft in Belgium, but studies have turned to an eventual replacement of tired and time-expired components only, such as the wings. The Alpha Jets are receiving an upgrading with modern avionics. This will keep them active until at least 2015, saving on maintenance costs and at the same time reducing the technology gap between these trainers and the MLU F-16. A prototype was modified by SABCA at Gosselies, and the first examples are now operational at Beauvechain. Series modification will be done at the base itself. Main components of the upgrade are a laser INS with embedded GPS, a SHUD (Smart Head-Up Display), a Multi-Function Display (HUD repeater) in the aft cockpit, a VOR-ILS receiver, a video recorder and modified control columns.

The 10 or so remaining Fouga CM.170 Magisters are the last operational examples of this type in Europe. The disbandment of No. 33 Sqn in December 1999 was a prelude to their deserved retirement, which has yet to come. After more than 40 years they are still whistling about, piloted by staff officers.

The future

A decision for the replacement of the C-130 has been taken, while long-term plans regarding the successor of the F-16, for which the F-35 (Joint Strike Fighter) is the prime candidate, will have to be made soon. Yet, disagreements between the government parties concerning this very costly programme may delay the new fighter, if not jeopardise it altogether. Acquisitions to replace 72 F-16s would amount to around BFr100 billion ($US2.2 billion). Possible alternatives are being put forward: restrict available funds to replace only the Hercules; participate in the F-35, maybe in a different way; reduce the number of F-35s... One possibility – to become a privileged development partner in the F-35 project – has already been postponed while parliamentary discussions continue.

The Hercules successor has already been ordered, although the aircraft only exists 'on paper'. During the 2001 Le Bourget air show, the Belgian government signed the Memorandum of Understanding (MoU) on the European A400M military airlift programme, and joined seven other European countries in the project. Belgium has committed itself to order seven A400Ms valued at an estimated $US937 million. Delivery of the first aircraft is anticipated to be around 2017, by which time the BAF's Hercules will be 45 years old.

The ever-restricted budget has meant that most aircraft types in the inventory are to be upgraded, to serve for more years. Even the five remaining Piper L-21Bs of the Luchtkadetten – Cadets de l'Air (Air Cadets), which are used as glider-tugs, are being completely rebuilt, and have received a new, more powerful engine.

Searching for a way to cope with a continuing budget reduction, the former Chief of Staff of the Air Force, General G. Vanhecke, was an ardent supporter of an integrated European air force. The establishment of the DATF, which has since been joined by Portugal, is an example of his efforts. He was one of the initiators for the setting up of a joint European pilot training programme by 2010. The European Air Chiefs' Conference (EURAC), held in early 2000 at his invitation, discussed a future European training system for fighter pilots. Named EURO-TRAINING, it fits entirely into the framework of his conviction. This concept would even see the development of a new European training aircraft. The current Chief of Staff will not only be responsible for further reducing the size of the air force, but will also focus on an increased flexibility of the service. The current upgrading of the available aircraft and the delivery of modern weapons will ensure that at least the hardware will be ready to face the challenges of the years to come.

Marine (Navy)

After the force reduction in the mid-1990s that resulted in almost a halving of the fleet and a personnel cutback from 4,800 to 2,700, the Belgian Navy tightened the long co-operation between itself and the navy of The Netherlands. An integrated operational command, known as ABNL (Admiral BeNeLux), was established at the Dutch port of Den Helder, allowing a more efficient use of the available and future assets of both navies. The area of operations of ABNL is the English Channel and the southern part of the North Sea. Although initially to be a dormant 'wartime only' headquarters, its function since 1996 has been activated to full-time status, with partial command of both navies. Full command authority remains with the respective nations, allowing individual decisions regarding operations, training and logistics. Leadership of ABNL is alternately the responsibility of the Commandant der Zeemacht in Nederland CZM-NED (Commander of the Navy in the Netherlands), and the Belgian COMOPSNAV (Commandant Opérations Navales, Commander Naval Operations).

Aerial assets

The first aircraft operated by the Belgian Navy were two Sikorsky HSS-1 helicopters used principally in the mine spotting and sweeping role. They operated alongside the SAR-dedicated S.58/HSS-1 of the air force's No. 40 Sqn at Koksijde, between 1962 and 1976.

To achieve some shipborne capability, the Belgian Navy received three Sud SA 316B Alouette III helicopters in 1971. A fourth example, previously used by the Protection Civile – Civiele Bescherming (Civil Defence Corps), was transferred to the Navy but never put into service, and was sold in 1991.

The flotation bag-equipped Alouettes are used for ship resupply, liaison, search and rescue, and casualty evacuation. At sea, they can only operate from two supply ships (BNS *Zinnia* and BNS *Godetia*), the sole Belgian Navy vessels in the fleet of 27 ships equipped with a helicopter deck. The helicopters are operated by the Heli Flight from Koksijde air base, where the unit is integrated into the Belgian Air Force's No. 40 Sqn. Although all operations and maintenance are conducted independently, the units share the available base infrastructure.

Belgische Luchtmacht – Force Aérienne Belge

UNIT	TYPE	BASE
1 Wing		
5 Smd/Esc	SF.260M/D	Beauvechain
7 Smd/Esc	Alpha Jet	Beauvechain
11 Smd/Esc	Alpha Jet, CM.170	Beauvechain
2 Wing		
1 Esc	F-16A/B	Florennes
350 Esc	F-16AM/BM	Florennes
10 Wing		
23 Smd (to disband)	F-16AM/BM	Kleine Brogel
31 Smd	F-16A/B	Kleine Brogel
349 Smd	F-16AM/BM	Kleine Brogel
OCU (to disband)	F-16B	Kleine Brogel
15 Wing		
20 Smd/Esc	C-130H	Melsbroek
21 Smd/Esc	ERJ-135/145, A310, Falcon 20, Falcon 900B	Melsbroek
40 Smd/Esc	Sea King Mk 48	Koksijde
Luchtkadetten/ Cadets de l'Air	L-21B, RF-5B, gliders	Beauvechain, summer camps at Weelde and Oostmalle

The 21 Smd/Esc staff/VIP transport fleet is completed by three Dassault Falcons: a single Falcon 900 (above) and two Falcon 20s (right).

Left: Five elderly Piper L-21B Super Cubs remain in service with the air cadets, having been bought from the Netherlands in 1975. They have been up-engined for their main role as glider-tugs. In an earlier era, the Belgian army received 157 L-18C Super Cubs for observation duties.

Right: The air cadets organisation, headquartered at Beauvechain but also operating summer camps, has a number of gliders on charge. This is a Grob G103A.

Below: The first taste of powered flight for many prospective Belgian air force pilots comes courtesy of the Fournier RF-5B motor-glider of the air cadets, based at Beauvechain. The Alpha Jets at the same base provide the young cadets with something to aspire to.

Right: 40 Smd/Esc's Sea King Mk 48s provide search and rescue along Belgium's North Sea coastline. Although the airframes are old, the Sea Kings have been progressivley updated, and are highly capable SAR platforms, with effective search radar and a strut-mounted FLIR turret below the nose on the port side.

Heli Flight, Koksijde

Sud SA 316B Alouette III   M-01/02/03 (OT-ZPA/-ZPB/-ZPC)   (3)

These venerable helicopters are scheduled to remain in service until at least 2005, by which time they will be 34 years old. The type of replacement helicopter has not been determined yet. A decision will depend on the required missions to be performed, the characteristics of the yet-to-be-ordered new frigates and, possibly, on the requirements of the Air Force and Army for a similar-sized helicopter.

The Belgian Navy's only air assets are the three SA 316B Alouette IIIs of the Heli Flight. Their primary task is to support ships at sea in a variety of utility roles, including liaison, casevac/medevac and light transport.

Licht Vliegwezen – Aviation Légère (Light Aviation)

Belgian Army Aviation was part of the Belgian Air Force when its first unit was established on 31 July 1947. The 369 Air Observation Squadron formed at Brasschaat, and a few months later was redesignated as 15 AO Sqn. Its aircraft did not arrive until April 1948, when the first Auster AOP.Mk 6 light aircraft were delivered. From July 1952, Piper L-18Cs gradually replaced the Austers. This allowed a second unit to be formed, No. 16 AO Sqn at Bützweilerhof near Cologne in Germany on 1 September 1953. After control of the two air observation squadrons passed to the Army on 1 April 1954, the units were redesignated as Light Aviation Squadrons.

Continued deliveries of the Piper Cubs, of which no fewer than 157 were received, allowed the establishment, on 19 June 1956, of the 17th Squadron at Werl and the 18th Sqn at Merzbrück on 3 July 1956, both in Germany. In order to provide the necessary crews to operate the growing numbers of aircraft, the 15th Sqn took over the advanced training task and was renamed Escadrille Instruction d'Aviation Légère – Opleidingsmaldeel van het Licht Vliegwezen (Esc I Lt Avn) (Light Aviation Training Squadron). A further redesignation to Escadrille Ecole d'Aviation Légère – Schoolsmaldeel van het Licht Vliegwezen (Light Aviation School Squadron) was effective on 1 April 1964, and resulted from the shedding of its secondary operational task. In March 1973 the school received its current name of Ecole de l'Aviation Légère – School van het Licht Vliegwezen (Light Aviation School).

From 1959 the Army also received a total of 80 Alouette II helicopters: 38 SE 313B Alouette II Artoustes and 42 SA 318C Alouette II Astazous. In 1959, No. 16 Sqn deployed some of its newly delivered Alouettes to Ruanda-Urundi, where they remained until this Belgian colony achieved independence in 1962.

The Alouette II and the L-18s were operated by all four squadrons and were supplemented from 1960 by 12 Dornier Do 27J-1 light STOL aircraft used by Nos 15 and 16 Sqns. The Dorniers, in turn, gave way to the same number of new Britten-Norman BN-2A twin-engined light aircraft in 1976, for use in the liaison and light transport tasks. The Piper Cubs were retired in 1969. In 1979 the Licht Vliegwezen van de Landmacht – Aviation Légère de la Force Terrestre (Light Army Aviation) received the status of independent arm within the Army command structure.

Aeromobility 1

In 1983, the Belgian Army announced its intention to replace 46 of its oldest Alouette IIs with 28 anti-tank and 18 liaison/transport helicopters, in a programme called Aeromobility 1. Among the contenders for the contract were the Aérospatiale SA 365M, Agusta A 109, Bell 406CS, MBB BK.117A, Sikorsky H-76 and the Westland Lynx 3. Although a decision was anticipated in 1984, it took four more years before the contract was signed: in December 1988 Agusta was declared the winner and was to supply 46 A 109II helicopters. The order comprised 18 A 109HO observation helicopters equipped with a Saab Helios observation turret, and 28 A 109HA anti-tank helicopters fitted with a HeliTOW missile system with four two-tube TOW-2A launchers. Later, all helicopters received the common designation A 109BA.

The decision to acquire the Agusta helicopters was subsequently widely criticised, not only for alleged corruption of politicians but also because the helicopters proved poorly suited to their tasks. Even before first delivery in January 1991, the A 109s were found to be some 100 kg (220 lb) heavier than specified. This resulted in modifications to doors and landing gear to reduce the weight. The range of the anti-armour version was inadequate and necessitated the installation of an auxiliary fuel tank in the cabin.

Subsequent mission-related modifications to the A 109BA have resulted in the following sub-types now in use:

■ Armed reconnaissance with the installation of two cabin-mounted FN (Fabrique Nationale) MAG 7.62-mm machine-guns
■ A close air support version armed with two 2.75-in

FFAR LAU-32 rocket pods replacing the TOW launchers. These pods were recovered from the retired air force Mirage 5 fighters
■ A transport version, which has been stripped of all specialised equipment and armament
■ A medical evacuation version with specialised equipment and a widened main cabin capable of taking up to two stretchers

Reorganisation

A major change took place in May 1993 with the formation of the Groupement d'Aviation Légère – Groepering Licht Vliegwezen (GAL/GLV, Light Aviation Group) and the redesignation of the three operational squadrons as aviation battalions. This coincided with the service introduction of the new Agusta helicopters, and preceded the return to Belgium in 1994-95 of the three Germany-based units, which found a new home at Bierset near Liège. This base had been vacated by the air force and provides ample space for the entire Group, which now houses all units, except for the pilot school. The GAL/GLV is responsible for highly mobile operations, and is directly controlled by the Operational Command of the Army. It also supports operations abroad, as in Somalia and Rwanda in 1993 and, more recently, as part of SFOR in Bosnia, Allied Harbour in Albania and KFOR in Kosovo.

Army pilots receive 60 hours of initial flight training with the air force on SF.260s at Beauvechain, before continuing to the LAS for another 170 hours on Alouette II and A 109. In all, some 20 months of training precede the award of Army Aviation 'wings'. The school operates a dozen Alouette IIs and a number of A 109BAs (as required), as well as six BN-2As.

Federal Politie – Police Fédérale (Federal Police)

The first aircraft acquired by the Belgian Rijkswacht – Gendarmerie (as it was known) were six Sud SA 318C Alouette II helicopters that were part of a 48-aircraft order by the Belgian Army. Delivered from 1967, these Alouettes were identifiable as operated by the police only by their registration numbers, in the A-90 to A-95 range. In those days, the service was still of a paramilitary nature and the Ministry of Defence had some control over it (together with the Ministries of Justice and the Interior). As a result, operation and maintenance was handled by the army at Brasschaat.

Three Sud SA 330L Puma helicopters were acquired in 1973, dramatically increasing the capabilities of the Gendarmerie. Not only could they be employed for the transport of troops and medical evacuation, they were also suitable for fire-fighting. The helicopters were delivered in a colour scheme of white with a Dayglo band, but were still flown and maintained by army personnel at Brasschaat.

After the Ministry of Defence lost its part in the control of the Gendarmerie, it was decided to form an integrated Luchtsteundetachement – Détachement d'Appui Aérien (Air Support Detachment) within the police service. Its Alouettes and Pumas vacated Brasschaat and in October 1993 moved to the air force base of Brussels/Melsbroek, a more central location. To facilitate a smooth transition to self-sufficiency, the army supported operations until late 1994. Meanwhile, the remaining five Alouette II helicopters received the same white colour scheme as the Pumas, and were fitted with high skids for easier ground handling.

The service embarked upon an expansion and re-equipment programme of its airborne assets. This was initiated by the delivery of a used Britten-Norman BN-2T in November 1993, followed by a Cessna 182Q and two Cessna 182Rs (all second-hand) from May 1994. However, things did not go well initially. In the absence of necessary funding for the overhaul

of two of the Pumas, it was planned to trade in the third to pay for the required work. On the way to maintenance in France in December 1993, G 03 was damaged beyond repair when it turned over while taxiing at Lyon. A few months later, a newly delivered Cessna 182 was written off at Melsbroek when it was blown upside-down while taxiing behind a Dutch C-130 that was running up its engines. So, in just a few months, the service lost one-quarter of its resources: two Pumas (G 01 was traded in) and a Cessna 182.

The delivery of two MD 900 Explorer helicopters in 1997 marked the start of the long-awaited re-equipment. Their service introduction allowed the phase-out of the last Puma, which was retired in May 1998, and three of the Alouette IIs. The Explorers have been fitted with specialised law enforcement equipment and a rescue hoist, and are fully IFR equipped. An option on a third helicopter has been taken up and was delivered in July 2001.

Latest acquisition for the service is a pair of MD 520 NOTAR helicopters, delivered in late

Alouette IIs remain in use for liaison and training after over 40 years of Belgian army service, having begun their careers alongside Super Cubs. This is an Astazou-powered SA 318C.

Its aircraft are made available to the LAG in times of crisis. One BN-2A is operated by the LAS on behalf of the Belgian Marine Environmental Control for pollution control along the Belgian coast, and has been modified with SLAR (Sideways Looking Airborne Radar) and other specialised equipment.

Maintenance of all aircraft and helicopters, as well as the Hunter UAVs of the Observation and Surveillance Battery of the 80th Artillery Battalion at Elsenborn, is handled by the Bierset-based 255th Maintenance and Storage Company.

The future

In contrast to a general reduction in the strength of the Army in the years to come, the GAL/GLV is set to enlarge. The new Armed Forces reorganisation plan will see a further increase in the capability of Belgium's Army Aviation. It is intended to redirect the paratroop

battalions into highly mobile airborne units, for which up to 15 medium helicopters are to be acquired by 2004 to provide their in-theatre transport.

Although the withdrawal of the BN-2A Islanders was announced in March 1989 as part of the Aeromobility 1 reorganisation, 10 remain in use. The Army intended to replace them, and it has been reported that the SOCATA TBM.700 single-engined turboprop was a possible choice, but it is not clear if this replacement will receive a go-ahead. Up to 19 light helicopters will be acquired to replace the Alouette II in the training and liaison role from 2006. A contract signature is planned for 2004, provided the new reorganisation leaves space for this urgently needed modernisation.

A programme to modify and upgrade the Agustas is in the planning phase. Operations in Kosovo have proved once more that these helicopters are not entirely suitable for combat, the foremost concern being that their power to weight ratio is inadequate, especially if armour protection is installed. This problem could be addressed by installing more powerful engines.

Despite all being designated A 109BAs in GAL/GLV service, the Agustas serve in a variety of configurations. Above is the scout version (previously A-109HO), with roof-mounted turret. This version augments the TOW-equipped helicopters in anti-tank companies, and also equips a dedicated reconnaissance platoon in each attack battalion. Transport versions without any combat equipment include medevac helicopters (below).

Nine BN-2A Islanders remain in use for liaison and utility transport tasks (below), serving with 16 BnHLn at Bierset and the LAS at Brasschaat. One further aircraft (below left) is equipped with SLAR for maritime pollution surveillance and research.

December 1999 and January 2000. They allowed the final retirement of the two remaining Alouette IIs by June 2000. A third example is on option.

The service is administered by the Ministry of the Interior, and accomplishes general police tasks on behalf of it. Although the merger of all of Belgium's police services into the Federal Police has raised questions among those involved, the air support detachment has not been affected substantially, if at all – although a change of aircraft livery may be imminent.

The federal police service's air support detachment operates from a corner of the main Brussels airport at Melsbroek, although it detaches aircraft as required around the nation to assist police work. The fleet is primarily helicopter-based, with two MD 'NOTAR' (no tail rotor) types in use, the MD 520N (above right) and the MD 900 Explorer (right). In addition, a fleet of three Cessna 182s (above) is used for general surveillance and patrols. These two are Cessna 182Rs, wearing differing colour schemes.

Federal Politie – Police Fédérale

Luchtsteundetachement/Détachement d'Appui Aérien (Brussels/Melsbroek)

Type	Serial	Notes
Cessna 182Q	G 01	White/blue c/s
SA 330L	G 02	WFU 2/5/98, up for sale
2 x Cessna 182R	G 03/04	
BN-2T	G 05	WFU after accident at Beauvechain on 10/10/2000
3 x MD 900	G 10/11/12	
2 x MD 520	G 14/15	
2 x SA 318C	G 94/95	WFU 6/00

Today, when the Tomcat grabs the headlines, it does so principally as a bomber, yet it should not be forgotten that the F-14 remains the world's most 'complete' fighter in terms of its range of air-to-air weaponry. It is a testament to the aircraft's existing weapon capabilities that it was felt unnecessary to equip it with the AMRAAM – the 'death ray' missile of the 1990s and 2000s. And it should not be forgotten that the F-14 also ranks among the world's most capable tactical reconnaissance aircraft. In an illustrious career spanning nearly 30 years, Grumman's last and finest 'Cat' has become a true icon of American military might, and joined the handful of aircraft that have transcended their world to enter the imagination of the public at large. When captured in a classic pose such as that demonstrated by this VF-103 F-14B, no aircraft symbolises the terrible power and beauty of the jet fighter better than the Tomcat.

With its replacement, the F/A-18E/F Super Hornet, entering Fleet service, the F-14 Tomcat is in its twilight years. In the 1990s the career of the fleet defender *par excellence* saw a dramatic resurgence with the adoption of the bombing role, and the F-14 soon established itself as the carrier air wing's prime long-range attack platform. The integration of LANTIRN allowed the Tomcat to deliver weapons with great precision, and to designate targets for other aircraft in the 'fast-FAC' role. In these duties the F-14 has seen considerable action over Iraq, Yugoslavia and now Afghanistan. Scheduled to be out of service before the end of the decade, the Tomcat will not disappear without a fight. In the 1990s the F-14 community claimed that 'The Cat is Back' – 10 years on and it has not gone away.

Northrop Grumman
F-14 Tomcat
US Navy today

Above: VF-103 was the unit chosen to bring the LANTIRN Tomcat into reality, in a remarkably swift and troublefree programme. The integration of the targeting pod allowed the Tomcat to join the F/A-18 Hornet as an equal partner in the attack role, and had other benefits, too. The most obvious of these was the addition of GPS (Global Positioning System), which significantly enhanced the F-14's capabilities in other areas.

Right: Milliseconds from the hook engaging a wire, an F-14B is about to hit the deck. The Tomcat's airframe and undercarriage has stood up well to the continuous bruising imparted by no-flare deck landings at high weights.

With only seven years remaining until the last front-line Tomcat is withdrawn, and with the rundown of the remaining fleet already underway, one would expect the F-14 to be kept operational with a minimum of expenditure, and with no real expansion of the type's role and responsibilities. In fact, the F-14 force is undergoing major changes, introducing dramatic improvements in capability, and is embracing more fully the air-to-ground role which it first picked up only as it entered the second half of its career.

For the first 15 years of its service life, the F-14 was very much a single-role aircraft – a dedicated fleet air defence interceptor – and underwent the minimum of changes and upgrades. Known weaknesses and problems were addressed, with the AIM-54C model of the Phoenix being rushed into service after the original model was compromised following the fall of the Shah in Iran, and with new variants being developed with new, more powerful and more reliable engines. Otherwise, remarkably little happened until the Cold War began to draw to a close.

Although the aircraft-carrier was essentially an offensive 'Power Projection' weapon, the defensive F-14 was regarded by many as being the most important element within every Carrier Air Wing (CVW), and the F-14 force became an élite. During the Cold War, US aircraft-carriers represented the most tempting targets possible for Soviet long-range bombers, which could often attack using very-long range stand-off weapons, including cruise missiles. Only the F-14, with its AWG-9 weapons system and AIM-54 Phoenix AAMs, could hope to intercept such attackers before they could launch their missiles, 400-500 miles out from the carrier, or to successfully intercept incoming cruise missiles.

Aircrew flying other types pointed out that 'Fighters are fun, but bombers are important', but they were seldom heard. The F-14 was good-looking (except in the circuit, when its ungainly appearance led to the aircraft's unflattering 'turkey' soubriquet), and was a technological triumph. The Navy itself promoted the Tomcat above all other aircraft types in its PR and recruiting effort. The first Tomcats in service also wore extremely colourful unit markings, and the aircraft was glamorised by Hollywood, lionised by the press, and adored by aviation enthusiasts.

Cold War air wings

At the height of the Cold War virtually every Air Wing (11 in total, plus two Reserve Air Wings) included two Tomcat squadrons, and the F-14 equipped 22 front-line squadrons, four Reserve fighter squadrons and two training units (one for each Fleet). A 12th Air Wing (CVW-10) even began to form with two more Tomcat squadrons, but this was disestablished during 1988 as part of a package of defence cuts.

Most carriers embarked a standard Air Wing (known as the Conventional CVW), with two 12-aircraft F-14 squadrons, two light attack squadrons with 24 F/A-18s, one medium attack squadron with 10 A-6E bombers and four KA-6D tankers, and single ECM/EW, ASW, AEW and SAR/ASW squadrons equipped with a total of 24 EA-6Bs, S-3s, E-2Cs and SH-3s or SH-60s. The USS *Midway* never

embarked any F-14s, instead having three F/A-18 units, while *Ranger*'s Air Wing embarked two F-14 squadrons and two A-6 units, but never embarked any F/A-18s.

At one time, it seemed likely that the Conventional CVW would be replaced by the so called 'Roosevelt Air Wing', with each Tomcat and F/A-18 unit reduced by two aircraft, with no dedicated KA-6D tankers, with a second A-6 squadron and with single extra EA-6B and E-2C aircraft being carried. It was then expected that the 'Roosevelt' and 'Conventional' Air Wings would give way to a 'Power Projection Air Wing', with two 12-aircraft F/A-18 squadrons, 16 A-6Es or AXs, and only 20 F-14s in two 'light' ten-aircraft squadrons. In fact, there were insufficient A-6s to allow two Intruder units (or even a single 16-Intruder squadron) to become 'standard' and, in the event, the A-6E was retired without being directly replaced.

The subsonic Intruder's integrated track and search radar, and target recognition/attack multi-sensor (TRAM) system, with its chin-mounted forward-looking infra-red (FLIR) and laser designator and receiver gave the aircraft an unparalleled all-weather low-level attack capability. The aircraft also had an impressive payload and long range. Unfortunately, however, the A-6E's slow speed, lack of agility and acceleration made it rather vulnerable, and its age made it maintenance-intensive and difficult to support. While the F/A-18A achieved 17 maintenance man hours per flying hour (MMH/FH), the A-6E fleet averaged 44 MMH/FH, making it one of the Navy's most expensive front-line aircraft to operate. Moreover, individual examples of the Intruder were also running out of fatigue life, and large numbers were grounded or subjected to severe *g*-limit restrictions.

The US Navy initially planned to replace the A-6E with a new Intruder variant, newly-built, with new smokeless General Electric F404-GE-400D engines, a new AN/APQ-173 Norden Synthetic Aperture Radar and new digital avionics. This was cancelled in 1988, shortly after the prototype's first flight. Attention then turned to the advanced, stealthy A-12 Avenger, though this programme soon became mired in technical difficulties, mismanagement and cost escalation, and it was then cancelled in January 1991. This led to a requirement for an alternative long-range strike aircraft for the US Navy's carrier air wings. The proposed A-X and later A/F-X were cancelled in September 1993.

By this time the Navy had already decided to acquire an advanced derivative of the Hornet as an interim type, pending the A/F-X, and when the latter was cancelled, the new Super Hornet was left as the Navy's only new fixed-wing combat aircraft. Moreover, after the debacle of the A-12, it was decided that development and production could not

be concurrent, making it impossible for the new aircraft to be ready in time to replace the A-6. To make things worse, plans to re-wing the remaining A-6Es were dramatically cut back, and the type was instead simply retired. The last Intruder unit, VA-75 'Sunday Punchers', finally decommissioned in early 1997, but the bulk of the fleet had gone several years earlier.

The retirement of the A-6 left the Carrier Air Wing without a sophisticated, long-range all-weather strike attack aircraft, and in the absence of any alternative, the Navy began to look at air-to-ground modifications and derivatives of the F-14 and F/A-18.

Super F-14s

It was always apparent that the F-14 had a number of attributes which offered great potential in the air-to-ground role, including its relatively long range, impressive payload and two-man cockpit. But it was a question of potential, since although the aircraft had always had a secondary, reversionary air-to-ground capability, it had never been exploited by the US Navy. When the original VFX specification was first released in June 1968 it included an important secondary close air support role, with a payload of up to 14,500 lb (6577 kg). Early Grumman publicity material for the winning design (303E) included illustrations of the 'Tomcat-to-be' toting heavy loads of air-to-ground ordnance, and even during the F-14 flight test programme at least one pre-production Tomcat was photographed

Not a 1973-vintage aircraft, 'Bullet 101' was the last F-14D(R) to be redelivered to the US Navy, and was painted in late 1995 in an almost exact replica of VF-2's first scheme to commemorate the 25th anniversary of the Tomcat's first flight. The markings inside the fin proudly proclaimed that 'The Cat is Back'.

Grumman products have dominated US Navy carrier decks for decades, but in the 2000s their days appear to be numbered. The Tomcat is due to disappear by 2008, while the EA-6B Prowler is scheduled for replacement soon after. The nature of its successor has yet to be determined, although EW versions of the F/A-18F and F-35 (JSF) have been proposed. This 'Cat' is a VF-2 F-14D.

A scene once unthinkable in the Tomcat community: inert Mk 83 1,000-lb (454-kg) bombs and LGTRs (on the trolley at left) wait to be loaded on to the VF-2 and VF-213 Tomcats in the background, in preparation for air-to-ground training work at NAS Oceana, Virginia.

Below right: In the 2000s the Tomcat's main Achilles heel is its time-consuming maintenance requirements and unreliability of what is now a true veteran. It has become commonplace to launch air spares on operational missions as an insurance against inflight technical faults. Suffering no such problems is this VF-31 F-14D, cruising with wings fully spread.

Below: Low, slow manoeuvring, as demonstrated by this LANTIRN-carrying VF-143 F-14B, has been made much safer by the incorporation of the DFCS (Digital Flight Control System), which inhibits the Tomcat's propensity to depart.

carrying 14 500-lb (227-kg) Mk 82 bombs attached to modified Phoenix pallets. Much later, when the one-off F-14B Super Tomcat prototype was being used for F-14D development work, the Tomcat was again extensively photographed with air-to-ground weapon loads (usually four Mk 83 1,000-lb/454-kg bombs) and these photos were used for marketing purposes. When the F-14D entered service it incorporated the necessary software and hardware to enable it to carry iron bombs, and the incorporation of more advanced weapons would have been relatively simple.

But this capability remained latent. For as long as A-6 Intruders were deployed aboard US Navy carriers, there was simply no incentive to add the air-to-ground role to the Tomcat squadrons' repertoire. But once the Intruder needed replacing, Grumman turned its attention to unlocking the air-to-ground potential of the Tomcat.

The first Tomcat derivative proposed as an A-6 replacement was the so-called Quickstrike, a minimum-change version of the F-14D with navigation and targeting FLIR and FLIR/designator pods, and with additional modes for the APG-71 radar, including Doppler Beam Sharpening and synthetic aperture. This would have brought the radar up to the same standard as the APG-70 used by the F-15E Strike Eagle. The cockpit was to have been fully NVG-compatible, with new colour displays, including a digital moving map. Quickstrike was also to have featured four underfuselage hardpoints, each with five sub-stations, and two underwing hardpoints, each with two sub-stations. The Quickstrike's warload was to have included LGBs, Harpoon, SLAM, Maverick and HARM. Despite its long range and two-man crew, the proposed Tomcat Quickstrike was judged by the US Congress as being inferior to even the basic F/A-18C in the air-to-ground role, because it lacked the Hornet's synthetic aperture ground mapping radar capabilities, and was not compatible with the full range of smart air-to-ground ordnance, but only with LGBs.

Super Tomcat 21

The relatively modest Quickstrike therefore soon gave way to the Super Tomcat 21, which was developed as both an Intruder replacement, and as a lower cost, multi-role alternative to the proposed NATF, claiming to offer 90 percent of ATF's capability at 60 percent of the cost. Incorporating all of the improvements offered by Quickstrike, with a new ISAR version of the APG-71 radar and helmet-mounted sights, the Super Tomcat 21 was to have had improved F110-GE-129 engines offering 'supercruise' capability, and thrust-vectoring. Supercruise is defined as the ability to attain and then sustain supersonic cruising flight without recourse to reheat, and the Super Tomcat 21 promised to do so at speeds of up to Mach 1.3. The aircraft also featured a new, single-piece wraparound windscreen, giving a much improved view for the pilot.

Fuel capacity was increased through the addition of reshaped wing gloves (which broadly matched the planview outline of a standard Tomcat's wing glove with the original vanes extended). These new LERXes added around 2,500 lb (1134 kg) of fuel.

To compensate for the increased weight of fuel and weapons, Super Tomcat 21 also featured modified, increased lift single-slotted Fowler-type flaps, increased chord slats and revised all-moving tailplanes, which were enlarged by extending the trailing edge aft. These improvements were intended to allow heavyweight take-offs (or take-offs in zero-wind conditions) and reduced landing speeds.

Grumman hoped for a programme go-ahead in 1990, leading to a 1993 first flight date, and production deliveries from 1996. The company's anticipated development costs

were a relatively modest $989 million, and the 233 planned new-production Super Tomcat 21's were expected to have a unit cost of $39 million, with another 257 being remanufactured from F-14Bs and F-14Ds at a unit cost of only $21 million.

Grumman's final 'Super Tomcat' proposal was the Attack Super Tomcat 21, which was based on the Super Tomcat 21, with further improvements and refinements. Structurally, the so-called AST-21 introduced thicker outer wing panels, containing increased capacity fuel tanks, while the aircraft also featured increased capacity external fuel tanks. The flaps and slats were redesigned and refined, further reducing approach speeds by an estimated 18 mph (29 km/h).

Some sources suggest that the new supercruise engine was a feature of the Attack Super Tomcat, rather than the original Super Tomcat 21, but this cannot be confirmed.

Attack Super Tomcat was designed to carrying the same navigation and targeting FLIRs as the other 'Super Tomcats', but also replaced the AN/APG-71 radar with a new electronically scanned phased array radar, perhaps the Norden set originally developed for the A-12. Defensive aids would also have been improved, with new jammers and 135 chaff/flare cartridges in launchers built into the LAU-7 missile rails. However, the Attack Super Tomcat was judged to be unaffordable, and the Navy finalised its plans to develop the F/A-18E/F Super Hornet instead.

Super Hornet v. Tomcat

The F/A-18E/F development contract was signed in June 1992, launching an aircraft that was advertised as being larger and more capable than the baseline F/A-18, offering a substantial increase in payload, range, bringback and internal volume (for fuel and avionics).

It is true that the Super Hornet cannot carry an A-6 payload over A-6 distances, but it can fly about 35-50 percent further than the F/A-18C, and can land back with 9,000 lb (4082 kg) of fuel and weapons instead of only 5,500 lb (2495 kg). Moreover, the aircraft is designed to operate in today's post Cold War world, in which the nature of the threat has changed. The disappearance of mass fleets of 'Backfires', each armed with armfuls of AS-6 cruise missiles, has allowed the US Navy to conduct littoral operations, in which the primary threat comes from fighter-type aircraft carrying Exocet-type missiles.

In 1994, accepting and recognising that littoral warfare marked a shift away from open-ocean warfighting and toward joint-service operations conducted from the sea, the Secretary of the Navy said that 85 percent of the Navy's potential targets were within 200 miles (320 km) of the coast, and thus within the F/A-18C's range, even with an aircraft-carrier operating 100 miles or more offshore. F/A-18Cs carrying four 1,000-lb (454-kg) bombs and external fuel tanks have an unrefuelled mission radius of about 340 miles (547 km), while the F/A-18E/F is projected to carry the same weapon load up to 520 miles (837 km), even without inflight refuelling.

With comparable warloads, and under the same conditions, it has been suggested that the F-14 has a radius of action of about 750 miles (1200 km). This is an impressive difference, but one which the Navy's experts believe to be irrelevant. If greater range is needed, the Navy's Tomahawk cruise missile has a range of about 805 miles (1300 km), and Air Force bombers have even greater range.

The question of whether the Super Hornet is a much better bet for the US Navy than any Tomcat derivative could ever be remains a controversial and much argued point of view. Super Hornet supporters maintain that the reduced long-range stand-off threat allows an F/A-18E/F with AMRAAM to represent a viable replacement for the Tomcat/Phoenix combination in the Fleet Air Defence role.

However, while the Super Hornet (as a derivative of the 'Legacy' Hornet) promised to be fairly quick and simple to develop (in the event this proved not to be quite the case), it was clear that something would have to be done if the

Despite attempts to tone down the fleet, colour has always been a feature of the Tomcat community, although now it is restricted to CAG and CO's aircraft. This was VF-31's 'CAG-bird' F-14D while assigned to Abraham Lincoln in late 1997.

Known as Operation Southern Watch, or OSW, the policing of Iraqi airspace south of the 32nd Parallel has occupied the US Navy since the end of the Gulf War in 1991. After a flourish of activity in late 1992/early 1993, the OSW mission became rather tedious, but in more recent times Iraq has increased its challenges to UN fighters overflying its territory, leading in turn to numerous strikes being mounted against Iraqi air defences. With full air-to-air armament, this VF-2 F-14D returns to 'Connie' after a 1995 OSW patrol.

With Desert Fox bomb drop markings on its nose, VF-32's 'CAG-bird' F-14B refuels from a Marine Corps KC-130. Carried on underfuselage TERs (Triple Ejector Racks) are two LGTRs (Laser-Guided Training Rounds), used to mimic the behaviour of full-size Paveway weapons. The F/A-18D from the USMC's VMFA(AW)-224 in the background also carries LGTRs.

Right: As well as three Sparrows, a single Sidewinder and an instrumentation pod, this VX-9 F-14B is carrying a live AIM-54C Phoenix. The underfuselage Sparrow is carried in a recess: three similar recesses are located further forward, under where the Phoenix pallets are mounted on this aircraft. Combined with the lower wing pylon stations, the recesses allow up to six AIM-7s to be carried.

F-14As surplus to Fleet requirements have found a useful role with NSAWC (Naval Strike and Air Warfare Center) at NAS Fallon, Nevada. NSAWC was created by the amalgamation of 'Top Gun' (NFWS), 'Top Dome' (CAEWS) and 'Strike U' (NSWC) and provides an air combat training centre for all Navy pilots. Tomcats are allocated to provide fighter adversaries.

withdrawal of the A-6 were not going to leave an unacceptably large hole in the Carrier Air Wing's capability mix, with a particular long-range gap. One obvious solution was to activate the F-14's long dormant air-to-ground capability.

'Bombcat' – modest but useful

Much has been made of the Tomcat's increasing adoption of an air-to-ground role as the so-called 'Bombcat', though this was initially, in truth, extremely limited.

Small sections of the Tomcat community had pressed to be allowed to reclaim an air-to-ground role, ever since the introduction of the Hornet had shown that one aircraft could perform both roles with aplomb. With the Cold War drawing to a close, and with increasing emphasis being

placed on multi-role versatility, there was an attitude that "if the FAGs (Fighter/Attack Guys) could do it, then so should the Tomcat community!"

F-14 air-to-ground capabilities were quietly explored by Naval Systems Command, culminating in the dropping of two inert 2,000-lb (907-kg) Mk 84 iron bombs by a VX-4 F-14A on 10 November 1987. OTEF tests followed in 1988, and front-line trials began during 1990. The first 'Bombcats' were the F-14A+s of VF-24 'Fighting Renegades' and VF-211 'Checkmates', which began developing air-to-ground tactics and techniques. VF-24 won the honour of becoming the first fleet F-14 squadron to drop air-to-ground ordnance, (four Mk 84 bombs), inaugurating a new role for the F-14. VF-211 participated in Desert Storm, but only in the interceptor and TARPS roles, since weapons clearance trials continued at such a slow pace that it was not until July 1992 that Fleet Tomcat squadrons actually received a full clearance to use even GP bombs.

In the interim, VF-101 took a lead role in training the F-14 fleet in strike warfare from late 1990, one of the squadron's instructors dropping two inert Mk 84s on 12 September 1990. VF-211 was the first Pacific Fleet unit to complete the Tomcat Advanced Strike Syllabus (TASS) in June 1992. This course is now known as AARP (Advanced Attack Readiness Program). Clearances for CBUs (cluster bomb units) and LGBs followed soon after, however, expanding the 'Bombcat's arsenal.

In May 1991, VF-143 claimed to have become the first fleet Tomcat squadron to drop live air-to-ground ordnance, during a detachment to NAS Fallon, though VF-24 had already achieved this distinction a year earlier. Adoption of the 'Bombcat' role was somewhat patchy and uneven, some Air Wings becoming entirely 'Bombcat'-qualified

almost immediately, with others remaining unqualified, and some converting only one of their two squadrons (usually the non-TARPS unit) to the bombing role. When the USS *Constellation* deployed in late 1994, without A-6Es, its F-14Ds still could not drop bombs because they lacked the necessary computer software.

'Bombcats' entered combat on 5 September 1995, when two F-14As from VF-41 participating in Operation Deliberate Force over Bosnia-Herzegovina dropped LGBs (designated by F/A-18 Hornets) on an ammunition dump in eastern Bosnia. The squadron also dropped dumb bombs on Serb targets during the same cruise, but whenever it used PGMs, it required targeting support from Hornets.

Expanding the 'Bombcat's 'bite'

With work proceeding on the F/A-18E/F, and with the 'Bombcat' in service in a limited air-to-ground role, attention was turned to giving the existing F-14 force a limited all-weather/precision attack air-to-ground capability to help replace the A-6 Intruder in the interim.

In the absence of the A-6, the Joint Conference Committee on the FY 1994 Defense Authorization Act directed the Navy to add an 'F-15E equivalent' capability to its F-14D aircraft, including the capability to employ modern air-to-ground stand-off weapons. This went beyond the Navy's intention, which was merely to add a 'more robust' ground attack capability.

A COEA (Cost and Operational Effectiveness Analysis) completed in December of 1994 examined different proposals for turning the in-service F-14 into a precision strike platform. The US Navy had already outlined a $2.5 billion two-stage upgrade for the F-14A and F-14B. The initial phase of the planned upgrade, known as the 'A/B Upgrade', consisted of structural modifications to extend the Tomcat's fatigue life to 7,500 hours, improved cockpit displays, improved defensive systems, and the provision of digital avionics architecture and new mission computers to speed data-processing time and improve software capacity. This A/B upgrade was to be incorporated into 76 F-14As and 81 F-14Bs, conferring a degree of commonality with the F-14D before the second phase would be added to all surviving Tomcats.

This second stage, confusingly known as 'Block I', was to have added a built-in FLIR, an NVG-compatible night-attack cockpit and enhanced defensive countermeasures. Overall, this was not felt to offer anything that was not already offered by the F/A-18C, and the 'Block I' Tomcat even lacked some important Hornet capabilities, including

compatibility with vital weapons such as HARM, Harpoon, SLAM, Maverick and Walleye. In the event, funds for the A/B structural and survivability modifications were authorised, but funding for the F-14 Block I ground attack upgrade was eliminated.

Ambitious upgrades

One alternative studied was an F-14D-based upgrade known as the F/A-14D, a rolling four-phase upgrade which was not intended to alter planned F/A-18E/F procurement, but which would improve the F-14's capabilities as an interim A-6 replacement.

Proposed by Grumman as an alternative to the planned 'Block I' upgrade to the F-14A and F-14B, and sometimes referred to as 'Phase II', the $9.2 billion programme would have seen some 210 Tomcats (198 F-14As and F-14Bs and 53 F-14Ds) brought to a common (digital) standard, all with F110 engines, AYK-14 computer (with XN8 memory upgrade), an attack FLIR, MIL STD 1760 weapons capability (for JSOW), new displays, a one-piece windscreen, frontal RCS reduction measures and dry foam fuel tank protection. The second phase would add a navigation FLIR, an NVG-compatible cockpit, the F/A-18C(N)'s digital moving map, a Raster HUD and an inert gas fuel tank protection system, together with an AN/ALE-50 towed radar decoy. The proposed third phase added software modes from the F-15E's radar, and the fourth and final phase added JSOW and JDAM. Grumman also proposed a more limited programme, applying the same upgrade only to the 53 remaining F-14Ds, at a cost of $1.5 billion, to begin in 1995, and with Opeval in 1997. The Navy judged this proposal to be unaffordable.

In October 1994, Robert C. Byrd, and David R. Obey, respective Chairmen of the Senate and House of Representatives and Committees on Appropriations, and Sam Nunn, and Ronald V. Dellums, respective Chairmen of

Top: In the line of their adversary duties NSAWC F-14s are called upon to mimic a variety of foreign fighter systems. Naturally the Su-27 'Flanker' figures prominently, for which a number of the unit's aircraft received this 'Flanker'-style camouflage. F-14s are also used to mimic MiG-31s, occasionally working with E-2s which can imitate the A-50 'Mainstay'.

Above: Among the NSAWC fleet are aircraft wearing Iranian-style camouflage (not to be confused with the last F-14 from Iran's 80-aircraft order which was embargoed and delivered to the US Navy). It has been reported in late 2001 that all NSAWC aircraft will adopt this colour scheme. This machine has its modified Phoenix pallets/bomb racks lowered down from the underside of the 'tunnel' between the engine trunks.

Naval Air Warfare Center – testing the F-14

Subordinate to Naval Air Systems Command (NAVAIR), the NAWC has three principal divisions: Aircraft, Weapons and Training. Two of these operate Tomcats on a permanent basis.

Above: The NAWC-AD's Strike Test Squadron operates this F-14B modified with a Digital Flight Control System, which improves high-g manoeuvring and low-speed handling. DFCS underwent its first sea trials in November 1996 aboard USS John C. Stennis.

Naval Air Warfare Center Aircraft Division

NAWC-AD at NAS Patuxent River, Maryland, reports to Commander Naval Air Systems Command, and is responsible for the development of air vehicles, propulsion systems, avionics, and items like catapults and arrester systems. The unit parents the USNTPS and has three Aircraft Test Squadrons. One of these deals only with rotorcraft, and of the other two, the **Naval Strike Aircraft Test Squadron** flies most (if not all) of the Tomcats based at Patuxent River.

Although the Tomcat is nearing the end of its career, modifications to the type have continued to provide a great deal of work for the Naval Strike Aircraft Test Squadron's F-14s. During 2000-2001, the squadron were heavily committed to testing (and expansion) of the F-14's new DFCS, integration of JDAM, improvements to the VDIG and retrofit of the AN/ALE-47 chaff dispenser.

During 2001-2002, the DFCS is being further expanded, and the F-14D is gaining a new back-up Navigation Guidance System (NGS) and an upgrade to the current mission computer. The Tomcats are also to gain LANTIRN pods with higher altitude capability.

Finally, the ageing F-14s may gain structural improvements, and the Naval Strike Aircraft Test Squadron is to examine loads on the wing (to determine its service life), and on the Nose Landing Gear Steering Collar (NLGSC), and to evaluate new stronger engine mounts for the F110 engine.

Above and right: The Naval Weapons Test Squadron – Point Mugu is part of the NAWC-WD, and was formerly the Pacific Missile Test Center (and Naval Missile Center before that). As its earlier names suggest, it is devoted to missile trials over the Pacific Missile Range, and has operated various Tomcats since the early days of the programme, firing its first Phoenix in 1972. This is one of the unit's NF-14Ds.

Naval Air Warfare Center Weapons Division

NAWC-WD at China Lake was formed by merging the Naval Weapons Centre at China Lake and the Pacific Missile Test Center at Point Mugu in January 1992. Today, the NAWC-WD is tasked with the development and testing of air-launched weapons and associated tactics, and can call upon a highly favourable climate, a large fleet of aircraft types and massive ranges to fulfil its duties. The NAWC-WD is estimated to have $3 billion of infrastructure.

The division now parents two flying Naval Weapons Test Squadrons, the Naval Weapons Test Squadron (NWTSCL) 'Dust Devils' flying Hornets, Harriers and Cobras from China Lake, while the Naval Weapons Test Squadron (**NWTSPM**) **'Bloodhounds'** at NAS Point Mugu, operates a mix of aircraft, including the YF-4J, QF-4N/S, NP-3D and NF-14A/D. In recent years, the latter unit's achievements have included the early completion of Operational Testing of the Operational Flight Program (the radar tape load) for the F-14B. While VX-9 at Point Mugu conducted Operational Test (OT) of the aircraft, the maintenance departments of NWTSPM and VX-9 combined into one unit to complete the work two months early, allowing VF-102 to deploy months ahead of schedule, thereby participating in operations over the Balkans.

Point Mugu is also home to the **F-14 WSSA** (Weapons System Support Activity). This is part of the Naval Air Systems Command (NAVAIR) Tomcat Integrated Product Team (IPT), which reports to the F-14 Program Office, known as PMA-241. This provides cradle-to-grave F-14 weapon system support, including reliability and readiness improvements, the correction of latent defects, the replacement of obsolete parts and periodic functional upgrades in response to changing threats, and to enable the aircraft to meet new requirements. PMA-241 has also strived to establish a common baseline avionics standard for the three in-service F-14 variants.

The WSSA can call upon a unique range of F-14 system rigs and other facilities, which allow software development and synthetic 'airborne' testing at a fraction of the cost of relying on airborne platforms alone. These rigs have proved their worth in integrating JTIDS on the F-14, and in issuing revised Operational Flight Program Software loads. The rigs consist of the forward fuselages of F-14A, F-14B (Upgrade), and F-14D aircraft, each fitted with appropriate and representative avionics. Real and simulated weapons can be connected to the rigs, allowing ground-based compatibility testing and missile-on-board aircraft RF testing.

the Senate and House of Representatives Committees on the Armed Services, released a damning report about the various Tomcat upgrade proposals.

These distinguished politicians carefully evaluated the implications of the Navy's decision to spend an estimated $2.5 billion between fiscal years 1994 and 2003 for what was described as "a limited ground attack upgrade and other modifications to 210 F-14 Tomcat fighters", consisting of 76 F-14As, 81 F-14Bs and 53 F-14Ds and found that the Navy had "not made a compelling case to proceed with its $2.5 billion plan", for a number of reasons, which it carefully outlined.

Although the Navy had justified its proposed F-14 attack upgrades as being necessary to replace some capability that would be lost with the retirement of the A-6E, it was clear that upgraded Tomcats actually would not be available to fill the gap between the retirement of the A-6E and the introduction of the F/A-18E/F. Delivery of the first upgraded F-14s was not scheduled to begin until some time after the A-6Es were retired, and it looked as though they might not even be available before the F/A-18E/F. No F-14s were scheduled to begin receiving upgrades until fiscal year 1998, a year after the last A-6s were retired, and none

was to be delivered until 1999. Two CVWs would by then have been without A-6Es for at least five years. With the F/A-18 E/F aircraft entering service during 2000 the gap which could have been filled by the upgraded F-14 would have been very short.

Attack gap

By default, carriers would have been deploying for several years without either A-6Es or upgraded F-14s, instead relying on extra F/A-18Cs for all attack missions. This was said to demonstrate the Navy's willingness to rely on the Hornet for its strike capability, although senior officers disputed this, claiming that the arrangement was a considered risk, and reflected temporary affordability constraints, and not a willingness to permanently forgo capability.

As well as failing to 'plug the gap', the proposed Tomcat did not offer the capability which the politicians expected from its $2.5 billion price tag. They noted with concern that current Navy plans would not provide F-14s with F-15E-equivalent capabilities, and that if Congress wished to provide these, the Navy's own estimates show that it would cost very much more.

A desert-camouflaged NSAWC F/A-18 peels away from VX-9's latest black-painted Tomcat, an NF-14D. Traditionally using the callsign 'Vandy One', the succession of black test aircraft (F-4s and F-14s) at Point Mugu used to wear the Playboy bunny insignia on the tail, but that was deleted in the interests of political correctness.

VX-9 is the Navy's operational test and evaluation unit for fighter/attack aircraft. The detachment at Point Mugu, California was formerly designated VX-4, and has operated Tomcats since their entry into service, being the first Navy squadron to get the F-14.

In March 1999 F-14Bs from VF-32 engaged in air combat exercises with F-16A/B Netz fighters of the IDF/AF over Israeli ranges. According to the hosts, the results were heavily in favour of the F-16s, but the nature of the engagements was not released and any assessment would be highly speculative.

of the F/A-18C. By contrast, even early F/A-18Cs, with APG-65 radar, enjoyed synthetic aperture ground-mapping with Doppler beam sharpening, and their capability was only improved by the addition of APG-73 radar from 1994.

They were also disappointed that no F-14s would be able to launch "current or planned precision munitions or stand-off weapons, except for LGBs". It was acknowledged that LGBs are a useful (and sometimes war-winning) weapon, but expressed concerns that the usefulness of laser targeting would be severely limited when targets were obscured by clouds, smoke, haze, dust or moisture – all of which could potentially prevent laser beams from illuminating and marking a target.

There were important weapons routinely carried by both the A-6E and the F/A-18 which could not be used by the upgraded Tomcat, including the AGM-88 High-speed Anti-Radiation Missile (HARM), the AGM-84 Harpoon anti-ship missile, the AGM-65 Maverick anti-armour missile, Walleye guided bomb and the Stand-off Land Attack Missile (SLAM), while other newer weapons were compatible with the F/A-18C but not with the planned F-14 upgrade. These included the Joint Direct Attack Munition (JDAM) and the Joint Stand Off Weapon (JSOW).

With tight budgets and numerous other priorities, the politicians judged that the planned F-14 upgrades "did not appear to be cost-effective", offering little or no improvement over current capabilities and probably being unavailable until after the F/A-18E/F began to enter service. They noted that the Navy itself, "In setting its priorities" had already eliminated the F-14 upgrade from its Program Objectives Memorandum, which they took to be a clear admission that the Navy had weighed its needs and found that it had more important priorities.

Not only did the upgraded F-14 fail to measure up to the F-15E, the politicians also judged that it would not offer "any capability not available or planned for the F/A-18C," while most upgraded F-14s would actually be considerably less capable than the F/A-18s then in service. They were particularly scathing of the fact that the planned upgrades would not include the kind of air-to-ground synthetic aperture radar required for precision ground-mapping, or which would permit crews to locate, identify and attack targets in adverse weather and poor visibility.

The bulk of the Tomcat force was thus effectively limited to clear-weather ground-attack missions. Only the 53 F-14Ds, with their APG-71 synthetic aperture ground-mapping radar, would have capabilities approaching those

'Cheap and cheerful' precision attack

In the end, the COEA report recommended the cheaper and quicker option of simply integrating a stand-alone laser designator and FLIR on all Fleet F-14s, to give rudimentary night capability and compatibility with the basic range of laser-guided bombs. Such weapons could already be carried by the 'Bombcat', but the F-14 relied on third-party targeting and designation. Giving the Tomcat a basic self-designation capability was therefore felt to represent a useful baseline capability.

As a result, the Navy applied the first stage of its planned upgrade to 76 surviving F-14As and to 81 F-14Bs, incorporating structural improvements to give a 7,500-hour fatigue life, together with a new dual MIL STD 1553B digital avionics architecture, with new mission computers, improved cockpit displays (with a new HUD for the F-14B), and

Above: This immaculate four-ship of F-14As is from VF-154, the Tomcat squadron forward-deployed in Japan at Atsugi and assigned to Air Wing Five aboard USS Kitty Hawk (CV 63). Unlike US-based units, Air Wing Five is 'always on deployment', and does not follow the standard 2-year work-up/ deployment cycle.

Right: 'Blacklion 111', an F-14D(R) of VF-213, is carefully lined up for launch from Carl Vinson during a Southern Watch cruise. The aircraft, BuNo. 161159, was the first of the 'retread' A-models to emerge from the Bethpage works as F-14Ds, and was redelivered to the Navy in late 1990.

improved defensive systems, including AN/ALR-67 RWR, a BOL chaff dispenser and a PTID programmable tactical information display in the rear cockpit.

These modifications brought the old versions up to a broadly similar avionics standard to the 53 remaining F-14Ds, resulting in the designations F-14A (Upgrade) and F-14B (Upgrade), or F-14A++ and F-14B MMCAP (Multi-Mission Capability Avionics Programme). At one time, it was hoped that this improved commonality would allow F-14s of all variants to be deployed in mixed squadrons. It soon became clear that mixing TF30- and F110-engined versions in single units would be impractical, but the integration of F-14Bs and F-14Ds seemed more realistic, and it came as a surprise when plans for mixed F-14B/D squadrons were quietly cancelled in 1997. It had been intended that VF-2, VF-102, VF-143, VF-103 and VF-31 would transition to a mix of F-14Bs and F-14Ds (in that order), with the 'Bounty Hunters' expected to be the first to deploy, in August or September 1999.

LANTIRN 'Bombcat'

Meanwhile work began on providing the F-14 with a rudimentary night/precision attack capability, using a FLIR and laser designator. The US Navy decided to see whether such a system could be integrated on the F-14 using funding originally set aside for the integration of JDAM on the Tomcat. This inferred the use of an off-the-shelf system, and the Navy carefully examined Loral's Nite Hawk pod (used by the F/A-18C) and the Martin-Marietta LANTIRN (Low-Altitude Navigation and Targeting Infrared for Night) pod used on the F-15E and F-16C. Lockheed Martin had been proposing a variant of the LANTIRN pod to the Navy since 1993, for use on the F-14, and in December 1994 a Navy report had urged the acquisition of such a system.

The Nite Hawk system naturally offered commonality advantages, but in the end, LANTIRN had a wider field of regard (a 150° cone around the boresight) and a 5.87° field of view for target acquisition, while Nite Hawk offered only 4°. LANTIRN also offered a higher degree of magnification.

Instead of following the usual route, commissioning industry to prototype a LANTIRN installation and then conducting trials at the Naval Air Warfare Center (with service evaluation following with VX-9), the US Navy adopted a more streamlined approach, managing the programme 'in-house' and achieving much greater input from the front-line at every stage. AIRLANT was then given the task of demonstrating the capabilities of the system, and the installation was trialled by a Fleet squadron. This was possible because LANTIRN was already a mature system, in use with the Air Force since the late 1980s.

Fairchild Defense produced design drawings for an interface between a hand controller in the F-14 cockpit and a LANTIRN pod. This was a virtually self-contained system, with minimal modification to the aircraft's existing software and hardware. The pod is not integrated into the F-14's computers and software, instead feeding images directly from the FLIR onto the RIO's PTID and onto the pilot's vertical display indicator (VDI) in the F-14A/B, or onto one of the two MFDs in the F-14D.

Other LANTIRN-equipped aircraft tended to use two separate LANTIRN pods, with an AN/AAQ-13 navigation pod combining a wide Field of View FLIR and Texas Instruments TFR, and an AN/AAQ-14 targeting pod combining a stabilised, steerable telephoto IR imager with a collimated laser designator. When integrating the LANTIRN system onto the F-14, Lockheed Martin decided to use only the AN/AAQ-14 targeting pod, albeit with increased stabilisation and accuracy, thanks to its new inertial measurement system. The pod also incorporated a built-in GPS/INU, so that the pod 'knew where it was' without having to interface with the aircraft's navigation system. Because the pod has a GPS, navigational accuracy of the Tomcat itself is also greatly improved. The pod computer also contained all necessary ballistics data.

With a pre-briefed known target, the pod's GPS allowed

the laser to be automatically cued onto the target, and could even generate steering cues in the pilot's HUD, in the VDI (Vertical Display Indicator) or superimposed on the FLIR picture. The pod could find targets without a radar or aircraft navigation system hand-off, and did not need to be accurately boresighted to the aircraft.

The RIO designates the target after the pilot 'pickles' the bomb, and the pod performs its own BDA, by video-taping the FLIR picture through to impact. The LANTIRN pod can be used against targets of opportunity, in 'Cue-to-HUD' or 'Snowplough' modes. In the former case, the laser's line of sight is locked to a particular spot in the HUD, which the pilot manoeuvres onto the target by pointing the nose of the aircraft at it. In the Snowplough mode, the pod's line of sight is similarly fixed, but depressed by 15°, and the pilot steers the 'dot' onto the target by reference to the FLIR picture.

Originally designated F-14A+, the F-14B introduced F110 engines but none of the other F-14D improvements. The MMCAP programme added a host of upgrades, the most important of which for the crew are the new HUD (pilot) and PTID (RIO). The latter provides an excellent display of LANTIRN and TARPS imagery.

This smart F-14A 'CAG-bird' from VF-14 participated in the April 2000 Fleet Week fly-by of New York.

With its wings still in the 'oversweep' position, a VF-2 F-14D taxis forward to the bow cat of Constellation. *Its blotchy complexion reflects the continuous application of paint along chipped panel lines and fastenings in the never-ending war against saltwater corrosion.*

With a live 'Buffalo' – as the AIM-54 is called – aboard, a VF-213 F-14D prepares to launch for an OSW mission. This squadron made the first (US) combat firing of a Phoenix, when two were fired at extreme range against Iraqi fighters.

Trials went exceptionally well, and the F-14B MMCAP's PTIDS big screen gave a better LANTIRN picture than could be obtained in the F-15E or F-16. After a series of shakedown flights, in which pod controls were explored and fine-tuned, the aircraft was used to drop four Laser Guided Training Rounds and four inert GBU-16s on the Dare County Range, all but one of the LGTRs scoring direct hits. The exception was dropped outside the weapon's wind limits. Hnarakis and Slade then dropped four live GBU-16s at the Vieques range in Puerto Rico, scoring three bullseyes and one miss as a result of system failure.

By June testing was complete and Lockheed Martin was awarded a contract for production-standard systems for 10 aircraft. VF-103 was awarded the newly instituted Vice Admiral Allen Precision Strike Trophy (named after the Admiral who had driven the programme forward), and 10 squadron aircraft were modified to accept the six LANTIRN pods procured. These aircraft then carried out the further trials necessary before the system could be declared ready for deployment, including a 'mini-cruise' aboard the USS *Enterprise* during April-May 1996. The squadron used its new LANTIRN pods to 'spike' for RN Sea Harriers, and various other aircraft types.

On 14 June 1996, the LANTIRN-equipped F-14 Precision Strike Fighter was formally unveiled as the centrepiece of a lavish official roll-out ceremony in NAS Oceana's Hangar 23, at which Secretary of the Navy John Dalton officially accepted the first pod. Less than 10 months (actually 233 days) had elapsed between the initial signing of the contract and the system being ready for operational use.

Smart procurement

The F-14 LANTIRN program represented a textbook example of streamlined 'smart' acquisition, and has been hailed as "one of the most astonishingly successful military acquisition programme in recent history". The industry/Navy Department/front-line team worked together with brisk efficiency, achieving their goals within the set timescales and under budget. This F-14 Precision Strike team's achievement was officially recognised with the award of the Secretary of Defense Superior Management Award.

On the Tomcat, the AN/AAQ-14 pod is carried on station #8B (the starboard wing station) and is controlled by the RIO in the rear cockpit, using a simple hand controller. These hand controllers were 'off-the-shelf' items, originally designed for the A-12, and similar in appearance to an F/A-18 stick top. The pod requires MIL STD 1553B databus architecture, so LANTIRN has to be fitted to an F-14D or an F-14 MMCAP (F-14A (Upgrade), F-14B (Upgrade) or F-14A++) aircraft, or to an aircraft which has been specially fitted with MIL STD 1553B databuses. PTID is not required, since LANTIRN imagery can be displayed (albeit with less fidelity) on the older display screens.

A VF-103 F-14B (BuNo. 161608, Modex 213) was chosen to be the LANTIRN testbed. The aircraft was returned to Northrop Grumman for modification and the test programme then began in March 1995, with the aircraft making its first flight with LANTIRN on 21 March, flown by Commander Alex Hnarakis (VF-103's XO) with Lt Cdr Larry Slade as RIO.

On 28 June 1996, VF-103 'Jolly Rogers' took nine LANTIRN-capable aircraft (and five non-LANTIRN TARPS-equipped jets) and six LANTIRN pods with them when they embarked on a Mediterranean cruise aboard the USS *Enterprise*. Because the LANTIRN hand-controller replaced the usual TARPS panel it was not then possible for aircraft to be both TARPS- and LANTIRN-capable, although a 'work-round' has since been developed, and aircraft can now be fully compatible with both systems. Six of the nine VF-103 LANTIRN-compatible aircraft were further modified to allow their crews to use MXV-810 'Cat's Eye' NVGs, which allowed pilots to 'look into the turn', while the LANTIRN FLIR kept looking forwards. These allowed the squadron's FAC(A)-qualified crews to practise their craft by

night, and proved entirely satisfactory, although in the event, the F-14 fleet has been provided with rival ANVIS-9 NVGs, which have a wider field of view, tripled light amplification performance and lower unit price.

Operational success

LANTIRN's first operational cruise was a triumph, and only seven failures were experienced in more than 460 sorties. Failures were quickly rectified, since Lockheed Martin contractors were on board the *Enterprise* throughout the cruise. The LANTIRN pod proved useful for reconnaissance (giving the Tomcat an 'after dark' recce capability) and even in the air-to-air role, proving better at identifying long-range targets than the usual TCS. As well as taking

Between 1993 and 1996 the US Navy slashed its Tomcat squadrons, reducing most air wings to just one F-14 unit instead of two. The training requirement was reduced accordingly, and was consolidated within one squadron (VF-101) at Oceana. The 'Grim Reapers' continue to train new Tomcat crews at both the home base (below) and on available carrier decks (above).

Many of the Tomcat modifications have been applied to the F-14A, allowing it to remain a viable warplane in its last years of service. This VF-41 aircraft, seen on its last cruise in 2001, displays the BOL Sidewinder launch rails which also house chaff dispensers.

part in missions over Bosnia the squadron flew a 690-mile (1110-km) round trip strike mission against targets in Israel as part of Exercise Juniper Hawk. The VF-103 Tomcats scored hits on their four assigned targets and were credited with killing all opposing aircraft, proving the Tomcat's formidable self-escort capability. During the same cruise, VF-103 took the LANTIRN pod to war over Bosnia.

Initially the Navy ordered 13 LANTIRN pods, and a shortage of pods was at first the only major problem with the Tomcat LANTIRN programme. During 1997, for example, both pods and modified aircraft were in such short supply that they had to be transferred from unit to unit as squadrons deployed, and while shore-based at NAS Oceana squadrons often had no suitably equipped aircraft for LANTIRN training. Thus, when VF-103 returned from

deployment on 20 December 1996, its LANTIRN pods and equipment were immediately transferred to VF-32 aboard USS *Theodore Roosevelt*, for use on the MMCAP-modified A-model Tomcats.

At least 25 more pods were quickly ordered, and there were soon sufficient pods for simultaneous deployed operations by several LANTIRN-equipped Carrier Air Wings. Next to deploy with LANTIRN were VF-41 and VF-14, who deployed to the Mediterranean and the Red Sea from spring 1997 until the late summer.

VF-2 became the first Pacific Fleet squadron (and the first F-14D unit) to deploy with LANTIRN, between 1 April 1997 and September 1997 on board USS *Constellation*. With 10 LANTIRN-equipped F-14Ds (which the 'Bounty Hunters' always insist on referring to as Super Tomcats), VF-2 modestly claimed to be "the most potent Strike-Fighter squadron to have ever deployed".

It was followed by VF-211 aboard the USS *Nimitz*, in September 1997. VF-102 deployed on board the USS *George Washington* in October 1997, while VF-154 at NAF Atsugi, Japan, received Upgrade- and LANTIRN-modified Tomcats in September 1997, before deploying to the Persian Gulf in January 1998. The deployment by VF-102 marked the first deployment by aircraft which could carry either TARPS or LANTIRN, three of its aircraft being so equipped.

LANTIRN at war

LANTIRN-equipped 'Bombcats' made their combat debut during Operation Desert Fox at the end of 1998. F-14Bs from VF-32 aboard the USS *Enterprise* were involved in the first wave of attacks, on 16 December 1998, dropping GBU-12s and GBU-24s on Iraqi air defence installations. USS *Carl Vinson* arrived in time for the F-14Ds of VF-213 to participate in the third day's strikes. An official release later stated that: 'The strength of the F-14/LANTIRN programme was ably demonstrated in Desert Fox, and has provided us with a firm bridge to the F/A-18E/F'.

LANTIRN Tomcats were soon in action again. Within nine days of embarking for a six-month Mediterranean cruise, the 'Black Aces' of VF-41 found themselves flying combat missions over Kosovo in support of Operation Deliberate Force. VF-41 flew 384 sorties, totalling more than 1,100 combat hours, and dropped more than 160 tons of laser-guided munitions. The squadron claimed an unprecedented 85 percent success rate.

Back in the Middle East, on 9 September 1999, VF-2's LANTIRN-equipped F-14D Tomcats led the rest of Carrier Air Wing Two in Operation Gun Smoke. The Carrier Air Wing destroyed 35 of the 39 Iraqi anti-aircraft artillery and surface-to-air missile site targets it was assigned, in a large-scale operation which marked the biggest expenditure of ordnance during a single day since Operation Desert Storm.

Above: VF-154's F-14As received individual nicknames, perhaps indicative of their distance from the centre of bureaucracy: they are forward-deployed at Atsugi. Being based in Japan provides less opportunities for carrier deck training during work-up periods.

Right: The 'Red Rippers' of VF-11 are significant in that, since the return of VF-14 and VF-41 in November 2001, they form part of the only air wing which retains two Tomcat squadrons – CVW-7 aboard John F. Kennedy. VF-11 has a LANTIRN speciality within the wing.

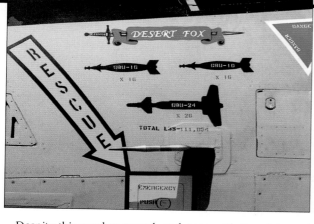

Despite this combat record, and even with the night and precision attack capabilities conferred by LANTIRN, the F-14 is not a true replacement for the A-6, nor even a real competitor to the F/A-18C. The FLIR's effectiveness can be severely constrained by the thinnest cloud or the lightest rain, and worse conditions can effectively ground the LANTIRN Tomcat.

Despite its limitations, LANTIRN is undergoing development to enhance its capabilities. Under the 'LANTIRN 40K' programme the Navy hopes to extend the firing limit from an altitude of 25,000 ft (7620 m) AMSL to 40,000 ft (12192 m), while achieving the specification ranges of 20 miles (32 km) (combat laser) and 12 miles (19.5 km) (training laser). Previously, the LANTIRN pod proved prone to arcing at higher altitudes, and required new, higher sensitivity laser receivers. 'LANTIRN 40K' components were laboratory-tested and installed in a targeting pod, and the laser was then successfully fired at simulated altitudes of up to 45,000 ft (13716 m) in a test chamber at Lockheed Martin's Orlando facility.

Flight testing of the prototype pods began in late August 2000, and 'LANTIRN 40K' component retrofit starting at the end of 2000. The first 'LANTIRN 40K' pods were scheduled for Fleet introduction in February 2001. LANTIRN Tomcats are also receiving new weapons, most recently the GBU-24E/B Enhanced Penetrating LGB and the GBU-31/32 Joint Direct Attack Munition (JDAM).

Modern weapons

Integration of the GPS-guided JDAM on the F-14 had been planned for many years, and the programme was even funded. In fact, LANTIRN integration was achieved using funding originally allocated for F-14/JDAM and, ironically, provided the F-14 with the GPS solution on which JDAM relies. Unlike an LGB, JDAM does not rely on laser designation, but instead has an INU, a GPS receiver and steerable tail surfaces, with the bomb being accurately 'flown' onto a given set of GPS co-ordinates. The weapon is therefore entirely unaffected by the weather and atmospheric conditions which may affect a laser-guided weapon, although accuracy may be slightly reduced. JDAM 'kits' (with new tails and side fairings) will allow existing 'dumb' bombs to be converted simply and cheaply.

JDAM is now in widespread service, and was used 'in anger' during operation Allied Force in Kosovo. Some 87,000 JDAM kits have been ordered by the US DoD, and the weapon will be used by the USAF, USN and USMC. The JDAM programme for the F-14 is reportedly progressing well. The Naval Strike Aircraft Test Squadron (part of the Naval Air Warfare Center Aircraft Division at NAS Patuxent River) completed separation tests for an envelope of up to Mach 0.95 with a minimum number of drops, and Weapons Test at Point Mugu quickly authorised a full-up JDAM drop from an F-14B Upgrade aircraft. The weapon was soon cleared for service, transforming the Tomcat into a GPS weapons player and freeing it from its previous long-standing reliance on unguided or laser-guided weapons. VF-102 is believed to have deployed to the northern Arabian Sea with full JDAM compatibility, though it remains to be seen whether Tomcats used the weapon during Operation Enduring Freedom.

While making strenuous efforts to expand the scope of the Tomcat's air-to-ground 'bite', the US Navy has not ignored the aircraft's defensive capabilities. Swedish BOL chaff dispensers were added (in the four underwing LAU-138 missile launch rails) as part of the MMCAP upgrade, though integration of these with the Tomcat's AN/ALE-39 expendable dispensing system was primitive. An AN/ALE-47 retrofit programme was therefore devel-

Above: An F-14B from VF-102 'Diamondbacks' leaps from the waist cat of Roosevelt. F110-powered F-14s have sufficient thrust in military (non-afterburning) power to launch without reheat, whereas TF30-powered F-14As must use Zone Three reheat.

Above left: F-14B operator VF-32 was the first unit to use the F-14/LANTIRN combination in action, during three nights of attacks on Iraq during Operation Desert Fox in December 1998. The squadron's bomb log (16 GBU-10s, 16 GBU-12s and 26 GBU-24s) is faithfully recorded on the nose of the 'CAG-bird'.

Below: A LANTIRN-carrying F-14D of VF-213 recovers aboard the 'Starship Vinson' during February 2001 work-ups. By October 2001 the squadron's Tomcats were in action over Afghanistan.

Above: The VF-41 squadron commander's aircraft received this nose art after the unit's fine showing in Operation Allied Force. The Tomcat was especially useful in the FAC(A) role, being used to remain on-station over designated 'kill boxes' to direct and designate for other attack aircraft after it had dropped its own ordnance. In this role the extra pair of eyes is of inestimable value.

Above: With LGBs in the 'tunnel' and LANTIRN clutched to station 8B, a 'Black Aces' Tomcat prepares to launch from Theodore Roosevelt during Allied Force. This campaign saw the 'Bombcat' come of age and proved the success of the LANTIRN integration. One former A-6 B/N, now an F-14 RIO, stated that the task of acquiring targets for designation was much easier in the Tomcat, mainly as a function of the embedded GPS.

Many of VF-41's missions over Kosovo were conducted by night. Recent Tomcat upgrades have made the cockpit displays fully NVG-compatible.

oped, under which the new system will replace the existing AN/ALE-39 systems on all surviving F-14Bs and F-14Ds. The replacement will involve a 'box for box' swap, together with the removal of unnecessary AN/ALE-39 components and the loading of a platform-specific Mission Data File (MDF) within the ALE-47's own Operational Flight Program (OFP), which is common to all Navy Aircraft. A new NVG-compatible Digital Control Display Unit (DCDU) will be fitted in the rear cockpit.

Integration of AN/ALE-47 will provide a step change in capability and reliability, and may even reduce support costs. The AN/ALE-47 will provide greater programming flexibility, and an expanded inventory of expendables, including BOL chaff/IR cartridges. The AN/ALE-47 will be fully integrated with all four of the Tomcat's BOL launchers, enabling complex deployment sequences using expendables from the BOL rails and the fuselage-mounted 'buckets', as part of a combined dispensing programme. The OFP supports seven different dispenser programmes.

Functional and carrier suitability testing of the ALE-47 on the F-14 was carried out by the Strike Aircraft Test

Squadron during the summer of 2000, leading to full deployment during 2001.

Upgrades do not always make things better. This was the case with the new HUD installed in F-14B (Upgrade) aircraft as part of the MMCAP programme. This was found to be 'marginally effective' and, with the erosion of the head-down Vertical Display Indicator's (VDI) reliability, caused real concerns over the impact on F-14B flight safety, as well as making interoperability difficult. Together referred to as the Vertical Display Indicator Group (VDIG), the HUD and VDI were controlled by an analog Display Indicator, and it was decided that all needed to be replaced.

Display replacement programme

The Strike Aircraft Test Squadron at Patuxent River received an F-14B Upgrade aircraft – ('Vandy 241') from VX-9 det Point Mugu – to complete testing of the replacement VDIG(R), and this aircraft was also used to complete all other F-14B Upgrade testing, including GBU-24E/B, JDAM and AN/ALE-47.

The replacement VDIG consisted of an advanced but off-the-self Flight Visions Inc Sparrow Hawk HUD, a new head-down VDI and a new colour video camera. The original analog Display Indicator was replaced by a new Modular Mission Display Processor (MMDP). The new HUD retains F-14B(U)-type air-to-air symbology, and uses F-14D-type symbology for take-off, cruise and landing, but offers an even larger field of view than the HUD installed in the F-14D. A so-called 'power carrot', which serves as a predictor of the aircraft's future energy state, and which is a feature of the F-14D HUD, will be incorporated in all HUD modes. These changes significantly improved the quantity and quality of information presented, and improved overall system reliability.

Initial flight tests of elements of the new VDIG(R) were conducted from November 1999 by NAWC's Weapons Division at Point Mugu, before a Developmental Test (DT) flight clearance recommendation was issued, allowing full testing to begin at the NAWC's Aircraft Division at Patuxent River. VX-9 then conducted operational assessment of the system, resulting in a fleet clearance in the autumn of 2000. Some 82 surviving F-14Bs are receiving this upgrade.

Taming the 'Turkey'

Although generally possessed of excellent handling qualities, especially by contrast with its predecessors, the F-14 does have some extremely undesirable flying quality characteristics in both the high angle of attack regime and in the landing configuration, and over the years these have resulted in a number of aircraft and aircrew losses, with engine failure/asymmetric thrust/stall-spin departures proving a particular problem.

Late in the Tomcat's career, a new Digital Flight Control System, developed by GEC Marconi Avionics (and based on that of the Eurofighter Typhoon), was procured for the F-14 fleet, under a 1996 $84 million contract. The DFCS programme has been conducted by a combined, integrated project team consisting of Navy and Industry personnel. GEC-Marconi Avionics provided the DFCS computer hardware, operational flight programme software and technical support. Northrop Grumman supplied flight test support and system integration support and conducted flying quality and structural analyses. The Naval Air Warfare Center Aircraft Division (NAWC-AD) at Patuxent River was responsible for development, integration and flight testing.

The DFCS team used two testbed aircraft, an F-14A (modex SD/207) and an F-14D (modex SD/230), and these completed clearance testing of the DFCS's mode I on board the USS *Enterprise* (CVN 65) in a variety of wind and sea conditions.

Fleet introduction of the F-14 DFCS (in its initial fleet release software version OFP 4.1.1) began in July 1999, with VF-14 becoming the first unit to deploy with the DFCS F-14A. DFCS was subsequently incorporated into all remaining F-14A, B and D variants under an aggressive and rapid transition schedule. All front-line F-14 squadrons

have now completed DFCS integration, with VF-102 completing the last AFCS deployment in April 2000.

The new DFCS has already been a great success story, even in its initial release form. The system greatly increases departure resistance and provides improved recovery capabilities when the aircraft does depart. The new DFCS also significantly improves handling qualities on approach. As well as enhancing flight safety, the new DFCS has proved more reliable and more maintainable than the original analog AFCS that it was designed to replace

The final DFCS software version (OFP 4.4), with improvements to the existing control laws for the automatic carrier landing system (ACLS), was released in August 2000, having completed flight testing aboard the USS *Enterprise* (CVN 65) in April 2000.

The new software load also included new control laws for the roll SAS, which eased manoeuvring flight envelope restrictions, and expanded the FCS self-test fault reporting capability.

Having undertaken three nights of operations during Desert Fox in December 1998, Enterprise was nearing the end of its operational deployment when Allied Force was launched against Serbia and Kosovo. The carrier had its deployment extended and arrived in the Mediterranean on 20 April 1999, the 27th day of the NATO campaign. After three days the Pentagon decided not to call upon the air wing, which included the F-14As of VF-14, for combat missions.

Paveway II-carrying F-14A Tomcats are seen during Mediterranean operations aboard Enterprise in April/May 1999. The 'CAG-bird' (left) displays special markings for the squadron's 80th anniversary, the unit claiming to be the oldest US Navy squadron. After return to the US at the end of this deployment, VF-14 became the first unit to field F-14As with the DFCS (Digital Flight Control System) installed. Other A-model units (VF-41, VF-154 and VF-211) followed swiftly after, as did B/D squadrons.

Two views show VF-32 F-14Bs recovering aboard USS Harry S. Truman during operations in the Persian Gulf during the carrier's first operational deployment in 2000/2001. The F-14 has always been somewhat tricky on the approach, even with the benefit of the DLC (direct lift control) which uses the automatic lowering and raising of spoilers to increase and decrease lift without altering aircraft attitude. Many of the problems arose from the high residual thrust of the turbofan engines, which required very low throttle settings where the engines are unresponsive, and a tendency to 'float' on the approach. Many of the approach problems have been alleviated by the DFCS.

The final ACLS configuration includes hardware and software modifications and has replaced the original pitch attitude command system with a new vertical velocity, or 'h-dot', command system with integrated direct lift control (DLC) giving extremely smooth glideslope control.

The lady vanishes

Many had hoped that the F-14's new capabilities and new usefulness as a long-range multi-role strike fighter would see the fleet being maintained at its late 1980s level, with two squadrons on every carrier deck. For a brief period following the withdrawal of the A-6, this was achieved, with the composition of the standard Air Wing changing to incorporate two slimmed-down F-14 squadrons and three squadrons of F/A-18Cs (often including a USMC unit). In the event this was judged to be impossible to sustain, since attrition and an uneven distribution of flying hours/fatigue led to a severe shortage of F-14 airframes. It became clear that maintaining a single F-14 squadron within each Air Wing would be a more realistic target, and this became the new 'standard' Air Wing composition. Between the end of Desert Storm and the end of 1996, the US Navy lost 14 F-14 squadrons – more than half the total. With 12 squadrons and 10 Air Wings, Tomcat numbers were sufficient to retain two Air Wings at what Tomcat supporters saw as the 'optimum' composition, with two squadrons of F-14s augmented by two Hornet units. The remainder transitioned to a one-Tomcat VF/three-

Hornet VFA squadron mix. In practise, the use of the Hornet rather than the Tomcat had few disadvantages in the post-Cold War world, since the newer Hornet proved more reliable, more maintainable and more capable than the ageing F-14.

Experience showed that there was a strong likelihood that in any given strike package, at least one F-14 was likely to abort for technical reasons, while Hornets tended not to, while the maintenance hours required to sustain a single Tomcat sortie remained very high, making it difficult for F-14 squadrons to maintain a high sortie rate, and requiring their maintenance departments to be large and well-manned. Finally, even with LANTIRN and all of the other upgrades, the Tomcat was not as versatile nor as effective as the Hornet, and offered no advantages, except where payload/range was an issue or where an extra pair of eyes was relevant, such as in the forward air control role.

When the 1997 Quadrennial Defence Review (QDR) suggested that production of the Super Hornet should be cut by almost 50 percent, from just over 1,000 to 548 units, many saw this as an opportunity for revitalising the Tomcat, though in truth, the F-14's fate had long been decided, and the aircraft will retire by 2008. If fewer Super Hornets are procured, they will instead be replaced by the new F-35 Joint Strike Fighter.

Recce Tomcat

If the Tomcat remains something of a 'poor relation' in terms of the scope of its air-to-ground capabilities, it remains the only carrierborne tactical reconnaissance asset. However, to infer that the Tomcat's usefulness in the reconnaissance role is a function of the lack of any alternative would be extremely misleading, since the aircraft has always had a fine reputation as a recce platform, thanks to the excellence of the TARPS (Tactical Air Reconnaisance Pod System) reconnaissance pod, the skill and elan of Tomcat TARPS crews, and the professionalism and dedication of those who process and exploit TARPS imagery.

The success of TARPS is perhaps surprising, since it originated as an interim solution to the US Navy's requirement for a carrierborne recce aircraft to replace the RA-5C Vigilante and RF-8G Crusader. Initial studies looked at developing and deploying a dedicated RF-14 reconnaissance variant of the Tomcat, but by 1974 it was clear that such an aircraft could not be ready in time, and the 'interim' solution of a Tomcat recce pod was adopted. This, it was confidently predicted, would soon be replaced by a dedicated RF-18 version of the Hornet, with a reconnaissance pallet in the former gun bay.

Development of TARPS began in April 1976, using an off-the-shelf system originally developed for the A-7 Corsair, but never placed into production or service. Prototype pods began flight testing in April 1977, on the fifth YF-14A (BuNo. 157984). The original (finned) version of the pod was carried on the right-hand intake duct, in place of a drop tank. During development the pod was moved to the right-hand rear fuselage Phoenix station (no. 5) and became more streamlined and refined in appearance.

Weighing 1,750-lb (794-kg) and 17 ft (5.18 m) in length, the TARPS pod contained four bays, or stations, with the fourth bay containing the electronics required to relay information to the RIO's display in the rear cockpit, and to the AN/ASQ-172 data display set, which may be used to mark the film to allow easier interpretation. Station 1 in the nose of the TARPS pod was designed to accommodate the KS-87B framing camera, used in the vertical or forward oblique mode with a 3- or 6-in (7.62- or 15.24-cm) focal length lens. Following a TARPS upgrade, this could be replaced by a new KS-153T camera, or an LLTV video camera. Station 2 was designed to hold the KA-99, a low-altitude, panoramic camera with a focal length of 9 in (22.86 cm) giving horizon-to-horizon coverage. The KA-99 is the primary sensor on most reconnaissance missions and represents the heart of the TARPS system, but since the TARPS upgrade this can now be replaced by a KS-153A or KS-153L. An AN/AAD-5 infra-red line scanner completed the TARPS pod's array of sensors, in Station 3.

The pod and its sensors are monitored and controlled by the Naval Flight Officer/Radar Intercept Officer (NFO/RIO) in the rear cockpit, who has a new TARPS display although the pilot is also provided with a camera on-off control on the stick.

Although TARPS imposes only a minimal penalty on aircraft performance and makes little demand on the aircraft systems, it does require power, signal and environmental control connections that are not normally available at Station 5. Aircraft therefore have to be specially converted and wired to carry the pod. Initially, some 65 F-14As were wired to carry TARPS, some of which were subsequently converted to F-14B standards. The 38 new-build F-14Bs were not wired for TARPs, unlike the 37 new-build F-14Ds and the 18 F-14D conversions, although a handful from Block 160 (163412, 163415, 163416 and 163417) have since been de-modified as NF-14Ds.

The F-14 retains significant defensive capabilities with the pod attached, although underfuselage AIM-54s cannot be carried. Outboard missiles (usually two AIM-7s and two AIM-9s) can be carried, and the 20-mm cannon can be fired while the pod is being carried. When not carrying TARPS, the aircraft can quickly be re-roled to full Phoenix or 'Bombcat' configuration.

TARPS enters service

After successfully completing testing, procurement of TARPS began in 1978. The system underwent OPEVAL in 1979 and the first operational deployment was undertaken by VF-84 in 1981. Thereafter, one squadron aboard each carrier was always TARPS-capable, deploying with several TARPS-compatible aircraft and a number of pods. When Air Wings went down to a single Tomcat squadron, the remaining unit was either the TARPS squadron, or took over the TARPS role.

By the 1980s, wet-film sensors were becoming increasingly old-fashioned. Imagery could not be datalinked, and film had to be processed (and sometimes even printed)

The F-14B is the most numerous version remaining in front-line service, equipping five squadrons. Most have been fitted with full LANTIRN and TARPS capability, and they have undergone the F-14B Upgrade programme. Among the less-visible features of the upgrade is a structural life extension to 7,500 hours.

Expendable countermeasures are released by the AN/ALE-39 dispensers under the rear fuselage and from the CelsiusTech BOL missile rail launchers. The new AN/ALE-47 system will allow a fully integrated and programmable release of chaff bundles or flares from all of the dispensers, significantly enhancing the Tomcat's protection against missiles. The AN/ALE-50 towed decoy system is unlikely to be applied to the aircraft.

USS **Enterprise** *(CVN 65) was nearing the end of a NorLant deployment when terrorists struck in the US on 11 September. The deployment was immediately extended as part of the US mobilisation response. The two Tomcat squadrons aboard were VF-14 (illustrated), and VF-41 both flying the F-14A. When they returned to the US in November, they became the first Tomcat units to transition to the Super Hornet.*

before it could be interpreted and exploited. This all took time (and expensive manpower) and forced a reliance on environmentally damaging chemicals, and as the performance of electro-optical sensors improved, the reconnaissance community generally began looking more and more at EO-based systems.

As the troubled ATARS system stalled due to technical and political difficulties, attention turned towards updating TARPS, to allow it to remain viable and useful through to the end of the Tomcat's life. The obvious solution was to convert the TARPS pod to carry EO sensors.

The Tomcat's new 'Digital TARPS' reconnaissance pod has already proved extremely successful, its EO-based sensors offering faster turnaround of imagery, better performance in poor light, poor weather and haze, while offering cost and manpower savings in processing and exploitation. The first version of digital TARPS, known as TARPS-DI, entered service in 1996 with VF-32, which deployed with the system in November 1996. TARPS-DI contained a Pulnix digital camera in the former KS-87B station (Station 1). The new Pulnix uses only the downward-facing

window and can store up to 200 images onboard. The RIO can review these images and transmit them to the carrier or any other suitably equipped receiver within a 186-mile (300-km) range. The system is able to downlink imagery in near real time for battle damage assessment, although only by 'line-of-sight'. The next version, TARPS-CD, began testing in 1998, adding real-time EO step-framing.

Both attack and reconnaissance operations have been revolutionised by the introduction of FTI (Fast Tactical Imagery), a real-time tactical datalink, first deployed with VF-14 and VF-41 in April 1999. This allows TARPS, TCS or LANTIRN imagery to be transmitted from 'stand-off range' to the carrier or to any other FTI-equipped platform. Moreover, LANTIRN can be used to obtain GPS-quality target co-ordinates, which can then be transmitted (with imagery) to other aircraft.

Tomcat today

Although the US Navy's Tomcat fleet is at its smallest ever size, and although the first front-line units have already begun conversion to the Super Hornet, and even despite its

A VF-41 F-14A refuels from a VS-24 S-3B on 5 October 2001, two days before Tomcats led the first US Navy strikes into Afghanistan as part of Operation Enduring Freedom. As well as delivering Paveway laser-guided bombs, the F-14s have also performed the 'fast-FAC' mission, using LANTIRN to designate targets for Hornets.

Clutching a pair of GBU-16s to its belly, a VF-41 F-14A launches from Enterprise for an Enduring Freedom mission on 18 October, while the squadron's 'CAG-bird' manoeuvres into position behind. After heavy involvement in the opening phase of the campaign, Enterprise and its two F-14 squadrons were withdrawn, replaced by Roosevelt.

Below: Along with Enterprise, initial Enduring Freedom missions were launched by Carl Vinson, whose single F-14D squadron (VF-213) was heavily involved. This scene from the third night of the war shows JDAMs (for F/A-18s) and GBU-16s, although the Tomcat appears to be armed with Mk 20 Rockeyes.

limited operational capabilities, the F-14 has continued to provide the US Navy with a vital asset, and one which has seen action on a number of occasions.

On 6 January 1999, an F-14D of VF-213 from the USS *Carl Vinson*, participating in Operation Southern Watch, fired two AIM-54 Phoenix AAMs at a pair of Iraqi MiG-25s, marking the first USN combat use of the Tomcat's big missile (it had been used in anger by Iranian Tomcats). The weapons missed their targets, which were able to turn away outside the Tomcat's relatively narrow radar gimbal limits at the long ranges involved, though parametric details of the engagement are naturally highly classified. The poor combat record of the AIM-54 in US Navy service has been echoed during exercises where, even in apparently ideal conditions, the AIM-54 seems to have a relatively poor 'strike rate'. Supporters of the Phoenix inevitably quote the results of the 'Six-on-Six' ripple fire test carried out by Commander John 'Smoke' Wilson, with Lt Cdr Jack H. Hawver in the back seat, at Point Mugu on 21 November 1973. The test was taken as proof that the Tomcat/Phoenix could successfully make a simultaneous interception of six targets, flying at different heights and airspeeds.

Others remain unconvinced even by the test, not least because only four of the drone targets were downed. One BQM-34E 'lost augmentation' and the missile missed, while another suffered a failure and missed the QT-33 drone it was fired at. Critics doubted the validity of a test which had been studiously pre-rehearsed (with drones flying at the same speeds and heights, and on the same headings in order to allow the crew to work out and practise the appropriate launch sequence). Others questioned the realism of the narrow 15-mile (24-km) front along which the targets

approached and the 2,000-ft (610-m) maximum separation between targets. It was also pointed out that the targets all had augmentation (to make them better radar targets) and were flying at 'easy' speeds of between Mach 0.6 and Mach 1.1, with no evasive manoeuvring, jamming or chaff. The test, they averred, presented a modest challenge, while no-one could expect an enemy bomber formation to behave so co-operatively.

Whether or not the test was the success which Grumman, Westinghouse, Hughes and the Navy claimed, it

Below and below left: When Theodore Roosevelt arrived in the war zone it brought with it the F-14Bs of VF-102 'Diamondbacks', these aircraft being JDAM-capable. Below is a night launch from 21 October, during the period in which F-14s flew combat missions from three carriers.

Considering its role and the amount of time it has been in service, it is somewhat surprising that the F-14 has only one confirmed air-to-air 'kill' in US Navy service – and that was over an Mi-8 helicopter during Desert Storm. This should not disguise the fact that the F-14 remains in the top drawer of air combat fighters. US Navy air combat training remains among the best in the world, although F-14 crews now have to work even harder to achieve the requisite skill levels in both air fighting and ground-attack regimes, and all the while operating a notoriously 'difficult' aircraft from a boat in the middle of the ocean. Compared with the F/A-18C, the Tomcat's two-man crew certainly aids air-to-ground work.

was certainly expensive – the 38-second sequence being costed at a staggering $154,000 (in 1973 dollars!) per second. "It was like setting fire to a 10-storey car park filled with brand new Cadillacs" recalled pilot Wilson later.

Testing of the improved AIM-54C began at Point Mugu in 1979, at the same time that Iran's F-14As and some 200 Phoenix missiles were falling into revolutionary hands. Point Mugu was forced to develop counter-countermeasures against its own AIM-54, and had to ensure that the capabilities of the new F-14A/AIM-54C would not be compromised by enemy knowledge of the earlier system. Development testing at Point Mugu included another spectacular 'Six-on-Six' test, this time conducted before a congressional committee. This demonstrated that the weapon system could simultaneously acquire and track six independent targets, and then launch and guide six missiles, each to a selected target, although it is not known whether the new test repeated the unrealistic test conditions of the first.

Although the AIM-120 AMRAAM cannot match the 'brochure range' figures claimed for the Phoenix, the missile is widely believed to be very much more effective. This seemed to be acknowledged when the US Navy opted to add AIM-120 AMRAAM capability to the F-14D when its computer software was updated. This plan was subse-

quently cancelled and the shorter-range F/A-18C, which does enjoy full AMRAAM capability, has assumed an increasing share of the air defence burden. Moreover, advanced derivatives of the AMRAAM have been developed with ramjet boosters which dramatically increase range, probably to beyond the reach of the Phoenix.

The AIM-54C was given another chance to prove its mettle in September 1999, when a VF-2 F-14D fired a single AIM-54 at a pair of Iraqi MiG-23s (or MiG-25s, according to some sources) during Operation Gun Smoke, missing again.

Enduring Freedom

Regular bombing and reconnaissance missions have continued over Iraq, and more recently over Afghanistan. When the USA launched retaliatory strikes following the terrorist attacks on the World Trade Center and Pentagon on 11 September 2001, they relied principally on ship- and submarine-launched cruise missiles, and on B-52 and B-1B bombers forward deployed to Diego Garcia, together with two Carrier Air Wings operating from aircraft-carriers in the northern Arabian Sea. Politically prevented from using most nearby land-bases in the Persian Gulf and in Iran and India, and unwilling to over-use bases in front-line Pakistan and Uzbekistan, aircraft-carriers proved the only way of applying tactical air power in Afghanistan, though their aircraft were operating at the limit of their range, and relied on air-to-air refuelling en route to and from the target. The air war over Afghanistan has a remarkably low profile, and very few details were released about its conduct, let alone about its effectiveness.

After an initial brief phase of night attacks, the carriers launched a handful of sorties on most days of the campaign, with the F/A-18Cs and F-14s operating in conditions of total air supremacy and with only the most primitive surface AA threat. They attacked targets from medium altitude, mainly using Paveway laser-guided bombs, partly switching to CBUs when attacks switched to the Taliban front line. Despite a low intensity of operations, carrier-based tankers were unable to meet the demand for fuel, and RAF and USAF tankers were active in supporting operations by the carriers' Tomcats and Hornets.

When Operation Enduring Freedom began, the US Navy could call upon USS *Carl Vinson* (with CVW-11 embarked, including the F-14Ds of VF-213) and USS *Enterprise* (with CVW-8 embarked, including the F-14As of VF-41 and

VF-14). *Enterprise*'s place was then taken by USS *Theodore Roosevelt*, whose CVW-1 included the F-14Bs of VF-102. Some reports suggest that these were the first F-14s to deploy with JDAM, though there is no confirmation of this. A fourth carrier, USS *Kitty Hawk*, was involved in Enduring Freedom, but operated as a Special Forces helicopter platform, and only embarked with some of CVW-5 (including F/A-18s and S-3s) but without the F-14 element, VF-154.

Quite apart from combat operations, the F-14 squadrons have also undertaken some useful and realistic training exercises. In September 1999, for example, F-14s from VF-2, VF-41, VF-143 and VF-211 sank the redundant cruiser *Belknap* using only free-fall, unguided bombs. One VF-2 pilot put two such weapons down the ship's smokestacks, proving the ability of the Tomcat to deliver unguided ordnance with great accuracy.

The F-14 has not yet had another opportunity to demonstrate its air-to-air prowess, however. In today's unstable world, it would take a brave man to predict that there will be no further chances for Tomcat aircrew to show their mettle.

All remaining F-14As are scheduled for retirement by 2003, the F-14Bs following by 2007 and with the last F-14Ds retiring by 2008. Many may bemoan the retirement of the Tomcat and its replacement by the shorter-ranged F/A-18F, but with the US Navy's shift from 'blue-water' to littoral operations, and with a diminished long-range bomber threat, the F/A-18E/F represents a better tool for the carrier air wing, and one which will, in any case, be augmented by CALCMs for longer range strikes.

VF-14 began to re-equip with the single-seat F/A-18E in late 2001, but the remaining units (VF-2, VF-11, VF-31, VF-32, VF-102, VF-103, VF-143, VF-154, VF-211 and VF-213) will re-equip with F/A-18F two-seaters. A front-line CVW's offensive/defensive capability will then be provided by four Hornet squadrons (like the experimental *Coral Sea* Air Wing deployed in the early 1980s), and this will remain the standard Air Wing composition until the F/A-18C/Ds are replaced by JSF. By the end of 2008, the Tomcat is due to have disappeared from front-line service altogether, and the 'Mighty Turkey' will soon be no more than a memory.

Jon Lake

For the time being it would appear that the sun is finally setting on the F-14. Whether the Super Hornet can adequately fill the vacant space on US Navy' decks left by the F-14's passing remains to be seen. Above is a VF-102 F-14B, while below is a VF-2 F-14D.

Tomcat stores and weapons

Air-to-air missiles

The AIM-54C Phoenix remains the F-14's most powerful air-to-air weapon, and is scheduled to see out the Tomcat's career. AIM-54s can be carried from the lower wing pylons (below) or from four dedicated pallets under the fuselage. At the other end of the AAM spectrum is the AIM-9M Sidewinder, fitted to the shoulder rails.

Lacking AMRAAM capability, the F-14 still employs the AIM-7 Sparrow (above) for medium-range engagements.

Laser-guided bombs

Paveway II bombs (identified by the gimbal-mounted seeker head) available to the Tomcat are the 500-lb (227-kg) GBU-12 (below), 1,000-lb (454-kg) GBU-16 and 2,000-lb (907-kg) GBU-10. All bombs are carried under the fuselage on adapted Phoenix pallets.

The GBU-27 Paveway III is available in standard or penetrating (above) forms. The Paveway III seeker offers greater accuracy and increased flexibility.

Training weapons

For dumb bombing practice various small-scale stores can be carried on Triple Ejector Racks (TERs). They mimic the ballistics of the Mk 80 series weapons. This is a Mk 76 simulator for the Mk 82 weapon. Full-size inert weapons are also routinely used.

For laser-bombing training the Tomcat can carry the LGTR (Laser-Guided Training Round). This has a Paveway seeker head, and its ballistics mimic those of a full-size bomb.

TARPS pod

Carried under the rear right Phoenix station, the TARPS pod provides multi-sensor reconnaissance. The Digital TARPS pod has replaced the traditional wet-film system used previously.

LANTIRN targeting pod

The LANTIRN pod gives the Tomcat its precision targeting capability. A laser designator is boresighted with an acquisition FLIR, which has two fields-of-view available: wide (5.87°) and narrow (1.68°). Normal magnifications are x4.1 (wide) and x10 (narrow), although x20 is available.

LANTIRN is carried on the starboard wing pylon. This aircraft (above) is also fitted with the BOL Sidewinder rail which incorporates a chaff/flare launcher in the rear.

Electronic countermeasures pod

The ALQ-167 'Bullwinkle' reconfigurable jamming pod is occasionally carried from an adapted Phoenix pallet for use against specific threats. It can also be used to provide an EW threat environment during training exercises.

VF-14). *Enterprise*'s place was then taken by USS *Theodore Roosevelt*, whose CVW-1 included the F-14Bs of VF-102. Some reports suggest that these were the first F-14s to deploy with JDAM, though there is no confirmation of this. A fourth carrier, USS *Kitty Hawk*, was involved in Enduring Freedom, but operated as a Special Forces helicopter platform, and only embarked with some of CVW-5 (including F/A-18s and S-3s) but without the F-14 element, VF-154.

Quite apart from combat operations, the F-14 squadrons have also undertaken some useful and realistic training exercises. In September 1999, for example, F-14s from VF-2, VF-41, VF-143 and VF-211 sank the redundant cruiser *Belknap* using only free-fall, unguided bombs. One VF-2 pilot put two such weapons down the ship's smokestacks, proving the ability of the Tomcat to deliver unguided ordnance with great accuracy.

The F-14 has not yet had another opportunity to demonstrate its air-to-air prowess, however. In today's unstable world, it would take a brave man to predict that there will be no further chances for Tomcat aircrew to show their mettle.

All remaining F-14As are scheduled for retirement by 2003, the F-14Bs following by 2007 and with the last F-14Ds retiring by 2008. Many may bemoan the retirement of the Tomcat and its replacement by the shorter-ranged F/A-18F, but with the US Navy's shift from 'blue-water' to littoral operations, and with a diminished long-range bomber threat, the F/A-18E/F represents a better tool for the carrier air wing, and one which will, in any case, be augmented by CALCMs for longer range strikes.

VF-14 began to re-equip with the single-seat F/A-18E in late 2001, but the remaining units (VF-2, VF-11, VF-31, VF-32, VF-102, VF-103, VF-143, VF-154, VF-211 and VF-213) will re-equip with F/A-18F two-seaters. A front-line CVW's offensive/defensive capability will then be provided by four Hornet squadrons (like the experimental *Coral Sea* Air Wing deployed in the early 1980s), and this will remain the standard Air Wing composition until the F/A-18C/Ds are replaced by JSF. By the end of 2008, the Tomcat is due to have disappeared from front-line service altogether, and the 'Mighty Turkey' will soon be no more than a memory.

Jon Lake

For the time being it would appear that the sun is finally setting on the F-14. Whether the Super Hornet can adequately fill the vacant space on US Navy' decks left by the F-14's passing remains to be seen. Above is a VF-102 F-14B, while below is a VF-2 F-14D.

Tomcat stores and weapons

Air-to-air missiles

The AIM-54C Phoenix remains the F-14's most powerful air-to-air weapon, and is scheduled to see out the Tomcat's career. AIM-54s can be carried from the lower wing pylons (below) or from four dedicated pallets under the fuselage. At the other end of the AAM spectrum is the AIM-9M Sidewinder, fitted to the shoulder rails.

Lacking AMRAAM capability, the F-14 still employs the AIM-7 Sparrow (above) for medium-range engagements.

Laser-guided bombs

Paveway II bombs (identified by the gimbal-mounted seeker head) available to the Tomcat are the 500-lb (227-kg) GBU-12 (below), 1,000-lb (454-kg) GBU-16 and 2,000-lb (907-kg) GBU-10. All bombs are carried under the fuselage on adapted Phoenix pallets.

The GBU-27 Paveway III is available in standard or penetrating (above) forms. The Paveway III seeker offers greater accuracy and increased flexibility.

Training weapons

For dumb bombing practice various small-scale stores can be carried on Triple Ejector Racks (TERs). They mimic the ballistics of the Mk 80 series weapons. This is a Mk 76 simulator for the Mk 82 weapon. Full-size inert weapons are also routinely used.

For laser-bombing training the Tomcat can carry the LGTR (Laser-Guided Training Round). This has a Paveway seeker head, and its ballistics mimic those of a full-size bomb.

TARPS pod

Carried under the rear right Phoenix station, the TARPS pod provides multi-sensor reconnaissance. The Digital TARPS pod has replaced the traditional wet-film system used previously.

LANTIRN targeting pod

LANTIRN is carried on the starboard wing pylon. This aircraft (above) is also fitted with the BOL Sidewinder rail which incorporates a chaff/flare launcher in the rear.

The LANTIRN pod gives the Tomcat its precision targeting capability. A laser designator is boresighted with an acquisition FLIR, which has two fields-of-view available: wide (5.87°) and narrow (1.68°). Normal magnifications are x4.1 (wide) and x10 (narrow), although x20 is available.

Electronic countermeasures pod

The ALQ-167 'Bullwinkle' reconfigurable jamming pod is occasionally carried from an adapted Phoenix pallet for use against specific threats. It can also be used to provide an EW threat environment during training exercises.

Airbrakes
Situated above and below the rear fuselage are door-type airbrakes, which operate simultaneously to avoid pitch changes. The upper door has an area of 8.6 sq ft (0.8 m²) and the lower door measures 7.4 sq ft (0.69 m²). The lower brake is restricted to 18° deflection when the undercarriage is lowered to remove the risk of grounding.

Intakes
Unlike the 'nodding' intakes of the F-15, those of the Tomcat are fixed. However, three large ramps which hinge down from the top of the intake alter the airflow pattern and increase/decrease 'throat' area to ensure optimum airflow. At supersonic speeds a considerable amount of air is spilled through prominent doors on the top surface of the intake trunk, while at low speeds these doors operate in the reverse direction as auxiliary intakes.

Laser-guided bombs
This aircraft is depicted carrying two GBU-24A/B bombs, the penetrating warhead version of the 2,000-lb (907-kg) class Paveway III. The Paveway III weapons, distinguished by their fixed seeker heads and larger wing assemblies, are considerably more accurate than the Paveway IIs as they use proportional guidance rather than full deflection of the control surfaces. This, in turn, means they manoeuvre less, and can convert more of the kinetic energy imparted by the launch aircraft into stand-off range. Another feature is the ability to follow a pre-programmed attack profile, depending on the target. Paveway III kits have only been applied to to 2,000-lb warheads, whereas the Paveway II kit is available for a range of warhead weights.

Northrop Grumman F-14D Tomcat
VF-213 'Black Lions'
CVW-11, USS *Carl Vinson* (CVN 70)

USS *Carl Vinson* and Air Wing Eleven were among the first US forces to be assigned to Operation Enduring Freedom, the US government's 'war on terrorism' launched after the attacks of 11 September 2001. While on a WestPac cruise, the carrier received orders to take up station in the Arabian Sea off the coast of Pakistan, where it awaited the call to launch raids into Afghanistan against Al Qaeda terrorist training camps and Taliban military positions. Such operations began on 7 October. At the forefront of the raids were the Tomcat squadrons of *Carl Vinson* (VF-213) and *Enterprise* (VF-14 and VF-41), the latter carrier having had its NorLant deployment extended to allow its participation in Enduring Freedom.

In the attack role the principal weapon of the Tomcat is the laser-guided bomb, aimed using the LANTIRN forward-looking infra-red/laser designator pod carried on the lower starboard pylon (station 8B). This aircraft is shown carrying a typical 'laser-bomber' loadout, with bombs carried on modified Phoenix pallets in the 'tunnel', as the underfuselage area between the engine trunks is known. It is assigned to the squadron commander, and carries the lion nose marking which appeared in early 2001.

Powerplant
The Pratt & Whitney TF30 turbofan had always been regarded as the Achilles heel of the F-14A, particularly in its susceptibility to compressor stalls. Although successive versions, culminating in the -414, alleviated many of the problems, a new engine in the form of General Electric's F110-GE-400 fully ended the Tomcat's long-running engine saga. Fitting the F110 (which has an 82 per cent parts commonality with the F110-GE-100 used in the F-16) proved straightforward, with only minor changes to secondary structures. The engine itself has a 50-in (1.27-m) section added downstream of the turbine, which moves the intake face further forward (as compared with the TF30) and the nozzle further aft.

Mass flow through the engine rises from the TF30's 250 lb (113.4 kg) per second at take-off to 270 lb (122.5 kg), while thrust is theoretically increased to 29,000 lb (129.05 kN), although in the Tomcat the thrust is reduced to 27,000 lb (120.15 kN) to match the engine better to the F-14's requirements. The extra thrust allows the Tomcat to launch without using afterburner unless at high weights. Further advantages of the F110 are carefree throttle handling, greater reliability and TBO (time between overhaul), and a significant reduction in fuel burn, equating to an average mission radius increase of around 62 per cent. The engine itself has a three-stage bypass fan and a nine-stage compressor providing a compression ratio of 31. Ahead of the fan is a bullet spinner and 20 fixed vanes, each with a variable flap on the trailing edge.

Electronic defences
As one would expect, the F-14 is well protected against a variety of threats. The principal warning system is the ALR-67, which receives across a 1 GHz to 16 GHz range. It can identify radars by cross-checking received signals with an onboard threat library, and presents an annotated display with azimuth and type details on a screen in the rear cockpit. Jamming equipment consists of the ALQ-165 ASPJ (Airborne Self Protection Jammer) in some aircraft or the older ALQ-126 DECM (deception ECM). ASPJ was to be fitted to all Navy aircraft, but these plans were cancelled. However, F-14Ds continue to use the equipment, even it does not meet its full specification. Some of the ALR-67 and ALQ-165 antennas are housed in a reprofiled leading-edge extension. Mechanical countermeasures include ALE-39 dispensers under the tail, and BOL Sidewinder launch rails which contain a dispenser in the rear. The ALR-43 ECA (Expanded Chaff Adaptor) can also be carried.

Internal fuel
The total internal capacity of 2,397 US gal (9074 litres) is carried in five main areas (left and right outer wing interspar voids, forward fuselage cells, rear fuselage cells and wing box carry-through). The left engine is usually fed by fuel in the left wing, rear fuselage and left side of the wing box, while the right engine draws from the right wing, forward fuselage and right side of the wing box.

OPERATORS FILE

UNITED STATES NAVY

Between the end of Desert Storm in 1991 and the end of 1996, the US Navy lost 14 F-14 squadrons – more than half the then total – leaving just 12 front-line squadrons, a training unit and a single USNR unit, which itself converted to the F/A-18 in 1999. F-14 units which have disbanded are as follows:

VF-1 'Wolfpack'	disestablished 1 October 1993
VF-21 'Freelancers'	disestablished January 1996
VF-24 'Renegades'	disestablished August 1996
VF-33 'Starfighters'	disestablished October 1993
VF-51 'Screaming Eagles'	disestablished 31 March 1995
VF-74 'Bedevilers'	disestablished 28 or 30 April 1994
VF-84 'Jolly Rogers'	disestablished October 1995
VF-111 'Sundowners'	disestablished 30 March 1995
VF-114 'Aardvarks'	disestablished 30 April 1993
VF-124 'Gunfighters'	disestablished 30 September 1994
VF-142 'Ghostriders'	disestablished 7 April 1995
VF-191 'Satan's Kittens'	disestablished 30 April 1988
VF-194 'Red Lightings'	disestablished 30 April 1988
VF-201 'Hunters'	disestablished 1999
VF-202 'Superheats'	disestablished 31 December 1994
VF-301 'Devil's Disciples'	disestablished 31 December 1994
VF-302 'Stallions'	disestablished 31 December 1995

Although F-14s still deploy aboard both Pacific and Atlantic Fleet carriers, Commander, Fighter Wing, US Atlantic Fleet provides logistics and administrative support to all 12 fleet F-14 Tomcat squadrons, and the F-14 Fleet Replacement Squadron (FRS), all of which are shore-based at NAS Oceana, Virginia.

During the course of the 2000s the F-14 will give way to the F/A-18E/F. The process began in late 2001 when VF-14 and VF-41 transitioned to the Super Hornet, becoming VFA-14 and VFA-41 in the process.

The 12 front-line squadrons equip 10 regular CVWs, two of which (Air Wing 7 aboard the *Kennedy* and Air Wing 8 aboard *Enterprise*) still embark two F-14 squadrons.

CVW-1	**VF-102** (F-14B)	*Theodore Roosevelt* (CVN 71)	Lant
CVW-2	**VF-2** (F-14D)	*Constellation* (CV 64)	Pac
CVW-3	**VF-32** (F-14B)	*Harry S. Truman* (CVN 75)	Lant
CVW-5	**VF-154** (F-14A)	*Kitty Hawk* (CV 63)	Pac
CVW-7	**VF-143, VF-11** (F-14B)	*John F. Kennedy* (CV 67)	Lant
CVW-8	**VF-41, VF-14** (F-14A)	*Enterprise* (CVN 65)	Lant
CVW-9	**VF-211** (F-14A)	*John C. Stennis* (CVN 74)	Pac
CVW-11	**VF-213** (F-14D)	*Carl Vinson* (CVN 70)	Pac
CVW-14	**VF-31** (F-14D)	*Abraham Lincoln* (CVN 72)	Pac
CVW-17	**VF-103** (F-14B)	*George Washington* (CVN 73)	Lant

These remaining squadrons have now started to convert to the F/A-18E/F Super Hornet, beginning with the squadrons of Air Wing Eight, which returned from duty over Afghanistan in late 2001. VF-14 is re-equipping with the single-seat F/A-18E, while VF-41 will receive two-seat F/A-18Fs. Next to convert to the F/A-18F will be VF-102 in early 2002, and VF-211 towards the middle of the year.

All the remaining units will re-equip with the F/A-18F, which is scheduled to have entirely replaced the F-14A by 2003, although there may be a change-over of variants between Tomcat squadrons, and units currently operating the A-model may survive after 2003 with F-14Bs or F-14Ds, while units now operating the later types may relinquish these and convert first. The last F-14Bs are scheduled to be replaced by the F/A-18F by 2007 and the last F-14Ds following before the end of the next year, 2008.

In addition to the regular fighter squadrons, FRS, adversary unit and operational evaluation squadron described below, a handful of Tomcats also serve with the Naval Air Warfare Center's test fleet at two sites: Patuxent River and Point Mugu. This NF-14B is allocated to NAWC-AD's Strike Test Squadron at the former.

VF-2 'BOUNTY HUNTERS'

Dormant since World War II, Fighting Two became the US Navy's second F-14 squadron in October 1972. As a Tomcat squadron, VF-2 won a succession of high-profile awards and established a reputation as one of the Navy's premier fighter squadrons. The awards included two COMNAVAIRPAC Battle 'E's, an unprecedented three consecutive Boola-Boola Awards from 1985 to 1987, and numerous victories in the West Coast High Noon Gunnery, TARPS, ECCM and Fighter Derby competitions.

VF-2 flew more than 550 combat missions and 1,900 combat flying hours during Operation Desert Storm – more than any other tactical squadron flying in-theatre during the 43-day war. VF-2 transitioned to the new F-14D in February 1993, and in July the squadron cross-decked to the USS *Constellation* (CV 64) when the ship returned to San Diego after completing its Service Life Extension Program. A 1994 deployment to the Arabian Gulf saw VF-2 achieving nearly 800 operational sorties and more than 2,050 flying hours, shooting more than 85,000 ft (25908 m) of TARPS film, and producing 12,000 8 x 10 prints.

In May 1996 VF-2 'led the pack', becoming the first West Coast F-14 squadron to relocate to NAS Oceana. VF-2's next cruise began in April 1997 – this time using its F-14Ds as 'Bombcat' strike-fighters, using the LANTIRN targeting pod, LGBs and 'dumb' bombs. With 10 of its 14

F-14Ds (which the 'Bounty Hunters' always call Super Tomcats) equipped for LANTIRN, VF-2 modestly claimed to be "the most potent strike-fighter squadron to have ever deployed". Equally notably, the squadron's remaining four F-14Ds deployed with the new Digital TARPS pod, using these operationally over Iraq, and transmitting imagery back to the ship in near real time. The squadron deployed again in June 1999, with *Constellation* taking over the Operation Southern Watch commitment from *Kitty Hawk* on 28 August 1999. This cruise marked the first use by the Tomcat of the Fast Tactical Imagery (FTI) system, demonstrating near real time targeting in-theatre for the first time, sending FTI imagery to an airborne F-14D aircraft to give the aircrew minute-old satellite imagery.

VF-2 encountered Iraqi anti-aircraft fire on almost every mission flown and, on one occasion, launched an AIM-54 against a pair of incoming MiG-23 'Floggers'. On 9 September 1999 LANTIRN-equipped VF-2 Tomcats led Carrier Air Wing Two in Operation Gun Smoke, destroying 35 of the 39 Iraqi anti-aircraft artillery and surface-to-air missile site targets assigned. The operation marked the biggest expenditure of ordnance in a single day since Operation Desert Storm.

Meanwhile, VF-2 has continued its award-winning prowess, scooping the 1995, 1997, and 1999 COMNAVAIRPAC Battle 'E's, the

1995 and 1997 Boola-Boola Awards, the 1996 Bombing Derby Award and the 1997 and 1999 Safety 'S' Awards.

VF-2 currently forms part of Air Wing Two aboard the USS *Constellation* (CV 64), and its aircraft wear the tailcode 'NE' and modexes 100-107 and 110-116. As the only Tomcat unit in CVW-2, VF-2 operates in the TARPS and LANTIRN roles. It is partnered by three F/A-18C units – VFA-137, VFA-151 and VMFA-323.

As a reminder of VF-2's rich history, VF-2's aircraft originally

retained the red, white, and blue 'Langley Stripe', which is similar to the markings used by the original VF-2 when deployed aboard the USS *Langley* in 1925, though since the toning down of unit markings, this has only been seen in full colour on CAG-birds and CO's aircraft, and in miniature form as a background to the unit badge on the tail.

VF-2's Tomcats still wear the 'Langley' stripe on the nose, albeit in toned-down form. Two stars adorn the rudder.

71

Wing surfaces

The Tomcat has small inboard trailing-edge flap sections operable only when the wing is fully forward, and larger outboard sections which can be used at intermediate sweep settings (up to 50°). Maximum flap deflection is 35° for landing and the flaps incorporate an upper-surface 'eyebrow door' which seals the wing/flap gap when they are retracted. The lower trailing edge of the wing has a 'cove door' surface which raises to form a slot between the wing and flap when they are fully deflected. The leading edge has slats which can be used for landing at up to 17° deflection, or for manoeuvring at up to 7° deflection. The flaps, too, can be deflected down by up to 10° for manoeuvring. Just forward of the flaps are overwing spoilers, which provide roll control at low speeds (they are locked shut beyond 57° wing sweep) and lift dumping on rollout. Maximum spoiler deflection is 55°.

Wing sweep

The F-14's outer wing panels can be swept from a leading-edge sweep of 20° back to 69° in flight. A 75° 'oversweep' position is provided to reduce span for deck stowage, although this can only be set manually with the aircraft at rest. Control of the wing sweep is effected by the pilot using a four-position thumb switch on the side of the starboard engine thrust lever. The standard setting is 'Auto', which hands control of the wing sweep angle to the CADC (central air data computer). This sets the optimum manoeuvring angle of sweep, based primarily on Mach number. Two other positions are 'Fwd' and 'Aft', which allow the pilot to override the CADC. The fourth position is 'Bomb', which is used in ground attack missions. This ensures that the manoeuvring flaps remain retracted, and that the wing sweep is not less than 55°. This simplifies the computations of the bombing computers. Inboard of the throttle quadrant is an emergency wing sweep lever, protected in normal flight by a hinged cover.

Wing profile

To provide sufficient strength with low weight, the F-14's wings (of NACA 64A2 profile) a thick for a supersonic aircraft, with a 10.2 per cent thickness:chord ratio at the root taperi cent at the tip. This also allows them to mount extensive high-lift surfaces to reduce appr By dramatically sweeping back the wings for supersonic flight, the thickness:chord ratio is reduced significantly.

Phoenix missile

Although not carried by this aircraft, the Phoenix remains an important Tomcat weapon. The current version is the AIM-54C+, which has a closed-cycle cooling system catering for much reduced cooling needs. Earlier missiles required a continuous feed of cooling oil from the F-14 itself, but the F-14D was not fitted to provide this capability, and can therefore only carry the C+ version. The C itself introduced new ECCM (electronic counter-countermeasures) and a revised proximity fuse which could handle all-altitude operations. Target discrimination was improved, as was the ability to make attacks from beam positions. Engagement range was also increased.

Radar

Although based on the F-14A's AWG-9 radar, and incorporating the six main functions (pulse-Doppler search, pulse-Doppler single target track, track while scan, range while search, pulse search and pulse single target track), the F-14D's APG-71 is greatly improved with a digital programmable signal processor which works at around six times the speed. More modes are available, including raid assessment which can distinguish between closely spaced targets, a long-range target identification function, and ground-mapping.

Undernose sensors

The key means of identifying the F-14D from the A and B is by the twin undernose sensor set, comprising the AXX-1 TCS (Television Camera Set) in the starboard pod and the IRSTS (Infra-Red Search and Track Set) in the port pod. These sensors, and the APG-71, can be interslaved.

VF-11 'RED RIPPERS'

Flying F-14As since 1980, VF-11 is the US Navy's longest continuously serving fighter squadron (VF-14 has served longer, but was briefly assigned a bomber role). The 'Red Rippers' joined Carrier Air Wing 14 (CVW-14) on 12 July 1992, and converted to the F-14D, becoming the first Fleet F-14D unit. The 'Red Rippers' were awarded the 'Mutha' award in 1993 for being the most outstanding and spirited fighter squadron at NAS Miramar. The squadron made the F-14D's first cruise, deploying on board USS *Carl Vinson* (CVN-70) for WestPac '94, during which the squadron flew missions in support of Operation Southern Watch. In 1994 VF-11 pioneered an NVG upgrade for the F-14, developing the necessary instrument/

VF-11 F-14Bs wear the unit's hog's head and lightning flash badge in toned-down colours on the fin. The insignia has barely changed since 1927.

lighting filters in-house, and then testing the modification on a squadron aircraft. The squadron deployed to the western Pacific with six NVG-compatible aircraft, and long-term Navy plans envisage the system being fitted to all F-14s. VF-11 deployed aboard the *Vinson* again in May 1996 for the ship's last cruise with CVW-14. During the cruise, VF-11 again flew missions in support of Operation Southern Watch and escorted B-52 bombers during Operation Desert Strike in early September 1996.

Like all Pacific Fleet F-14 squadrons, VF-11 moved to NAS Oceana during early 1997, and almost immediately

started to convert from the F-14D Tomcat to the older, less capable F-14B, completing the process in May 1997. The limited number of F-14D airframes available seemed to make it impossible to support three active squadrons, as well as the RAG and various test units. The 'Red Rippers' joined CVW-7 for its 1998 cruise, which was also the first operational deployment of the USS *John C. Stennis* (CVN 74), then the Navy's

newest carrier. *Stennis* relieved *George Washington* in the Persian Gulf.

VF-11 currently forms part of Air Wing Seven aboard the USS *John F. Kennedy* (CV 67), and its aircraft wear the tailcode 'AG' and modexes 200-216. It is partnered by VF-143 'Pukin Dogs' and two F/A-18C units – VFA-131 and VFA-136. While VF-143 handles CVW-7's TARPS requirements, VF-11 has a LANTIRN commitment.

VF-14 'TOPHATTERS'

VF-14 claims to be the oldest US Navy squadron in existence, tracing its lineage back to 1919, through many re-designations. Before becoming VF-14 on 15 December 1949, the 'Tophatters' were known as VF-1, VS-41, VB-4, VA-1A and VA-14. VF-14 converted to the F-14 in September 1974, the first Atlantic squadron to deploy with the F-14A and followed much the same pattern as other Tomcat units, including participation in Operation Desert Storm. VF-14 began to work up an air-to-ground capability in December 1991, starting with the Tomcat Advanced Strike Syllabus (TASS) and progressing to air wing workups at NAS Fallon. Though VF-14 was not the first unit to become 'Bombcat'-qualified (VF-24 and VF-211 practising the role even before Desert Storm) it was the first to make a 'Bombcat' carrier deployment. *Kennedy* and its squadrons were emergency-deployed in July 1992 as tensions in the Persian Gulf increased, but the carrier was recalled within days as the problems cooled. The scheduled cruise began in October 1992 and VF-14 participated in Operation Deny Flight sorties over former Yugoslavia.

VF-14 left CVW-3 in late 1995, and was directly assigned to Fighter Wing Atlantic at NAS Oceana, awaiting reassignment. At one time it seemed likely that the squadron would convert to the F/A-18 Hornet and become VFA-14. During this period, the 'Tophatters' continued to work up in the air-to-ground

role and served as the testbed unit for the Tomcat air-to-ground rocket programme. However, the decision was taken to retain VF-14 as an F-14 squadron and, in 1996, the squadron participated in its first cruise for several years, joining CVW-8 aboard the USS *John F. Kennedy* for a Mediterranean cruise. This finally restored CVW-8 to two F-14 squadrons, VF-14 operating alongside VF-41. VF-14 made another Mediterranean Sea/Arabian Gulf cruise in spring 1997, participating in Operation Allied Force. Both CVW-8 F-14 squadrons had by then received LANTIRN-capable Tomcats.

At the end of 1998 VF-14 re-equipped with the new F-14A DFCS, deploying with these on 26 March 1999 aboard USS *Theodore Roosevelt* for a scheduled six-month cruise to the Mediterranean

and the Gulf. During this deployment, VF-14 was successfully involved in NATO's Operation Allied Force and in Operation Southern Watch.

VF-14 has continued to add to its haul of awards, which already include two Presidential Unit Citations, the Navy Unit Commendation, two Meritorious Unit Commendations, five Battle stars, four CNO Aviation Safety awards, and seven COMNAVAIRLANT Battle Efficiency 'E' awards – in 1998 VF-14 gained the Admiral Joseph C. Clifton award and the Arleigh Burke Fleet Trophy, awarded annually to the most improved combat unit (ship, submarine or squadron) in the US Atlantic Fleet (CINCLANTFLT). This award had never before been won by an F-14 squadron.

VF-14 currently forms part of Air Wing Eight aboard the USS *Enterprise*

(CVN 65), and its aircraft wear the tailcode 'AG' and modexes 200-216. It is partnered by VF-41 'Black Aces' and two F/A-18C units – VFA-15 and VFA-87. Unusually, both of CVW-8's Tomcat units have a LANTIRN capability.

Enterprise departed from Norfolk for a six-month Mediterranean/Gulf deployment on 27 April 2001, transiting via the UK for exercises in the North Sea. The carrier entered the Persian Gulf on 1 August 2001, and relieved *Constellation* on Operation Southern Watch on 4 August 2001. *Enterprise* was itself relieved by *Carl Vinson* on 16 September, but then moved to the northern Arabian Sea in support of Operation Enduring Freedom.

Between 21 and 22 October *Enterprise* completed a complex resupply operation, transferring the remaining ordnance to *Roosevelt*, before leaving the northern Arabian Sea. The carrier completed passage through the Suez Canal on 28 October, and passed through the Straits of Gibraltar on 3 November.

After completing this final cruise aboard *Enterprise* (between 25 April 2001 and November 2001), including participation in operations over Afghanistan, VF-14 returned to Lemoore to begin transition to the F/A-18E, the only F-14 unit to transition to the single-seat version of the Super Hornet.

Two bomb-carrying VF-14 F-14As are seen in January 2001 during exercises with the Royal Navy off Scotland.

VF-31 'TOMCATTERS'

VF-31 is usually said to be the US Navy's second oldest fighter squadron, and enjoys the unique distinction of having scored kills in World War II, Korea and Vietnam. The squadron received F-14s in 1981, and transitioned to the F-14D in 1992, joining CVW-14 that July. Partnered with VF-11, the 'Tomcatters' embarked on USS *Carl Vinson* for another WestPac deployment in 1995, and then again in 1996. During this latter deployment, the *Carl Vinson* Task Group took part in Operation Southern Watch and in Operation Desert Strike, during which USN and USAF forces conducted TLAM and CALCM strikes against Iraq in response to Baghdad's invasion of Kurdish-held territory in northern Iraq. VF-31 escorted B-52 aircraft in support of their CALCM strikes and subsequently flew numerous sorties to enforce the

'no-fly' zone which had been expanded to 33° north.

VF-31 became CVW-14's only F-14 unit in 1998, when VF-11 joined CVW-11. The 'Tomcatters' deployed on USS

Abraham Lincoln again for WestPac 98, participating in Operation Southern Watch and in maritime interdiction operations in the Arabian Gulf.

VF-31 still forms part of Air Wing

Fourteen aboard USS *Abraham Lincoln* (CVN 72), and its aircraft wear the tailcode 'NK' and modexes 100-116. It is partnered by three F/A-18C units – VFA-25, VFA-113 and VFA-115.

VF-31's 'Felix' badge is one of the best-known military aircraft markings, dating back to the late 1920s. Here it is worn in 2001 by a Phoenix-toting F-14D.

VF-32 'SWORDSMEN'

VF-32 remained with CVW-3 even after long-time partner unit VF-14 moved across to CVW-8 to join VF-41. Air Wing Three itself moved from *Kennedy* to *Eisenhower* for a 1994-95 cruise, and then on to *Roosevelt* for cruises which took place between November 1998 and May 1999, and between November 2000 and May 2001. In the course of the first of these cruises, VF-32's Tomcats exercised with Israeli F-16s in March 1999. VF-32, a long-term home of recce expertise and excellence within the Tomcat community, was among the first units to receive the new digital TARPS

Like most 'CAG-birds, that of VF-32 wears colourful markings. The squadron flies the F-14B from Truman.

reconnaissance pod, carrying out much of the trials and development work.

VF-32 currently forms part of Air Wing Three aboard USS *Harry S. Truman* (CVN 75), and its aircraft wear the tailcode 'AC' and modexes 100-116. As the only Tomcat unit in CVW-3, VF-32 operates in the TARPS and LANTIRN roles. It is partnered by three F/A-18C units, VFA-37, VFA-105 and VMFA-312. The carrier's first deployment in 2001 involved a period of duty on Operation Southern Watch in the Persian Gulf.

VF-41 'BLACK ACES'

The 'Black Aces' transitioned to the F-14A Tomcat in 1976 and joined Carrier Air Wing Eight aboard USS *Nimitz* (CVN 68) in January 1978. The squadron participated in Operation Desert Storm, but did not deploy during the March-September 1993 cruise aboard *Roosevelt*, its place being taken by VMFA-312. VF-41 remained part of CVW-8, ready to deploy if required, though many expected that this was the prelude to disestablishment. In fact, VF-41 conducted intensive training, including participation in Exercises Red and Maple Flag, and in early 1994 the 'Black Aces' grew to a 14-aircraft squadron and received its first TARPS-equipped aircraft and additional

personnel. Under the command of Captain 'Sodbuster' Benson, skipper from February 1992 to May 1993, VF-41 led the Tomcat community into the multi-mission strike role. Fighting Forty-One played a pivotal role in Kosovo as a result, and Benson was later voted 'Black Ace of the Century'. Some had expected VF-41's departure to be the beginning of a permanent arrangement, with VF-84 continuing as CVW-8's sole F-14 unit. Instead, VF-41 rejoined *Roosevelt* as an integral part of CVW-8, deploying for a six-month deployment to the Mediterranean Sea, Red Sea, Arabian Sea, Arabian Gulf, Persian Gulf and Adriatic Sea from 22 March 1995. During this deployment, VF-41 participated in Operations Deliberate Force and Deny Flight over Bosnia-

In its final Tomcat deployment, VF-41 undertook bombing missions over Afghanistan in the opening three weeks of Enduring Freedom.

Herzegovina and in Operation Southern Watch over Iraq, amassing 530 sorties and logging more than 600 combat flying hours. During Deliberate Force VF-41 became the first F-14 unit to drop bombs 'in anger'.

VF-84 did not deploy, its place taken by a Marine F/A-18 unit, and it was disestablished after the cruise. In March 1996, VF-41 made a brief deployment aboard *Stennis*, as part of the new CVN 74's shakedown cruise. VF-41 was not destined to remain as the sole Tomcat unit within CVW-8, however, being partnered by VF-14, previously part of Air Wing Three. VF-14 and VF-41 have remained partnered within CVW-8 ever since.

On 26 March 1999 VF-41 embarked for a six-month deployment, and was flying combat missions over Kosovo within nine days of leaving home, operating in support of Operation Allied Force. The squadron undertook 384 sorties and logged over 1,100 combat flying hours, dropping more than 160 tons of LGBs and achieving an

unprecedented 85 per cent success rate. In doing so the 'Black Aces' became the first Tomcat squadron to prove LANTIRN in combat. VF-41's Tomcats also operated in the forward air control role, guiding the crews of other aircraft as they delivered more than one million pounds of ordnance. During the same cruise, USS *Theodore Roosevelt* was ordered to the Persian Gulf where VF-41 operated in support of Operation Southern Watch, dropping bombs in two theatres in a single cruise. When the squadron returned to Oceana in late September it had flown more than 1,200 combat sorties, and had dropped over 200,000 lb of ordnance, including 400 laser-guided bombs.

VF-41's last assignment as an F-14 unit was as a part of Air Wing Eight aboard *Enterprise* (CVN 65), and its aircraft wear the tailcode 'AG' and modexes 100-116. Its aircraft had both LANTIRN and TARPS capabilities, and were partnered by VF-14 'Tomcatters' (which see) and two F/A-18C units, VFA-15 and VFA-87. VF-41 participated in Operation Enduring Freedom, following a similar pattern of operations as VF-14, as described in the 'Tophatters' entry. On return to the US the squadron began conversion to the F/A-18F.

VF-101 'GRIM REAPERS'

VF-101, then the Atlantic Fleet F-4J Readiness Squadron, assumed the additional role of training F-14 aircrews and maintenance personnel in January 1976, convening its first conversion course (for aircrew from VF-41 and VF-84) that June. On 5 August 1977, VF-101 split in two, with the F-4 element becoming VF-171.

As the East Coast F-14 FRS VF-101 kept abreast of every development in the wider Tomcat community, thus in April 1988, VF-101 received its first F-14B, and in September 1990 began training the fleet in strike warfare. VF-124 'Gunfighters' (the west coast F-14 FRS) disestablished on 30 September 1994, leaving VF-101 as the sole F-14 Fleet Replacement Squadron. VF-101

maintained aircraft on the west coast (Det Miramar) while front-line units were still based there. The squadron's aircraft wear a stylised 'grim reaper' insignia, in which the skeleton is said to represent sudden death to the USA's enemies, with the scythe being symbolic of the Tomcat's powerful armament.

While it may be a training unit, VF-101 has a front-line ethos, exemplified by its oath: "To engage the enemy whenever and wherever he is met with a fury and aggressiveness that will ensure the success of our mission and to do this not with the thought of attaining personal honor, but because by our actions, we will contribute to the ultimate defeat of our enemy and the glory of the US Navy. Mow 'em down!"

VF-101 operates all three front-line Tomcat variants for type conversion. Its fleet and flight hours are due to reduce as the requirement for new F-14 crews dwindles.

VF-102 'DIAMONDBACKS'

Following participation in Operation Desert Storm and the usual round of carrier deployments with CVW-1, VF-102 'Diamondbacks' became Carrier Air Wing One's sole Tomcat squadron following the disestablishment of VF-33 in July 1993. VF-102 received four additional aircraft, taking its complement to 14 F-14As.

During the Mediterranean deployment which began in early August 1993, CVW-1 supported Operations Provide Promise and Deny Flight, transiting the Suez Canal in late October to participate in Operation Restore Hope in Somalia.

The Air Wing then went on to support Operation Southern Watch in Iraq from mid-December, breaking records in total flying hours and sorties flown.

After an Orange Air detachment to Roosevelt Roads, Puerto Rico, in June 1994, VF-102 returned to Oceana and began conversion to the F-14B. The squadron completed carrier qualifications aboard USS *America* in July and USS *Enterprise* in October.

The squadron embarked aboard USS *America* in December 1994 for Refresher Training (REFTRA) prior to an August 1995 cruise. VF-102 became the

first Tomcat squadron to deploy to MCAS Yuma for SFARP in 1995, and provided students for the Navy's first ever FAC(A) training course, producing four fully qualified crews.

During its final 1995-96 Mediterranean cruise USS *America* made an emergency diversion to the Adriatic to take part in Operation Deliberate Force. Most of the cruise was then spent in the Adriatic, although in November the Air Wing participated in Exercise Bright Star with the Egyptians. Reaching the Persian Gulf, VF-102 flew missions in support of operation Southern Watch, but these were cut short when the deployment of US ground forces in Bosnia led to a quick

dash back to the Adriatic in December.

VF-102 transitioned to the F-14B Upgrade during the 1996-97 turnaround cycle. The new sub-variant featured a number of software upgrades and full compatibility with the LANTIRN targeting pod. At the annual 'Fighter Fling', VF-102 won the prestigious new VADM 'Sweetpea' Allen Precision Strike Award for its role in expanding the F-14's strike warfare capabilities and tactics.

Between October 1997 and April 1998, CVW-1 made a Mediterranean cruise aboard USS *George Washington*, and VF-102 again participated in Bright Star. *Washington*'s Battle Group was sent to the Arabian Gulf in November to

reinforce Southern Watch, following worsening relations with Iraq as the UN's Weapons Inspection Process began to disintegrate.

Between September 1999 and March 2000, CVW-1 deployed aboard USS *John F. Kennedy*, but VF-102 now forms part of Air Wing One aboard *Theodore Roosevelt*. Its aircraft wear the tailcode 'AB' and modexes 100-116. As the only Tomcat unit in CVW-1, VF-102 operates in the TARPS and LANTIRN roles. It is

A 'Diamondback' F-14B cruises over the Adriatic during operations over Bosnia. In 2001 the unit went to war over Afghanistan.

partnered by three F/A-18C units – VFA-82, VFA-86 and VMFA-251.

After the completion of the Tomcat's last cruise aboard *Roosevelt* (scheduled to take place between September 2001 and March 2002), VF-102 will transition to the new F/A-18F Super Hornet at

NAS Lemoore, probably cascading its F-14Bs to a unit currently operating older A-models. Meanwhile, *Roosevelt* reached the northern Arabian Sea in late

October 2001, and began combat operations over Afghanistan in support of Enduring Freedom, relieving *Enterprise*.

VF-103 'JOLLY ROGERS'

VF-103 was originally known as the 'Sluggers' before it adopted the historic 'Jolly Rogers' name and symbol in late 1995. As the 'Sluggers', VF-103 pioneered the use of the LANTIRN targeting pod on the F-14, conducting extensive trials in March/April 1995. The squadron deployed to the Mediterranean on 28 June aboard *Enterprise*, taking nine LANTIRN-capable aircraft and six pods. This marked the first operational deployment of LANTIRN for the US Navy.

When VF-84, the original 'Jolly Rogers', disestablished as part of planned (budget-driven) cuts on 29 September 1995, VF-103 requested permission to adopt the 'Jolly Rogers'

name, traditions and insignia, and formally took them over the next month.

In May 1997 VF-103 moved over to USS *Dwight D. Eisenhower* (CVN 69), and in June the next year deployed aboard 'Ike' for a cruise to the Adriatic, ready to undertake possible air strikes to protect the province of Kosovo.

VF-103 currently forms part of Air Wing Seventeen aboard the USS *George Washington* (CVN 73), and its aircraft wear the tailcode 'AA' and modexes 100-116. As the only Tomcat unit in CVW-17, VF-103 operates in the TARPS and LANTIRN roles. It is partnered by three F/A-18C units – VFA-34, VFA-81 and VFA-84.

Two 'Jolly Rogers' Tomcats display the standard (background) and high-visibility schemes used by the squadron, the full-colour aircraft also wearing the unit-significant modex of '103'. 'AA' tailcodes are worn on the inner sides of the fins.

VF-143 'PUKIN' DOGS'

In August 1992, the 'World Famous Pukin' Dogs' and the rest of Carrier Air Wing Seven were reassigned to USS *George Washington* (CVN 73), then the Navy's newest aircraft-carrier. Despite

its 'politically incorrect' name, VF-143 survived the reduction of CVW-7 to a single F-14 squadron in April 1995. The squadron was directed to remove the 'Pukin' from its name, though VF-143

never seems to have complied.

VF-143 deployed aboard *Washington* on its maiden 'shakedown' cruise, and then again for the first full Mediterranean deployment in May 1994. In December 1995, the 'Pukin' Dogs' departed on another cruise

aboard CVN 73, and soon began flying missions over Bosnia in support of Operation Decisive Endeavor, and later over Iraq in support of Operation Southern Watch.

CVW-7 (with the 'Pukin' Dogs') transferred to USS *John C. Stennis* (CVN 74) for the new carrier's maiden deployment. VF-143 was by then equipped with LANTIRN, night vision goggles and digital TARPS. At the same time, CVW-7 gained a second F-14 squadron, in the shape of VF-11. Air Wing Seven's next cruise (beginning in February 2000) was aboard USS *Dwight D. Eisenhower* (CVN 69).

VF-143 now forms part of Air Wing Seven aboard the USS *John F. Kennedy* (CV 67), and its aircraft wear the tailcode 'AG' and modexes 100-116. Its aircraft include some equipped with the digital TARPS pod. It is partnered by VF-11 'Red Rippers' and two F/A-18C units – VFA-131 and VFA-136.

By the end of 2001 CVW-7 aboard 'JFK' was the only air wing with two Tomcat squadrons. VF-143 flies the air wing's TARPS-capable aircraft.

VF-154 'BLACK KNIGHTS'

When VF-21 disestablished in January 1996, VF-154 was left as the sole F-14 squadron within Air Wing Five. CVW-5 was attached to USS *Independence* (CV 62), home-ported at Yokosuka, Japan, and its units were forward-deployed at nearby NAS Atsugi. *Independence* was replaced by USS *Kitty Hawk* (CV 63) during 1998.

1999 was a particularly busy year for VF-154, with training detachments in the USA, two Phoenix missile shoots, and Exercise Tandem Thrust all taking place before the end of March. The period saw VF-154 making its first tactical use of FTI, the employment of two GBU-16s, and the first-ever FAC(A) participation in a Naval Gun Fire Exercise, controlling live fire from USS *Chancellorsville* (CG 62). Next the squadron deployed to the Gulf to take part in Operation Southern Watch, doing so with aircraft just modified with the Digital Flight Control System (DFCS),

A VF-154 F-14A rests on the deck of Kitty Hawk during a 2001 visit to Australia.

making the 'Black Knights' the first F-14 squadron to deploy with the new system. The aircraft also featured the new Fast Tactical Imagery system, giving F-14 crews the ability to transmit and receive imagery and bomb damage assessment in near real-time. During the cruise, VF-154 flew 397 sorties in support of Operation Southern Watch, and participated in three separate strikes against Iraqi targets, destroying 67 per cent of assigned targets. The cruise gave the opportunity for exercises with the Royal Air Force of Oman, before the F-14s returned to NAF Atsugi in August.

In October VF-154 again deployed as part of CVW-5, participating in Exercises Foal Eagle and ANNUALEX. All VF-154 FAC(A) aircrew participated in close air support missions in South Korea, including operations to within 10 nm of

the DMZ, co-operating with other Navy, Air Force and ROK assets. VF-154 also developed innovative tactics using the F/A-18's Laser Spot Tracker in conjunction with the F-14's LANTIRN.

VF-154 remains part of Air Wing Five aboard the USS *Kitty Hawk* (CV-63), and its aircraft wear the tailcode 'NF' and modexes 100-107 and 110-116. It is

partnered by three F/A-18C units – VFA-27, VFA-192 and VFA-195.

When *Kitty Hawk* departed from Yokosuka to take part in Operation Enduring Freedom, it did so for primary use as a floating base for special operations helicopters and troops. Much of its air wing was left behind, including VF-154.

VF-211 'CHECKMATES'

VF-211 originally transitioned to the F-14A in 1975, converting to the more powerful F-14B in 1989. Following participation in Operation Desert Storm, the 'Fighting Checkmates' transitioned back to the F-14A in 1992, when it was decided to concentrate all F-14Bs within the Atlantic Fleet. The squadron moved from NAS Miramar to Oceana in August 1996, and became Carrier Air Wing

Nine's sole Tomcat unit when VF-24 disestablished on 31 August 1996. VF-211 made one 'solo' deployment aboard USS *Nimitz* before CVW-9 transferred to USS *Stennis*, making a first deployment from January 2000.

VF-211 currently forms part of Air Wing Nine aboard the USS *John C. Stennis* (CVN 74), and its aircraft wear the tailcode 'NG' and modexes 100-107

VF-211's 'CAG' aircraft has the fin checkers in red/white. Regular squadron aircraft have a checkerboard in toned-down greys.

and 110-111, 113 and 116. As the only Tomcat unit in CVW-9, VF-211 operates in the TARPS and LANTIRN roles. It is partnered by three F/A-18C units – VFA-146, VFA-147 and VMFA-314.

After the completion of the Tomcat's last cruise aboard the *Stennis* (due to take place between January and July 2002), VF-211 will transition to the new F/A-18F Super Hornet at NAS Lemoore.

VF-213 'BLACK LIONS'

After participation in Desert Storm, VF-213 deployed aboard USS *Abraham Lincoln* for the second time in 1993, participating in Operation Southern Watch over Iraq and Operation Restore Hope in Somalia. VF-154 became the only Tomcat unit within CVW-11 with the disestablishment of VF-114 'Aardvarks' on 30 April 1993. From April to October 1995, VF-213 made another cruise aboard the 'Honest Abe', again flying in support of Operation Southern Watch.

VF-213 then moved (with the rest of CVW-11) to the USS *Kitty Hawk*, deploying for six weeks for Exercise RIMPAC '97 and for six months for a WestPac '97 cruise. During RIMPAC '97, VF-213 fired twenty-six Phoenix and six Sidewinder missiles, including an unprecedented simultaneous six-Tomcat, 12-missile Phoenix shoot.

On returning from the WestPac cruise in April 1997, VF-213 disembarked to NAS Oceana, the unit's new home. A shortage of F-14As forced

The 'Black Lions' have been busy recently, with time spent on Southern Watch and now Enduring Freedom.

the squadron to re-equip, even though the US Navy had previously gone from three to two F-14D units because of a similar shortfall. Nevertheless, the 'Black Lions' immediately began conversion to the F-14D, completing the process in December 1997. Air Wing Eleven and VF-213 then moved to *Carl Vinson*. A RIMPAC '98 exercise followed, during which one Sidewinder and six Phoenix missiles were expended, one AIM-54C being launched at night by a crew using NVGs.

Two months into *Vinson*'s 1998/99 WestPac deployment to the Arabian Gulf, the carrier participated in Operation Desert Fox. VF-213 became the first unit to launch an AIM-54C in anger, firing two missiles against Iraqi fighters violating the Iraqi 'no-fly' zone. Both missiles missed their targets.

VF-213 currently forms part of Air

Wing Eleven aboard the USS *Carl Vinson* (CVN 70), and its aircraft wear the tailcode 'NH' and modexes 100-107 and 110-116. As the only Tomcat unit in CVW-11, VF-213 operates in the TARPS and LANTIRN roles. It is partnered by three F/A-18C units – VFA-22, VFA-94 and VFA-97.

Vinson departed from Bremerton for

a six-month WestPac/Gulf deployment on 25 July 2001, subsequently embarking VF-213 as part of Air Wing 11. The carrier relieved *Enterprise* on Operation Southern Watch on 16 September 2001, moving to the northern Arabian Sea in early October to take part in Operation Enduring Freedom.

VX-9 'VAMPIRES'

VX-9, a test and evaluation unit based at NAS China Lake, is a tenant command of NAWS China Lake, and was formed on 29 April 1994 by combining VX-4 at Point Mugu and VX-5 at China Lake. It is tasked with the operational evaluation of aircraft, weapons systems and equipment, and to develop tactical procedures for their employment. China Lake incorporates massive ranges, lying under some 17,000 square miles (44000 km²) of joint-service restricted airspace. At China Lake, VX-9 operates all versions of the F/A-18 Hornet, the AV-8B Harrier II, the Grumman EA-6B Prowler and the Bell AH-1W. The unit's F-14s (drawn from all variants) are operated from NAS Point Mugu, by a separate permanent detachment. The main element of VX-9 at China Lake has essentially taken over the role (air-to-ground ordnance and tactics testing and trials) and duties of the former VX-5, while the Point Mugu detachment has

taken over the responsibilities of the former VX-4.

Like VX-4, the VX-9 Detachment at NAS Point Mugu conducts testing on all facets of the air-to-air fighter role, including weapons, aircraft systems and software. In effect, this restricts the

scope of the squadron's activities to the F-14 Tomcat, the US Navy's only dedicated interceptor.

With an overall total of 28 aircraft, and two separate operating locations, VX-9 sometimes resembles two squadrons, though they all wear a

Two VX-9 F-14Bs display the black-finned and black-tanked scheme adopted as standard by this operational evaluation and trials unit.

common badge. This is the traditional Vampire bat insignia of VX-5, with four stars added in acknowledgement of the absorption of VX-4.

VX-4 had for many years operated a number of 'flagship' aircraft in an overall glossy black paint scheme, as 'Black Bunnies'. This tradition has been continued by VX-9's Point Mugu detachment, although the 'Vampires' current flagship, a gloss black F-14D (callsign 'Vandy One') has the unit's bat insignia in place of the traditional Playboy bunny.

Another VX-9 Det. Point Mugu F-14B ('Vandy 240') had its tails, ventral fins and external tanks painted black to match those of the flagship, and was followed by another F-14B (upgrade), 'Vandy 241'. This was then adopted as the unit's standard colour scheme.

NSAWC

NSAWC (pronounced 'N-Sock') formed through the merger of three separate units on 11 July 1996. NSAWC's components are the former Naval Strike Warfare Center ('Strike U') at Fallon (and latterly Lemoore), the Naval Fighter Weapons School ('Top Gun') at NAS Miramar and the Carrier Airborne Early Warning Weapons School ('Top Dome') also from NAS Miramar. Consolidation of these three units brought with it efficiency savings, but also helped to standardise and co-ordinate training and communication between various naval aviation communities.

NSAWC flies a mix of about six F-14As, and about 20 F/A-18As and F/A-18Bs, together with with three or four SH-60F/HH-60Hs forming a Combat

Search and Rescue element. Like 'Top Dome' before it, NSAWC relies on E-2Cs temporarily drawn from the front-line fleet for its courses.

NSAWC's mission is two-fold, providing 'graduate training' in tactics for selected front-line aircrew (who then return to their units to pass on their

newly acquired knowledge and expertise as instructors) and also providing pre-deployment training for Carrier Air Wings in air-to-air and strike warfare. CVW Integrated and Advanced Training Phases (ITP/ATP) conducted at NAS Fallon are large-scale exercises, and may involve as many as 50 aircraft,

serving as invaluable 'dress rehearsals' for scenarios which the Air Wing might meet 'on deployment'. This dual task has remained basically unchanged since NSAWC's three elements were separate units, although new courses have been added. NSAWC also provides *ad hoc* adversary training for Fleet units, and for the West Coast F/A-18 FRS (VFA-125).

NSAWC aircraft wear the traditional and long-standing 'Top Gun' 'MiG in the pipper' badge, though this is superimposed on the lightning bolt insignia traditionally associated with 'Strike U'.

A 'plain Jane' NSAWC F-14A (foreground) flies in company with VX-9's all-black F-14D. It is expected that all NSAWC aircraft will adopt an Iranian-style desert camouflage for their adversary work.

Grupo Aéreo 4 de Caza
Argentina's fighter school
Photographed by Marnix Sap

Escuadrón I – MS.760 Paris
The Fuerza Aérea Argentina acquired 48 MS.760s to operate in the advanced/weapons training role. Of this total, 36 were assembled locally by DINFIA (Dirección Nacional de Fabricaciones e Investigaciones Aeronáuticas). The first Paris to fly in Argentina was A-01, the third French-built aircraft. By September 1959 three were in service at El Plumerillo, and soon after the serial block changed to E-201 onwards. The Paris also served with the Escuela de Aviación Militar at Córdoba, but in 1987 the surviving fleet was concentrated in the Escuela de Caza (Grupo 4) at El Plumerillo. The weapons training role was assumed by the IA-63 Pampa from 1990.

Today, Escuadrón I (also known as the Escuadrón Operativo) operates 10 MS.760s, and is the last military user of the Paris in the world. Eight of the aircraft are in 'standard' configuration and are often fitted with two 7.62-mm machine-guns in the nose and a 150-kg (331-lb) bomb under each wing. Having lost their fighter lead-in training role, they are used mainly as a 'holding' squadron for pilots awaiting a place on the Pampa course. Two MS.760s are in 'Manguero' configuration, used for towing banner targets. For this role they have orange-painted noses, tails and wing tanks.

In 1999 the Paris clocked up 40 years of service, and the first aircraft delivered, E-201, was given a special commemorative scheme (below). Although the threat of retirement has hung over the Paris on several occasions in the past, it is now expected that they will serve until 2003.

Mendoza memories

Douglas A-4C Skyhawk *(below)*
Grupo 4's Escuadrón I operated all 25 A-4Cs delivered to Argentina, while the group's other squadrons flew the F-86F Sabre and MS.760. Grupo 4 Skyhawks were sent to San Julian during the Falklands/Malvinas War, losing nine aircraft to enemy action during the conflict. Soon after, Grupo 4's seven survivors were transferred to Grupo 5 to join the A-4B survivors. This preserved aircraft, complete with ship 'kill' marking, wears the badges of both units.

Dassault Mirage IIICJ *(above)*
From their delivery from Israel in late 1982/early 1983 to 1991, 19 Mirage IIICJs and three IIIBJs were flown from Mendoza by the newly-created Escuadrón 55, established in memory of the 55 FAA servicemen who lost their lives in the Guerra del Atlántico Sur (Falklands War) in 1982. The unit functioned as the Mirage operational conversion unit.

Located near the city of Mendoza, close to the Andes mountains and the Chilean border, Base Aérea Militar El Plumerillo is home to IV Brigada Aérea, whose Grupo 4 (Escuela de Caza) is the main combat training unit for the Fuerza Aérea Argentina.

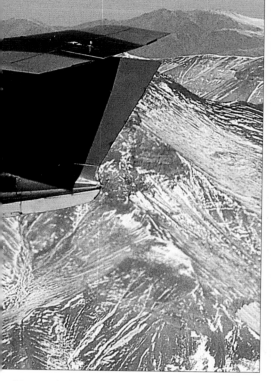

Escuadrón II – IA-63 Pampa

Future Argentine fighter pilots arrive at El Plumerillo from the Escuela de Aviación Militar at Córdoba, where they flew the Beech Mentor and EMB-312 Tucano. Combat training is then given by Grupo 4's Escuadrón II, the heart of the Escuela de Caza (fighter school). Students fly the Pampa during the Curso de Estandardarización para Aviones de Combate (CEPAC – fighter standardisation course). Having successfully completed the course, they are then posted to operational conversion units, with most beginning their combat careers flying the Pucará with Grupo Aéreo 3 de Ataque at BAM Reconquista.

Fábrica Militar Argentina (FMA) built 15 IA-63 Pampas for the FAA, the first prototype flying on 10 October 1984. The first service aircraft was delivered to El Plumerillo on 9 May 1988 to begin the reformation of Escuadrón II, which also became known as the Escuadrón Pampa. The final aircraft was handed over on 28 September 1999. A further 12 IA-63s have been ordered from Lockheed Martin Aircraft Argentina SA (LMAASA – the successor to FMA). They will feature a new 'glass' cockpit, and the earlier batch will be upgraded to this new standard.

Escuadrón III – SA 315B Lama

Argentina purchased six Aérospatiale SA 315B Lamas in 1973, initially for service with VIII Brigada Aérea at Morón. On 15 August 1977 they were transferred to the Escuadrón Búsqueda, Rescate y Tareas Especiales within IV Brigada at El Plumerillo. The outstanding high-altitude performance of the type was ideal for mountain SAR tasks and for the Campañas de Limites (border campaigns) missions. This was not, as the English translation might suggest, a conflict, but rather an effort by Argentina and Chile to define the exact border between the two nations, which runs for most of its length along the Andean Cordillera. Working with Chilean Lamas, the helicopters from El Plumerillo were used to place cones along the border in the high Andes, a task which lasted from 1975 to 1997.

Today Escuadrón III (also known as Escuadrón Lama) has two for SAR work, one having been lost on 18 September 2001. The squadron also operates three DINFIA-built Cessna 182s and a Rockwell 500U Commander on liaison duties. The hard-working Lamas are in need of replacement, but few current helicopter types can match their high-altitude capability.

Escuadrón IV – Sukhoi Su-29AR *(opposite page)*

In the mid-1990s the Fuerza Aérea Argentina took the decision to re-establish a national aerobatic team. The 'Cruz del Sur' (Southern Cross) team had been formed in 1961 at El Plumerillo to fly the F-86F-30 Sabre in the FAA's 50th anniversary year, but was disbanded in 1962. For its new team, the FAA evaluated the use of jet trainers, such as the Pampa or even Paris, but eventually decided to procure a high-performance modern aerobatic aircraft.

Accordingly, an order for eight two-seat Sukhoi Su-29ARs was placed in early 1997. In July FAA personnel travelled to Moscow to oversee the final assembly of the first two aircraft and to subsequently flight-test the finished product. The first two were then sea-freighted to Argentina, arriving at Buenos Aires on 9 October 1997. They were sent to the Area Material Rio Cuarto facility for reassembly. On 12 November 1997 the first Su-29AR reached El Plumerillo.

On 2 February 1998 Escuadrón IV was created within Grupo 4 at El Plumerillo, resurrecting the 'Cruz del Sur' team. Aircraft were painted with the Southern Cross marking on the fin. A stunning display routine was devised, utilising much of the Su-29AR's +12/-10 *g* envelope and including new aerobatic manoeuvres such as the 'Viva Argentina', and the team has performed many times throughout South America. When not performing, Escuadrón IV is involved in display work-up and practice.

Army Lamas

Sección Aviación de Ejército de Montaña 8

This Comando de Aviación del Ejército (CAE, Army aviation command) unit was formed on 6 November 1990, and received its first SA 315B Lama from Campo de Mayo (the Army's principal helicopter base) on 9 April 1991. SAE 8 Lamas support Army units operating in the Andes and, like the FAA helicopters, are painted orange for high-visibility in the snowfields. The unit's Lamas were initially hangared alongside the Escuadrón III helicopters, but in late 1995 SAE 8 moved to its own facility at El Plumerillo. The section currently has two Lamas assigned, but only one is serviceable. The only other CAE Lama is operated by Sección Aviación de Ejército 6 at Neuquen.

Super Puma and Cougar
AS 332, AS 532 and EC 725

Turning to the more powerful Makila turboshaft allowed Aérospatiale to develop the Puma airframe into a larger and more versatile helicopter, while retaining the agility and performance of the original design. Ongoing development, including two fuselage stretches, has led to a family of helicopters which can answer a wide range of military requirements.

It is a tribute to the soundness of the basic SA 330 Puma design that in 1974, a full nine years after the prototype had flown, the aircraft remained in large-scale production. Aérospatiale decided to base its new medium helicopter on the same basic airframe. It must be remembered that the pace of technological change during the 1970s was still very rapid, and at the very time that Aérospatiale chose to develop its Puma into the AS 332 Super Puma, many of its competitors were turning to all-new designs: Sikorsky with its S-70 and S-76, Boeing's Model 179, and the Westland WG.30. Only Bell, evolving its Model 212 into the 412, and Russia's Mil, turning the Mi-8 into the Mi-17, followed the same path as Aérospatiale.

Right: The first prototype AS 332 Super Puma displays the type's good underslung load capability. The extra power of the Makila engines can be harnessed to lift up to 4.5 tonnes – more than the empty weight of the helicopter itself.

Moreover, the Super Puma was directed primarily at civil customers. They had accounted for only about 130 SA 330 sales, and might have been expected to place greater emphasis on the advantages that might be offered by an entirely new aerodynamic design, and by an aircraft with a cabin that was optimised from the start for carrying passengers.

In 1974, when design work on the Super Puma began, the first Turmo IVC-engined Pumas were becoming available. Aérospatiale

had already decided that its new design would require greater power than the Turmo could provide, and that civil customers, particularly, would require the kind of operating efficiencies that only a more modern engine could offer. The Super Puma was therefore designed around a pair of Turboméca's new Makila turboshafts. They promised an improved power-to-weight ratio, reduced maintenance requirements, and an 18 per cent reduction in specific fuel consumption. The new engine could wind up from idle to full power in only 1.5 seconds.

The first Makila-powered Puma was a converted SA 330 – the second SA 330 prototype, F-ZWWO – which first flew with its new Makila engines in June 1977. Its airframe was otherwise unmodified. More recently, some 10

Right: Spain was an important customer for the original short-fuselage AS 332B/AS 532UC, operating the type on a variety of duties including VIP transport, SAR and assault work. The latter occupies the 18 AS 332Bs operated by the Spanish army (locally designated HU.21 – HT.21 until January 1999). This aircraft is seen on UN peacekeeping duties in Bosnia. The FAMET subsequently acquired 15 stretched AS 532ULs (HU.21L).

Stretching the fuselage in the AS 332M/AS 532UL allowed the standard seating to rise to 25 troops, the aircraft being easily distinguishable by the additional cabin window. Among the customers are Jordan (below), which bought eight, and Switzerland (left) which purchased 15. Another 12 AS 532ULs are in the process of being delivered, of which 10 are being built in Switzerland under sub-contract to Eurocopter.

Portuguese SA 330Cs have been re-engined successfully with Makilas to create the SA 330S, again without requiring major airframe modifications.

Aérospatiale was determined to provide several means of differentiating the new Super Puma from the original design. The first was to use a new designation prefix, reversing the SA of Sud Aviation to AS for Aérospatiale, while continuing in the same numerical designation series. The Super Puma gained a new, swept ventral fin below the tail rotor pylon, at the aft end of the tailboom, and a new, pointed nosecone. These features undeniably brought with them some aerodynamic benefits, albeit quite limited; their primary purpose was almost certainly to give the new model a distinctive and sleeker profile, and provided a neat space for a weather radar to be installed.

More significant, but rather less obvious, was a slatted half tailplane that improved attitude control at slow climbing speeds. The rotor blades themselves were reshaped, and the rotor head was capped by a domed saucer fairing that smoothed the wake caused by the rotating rotor hub.

It was anticipated that the Super Puma would probably 'grow' as the original aircraft had done, with new sub-variants operating at progressively higher all-up weights. The initial version of the Makila engine, the 1A, was certificated in 1980 with a maximum contingency rating of 1327 kW (1,780 shp), allowing Aérospatiale to offer 'standard' and 'stretched' versions of the AS 332 from the start, virtually simultaneously.

Heavy-duty undercarriage

In addition to operating at higher all-up weights, it was anticipated that the Super Puma would be particularly attractive to operators in the offshore oil support business. Therefore, the undercarriage was redesigned to permit landings on small oil-rigs and ships, with a more crashworthy, high energy-absorbing landing gear than the original SA 330. This featured entirely new single mainwheel units, replacing the original aircraft's twin wheels. The new levered oleo was anchored to a pivoted axle beam mounted to one of the fuselage mainframes at (or just below) cabin floor level. A retraction jack ran from the top of the oleo (close to the outer end of the axle) diagonally backwards and upwards to an anchor point on another mainframe, at roughly window height. This jack was covered by a new fairing which ran up from the oleo, providing another visual cue of the Super Puma's identity.

The needs of military customers were not ignored, and the gearbox was redesigned to give greater battle damage tolerance. Many of the standard Super Puma features were also of direct relevance to military operators. The Super Puma's proven all-weather capability (even in icing conditions) was highly prized by military operators, since it gave improved high mission readiness. The aircraft's manoeuvrability, high performance, rapid throttle response times and wide power margins all helped improve survivability, and helped make the type a more versatile and more useful multi-role tool, capable of adaptation to meet a variety of roles. The Super Puma's composite rotor blades – in addition to conferring improved serviceability and an unlimited useful life – were impervious to corrosion. For military operators it was significant that, by comparison with blades incorporating metallic components, the Super Puma's all-composite blades also had lower vulnerability to battle damage. The ruggedness of the Makila engines was highly valued by military operators, while the simple rotor head and other features that endowed the aircraft with a high degree of maintainability also tended to improve resistance to battle damage.

The manufacturers did not have to rely solely on those features already incorporated in the civil AS 332 to appeal to military customers, however. The design team was soon able to offer a variety of optional features intended to appeal to military users, including armoured crew seats, crashworthy troop seats and a range of defensive systems, including radar, laser and missile approach warning sensors. The aircraft can be fitted with exhaust diffusers which give a reduced IR signature, providing a degree of protection against heat-seeking missiles, together with sophisticated infra-red and electromagnetic jammers, and expendable countermeasures systems.

The aircraft's versatility makes it an extremely useful multi-role military helicopter, and it can do far more than transport men and material,

In South Africa Denel produced its own 'Super Puma' in the form of the Oryx (originally Gemsbok). Although the airframe is that of the original SA 330, the aircraft has the Super's Makila engines and a ventral fin. The excellent hot-and-high performance is much appreciated by the South African Air Force.

thanks to its excellent performance characteristics and spacious cabin. The aircraft has a 4.5-tonne (4.43-Imp ton) capacity external load hook for lifting even the heaviest underslung loads, and some variants have a restressed cabin floor that lets heavy freight be carried internally. The Super Puma can be equipped with a 245-kg (540-lb) capacity hoist, useful for SAR and CSAR duties, and can be armed with door-mounted machine-guns or with pod-mounted cannons, rockets and a variety of specialised anti-submarine or anti-surface weapon systems. The Super Puma's lifting capability even allowed Aérospatiale to offer variants which carried a pair of massive AM.39 Exocet ASMs, which almost dwarf the aircraft.

Enter the Cougar

In January 1990 the Cougar name was adopted for all military variants of the Aérospatiale-built Super Puma, and military Super Puma designations were changed from AS 332 to AS 532. On 16 January 1992, Aérospatiale's helicopter division merged with that of MBB (DASA) to form the new Eurocopter Group, owned 70 per cent by Aérospatiale (which became Eurocopter France) and 30 per cent by Daimler Aerospace (DASA, which became Eurocopter Germany). The first all-new family of variants produced since then (the Super Puma and Cougar Mk 2+) have adopted new designations. Their EC

prefix and 225 and 725 model numbers, which fit in with other Eurocopter helicopters, end the historic link with Sud Aviation's original numbering and designation system.

The original SA 330 was built in nine basic versions, all of which were essentially the same with the exceptions of their powerplant installations, and whether they had trooping or airline-type doors and composite or conventional rotors. The Super Puma, by contrast, has already been built in three different cabin lengths, and there are other obvious major differences between the several distinct families. This makes it very much easier to identify

a Super Puma or Cougar simply by looking at it, although differentiating between sub-variants within the same family remains a potential minefield for the unwary.

Over 500 examples of the Cougar/Super Puma family have now been completed. The total includes a small number of license-built Indonesian aircraft, but does not include the enigmatic Oryx, South Africa's unique Puma/Cougar hybrid. Military and government customers have accounted for just over half of the Cougar/Super Puma orders, even though the 40 or so air arms which have ordered the type have tended to do so in small numbers.

Above: The Armée de l'Air operates a few Super Puma/Cougars, including these AS 332Ls operated by Villacoublay-based EH 3/67 'Parisis' in the VIP transport role. The aircraft display two options normally specified for this role: revised cabin door incorporating a standard airline-style door and stairs, and an air conditioning pack scabbed on to the port forward fuselage. Other AdA Super Puma/Cougars fly on special forces transport duties, mountain SAR, CSAR and nuclear test facilities support.

Left: Dubbed Cougar Mk II, the AS 532U2 (unarmed) and A2 (armed) introduced a further cabin stretch to seat 29 troops, distinguished by an enlarged rear window and a box fairing. The Netherlands was the first major military customer, buying 17 AS 532U2s for service with 300 Squadron, part of the THG at Soesterberg.

could be seen as giving the aircraft a useful niche, falling as it does between smaller and larger competitors. Unfortunately, though, army requirements tend to be based around fairly standardised squad and platoon sizes, and to some operators, the aircraft appears to fulfil neither requirement. This explains the continuing popularity of the original, short-fuselage Cougar among military customers, which prize the original Puma's ability to carry a standard-sized infantry squad and do not feel they need an aircraft that can carry one and one-half squads.

However, the end of the Cold War has brought a change in the structure of army units. New peacekeeping and peace enforcement roles sometimes require the carriage of bulky kit and extra supplies, local police personnel, interpreters or liaison officers, so the larger Cougar's ability to carry extra personnel may become more useful.

Revising the SH role

As air forces have gained more experience in using support helicopters, less emphasis is being placed on carrying 'bayonets', which is regarded by many of the experts as a wasteful use of scarce, expensive and vulnerable assets. Instead, support helicopters are increasingly tending to be used for moving specialist troops, air defence teams and communications units, for carrying underslung loads of artillery pieces, ammunition, fuel and other vital supplies: embracing a logistics support role rather than a simple transport role.

Moreover, there are a host of roles for which extra cabin volume is highly prized, including combat SAR, casevac, and some command/ control and reconnaissance/surveillance roles, for which bulky equipment and operators may require a well-ventilated and spacious working environment.

Eurocopter has demonstrated its commitment to the future of the Super Puma and Cougar (not least by launching the modernised Mk 2+ versions) and continues to market the type aggressively. For the more cost-conscious and 'cash-strapped' customers, the company offers austere variants with a standardised avionics fit and fixed undercarriage. The Super Puma's manufacturers are certainly making every effort to ensure that the type remains a major player in the market.

There has not been a large domestic military market for the type, and the most important customers so far have been Singapore (with 36 delivered) and Turkey (with orders for 50).

Its range of fuselage lengths means the Super Puma/Cougar can seat between 21 and 29 troops, while the proposed Mk III will carry even larger numbers. This latest stretch is probably necessary if the aircraft is to gain significant additional orders. It faces competition from the smaller NHI NH 90 (accommodating 14-20), and the 22-troop Sikorsky S-92, and from larger helicopters like the Mi-17 (which seats 30 troops) and larger military helicopters like the EHI EH101 Merlin (30 seated troops, or 45 on the floor), the Boeing Vertol CH-47 Chinook (33-55 troops) and the Sikorsky CH-53E (55 troops). The Super Puma's capacity

Jon Lake

Short-fuselage versions

SA 331

The SA 331 designation was first applied to a proposed 'Super Puma' during the early 1960s. The aircraft was described as a "projected variant with a ducted fan and a Vee tail replacing the tail rotor."

The SA 331 designation re-emerged during the early 1970s, when a new Super Puma was conceived as a replacement for the basic SA 330. The upgrade was relatively modest, with new, more powerful Turboméca Makila engines and other refinements. The first Super Puma was a converted SA 330 (F-ZWWO, previously the second SA 330 prototype), and first flew with its new Makila engines, as the SA 330Z, in June 1977. The first newly-built pre-prototype (F-WZAT) was converted using an uncompleted Puma fuselage (c/n 541) and first flew on 5 September 1977. This aircraft may have used the designation SA 331-001 and SA 330R, although this designation has sometimes been associated with the stretched fuselage of the AS 332L. It had originally been intended that the new type would feature a Gazelle-type fenestron shrouded tail rotor, but although it was tested on another converted Puma prototype (the SA 330Z), it was not adopted for production.

AS 332 Super Puma

Although some standard Pumas have been re-engined with Makilas (notably Portugal's aircraft) without major airframe modification, the production Super Puma features a new ventral tailfin to give greater keel area, and a reshaped nose. The first of six true Super Puma prototypes (F-WZJA) made its maiden flight on 13 September 1978. Powered by Makila engines, and fitted with composite main rotor blades and the distinctive new ventral fin, the aircraft retained a standard Puma-type airframe, with the same cabin window arrangement, but with a new, slightly pointed nose radome that could accommodate RDR 1400 or RCA Primus weather radar.

F-WZJA was the first true Super Puma prototype, and is seen here during tests with additional nose instrumentation.

AS 332B Super Puma and AS 532UC/AC Cougar Mk 1

The first production Super Puma was the AS 332B. This military utility version retained the original, short SA 330-type fuselage. It was capable of carrying 21 fully armed troops, and was offered with a variety of radar warning and missile detection systems, as well as chaff/flare dispensers. The basic B was soon augmented (and then replaced) by the AS 332B1 with a strengthened cabin floor stressed for loads of 1500 kg/m² (307 lb/sq ft), and was capable of seating three extra troops in the same cabin area. The type remains available, and is offered with a range of options including undernose FLIR or search radar, flotation gear and specific role equipment for SAR, as well as an NVG-compatible cockpit and crashworthy seats.

Even after the introduction of the stretched AS 332L (and the similar military AS 332M), the original short-fuselage AS 332 remained popular with military customers, not least because it is 150 kg (330 lb) lighter than any stretched variant. The AS 332C was nominally the civil equivalent of the AS 332B, fitted out for carrying up to 17 passengers. Several were sold to military operators.

The AS 332B1 Super Puma remained in production long enough to be redesignated the AS 532UC/AC Cougar Mk I in 1990. The AC is the designation for the (so far unsold) armed version that has provision for cabin-mounted machine-guns and for 20-mm gun pods or 68-mm rocket-launchers.

'Short' AS 332Bs and AS 332Cs were delivered to Abu Dhabi, Argentine army, the Brazilian air force (as the CH-34) and the Brazilian navy (as the UH-14), the Chilean army, Ecuador, France, Nigeria, Oman and Spain. The AS 532UC has been offered to Austria, where it is believed to be the government's 'political' choice, although the air force may prefer the S-70.

Spain's AS 332Bs have had a bewildering array of local designations. Ten were delivered as SAR aircraft to the Spanish Air Force as HD.21s (eight of which were described as AS 332Fs by some sources), two more being delivered as VIP aircraft under the HT.21 designation. All were fitted with enlarged sponsons, the SAR aircraft also having comprehensive emergency flotation gear. This was not fitted to allow 'on the water' operations, but rather to permit the aircraft to be recovered if it had to alight on the water. The VIP aircraft had an external cabin air conditioning pack mounted on

Right: Argentina was one of a number of nations which followed up SA 330 purchases with AS 332s. Seen while under test at Aérospatiale's Marignane factory, this AS 332B was fitted with nose radar, large sponsons and flotation gear for service with the Argentine army's Grupo de Helicópteros de Asalto 601, which also flies the remaining SA 330L.

AS 332B

- Slatted tailplane on port side
- Makila 1A turboshafts
- Revised nose shape with weather radar
- Ventral fin
- Short fuselage with five cabin windows

Eight AS 332Bs of the Spanish air force's HD.21 fleet are configured for SAR duties, serving with 802 Escuadrón at Gando in the Canaries, and 803 Escuadrón at Cuatro Vientos. The fleet also has a limited combat SAR role, although it does not have any additional equipment for this tasking.

Most AS 332Bs were completed with small cabin windows, like this Abu Dhabi Air Force aircraft. Later machines, notably the Spanish army aircraft, have larger windows.

the port side of the forward fuselage, aft of the flight deck.

Some 18 AS 332Bs were also delivered to the Spanish army as HT.21s, although they were subsequently redesignated (in January 1999) as HU.21s. It is unclear whether the single surviving VIP HT-21 has been similarly redesignated.

Most early Super Pumas (of all sub-variants) were powered by a pair of 1327-kW (1,780-shp) Makila 1A turboshaft engines, but later aircraft switched to the more powerful 1370-kW (1,837-shp) Makila 1A1.

AS 332C Super Puma Mk 1

Left: *This AS 332C was delivered to the Armée de l'Air for liaison/VIP transport.*

Below: *Highly capable SAR platforms, Greece's four AS 332C1s have undernose search radar and FLIR. The intakes are fitted with simple wire mesh filters.*

The AS 332C was the civil 'airliner' version of the AS 332B, seating up to 17 passengers. Short Super Pumas delivered to military customers included at least five standard AS 332Cs, three going to France for use by EH 1/67 at Cazaux and EH 6/67 at Solenzara, and two going to Oman's Royal Flight.

AS 332C1 SAR Super Puma Mk 1

The Greek Ministry of the Merchant Marine signed a $US60 million contract with Eurocopter for the purchase of four AS 332C1 Super Puma helicopters on 20 August 1998. Intended for search and rescue work in the Aegean, the AS 332C1 is based on the short-fuselage, 1400-kW (1877-shp) Turboméca Makila 1A1-powered version of the civil Super Puma.

The Greek AS 332C1s are fitted with a nose-mounted Bendix 1500B radar (capable of detecting small boats at long ranges), a Thomson-CSF Chlio FLIR system, a Spectrolab searchlight, hailers, a 272-kg (600-lb) capacity hoist,

jettisonable liferafts, and emergency medical facilities. They also feature a Sextant Avionique Nadir Mk 2 autonomous navigation system coupled to an SFIM 155 supermode-capable autopilot, which can perform fully-automatic transitions and hovering.

The Greek authorities took delivery of the first two SAR Super Pumas at Marignane on 21 December 1999. The remaining pair was delivered in March 2000.

Although owned by the Ministry of the Merchant Marine, the SAR Super Pumas are operated by 358 Squadron at Elefsis.

AS 532UB Cougar 100

Competition from the Sikorsky S-70 and cheaper Russian helicopters like the Mi-17 prompted Eurocopter to offer a simplified version of the Cougar, seeking to offer a variant that would be 15-20 (or even 20-30) per cent cheaper

than the original AS 532UC/AC. This was achieved by producing a completely standardised version with no customer options, reducing the need for extensive installation work for specially-specified equipment and thus

shortening production times. The avionics consist of a cheaper but still comprehensive IFR package, with TACAN, GPS and radar altimeter.

The aircraft has a simplified fuel system and fixed, unfaired landing gear, which reduces cruising speeds by about 5 kt (9 km/h). Otherwise, the new variant has identical mission capability

to the standard Cougar. Several simplified Cougar 100 variants have been described, the AS 532UB and armed AS 532AB being based on the short-fuselage AS 532UC, and the AS 532UE being based on the longer AS 532UL. Only the latter version (described separately) is currently being marketed.

AS 332F Frégate and AS 532SC Cougar Mk 1

The final short-fuselage Super Puma variant is the AS 332F or AS 332F1 Frégate, optimised for anti-surface warfare (ASuW) and anti-submarine warfare (ASW). The type was originally offered with an undernose radome for a 360° OMERA ORB-32 ASD radar, or a Thomson-CSF Agrion. The type had provision for a pair of AM.39 Exocet

ASMs (one on each side of the cabin) carried on externally-braced outrigger pylons, or could replace these weapons with torpedoes. The aircraft could also be fitted with a variable-depth dipping sonar (lowered via the structural cut-out provided for the external load hook) and towed magnetic anomaly detector (MAD). For shipborne operation, the

AS 332F was fitted with a folding tail rotor pylon, anti-corrosion measures, and a deck-landing assistance 'harpoon' system. Two of these potent missile-armed helicopters were delivered to the Abu Dhabi element of the UAE air forces in 1982, and five more 'short' Abu Dhabi AS 532UCs are to be retrofitted to a similar standard. Kuwait

received six AS 332F1s in 1985.

The AS 332F/F1 Frégate was redesignated the AS 532SC Cougar Mk 1 in 1990. The Chilean Navy purchased seven of the type in 1991, which became the first Cougars to undertake ship-borne operations routinely, being deployed aboard the 'County'-class destroyers *Blanco Encalada* and *Cochrane*, and the 'Leander'-class frigates *Lynch* and *Condell*. The Royal Saudi Navy Force

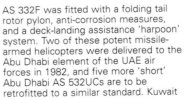

The Força Aeronaval da Marinha do Brasil operates AS 332F1s in the utility/transport role, locally designated UH-14. Although they do not have any specialised ASW/ASUW features, they are fitted with a folding tail rotor for shipborne operations.

AS 532SC — Folding main rotors — Folding tail boom — Dipping sonar option, deployed through cabin floor cutout — Undernose search radar — AM.39 Exocet capability

has 12 Cougars, of which six are AS 532SCs with Exocet capability. The other six are AS 532UC standard transports.

The AS 532SC Cougar continues to be marketed aggressively, though its avionics and equipment fit may be quite different to those fitted to early AS 332Fs. The aircraft is now equipped with a sophisticated electronic package, integrating the latest-generation sensors with powerful computing equipment. The radar currently being offered to potential AS 532SC customers is the panoramic, multi-mode, pulse-compression VARAN radar that is optimised for active detection of small targets in rough sea states and in conditions of severe electromagnetic interference. The aircraft also carries wide-band omni-directional DR 2000/DALIA passive ESM equipment.

It is claimed that a single AS 532SC Cougar, in one five-hour sortie, is able to survey the same area as a frigate during 24 hours. The AS 532SC Cougar has demonstrated the ability to operate from helicopter-carriers, destroyers or frigates, and can be equipped with the HARPON deck lock.

The AS 332F/AS 532SC has proved popular in the Gulf, operated by Kuwait, Saudi Arabia and the UAE. This aircraft is one of the UAE's machines, displaying the heavy stores pylons used to carry the AM.39 Exocet anti-ship missile.

The AS 532SC Cougar was offered to South Africa to meet its navy's Maritime Helicopters Programme, which called for a maritime helicopter able to operate from patrol corvettes. Eurocopter, with Denel as prime contractor, offered South Africa four to six new AS 532SCs, to be fitted with a locally-developed and integrated avionics and tactical system, closely based on that being developed for Denel's indigenous Rooivalk attack helicopter.

The AS 532SC Cougar was an attractive option for South Africa, enjoying significant commonality with the existing SAAF Oryx. This would have meant that the new type would require minimal logistic support requirements, significantly reducing total system life cycle and support costs. Despite these advantages, the AS 532SC lost out to the Super Lynx.

AS 532MC Cougar

The AS 532MC is an unarmed, short-fuselage maritime version of the AS 532SC for SAR and surveillance duties. No customers have been found, although it is believed that this was the variant offered to meet the 1996 US Navy requirement for a new VertRep helicopter.

Long-fuselage versions

AS 332L Super Puma

The improved performance of the AS 332 Super Puma soon led to efforts to enlarge the aircraft's cabin, which was identical to that of the 'standard' Puma and, as such, was regarded as being somewhat 'cosy', accommodating 20-21 troops in some discomfort, or 17 passengers. The obvious solution was to insert a modest fuselage plug, adding 0.76 m (2 ft 6 in) to the cabin length and increasing cabin volume from 11.4 m³ (402.6 cu ft) to 13.3 m³ (469.7 cu ft). This allowed four extra passenger seats to be added, and two extra cabin windows (one per side, aft of the flight deck). The result was the civil AS 332L, whose prototype (F-WJZN) flew for the first time on 10 October 1980, though

Japan's three AS 332Ls were originally ordered for use during the 1986 Tokyo Summit, and were subsequently transferred to the JGSDF for VIP transport duties with the Tokubetsu Yuso Koku-tai (special transport squadron).

some sources suggest that this aircraft was preceded by the SA 330R, a stretched conversion of a standard Puma also known as the SA 331-001.

The basic AS 332L Super Puma soon gave way to the AS 332L1, which had a reinforced floor, airliner-type 'pilots' seats, and accommodation for 24 passengers instead of 21. Two VIP aircraft for Thailand, delivered in 1997, were designated AS 332L2, and are

believed to be Mk 2 aircraft with the further stretched cabin. They are described separately.

Although ostensibly a civil variant, the AS 332L/L1 attracted several military customers, especially for use in the VIP role. They included Cameroon, China, the Democratic Republic of Congo

(Zaïre), France, Iceland, Japan, South Korea, Mexico, Nepal, Oman, Thailand and the United Arab Emirates.

The AS 332L Super Puma has not been redesignated and the Cougar name should not be applied to the type, even to aircraft operated by military customers.

AS 332M Super Puma and AS 532UL Cougar Mk 1

The AS 332M was offered as a dedicated military equivalent of the stretched AS 332L, and the demonstrator (F-WJZN) previously had served as the AS 332L prototype. In a military seating fit, the 'long' version can carry up to 25 troops, or six stretcher cases and 10 medical staff or walking wounded. The increased capacity

Escuadrón 402 of Ala 48 flies the AS 532UL (HT.21A) on VIP transport duties for the Spanish air force, alongside AS 332Bs (HT.21). The aircraft have airliner-style doors.

imposed a weight penalty, however, and sales of the AS 332M were sluggish; many military customers preferred the more compact AS 332B/AS 532UC.

When Eurocopter adopted the Cougar name and AS 532 designation for military versions of the Super Puma, the AS 332M became the AS 532UL Cougar Mk 1. Delivered in its basic, unarmed utility form to Brazil, Chile, France, Jordan, Singapore, Spain, Sweden, Switzerland and Turkey, the AS 332M/AS 532UL is capable of lifting a 4.5-tonne (4.43-Imp ton) underslung load, and has proved a worthy

Large sponsons and flotation gear optional, standard small sponsons shown

Makila 1A1 turboshafts

Undernose search radar option

Long fuselage with six cabin windows

AS 532UL

Sweden's HKP 10s were procured for SAR duties from nine locations around the country. They are well equipped for the task, including rear-view mirrors for the pilots. In the winter months they often operate with ski pads attached.

recent reports have gone back to reporting a 30-aircraft total, however. Except for two initial 'pattern' aircraft, all Turkish Cougars are being assembled in Turkey under the auspices of the EUROTAI consortium established by Eurocopter and Tusas Aerospace Industries.

The Turkish Land Forces received the first Cougar helicopter from the TAI production line in May 2000, with Jean-François Bigay, Chairman of the Eurocopter Group Supervisory Board, handing over the keys to General Attila Ates, Commander of the Turkish Land Forces. Six army AS 532ULs were produced initially, at the rate of one helicopter every two months. Production then ramped up to a rate of one per month (interspersed with AS 532ALs for the air force), and deliveries are expected to be completed in February 2003.

The ALAT's small Cougar force is operated by two rapid-reaction Escadrilles d'Hélicoptère de Manoeuvre at Phalsbourg, and a special forces transport unit at Pau.

competitor to the smaller Sikorsky S-70/UH-60 Black Hawk. Sales have sometimes been slow, but the AS 532UL is an excellent aircraft, with many fine qualities, and Eurocopter has offered offsets and local production where necessary. It has been

suggested that the Spanish order could only be secured by Eurocopter accepting seven CN.235s to sell at the helicopter manufacturer's own risk.

Many operators of the stretched AS 332M and AS 532UL have applied local designations to the helicopters. Brazilian Air Force are known as CH-34s, while Sweden's 12 aircraft are known locally as the HKP 10. Four AS 332M1s delivered to the Spanish Air Force in 1991 were designated HT.21A. The 15 AS 532ULs delivered to the

Spanish army in 1996 initially were designated HT.21UL, becoming HU.21Ls in January 1999. Swiss AS 332Ms have little-used local designations of TH86 (three aircraft) and TH89 (12).

Turkey signed a FF2.5 billion contract for 10 AS 532ULs (army) and 20 AS 532ALs (air force) in February 1997. The number of Cougars on order for the army was reported subsequently to have been increased to 20, or even 30, according to some sources; more

Two South American AS 532UL operators are the Chilean army (left), which has one, and the Brazilian air force (below). In FAB service the helicopter is designated CH-34, eight serving with 3° Esq/8° GAv 'Puma' at Afonsos.

AS 532UL Cougar HORIZON

Following the success of the original Orchidée demonstrator Puma during the Gulf War, the programme was resurrected by the French army in 1993, albeit on a reduced scale. The programme gained a new acronym – HORIZON (Hélicoptère d'Observation Radar et d'Investigation sur Zone) – and gained much-needed new impetus.

Following an eight-month definition phase, a single AS 532UL-based prototype (F-ZVLJ) was flown with the full-standard HORIZON radar on 8 December 1992, and flew with the full system from 1994.

The first aircraft was delivered to the French army on 24 June 1996, followed by a second (plus the first air-deployable, vehicle-mounted ground station) in December 1996. The third and fourth aircraft followed in 1997 and 1998, with a second ground station.

The HORIZON Cougar's I-band (8-10 GHz) multi-mode pulse-Doppler radar is served by a massive, plank-like 3.5 x 0.8-m (11.48 x 2.62-ft) retractable antenna array, which drops down and rotates slowly (at 2° 4' or 8° per second) below the rear part of the cabin. The Thomson-developed radar has a formidable moving target indication capability, making the HORIZON system effectively a low-cost, tactical equivalent to the 'big picture' E-8 J-STARS, which it can complement.

The radar has a range resolution (accuracy) of approximately 40 m (131.23 ft) and a target velocity accuracy of +/- 7 km/h (4.3 mph). It can detect and classify up to 4,000 moving objects and vehicles (including low-flying

helicopters) at ranges of up to 150-200 km (93-125 miles) (depending on aircraft height), with sufficient accuracy to supply targeting data to systems like MLRS. The aircraft can stay on station for up to four hours, flying at heights of up to 10,000 ft (3048 m). In a high-threat environment the helicopter can pop up from low level to take a quick peek, using a so-called 'snapshot mode' that enables it to scan a 20000-km² (7,722-sq mile) area in only 10 seconds.

The HORIZON Cougar can operate in an autonomous mode, in which the onboard operator controls the radar and tailors the mission to achieve his briefed objectives, analyses raw radar data, and then sends processed information via HF or VHF to a single command vehicle.

The ALAT's four HORIZON Cougars are based at Phalsbourg with a special squadron within the 1er RHC. This is the first aircraft, seen with the radar extended during trials.

Alternatively, the aircraft can be controlled from the ground station (consisting of multiple vehicles for command, control, and processing), to which it may be linked via a secure single-channel Dassault Electronique AGATHA (Air/Ground Anti-jam Transmission from Helicopter or Aircraft) microwave datalink. Many scenarios envisage the co-ordinated use of two HORIZON-equipped Cougars, each controlled from a single ground station.

The HORIZON ground surveillance system-equipped Cougar is another version being offered for export.

AS 332M Super Puma and AS 532AL Cougar Mk 1

The armed version of the AS 332M/ AS 532UL is known as the AS 532AL. Turkey has also acquired the basic armed utility Cougar Mk 1, but in a slightly different form, optimised for CSAR. This is described separately, below.

AS 532AL SAR Cougar Mk 1

In 1997, the Turkish government signed the FF4.45 billion Phenix 2 contract for 30 Cougar Mk 1 helicopters, 28 of which were to be built locally by a newly-formed consortium, known as EUROTAI, established by Eurocopter and Tusas Aerospace Industries Inc. In the EUROTAI consortium, TAI was tasked with airframe manufacture and assembly and with acceptance testing. Eurocopter and TAI also signed a regional joint marketing agreement that allowed Turkish industry to market and sell the Cougar helicopter. The contract covered 10 AS 532UL Cougars for the Turkish army, and 20 AS 532UL/AL Cougars for SAR and Combat SAR duties with the air force. The Turkish air force aircraft will consist of six aircraft configured for CSAR and 14 for 'normal' SAR operations.

The AS 532AL SAR Cougar Mk 1 features an undernose 360° search radar, a nose-mounted FLIR, and emergency flotation gear on the sponsons and in a 'horse-collar' around the nose. The type appeared broadly similar to the Greek SAR Super Pumas,

albeit with a blunter nose and different air intake filters.

The first Turkish air force AS 532AL SAR Cougar Mk 1 was ceremonially handed over to the Chief of the Turkish Armed Forces, General Hüseyin Kivrikoglu, at Marignane on 1 May 2000.

A second followed before the next 28 Turkish Cougars (18 of them SAR-configured) followed from the TAI assembly lines between late May 2000 and February 2003.

Like its neighbour, Greece, Turkey has opted for the AS 532 to provide rescue coverage, although it has chosen the long-body (AL) version as the basis. The aircraft operate in detachments around the country.

AS 532UE Cougar 100

The AS 532UE is an austere 'budget' variant of the stretched Cougar Mk 1, similar to the AS 532UB. It has the same simplified fuel system and fixed, unfaired landing gear, but is based on the longer AS 532UL airframe. Similarly intended as a competitor to cheaper Eastern Bloc helicopters like the Mi-17 (and even to second-hand machines from other sources), the UE promises to be 15-20 per cent cheaper than the AS 532UL.

The aircraft can transport 25 troops in addition to the crew, and is offered 'ready for use' for the tactical transport and logistical support roles. It features the basic minimum of radio and navigation equipment required for these tasks.

A prototype had been expected to fly during 2000 but development has been suspended.

Stretched versions

AS 332L2 Super Puma Mk 2

The Mk 2 version of the Super Puma flew in prototype form on 6 February 1987. The longest current variant of the Super Puma/Cougar line, the Mk 2 has a cabin further lengthened by 55 cm (21.6 in), giving a total volume of 15 m³ (530 cu ft). This is claimed to be the biggest cabin volume for any helicopter in the Super Puma's category.

The Mk 2 introduced an improved Spheriflex main and tail rotor hub system without lubricated bearings, and the new main rotor featured parabolic, anhedral section tips. The aircraft has a new four-bladed tail rotor.

It is powered by uprated 1569-kW (2,104-shp) Makila 1A2 turboshafts. The aircraft has a reinforced central structure, and can carry 28 passengers, 29 troops or 12 stretchers, or an underslung load of 5 tonnes (4.92 Imp tons). Improvements were made inside the cockpit, too, such as a four-screen

(CRT) 'glass' cockpit and a new, four-axis autopilot with built-in coupler. The aircraft is also fitted with HUMS (Health and Usage Monitoring System).

By the time the type gained its French certification, in April 1992, the military utility version had been

redesignated the AS 532U2, although three VIP aircraft for the Royal Thai Air Force were delivered as AS 332L2s (still used as the civil designation) in 1997.

There are utility, combat search and rescue, and armed versions of the Mk 2, all of which are described separately.

The Royal Thai Air Force Royal Flight operates three AS 332L2s, two of which are appointed with a luxurious 10-seat interior for royal use. The third has a 14-seat layout for government use.

AS 532U2 Cougar Mk 2

The basic military utility version of the Cougar Mk 2 has been delivered to the Royal Netherlands Air Force, which received 17 AS 532U2 helicopters from 1996, and the German Luftwaffe, which received three in 1997. The latter aircraft are used mainly for VIP work

By 2001 the only customers for the basic transport Cougar Mk 2 were the Netherlands (below right) and Germany (below). The Luftwaffe machines are in VIP fit, with airliner-type doors.

with the 3. Flugbereitschaftsstaffel at Berlin-Tegel.

With the advent of the EHI EH101 and Sikorsky S-92, the Cougar Mk 2 has a number of larger, modern competitors, while smaller helicopters like the AB 139 and NH 90 compete with smaller Cougar variants. Eurocopter had to fight hard to win the Dutch order, and the value of offset business eventually reached 120 per cent of the total order value. The cost of the basic utility Cougar Mk 2 has been

estimated at FF75 to 82 million, depending on equipment.

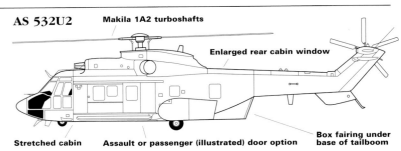

AS 532U2 — **Makila 1A2 turboshafts** — **Enlarged rear cabin window** — **Box fairing under base of tailboom** — **Stretched cabin** — **Assault or passenger (illustrated) door option**

Since being delivered to No. 300 Squadron at Soesterberg in April 1996, some Dutch Cougars have undergone a number of interesting modifications. In 1998 the Dutch borrowed skis from the Swiss Air Force for a winter exercise, and may now have bought sufficient skis for about five aircraft. From December 1999, four aircraft were modified by Aérospatiale to be able to carry chaff/flare dispensers, radar warning receiver and missile approach warning system equipment, and a door gun. Four more were due to follow during 2000-2001.

AS 532U2/A2 RESCO Cougar Mk 2

The RESCO Cougar Mk 2 was developed to meet an Armée de l'Air requirement for a Puma replacement in the Combat SAR role, RESCO being an acronym for REcherche et Sauvetage en COmbat. The total requirement is for an estimated 14 helicopters, though only four are being acquired under the present procurement programme, replacing three Pumas currently used in the role. The Pumas operated with a relatively large crew, and bulky internal equipment limited their capacity and range. The Armée de l'Air conducted an intensive evaluation of the prototype (F-ZVLA) aircraft in July-August 1999, logging more than 100 flying hours.

The CSAR role may require operation close to or even behind enemy lines, in all weathers and by day or night. Accurate navigation is essential, and in the Cougar Mk 2 this is provided by a self-contained navigation system which integrates the GPS, inertial reference system, Doppler and VOR/TACAN/DME. The Cougar crew uses an encrypted Personal Locator System (PLS) to find downed aircrew, and this helps to 'hide' the incoming helicopter and survivors from an enemy. In the search area, the crew can look out through bubble observation windows on the cabin doors, and have a FLIR, a searchlight, and a panoramic detection radar with a PLS homing function. The Cougar Mk 2 already has complete NVG

The first AS 532A2 RESCO for the Armée de l'Air is seen during tests. The FLIR turret is prominent, as is the heavy-duty winch. The aircraft is fitted with a dual-band searchlight.

compatibility throughout the cockpit and cabin, allowing the crew unrestricted use of third-generation night vision goggles during night missions.

'Ordinary' air-sea rescue forms an important part of the RESCO Cougar Mk 2's role, and this is made easier by the Sextant Avionique NADIR navigation system, which incorporates an Integrated Flight Display System (IFDS) with a four-axis SFIM PA-165 autopilot. All normal SAR mission manoeuvres can be automated, including the descent, transition and hover manoeuvres over the survivor. The aircraft has a 272-kg (600-lb) capacity primary hoist with a back-up emergency hoist.

The RESCO Cougar Mk 2 has a larger cabin than most of its competitors in the 10-tonne (9.84-Imp ton) class and is therefore better able to carry more of the vital equipment and crew required in the CSAR and SAR roles, including hoist operators, dedicated rescue personnel, an operator's search and navigation console, doctors and paramedics, stretchers, medical equipment, and the usual life rafts, smoke floats and flares.

In order to rescue shot-down aircrews from hostile territory, the

Armée de l'Air required that the helicopter be able to fly up to 250 nm (463 km) behind enemy lines, hover there for half an hour, then return at low level. For very-long-range operations, the RESCO Cougar Mk 2 can operate at a gross weight of 11200 kg (24,691 lb) compared to the normal maximum mission weight of 9750 kg (21,495 lb). Fuel tanks in the enlarged landing gear nacelles increase the range of the aircraft, and another tank can be fitted in

the aft cabin. This allows the Cougar to rescue and recover two survivors from a location up to 400 nm (740 km) from base.

As an aircraft designed to go 'in harm's way', the RESCO Cougar Mk 2 has external weapon struts for a variety of self-defence/fire suppression weapons, including podded 20-mm cannon or a variety of rocket pods. It can also can carry two fuselage-mounted 7.62-mm machine-guns, behind the forward-sliding domed observation windows in the cabin.

The aircraft has a number of survivability features designed to maximise resistance to battle damage. The fuel cells are self-sealing and crash-resistant, and a high level of built-in redundancy is provided in the vital systems (flight controls, fuel, hydraulic and electrical systems, and the autopilot). The Spheriflex-type rotor heads have high impact tolerance and the gearboxes can operate without lubrication for 30 to 90 minutes. The pilots sit on armoured seats. For self-protection, a radar warning receiver and missile approach warner can be installed, coupled with flare and chaff

In original form the AS 532A2 RESCO had a four-bladed main rotor but is being retrofitted with the five-bladed rotor and uprated engines of the EC 725.

dispensers. It is obviously better to avoid detection by the enemy, so the RESCO Cougar Mk 2 uses technology developed by ONERA (the French Aerospace Research Centre) to reduce its acoustic, radar and infra-red signatures, including engine exhaust IR suppressors and special low IR-reflectance paint.

The French Air Force received the first RESCO Cougar Mk 2 (F-ZVMC) from Eurocopter's Marignane plant on 9 September 1999. The helicopter had its instrumentation fitted at the Istres Flight Test Centre before being handed over to the CEAM (the French Military Experimental Centre) for further operational evaluation, and for the development and definition of operating procedures.

By the time it was delivered, the AS 532-based RESCO Cougar had been overtaken by events, and the remaining three aircraft in the order were delivered to improved Cougar Mk 2+ standards. The first aircraft was subsequently retrofitted to this standard, which is described separately.

AS 532A2 CSAR Cougar Mk 2

Saudi Arabia ordered 12 Cougar Mk 2s for CSAR duties in July 1996, paying a reported FF3 billion ($US600 million), and deliveries began during 1998. They are similar to the Armée de l'Air RESCO Cougar Mk 2, but use the Anglicised designation CSAR Cougar Mk 2.

The Saudi aircraft are equipped for inflight refuelling from a Hercules tanker, using an extendable air-to-air refuelling probe installed on the left side of the fuselage. This system was proved in a two-phase programme from BA125 Istres, using a KC-130H Hercules tanker and a CSAR Cougar Mk 2 helicopter on loan from the Saudi Air Force. Aerodynamic and flight envelope aspects (including 'dry prods') were tested during June 2000, before full fuel transfers (of up to 5,500 lb/2495 kg) were demonstrated in October 2000. The CSAR Cougar Mk 2 refuelled from the KC-130's port and starboard wing pods, in various configurations, and at up to maximum all-up weight, while carrying a full load of external stores.

The Saudi aircraft also featured new engine exhaust suppressors that direct hot exhaust gases into the rotor disc.

Greece has ordered six CSAR-configured Cougar Mk 2s for the air force, and they may be to a standard similar to that of the Saudi aircraft.

The AS 532 Cougar Mk 2 has also been offered to meet two Canadian Armed Forces requirements. The $C600 million Canadian Support Helicopter requirement called for 15 aircraft, while the $C2 billion Maritime Helicopter Programme required 32 aircraft, equipped with Inverse Synthetic Aperture Radar, ESM, an EO sensor, active dipping sonar, sonobuoy processing and MAD equipment, and capable of carrying Mk 46 torpedoes and/or unspecified anti-ship missiles. Eurocopter teamed with local companies Conair, IMP Aerospace (which would be responsible for completing, supporting and overhauling aircraft), SNC Lavalin (programme management) and Spar Aviation Support (logistics support and overhaul of dynamics) to form Team Cougar.

An AS 532A2 CSAR destined for the Royal Saudi Air Force sits outside the Marignane factory. Saudi aircraft can be armed with gun and rocket pods, and door-mounted weapons.

AS 532A2   **Window- and door-mounted guns**   **Extensive defensive systems**
Undernose FLIR turret   **Upturned exhausts**
Retractable inflight refuelling probe   **Weapons pylon (both sides)**

Five-bladed versions

EC 225 Super Puma Mk 2+

The civil Super Puma reportedly will be offered in further upgraded form as the EC 225 Super Puma Mk 2+. The military Mk 2+ flew first, however, and the relevant modifications are therefore described under the EC 725 Cougar Mk 2+ heading. JAR 29 European civilian certification of the EC 225 is scheduled for the end of 2002.

EC 725 Cougar Mk 2+

The Mk 2+ is the latest member of the Super Puma/Cougar line, although it uses a new EC (for Eurocopter) designation prefix in place of the AS (for Aérospatiale) applied to previous Super Puma and Cougar variants. It also uses new model numbers, relating to other new Eurocopter designs rather than to the old system based on Sud Aviation models. Civil variants are EC 225s, while military versions are referred to as EC 725s.

Early marketing efforts emphasised the newness of the aircraft: Eurocopter stressed that it "selected the basic Super Puma/Cougar Mk 2 airframe structure" (inferring that an all-new airframe design had been considered) because of the "outstanding quality" it had demonstrated.

The Mk 2+ is designed to offer substantially enhanced performance, especially in terms of payload/range, as well as improved economy, reliability and maintainability through the use of advanced technologies. The new variant has a new powerplant, a reinforced main gearbox, a new main rotor system, and a new integrated flight and display system.

The new powerplant consists of a pair of Turboméca Makila 1A4 turboshaft engines, which use state-of-the-art materials and improved airflow design to offer an emergency power rating of up to 1800 kW (2,413 shp) – 14 per cent more than the previous version of the Makila. A duplex (two-channel) Full Authority Digital Engine Control (FADEC) system and 'blade-shedding' free turbine architecture provides great reliability, while maintainability is ensured through the engine's modular design. Each engine is a 'power egg' – a self-contained unit incorporating all the systems, equipment and accessories required for its operation.

The main gear box is reinforced to cope with the increased power output of the Makila 1A4s, and the increased MTOW. The gear train of the original engine has been kept, but the spiral bevel gears will integrate deep nitriding technology and the latest optimised tooth profiles. The lubrication system includes an emergency spraying sub-system which allows 30 minutes of flight without oil.

Spheriflex main and tail rotor heads are retained on the Mk 2+, although the rotor head has been redesigned to incorporate five new state-of-the-art blades. The slow-turning, 16.2-m (53.15-ft) diameter, five-bladed configuration was selected to give the lowest possible vibration levels and noise signature. Each blade has a composite spar with multiple box structures, and tip caps. The parabolic blade tips have an anhedral profile. The rotors and the horizontal stabiliser can be fitted with a de-icing/anti-icing system.

The new variant features an Integrated Flight and Display System (IFDS) incorporating a new four-axis autopilot, integrating the presentation of flight data and management of the sub-systems. The Flight Display System (FDS) is based around four 6 x 8-in (15 x 20-cm) liquid crystal multi-function displays (LCD) and two 4 x 5-in (10 x 13-cm) liquid crystal displays.

The new medium-lift (11-tonne/10.82-Imp ton) Cougar/Super Puma Mk 2+ prototype (F-ZVLR) performed its 50-minute maiden flight at Marignane

F-ZVLR is the first EC 725, originally flying in a standard ALAT camouflage scheme. The airframe is basically the same as the AS 532U2/A2, but has an all new dynamic system.

EC 725   **Makila 1A4 turboshafts**   **Five-bladed main rotor**
Revised cockpit displays
Retractable refuelling probe option   **Based on AS 532U2/A2 airframe**

Although it does not offer any additional cabin volume over the Cougar Mk 2, the EC 725 Cougar Mk 2+ offers much improved performance and greater load-lifting capability.

on 30 November 2000. The crew consisted of test pilot Hervé Jammayrac, Bernard Turcat as flight test engineer and Daniel Sémioli as flight test mechanic. The prototype flew in basic utility form, without armament or inflight-refuelling equipment. This will be an option on some military sub-variants, using the system successfully tested on the Cougar Mk 2.

The EC 725 has already been ordered by the Armée de l'Air to fulfil its requirement for a CSAR helicopter, changing an existing order for three AS 532A2s into an order for EC 725s. The RESCO version of the aircraft is expected to receive its French military release-to-service qualification in 2003.

EC 725 RESCO Cougar Mk 2+

The first military version of the Cougar Mk 2+ to enter service will be used by the Armée de l'Air to perform Combat SAR missions for the French armed forces. Three helicopters previously ordered (as AS 532A2 RESCO Cougar Mk 2s) will be delivered to the new standard in 2003. The RESCO Mk 2+ will include an inflight-refuelling probe, already validated on Saudi CSAR Cougar Mk 2s. The Mk 2 version that has already been delivered will then be brought up to the same EC 725 standard. The Armée de l'Air currently requires 14 of these aircraft.

The new EC 725 has already been flown by the French Air Force Chief of Staff, General Jean-Pierre Job, at Marignane.

F-ZVLR, the EC 725 prototype, has been tested with a refuelling probe for the EC 725 RESCO version. It appeared in this guise at the 2001 Paris air show.

Super Puma and Cougar Mk 3

In 1998, Eurocopter revealed a proposed growth version of the Mk 3 that offered a 25 per cent increase in cabin volume (to 20 m³/706 cu ft), achieved through another modest (70-cm/27.5-in) stretch in length, coupled with increases in width (25 cm/9.8 in) and height (35 cm/13.8 in). The new type was expected to have a 14 per cent increase in power, allowing a 10 per cent hike in MTOW, to 10 tonnes (9.84 Imp tons). The type was envisaged as a competitor to the S-92, in both civil and military markets.

Overseas production

Denel (Atlas) Gemsbok/Oryx

The Oryx is an improved South African Puma derivative, incorporating some features from the Super Puma, although it is not an AS 332 or 532 variant in the strictest sense. The Oryx has been described as "The most 'Super' Puma and not just an AS 332 Super Puma". The type was acquired as a Puma replacement while South Africa was still practising apartheid and weapons procurement was complicated by sanctions. Details of the Oryx programme thus remain unclear.

The Oryx drew on lessons learned from the attack helicopter programme that eventually bore fruit with the Rooivalk. A pair of ex-SAAF Pumas was sold to Atlas for use as demonstrators and testbeds, and the first of these became the XTP-1. This aircraft incorporated a number of engine, dynamics system and airframe improvements (in addition to its weapons systems and armament), which formed the foundation of the basic Puma replacement programme. The new assault transport 'Super Puma' was initially known as the Gemsbok, but was soon renamed the Oryx.

The official line is that the Oryx is a new-build aircraft, based on the SA 330 Puma but wholly manufactured in South Africa by Atlas (now Denel) following a gradual programme under which Puma components, sub-assemblies and, eventually, whole airframes were locally manufactured. Others believe that the Oryx was produced locally by assembling and upgrading existing Puma airframes. The SAAF's existing Pumas were largely accounted for, however, though Puma airframes may have been obtained from Romania or even France.

A Portuguese businessman took Eurocopter to court in 1996, claiming that his company, Beverley Securities Inc. (BSI), was owed substantial commission relating to a $US2 billion sale of helicopters, in kit form, to South Africa. He claimed that these kits had been supplied to South Africa via Portugal's OGMA, that they had been described as 'spare parts' for existing Pumas (and thus not subject to the

The Oryx fulfils a number of important roles within the SAAF, including rescue and assault transport. They were heavily employed during the Mozambique flood disaster, making countless rescues.

South Africa's Oryx fleet is spread between four squadrons – Nos 15, 17, 19 and 22 – the last of which is responsible for providing naval support, fire-fighting and rescue. Both of these aircraft have the nose radar fitted, while the aircraft above has flotation equipment for overwater operations.

Denel Oryx

Intake filters standard

Topaz turboshafts (Makila 1A1)

Based on SA 330 airframe

Ventral fin as standard

Weather radar usualy fitted

Most with large sponsons, some with flotation gear

embargoes then in force) and that they had been sold to a front company in Zaïre. BSI's court action failed, though the number of kits said to be involved tallied exactly with the number of 'production' conversions.

It is believed that an ex-SAAF SA 330L Puma, serial number 177 (one of the XTP-1s), was converted to serve as the Oryx prototype, gaining the serial 1250. No first flight date is known for the Oryx prototype, though the type made its first public appearance in 1991. The first delivery to the SAAF was made in 1988 and the type entered full service in early 1994, with No. 19 Squadron. All 50 had been delivered by

14 May 1996. Some sources suggest that Oryx 1200 was the prototype, built in France and followed by 49 new-build South African aircraft, and that 1250 was merely a single converted SA 330.

The Oryx is powered by a pair of locally-built Topaz engines – broadly equivalent to the 1400-kW (1,877-shp) Makila 1A1. The aircraft has a Super Puma-style ventral fin and a slatted tailplane. The Oryx did not have the revised undercarriage of the Super Puma, and thus did not have the vertical hydraulic retraction jack lying vertically along the side of the rear fuselage, under a distinctive fairing. Some later Oryxes did have an external bracing

strut running diagonally down from the side of the cabin to the outer 'corner' of the main undercarriage sponson, like that fitted to some later SAAF Pumas. Most, but not all, Oryxes were fitted with larger sponsons, containing extra 350-litre (77-Imp gal) fuel tanks. The Oryx retained the same basic nose shape as the standard Puma, rather than the more pointed nose of the Super Puma. This did, however, mount a small thimble radome, housing an Allied Signal 1400B weather radar.

The Oryx is used by the SAAF in the assault transport, utility and SAR roles, and also for shipborne SAR and replenishment duties (two aircraft

having been painted in a maritime grey colour scheme) and for Antarctic support duties (at least two aircraft, including 1238 and 1249, having been painted red and white).

Denel has actively promoted the Oryx to a number of potential export customers, and has signed reciprocal support agreements with Eurocopter under which Denel could support Pumas and Super Pumas in Africa, while Eurocopter could support Oryxes in some other areas.

Two helicopters are used by the SAAF for Antarctic support duties. They are designated Oryx M2.

Denel Oryx OCJ/SOCJ

Four Oryxes were converted to, or built as, Stand Off Communications Jammers (SOCJ). They have a Grintek System Technologies GSY 1500 20-500 MHz communications jammer, served by a massive antenna array mounted on the starboard side consisting of a horizontal rod projecting outwards from the flat fuselage side, supporting a series of vertical dipoles, tapering in height so that the shortest poles were farthest outboard. The horizontal rod is

attached to a vertical support which, in turn, is attached to the aircraft above and below the sliding door, leaving room for the door to move below it. The jammer is believed to have a range of up to 450 km (280 miles), and is capable of jamming up to 20 prioritised frequencies. Two SOCJs are used by No. 17 Squadron and two more by No. 19 Squadron. The variant was first identified in late 1993, but was not unveiled officially until 2000.

Denel Oryx SORJ

Denel converted four Oryxes to Stand Off Radar Jamming (SORJ) configuration, with a Sysdel L-Band and S-Band ECM system. These aircraft had

a massive antenna array fitted in place of the starboard door, which took the place of a massive square box running on the normal door rails. Two aircraft were assigned to No. 17 Squadron and two to No. 19 Squadron.

IPTN NAS 332B/C/F/L

Following its licensed manufacture of 11 examples of the standard SA 330 Puma (which ended in 1981), the Indonesian aerospace company IPTN switched to production of the AS 332 from 1983, principally to meet local needs but also for export to some Asian countries. The first 18 Indonesian-built Super Pumas were short NAS 332Bs and NAS 332Cs, and may also have included a number of maritime ASW aircraft equivalent to the AS 332F, possibly designated NAS 332F ASW/MA. At least four of these have been positively identified in Indonesian service, carrying the serials HU-440 to 443, armed with AM.39 Exocet missiles and fitted with undernose radar.

The first Indonesian-built Super Puma was a civil NAS 332C, delivered to Pelita on 22 April 1983. Seven more civil

aircraft were reportedly sold to Iran for offshore oil rig support duties. Three paramilitary NAS 332Ls were delivered to the Malaysian government for VIP duties as M36-01, 02 and 03, and at least two VVIP and four utility transport NAS 332B/Cs went to Indonesia's armed forces.

Indonesian Super Puma production switched to the longer NAS 332L from the 19th aircraft (or from the 14th aircraft, according to some sources).

The exact breakdown of military versions for the Indonesian armed forces remains unknown, but it has

been suggested that the Indonesian Air Force requires 16, comprising either two VIP, one VVIP, seven transport and six CSAR, or two VVIP, nine transport and five CSAR. This may be in addition

to 16 aircraft already in the process of being delivered. The split between long- and short-fuselage variants has not been revealed, however, and the situation remains confused.

Carrying the badge of Skwadron Udara 17, this Indonesian air force NAS 332L1 is used for VIP transport duties from Halim-Perdanakusuma.

Developed under the joint YuRom programme, the IAR-93/Orao emerged as a punchy, if uncomplicated, attacker in the mould of the Anglo-French Jaguar. Its continued development was cut short by the tumultuous events which occurred in the countries which created it.

IAR-93 and Orao
Balkan Warrior

Prior to World War II, Romania had developed a self-sufficient aviation industry. During the war it produced more than 1,300 aircraft, of which 450 were IAR-80 and IAR-81 fighters and dive-bombers, delivered by Industria Aeronautica Romana (IAR) in Brasov. They fought on three fronts: in the Eastern campaign against the Soviet Union; in the defence of the oil refineries around Ploiesti, against Allied bombers; and in the Western campaign, for the last nine months of the war, on the Allied side and against the Germans. Despite this late shift of allegiance, the peace treaty did not accord Romania co-belligerency status and the country was forbidden to produce combat aircraft after the war.

Right: This model shows the IAR-91 design proposed by the Romanians for the Yurom fighter. The intended powerplant was two non-afterburning RD-9Bs. Two guns were mounted on the sides of the nose and four hardpoints were provided.

Facilities were set up or retained for the overhaul of Soviet types newly entered into service, as well as workshops for small-scale production of light aircraft and gliders. Although IAR in Brasov no longer existed, 'IAR' remained the trademark of several aircraft designed and/or built in Romania during that period and afterwards (and was even adopted as a local designation for licence-built aircraft).

In the 1960s Romania began to detach itself from the influence of the Soviet Union, even though it was a member of the Eastern Bloc and remained Communist. This became more evident after 1965 when Nicolae Ceausescu became the new leader. Within the general reorganisation of the country's economy, it was decided in September 1968 to develop a

Above: The unpainted, canopy-less Romanian prototype undergoes final checks with IRAv at Bacau. The fuselage mark served as an sighting aid for centre of gravity measurements.

Left: Romania's IAR-93 prototype (001) first flew on 31 October 1974. The Soviet-style star national insignia gave way to roundels in 1984.

Left: Today the IAR-93/Orao remains in service only in Yugoslavia (Serbia) and the Bosnian Serb Republic, an unknown number having escaped the NATO onslaught during Allied Force operations in 1999. This quartet of IJ-22 Orao 1s is seen prior to the conflict.

Left: Today the IAR-93/Orao remains in service only in Yugoslavia (Serbia) and the Bosnian Serb Republic, an unknown number having escaped the NATO onslaught during Allied Force operations in 1999. This quartet of IJ-22 Orao 1s is seen prior to the conflict.

modern aviation industry by co-operating with countries outside the Eastern Bloc, especially those from western Europe.

A special institute for research and design in the aeronautical field was set up in Bucharest in 1968 as ICPAS (Institutul de Cercetari si Proiectari Aerospatiale – Aerospace Research and Design Institute), which in 1970 became IMFCA (Institutul de Mecanica Fluidelor si Constructii Aerospatiale – The Institute for Fluid Mechanics and Aerospace Construction) and later INCREST. Within the nucleus of the design team was a group of engineers from URA (later IRAv) in Bacãu, led by Dipl. Eng. Theodor Zanfirescu. At URA the team had performed the initial design of the IAR-90 business jet, followed by the IAR-91 and IAR-92 combat aircraft projects.

The first important project from ICPAS was to be a combat aircraft, designed in co-operation with VTI (Vazduhoplovno Tehnicki Institut – Aeronautical Technical Institute) from Zarkovo, near Belgrade in Yugoslavia. Militarily, Yugoslavia was the ideal partner for such a programme – it was not a member of the Warsaw Pact, it was near Romania and had similar industrial potential and military needs.

It had become apparent that a combat aircraft was needed to equip Romanian fighter-bomber units, and the requirements were for a subsonic multi-role aircraft capable of acting as a fighter against subsonic aircraft and cruise missiles, and of undertaking air combat and ground attack missions. The specification for the joint Romanian/Yugoslav aircraft was quickly defined by military specialists from the two countries during a meeting in Belgrade between 10 and 20 December 1969, and a close air support aircraft was stipulated.

Design work started in 1970 and on 20 May 1971 the two countries signed a governmental agreement for the YuRom project. The first programme managers were Dipl. Eng. Teodor Zanfirescu for the Romanian party and Colonel Vidoje Knezevic for the Yugoslavs.

The Romanians proposed the IAR-91 design, which had RD-9B turbojets for the powerplant and a general layout similar to that of the Sukhoi Su-25 (which was under development at that time). Agreement was finally reached on the Yugoslav proposal, which had several similarities with the Jaguar and featured Rolls-Royce Vipers.

It was decided that the aircraft would be named IAR-93 in Romania and J-22 Orao (Eagle) in Yugoslavia (J came from *jurisnik* = close support fighter).

Construction begins

The construction of a single-seat prototype started in each country in May 1972. IRAv (today Aerostar SA) in Bacãu was the main contractor and was responsible for fuselage construction, general assembly and testing of the Romanian prototype; IRMA Baneasa (today Romaero SA) in Bucharest built the wings, and ICA Ghimbav-Brasov produced the control surfaces. The construction of the Yugoslav prototype took place at the factories in Mostar (SOKO), Pancevo (UTVA) and Trstenik. Within

Above and right: 25001 was the Yugoslav prototype, completed without gun armament. It is shown above at Batajnica with four rocket pods. In Romania the IAR-93 remained a closely-guarded secret until the early 1980s, whereas the Orao prototype was shown at the Yugoslav Air Force Day display at Batajnica on 15 April 1975. The first Orao was placed on display in the Yugoslav Aeronautical Museum at Surcin.

the framework of the YuRom programme, Romania was responsible for the forward fuselage, fin and auxiliary tanks, and Yugoslavia for the wings, aft fuselage and tailplane.

The selected powerplant was two Rolls-Royce Viper Mk 632-41R turbojets with a maximum thrust of 4,000 lb (17.79 kN) each, installed side-by-side in the aft fuselage. The turbojet was to be built under Rolls-Royce licence in both countries. In Romania, the newly founded Turbomecanica in Bucharest was awarded the production licence; for the Yugoslav aircraft, the Orao factory at Rajlovac, near Sarajevo, was selected.

Prototype flight testing

The first Romanian prototype, White 001, made its first flight on 31 October 1974, with approval for the flight apparently coming from Nicolae Ceausescu himself. It took off at 12:08 p.m. local time on a flight that lasted 21 minutes, with Colonel Gheorghe Stanicã at the controls. The flight took place at speeds up to 500 km/h (310 mph) and heights up to 3000 m (9,840 ft). The aircraft performed several high-speed taxi tests prior to the first flight; the initial braking system caused several tyre blow-outs, and the system was later changed.

On the same day and at almost the same time, the first Yugoslav prototype, 25001, flew from Mostar. Major Vladislav Slavujević was at the controls and this flight also lasted around 20 minutes. For their inaugural flights, both prototypes were equipped with Martin-Baker Mk 6 ejection seats provided by the Yugoslavs, and both lacked guns.

On 18 July 1975 the Romanian prototype was demonstrated to Nicolae Ceausescu at Bacãu airfield. On 15 April 1975 the Yugoslav prototype was displayed on the occasion of

Colonel Gheorge Stanicã (below) performed the first IAR-93 flight, while Major Vladislav Slavujević (right, standing on right) handled the Orao's maiden flight. The pilot on the left is Colonel Franc Rupnik, another well-known Orao test pilot and commander of the Yugoslav Vazduhoplovni Opitni Centar (Air Test Centre).

Romania's second prototype was an IAR-93DC two-seater. The fuselage is seen while under construction at IRAv Bacău (above) before it was moved to Craiova for completion. The aircraft now rests in the Otopeni Aviation Museum (left).

Yugoslav Air Force Day, at Batajnica airport. It was later converted to the same standard as the first production aircraft, including the installation of guns. After the completion of its flying career, in 1988 the Yugoslav prototype was put on display at the Muzej Jugoslovensko Vazduho-plovstva (Yugoslav Aeronautical Museum) at Surcin near Belgrade, being towed there by road.

Move to Craiova

From 1975 the Romanian programme was moved from IRAv Bacău to IAv Craiova, which was founded on 7 April 1972 specially for the series production of these aircraft. In 1974, the CIZ (Centrul de Incercări in Zbor – Flight Test Centre) was established in Craiova for extensive testing of all Romanian-built aircraft, particularly the IAR-93 and later the IAR-99. On 21 December 1975 prototype 001 was moved to Craiova in a ferry flight.

Before IAv Craiova started to work at full capacity, six forward fuselage sections were built by IRAv in Bacău. IRMA in Bucharest produced two central fuselage sections.

The first two-seat Romanian prototype, IAR-93DC (*dubla comanda* = dual controls) White 002, made its maiden flight on 29 January

Two batches of IAR-93A pre-production aircraft were built, comprising 11 Preserie 1 aircraft (right), and 15 Preserie 2 machines (below), which introduced nose strakes and LERXes. Pre-production IAR-93As were delivered for service with Regimentul 67 from 1981.

1977. Its construction began in Bacău but was completed in Craiova. This aircraft is now preserved at the Muzeul Aviatiei (Aviation Museum) in Bucharest, near Otopeni international airport. The Yugoslav two-seat prototype, 25002, made its first flight in November 1976 from Batajnica airfield with Major Vladislav Slavujević at the controls.

IAR-93DC No. 003 was a pre-production two-seater that made the first flight on 4 July 1977; it was lost on 24 November 1977 during its 15th test flight, intended to determine the maximum level speed at 900 m (1,984 ft). Tail flutter caused the left stabiliser to break at a speed of 1045 km/h (650 mph) and an altitude

of 500 m (1,102 ft), and the aircraft entered an uncontrollable spin. The crew, Colonels Gheorghe Stanică and Petre Ailiesei, ejected safely. After this event, the aft fuselage structure was reinforced with a view to increasing the critical flutter speed.

Aircraft 004 was a pre-production single-seater, also named IAR-93SCH (*simplă comandă hibrid* – hybrid single-seater), that made its first flight on 31 October 1978. It was formally delivered to Regimentul 67 Vânătoare-Bombardament (67th Fighter-Bomber Regiment) at Craiova airfield on 8 December 1978. It was lost on 20 February 1979 and its pilot, Captain Eng. Dobre Stan, was killed; this was the only

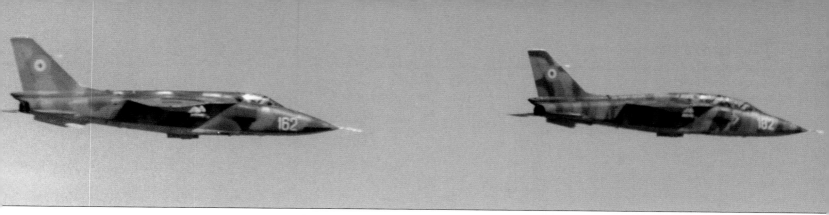

casualty of the development programme. One of the Yugoslav prototypes used for flutter tests was lost in 1980 near Mostar due to foreign object/bird ingestion.

The first deliveries

Delivery of pre-production aircraft was performed two years behind schedule. One reason for the delay was the need to reduce aircraft weight, the prototypes being about 1000 kg (2,205 lb) heavier than initial estimates.

The prototypes were built separately in each country, but all other aircraft were built as follows: IAv Craiova in Romania produced the forward fuselage, fin and auxiliary tanks for all aircraft built in both countries, and performed the general assembly for the Romanian IAR-93s. In Yugoslavia, the UTVA factory at Pancevo near Belgrade built the aft fuselages, ailerons and pylons, and SOKO in Mostar built the wings and rudder and performed the assembly of the Oraos.

In 1979 the first IAR-93A pre-production batch in Romania, named Preserie 1 (Preseries 1), covered 11 single-seat IAR-93As (aircraft numbers 109 to 119) and four two-seat IAR-93DCs (numbers 005 to 008). The Preserie 1 aircraft featured Romanian-built Viper 632-41 engines. Most had Martin-Baker Mk 10 ejection seats as standard, instead of the Mk 6s of the prototypes, although the two were interchangeable. The cockpit was equipped with the ASP PFD-21 gyro gunsight from the MiG-21.

On 23 August 1979 three IAR-93s (001, 002 and 005) were presented in flight during the military parade marking the national holiday of Romania. In August and September 1979, IAR-93DCs 005 and 006 were delivered to Regimentul 67, followed later by 007.

The first Romanian prototype was lost during the test programme when the aircraft, flown by Colonel Ilie Botea, crashed on 20 September 1979 following an engine flame-out. The pilot ejected safely. Modifications to the combustion chamber (which were made retroactively to aircraft already delivered) prevented such events from recurring.

The IAR-93A single-seat Preserie 2 aircraft were complemented by five IAR-93DC two-seaters, an example of which is seen below carrying bombs, and above in company with an IAR-93A Preserie 2. Romanian air force service began in 1981 with Regimentul 67 Vânătoare-Bombardament at Craiova, initially with Preserie 1 aircraft. The first Preserie 2 aircraft arrived in 1982, and the unit remained the only IAR-93 operator until 1989, when Regimentul 49 began operations from Ianca.

The first Yugoslav pre-series aircraft began to be produced at the end of 1977 and the first flew in 1978. The pre-production batch included 10 IJ-22 single-seaters (serial numbers 25701 to 25710) and five INJ-22 two-seaters (25601 to 25605). These aircraft were later named Orao 1. They were used for reconnaissance duties and some had no guns, the installation of which involved structural changes.

Aerodynamic refinements

IAR-93A Preserie 2 aircraft followed from 1980, and comprised 15 single-seaters (numbered 150 to 164) and five IAR-93DC two-seaters (180 to 184). The standard Preserie 2s featured strakes on the sides of the nose (their installation was required by the Yugoslavs) and wing leading-edge root extensions (although they were not present on several Preserie 2 aircraft). These aircraft also had Dowty hydraulic amplifiers replacing the Russian BU-45 (for ailerons) and BU-51M (for stabilisers) installed on early aircraft, a rudder hydraulic amplifier, Marconi artificial stability augmentation system (SAS) and autopilot, and a nosewheel steering system. Also, fuel tanks numbers 1 and 2, situated behind fuselage

Oraos of the 241.LBAE/98.AB are seen at Petrovec airfield near Skopje, Macedonia – now a major site for NATO operations in Kosovo and Macedonia. The aircraft in the foreground with tactical code '701' was the first pre-production IJ-22 built for the JRV.

frame number 16, were removed on Preserie 2 aircraft.

In 1980 construction began of the first production batch of Yugoslav aircraft, comprising 15 IJ-22 single-seaters (numbers 25711 to 25725) and three INJ-22 two-seaters (25606 to 25608). The aircraft differed from pre-production aircraft in the shape of the wing planform (leading-edge root extensions) and certain aerodynamic devices (strakes, fences). The first production single-seater flew in January 1981. The aircraft entered service with the JRV (Jugoslovensko Ratno Vazduhoplovstvo – Yugoslav Air Force) mainly for reconnaissance duties, along with the pre-production aircraft. The single-seat IJ-22s were declared operational in 1982, followed by the two-seat INJ-22 in 1983.

Initial deliveries to combat units were made to 353.IAE/97.AB (Avijacijska Brigada = Aviation Brigade) based at Ortješ Airbase,

Aircraft 200 ushered in a new era for the IAR-93 – it was the prototype for the IAR-93B series which featured afterburning Viper Mk 633-47 engines. The twin ventral fins, which had been found to be superfluous, were removed. The aircraft remained with the CIZ (Romanian flight test centre) throughout its career, until lost in a non-fatal crash.

Type Analysis

25201 was the Yugoslav prototype for the afterburning Orao, becoming the first of the breed to fly supersonically (albeit in a shallow dive). The second J-22NS was displayed at the 1985 Paris air show. Unlike the Romanian IAR-93MBs, Yugoslav Orao 2s retained ventral fins.

Above: The first J-22NS (also designated SY-1, later simplified to J-22) was placed on display in the UTVA factory complex at Pancevo.

Mostar, which was a reconnaissance unit supporting the Yugoslav Navy. Two INJ-22s were lost near Tuzla in the mid-1980s.

The second unit to receive Oraos was 351.IAE/82.AB at Cerklje Airbase, in eastern Slovenia. It also operated IJ and INJ-22 aircraft in the reconnaissance role, in support of the two attack squadrons also based at Cerklje and of the Yugoslav 5th Army in general.

One INJ-22, no. 25606, was converted at the Soko factory into a maritime surveillance version, named INJ-22M (M from *morski* = naval). The aircraft had all equipment and controls removed from the rear cockpit, replaced by a new display which included a large CRT. Under the belly was a pod housing an Ericsson Doppler surveillance radar. Several test flights were made from Orteš, near Sarajevo, in 1984. The fate of the aircraft is unknown.

Enter the IAR-93B and Orao 2

In 1981, the modified design for production aircraft was completed under the leadership of Colonel Eng. Alexandru Filipescu and Colonel Eng. Milos Petric. The series production aircraft were to have the airframe and systems as in the initial specification, with certain aerodynamic improvements, and to be fitted with afterburning Viper engines. The first afterburner system, built in 1979, was rejected for reasons related to weight and automatic system functioning; a second system using microjet technology was certified in 1983.

On 30 April 1984, the first aircraft in the IAR-93B series, wearing registration number 200, received flight authorisation. Its configuration was that of production aircraft. It was equipped with two afterburning Viper Mk 633-47 turbojets each rated at 4,000 lb (17.79 kN) dry and 5,000 lb (22.24 kN) with reheat. The IAR-93B had its ventral fins removed, as they had been on IAR-93DC Preserie 2 No. 180 and on the last IAR-93A Preserie 1, No. 119. Ventral fins were removed from production aircraft because they had proved inefficient on earlier aircraft.

Aircraft No. 200 made its first flight on 12 July 1984, with Viper 633-47 turbojets carrying serial numbers R1003 and R1004. Up to 2 July 1985, it logged 30 hours and 29 minutes in 48 flights. The aircraft had provision for the installation of guns, but they were not installed

when flight test instrumentation was carried inside the ammunition boxes.

IAR-93B No. 200 crashed on 26 November 1996, after more than 12 years of extensive testing with CIZ. The pilot, Captain Commander Matei Constantin Bebe, ejected safely.

The first Yugoslav aircraft equipped with afterburning engines (serial number 25101), designated SY-1 or J-22NS (*naknadno sagorevanje* = afterburner), made its first flight on 20 October 1983. On 22 November 1984 test pilot Marijan Jelen broke the sound barrier with this aircraft in a 25° dive, reaching Mach 1.032. This aircraft today is displayed inside the UTVA factory at Pancevo.

Due to problems encountered in the development of the engines fitted with afterburners, delivery of production aircraft started only in 1986. The JRV adopted the simple designation of J-22 for the single-seaters, while in the West they were named J-22 (M) or Orao 2. A total of 43 J-22 single-seaters was delivered, with serials 25101 to 25124, 25151 to 25154 and 25161 to 25175.

The first NJ-22 two-seater with augmented engines flew for the first time on 18 July 1986. A total of 12 NJ-22s (named Orao 2D in the West), with serials from 25501 to 25512, entered service with the JRV, the first being delivered in 1987.

Another eight J-22s and six NJ-22s were delivered, with serials 25201 to 25208 and 25526 to 25531, respectively. Some sources indicated they were converted from early IJ-22s and INJ-22s, respectively, the conversion being possible due to almost identical airframes.

Two attack squadrons received J-22 and NJ-22 aircraft: 238.LBAE/82.AB at Cerklje and 241.LBAE/98.AB at Petrovec Airbase, Skopje. A third attack squadron, 242.LBAE (s)/172.LAP, at Golubovci Airbase, Titograd (now Podgorica),

The 351.IAE/82.AB at Cerklje ob Krki in Slovenia was the second JRV unit to receive Oraos. The aircraft nearest the camera (tactical code '605') was the last of five pre-production INJ-22 Orao 1 trainers built. They were followed by three full production INJ-22s. Six INJ-22s were later converted to NJ-22 standard.

Variants and production

Romania
Prototypes: one single-seater (001) and one two-seater (002)
Pre-production: one two-seater (003) and one single-seater (004), latter also known as IAR-93SCH
IAR-93A: the first production version delivered to the Romanian AF, in the form of 11 Preserie 1 machines (serialled 109 to 119) and 15 Preserie 2 (150 to 164) aircraft. The IAR-93A featured non-augmented Viper Mk 632-41 engines
IAR-93MB: airframe identical to IAR-93B, but fitted with Viper Mk 632-41 engines. Fifteen aircraft produced (201 to 215)
IAR-93B: definitive production version, featuring reheated Viper Mk 633-47 engines, leading-edge root extensions, ventral fins and no fuselage strakes. Prototype IAR-93B (200) followed by 27 production aircraft (216 to 242)
IAR-93DC: general designation applied to all IAR-93 two-seaters (IAR-93A, B or MB). Fifteen aircraft comprising 005 to 008 (Preserie 1), 180 to 184 (Preserie 2) and 600 to 605 (IAR-93MB/B)

Yugoslavia
Prototypes: one single-seater (25001) and one two-seater (25002)
Pre-production: ten single-seaters (25701 to 25710) and five two-seaters (25601 to 25605)
IJ-22 Orao 1: reconnaissance variant, single-seater, airframe similar to IAR-93A (I comes from *izvidjac* = reconnaissance). Fifteen aircraft serialled 25711 to 25725
INJ-22 Orao 1: two-seat version of IJ-22 for pilot training in reconnaissance role. Three aircraft serialled 25606 to 25608
J-22: (Orao 2 in the West) primary attack version, single-seater with reheat, similar to IAR-93B. New-build construction accounted for at least 43 aircraft (25101 to 25124, 25151 to 25154, and 25161 to 25175), while another eight (25201 to 25208) were probably converted from IJ-22s.
NJ-22: (Orao 2D in the West), two-seat version of J-22 Orao 2 for pilot training in the attack role (first flight on 18 July 1986); N comes from *nastavi* = trainer. Twelve built from new (25501 to 25512) plus another six (25526 to 25531) believed to be produced by conversion from INJ-22

98

Specification – IAR-93 and Orao

Dimensions
Wing span: 9.30 m (30 ft 6.25 in)
Length overall, including nose pitot probe: single-seater 14.90 m (48 ft 10.6 in); two-seater 15.38 m (50 ft 5.5 in)
Height overall: 4.52 m (14 ft 10 in)
Wings area, gross: 26.00 m² (279.86 sq ft)

Weights
Empty, equipped: IAR-93A 6150 kg (13,558 lb); IAR-93B 5750 kg (12,676 lb); J-22 5500 kg (12,125 lb); IJ-22 5755 kg (12,687 lb)
Maximum take-off: IAR-93A 10326 kg (22,765 lb); IAR-93B 10900 kg (24,030 lb); J-22 11080 kg (24,427 lb); IJ-22 9500 kg (20,944 lb)

Performance (for IAR-93B normal take-off weight of 8400 kg/18,518 lb)
Maximum level speed: 586 kt (1086 km/h; 675 mph) at sea level
Maximum rate of climb: 3900 m (12,800 ft) per minute at sea level
Service ceiling: 13600 m (44,620 ft)
Take-off run: 800 m (2,625 ft)
Landing run: 1050 m (3,445 ft); 690 m (2,263 ft) with brake chute
Tactical radius: 270 nm (500 km) with one auxiliary fuel tank, hi-lo-hi
Max range: 722 nm (1337 km) in clean configuration at 9144 m (30,000 ft)
g limits: +8.0/-4.2

provided operational conversion/advanced training for the type.

Viper 633-47 engines were not initially available for production IAR-93Bs, so the first 15 aircraft delivered from 1982 were equipped with Viper 632-41s and known as IAR-93MBs (MB = *motor de baza* – basic engine). Aircraft 216 to 242 were production IAR-93Bs with Viper 633-47 engines and were delivered after 1987. All aircraft from 201 onwards had the ventral fins and inboard wing fences removed, and from 216 onwards the fuselage strakes were removed.

Seat testbed

A batch of six two-seaters (600 to 605) was finished and associated with the production batch of IAR-93B/MB. The first, No. 600, was assigned to CIZ and used for several purposes, such as flight testing the Romanian SC-HV-0 ejection seat, which was installed in the aft cockpit and built by Aerofina. For flight test measurement purposes, yellow scale markings

were painted on the sides of the aft fuselage (horizontal) and on the fin (vertical). Other flight tests necessitated the installation of small fixed foreplanes (canards) and occurred in 1991 in three different configurations: without canards (in July), with fixed canards at 0° incidence (in October) and at 2° incidence (in November). Results indicated that the configuration at 2° incidence provided better overall performance, including better turn rates.

Aircraft No. 605 was used as a demonstrator for an upgraded IAR-93, with a Collins avionics package (identical to that installed on IAR-99 No. 712) and a 'glass' cockpit. Flight tests in this configuration started in 1992.

IAR-93 in service

In 1981 the IAR-93 entered service with Regimentul 67 Vânâtoare-Bombardament (67th Fighter-Bomber Regiment) at Craiova airfield, with six aircraft on strength (including two-seat prototype 002) and 10 pilots certified for the type. The first sortie of a single-seat aircraft

On 28 June 1996 a sizeable number of Oraos was handed over by the JRV to the Yugoslav Aeronautical Musuem as the result of the November 1995 Dayton Peace Accords treaty which limited Yugoslavia to 155 combat aircraft. This INJ-22 (25606) was the aircraft used to test a maritime reconnaissance configuration.

with that unit was on 14 November 1981, by Lieutenant Colonel Paul Alexandrescu. At that time, single-seat aircraft 109 to 112, as well as

Romanian testbeds

The IAR-93DC two-seater 600 was fitted with small canards (left) in place of the nose strakes to test their effect on turn performance. The aircraft was tested with the canards at 0° and 2° incidence, with the results being plotted against the aircraft flown without canards. The aircraft is seen below in the CIZ hangar at Craiova in 1992, just after the test programme.

From 1992 IAR-93DC 605 (below) was used to trial an upgraded IAR-93 cockpit configuration. The front cockpit (right) featured a wide-angle head-up display and two 3-in (7.62-cm) monochrome multi-function displays.

This is the SIAR-93B simulator used to train IAR-93B pilots, developed by ICSIT-Av (later Simultec). This was derived from the SIAR-93A simulator which had been developed for the earlier variant.

This J-22 was assigned to the 238.LBE/82.AB at Cerklje ob Krki in Slovenia. After Slovenian forces attacked Cerklje air base with mortars during Slovenia's brief war for independence in June/July 1991, the Oraos were withdrawn but were employed on ground attack missions from bases outside Slovenia. They mainly used rockets and BL755 cluster bombs, although an attack with Durandal runway-cratering munitions against Ljubljana airport was aborted due to bad weather.

the two-seaters 005 to 008, had been delivered to Regimentul 67.

Deliveries continued in late 1981 and in the following year with the single-seat Preserie 1 aircraft 113 to 119 and Preserie 2s 150 to 154. At the end of 1982, 23 aircraft were in the inventory of Regimentul 67 and 27 pilots were

flying the type. On 7 March 1983 the aircraft, led by Colonel General Fabrikov, undertook combat exercises and live bombing with 100-kg (220-lb) and 250-kg (551-lb) bombs as well as rockets and guns, firing against ground targets in front of a delegation of the Warsaw Pact countries.

On 8 March 1983, IAR-93 Preserie 1 No. 113, flown by Major Ion Tănase, crashed on landing, following pilot error; the pilot ejected safely. On 23 August 1984, a formation of 12 IAR-93s took part in the military parade.

IAR-93A Preserie 1 No. 114 is now preserved at the Muzeul Aviatiei in Otopeni, and IAR-93A Preserie 2 No. 153 is at the Muzeul Militar National (National Military Museum) in Bucharest. Unusually, No. 153 has no wing leading-edge root extensions (LERXes), which were standard features on Preserie 2 aircraft.

Up to 1987, another 24 aircraft were delivered to Regimentul 67, including IAR-93 Preserie 2 Nos 155 to 160 and 163, and IAR-93MBs Nos 201 to 205, 207, 208, and 210 to 215.

After initial preparations in 1988, in the following year 10 IAR-93s were deployed to Regimentul 49 Vânătoare-Bombardament (49th Fighter-Bomber Regiment) at Ianca airfield, situated near the city of Brăila. They were returned to Craiova in 1990, when operations were stopped after IAR-93DC No. 601 was damaged. Between 1996 and 1997, 11 IAR-93MBs (Nos 201 to 211) and three two-seat IAR-93DC Preserie 2s (180, 182 and 183) were also assigned to Grupul 49 Vânătoare-Bombardament at Ianca airfield; they were later replaced in active service by IAR-99s and L–39ZAs. Some of the aircraft returned to Craiova, but a number of them (202, 207, 208 and 209) remain. At Ianca AB, the IAR-93s were used as interim replacements for the retired MiG-15s.

The Romanian IAR-93s never saw combat action, although between 23 and 24 December

IAR-93/Orao cockpit

Right: This 1990s vintage Orao cockpit shows noticeable differences when compared with the IAR-93 cockpits below, although the basic panel layout is similar. The primary flight instruments have a different arrangement, with the primary attitude indicator positioned higher in the Orao than in the IAR-93.

Above: This is the cockpit of an IAR-93A Preserie 1, fitted with a Martin-Baker Mk 6 ejection seat (production aircraft used the Mk 10). The gunsight is the ASP PFD-21 unit used in the MiG-21. The HSI instrument is missing from the panel.

Below: Taken with the seat removed, this photo shows the standard cockpit of the IAR-93MB. The instrument layout is entirely conventional with primary flight instruments grouped in the left-centre panel, and engine instruments to the right.

1989, during the Romanian revolution against the Communist regime, Regimentul 67 Vânătoare-Bombardament flew 17 sorties totalling 15 hours and 18 minutes. The aircraft were scrambled each time the airspace surveillance radars indicated unidentified light aircraft flying in the area.

In 1990, IAR-93s equipped Escadrilas 1, 2 and 3 of Regimentul 67 Vânătoare-Bombardament in Craiova, in addition to S-102s and MiG-15UTIs (replaced from 1991 by MiG-21s).

On 25 August 1992, IAR-93DC No. 602 stalled during evolution and was lost; the crew, Major Dan Cosăceanu and Captain Traian Neagoe, ejected safely. Between 1990 and 1995, the unit recorded 32 incidents with IAR-93s, half attributed to technical causes and a quarter to pilot error. On 17 October 1992, IAR-93DC Preserie 2 No. 184 with Major Ion Mârculescu and Second Lieutenant Nicolae Tâlpeanu started to bank after take-off due to defective installation of the aileron controls; the crew managed to land the aircraft safely.

On 1 September 1995, Grupul 67 Vânătoare-Bombardament (67th Fighter-Bomber Group) was established at Baza Aeriană 67 (67th Airbase), Craiova, by the reorganisation of Regimentul 67 Vânătoare-Bombardament.

In the afternoon of 9 July 1997, IAR-93MB No. 210 was loaded with the SEBAV sub-munitions dispenser containing live M.648 ammunition. The ammunition exploded during ground testing, killing 16 people (five from the 67th Airbase) and destroying the aircraft. On 9 April 1998, a single-seat IAR-93B from Grupul 67 crashed near the village of Ghercesti, Olt; the pilot, Commander Ion Mârculescu, ejected safely. This is the last known crash of an IAR-93 before the type was grounded later that year.

Weapons

IAR-93 armament consists of two airframe-mounted 23-mm GSh-23L twin-barrelled cannon on the lower front fuselage, below the engine air intakes, with 200 rounds per gun (also installed on Yugoslav Oraos). The aircraft has five external stores stations, of which the inboard underwing pair and fuselage centreline station are plumbed for 540-litre (119-Imp gal) drop tanks and are each stressed for loads up to 500 kg (1,102 lb). The outboard underwing stations are stressed for up to 300 kg (661 lb) each, giving a maximum external stores load of 1500 kg (3,307 lb) on the IAR-93A and 2500 kg (5,511 lb) on the IAR-93B. Typical weapon loads, on single or multiple launchers, can include free-fall bombs such as the BE-50

(50 kg/110 lb); up to 16 BE-100 or BEF-100 (100 kg/220 lb); up to four BM-250 or BEM-250 (250 kg/551 lb); up to five BA-500, BE-500 or BM-500 (500 kg/1,102 lb); four LPR 57-16 (UB-16) or LPR 57-32 (UB-32) rocket launchers each with 16 or 32 57-mm rockets; four LPR 2-122 launchers each with two PRND-122 rockets of 122-mm calibre; and a centreline GSh-23L cannon pod. Some IAR-93Bs were equipped to carry K-13 (AA-2 'Atoll') air-to-air missiles on the underwing stations. The LPR-57-16 launchers can be carried in pairs on GA adapters, the 250-kg bombs can be carried in pairs on LMB 2x250 bomb racks, and the 100-kg bombs on triple (LMB 3x100) or quadruple (LMB 4x100) bomb racks.

For ground pilot training, the specialised section within ICSIT-Av (as INCREST was also known) started to build simulators for the IAR-93 (in the 1990s this facility was restructured as an independent company for the design and production of simulators, and named Simultec). The SIAR-93A2 (used for training pilots for the IAR-93A) is now displayed at the Muzeul Aviatiei. Between 1986 and 1987, SIAR-93B1 and SIAR-93B2 were built for training pilots destined for the IAR-93B.

Paint schemes and camouflage of the Romanian aircraft differed from batch to batch, but were variations of brown and yellow spots on a dark green background on the upper surfaces, with light blue on the lower surface, having the numbers painted in white with a red outline on the fuselage nose sides. Some IAR-93MBs had the numbers painted in red, outlined with white. For example, No. 200 was painted white with red wingtips, with the dorsal spine and the number in black; No. 605

Information published in Romanian magazines revealed that an extensive upgrade was intended for the IAR-93, including the redesign of the forward fuselage for a ranging radar installation; the addition of fixed canards (as tested on aircraft No. 600); the redesign of the wingtip for the installation of a missile launch rail; and the incorporation of an integrated aircraft ladder. Further modifications were to be made to the hydraulic system (replacement of seals), and the main landing gear would be redesigned. The introduction of fly-by-wire (FBW) controls was also intended. The cockpit was to be equipped with HOTAS controls, HUD with UFCP and displays. The avionics package would include an inertial navigation system (INS) coupled with a GPS, and VOR/ILS, DME and Radar Warning Receiver (RWR) systems were to be installed.

The final Romanian production version was the IAR-93B, which had the definitive Viper 633-47 engines installed and dispensed with the ventral fins, nose strakes and inboard wing fences. This aircraft was one of the last built, and is displayed with an array of weaponry. On the inner wing pylons are twin LPR 2-122 launchers, each holding two 122-mm (4.8-in) PRND-122 rockets. The outer wing pylons mount UB-16 rocket pods, also known as LPR 57-16 (each holding 16 57-mm rockets). On the ground are two more UB-16s, four 500-kg (1,102-lb) bombs, five 250-kg (551-lb) bombs and 12 100-kg (220-lb) bombs carried on LMB triple racks, along with 23-mm ammunition for the two GSh-23L twin-barrelled cannon and the maximum load of 64 57-mm rockets (representing four UB-16 pods).

had a desert-type camouflage. Some IAR-93s had the tips of the nose and the tailpipe painted red, and prototype 001 had 'IAR-93' written on the air intakes. The prototype was already wearing camouflage for the first flight, with the Romanian flag on the rudder.

A total of 74 IAR-93s (all versions) was declared to be in the inventory of the Romanian Air Force. They have been grounded since 1998 and it is most likely that they will be retired soon. Around 13 are IAR-93DC two-seaters. Most served with two squadrons of Grupul 67 Vânãtoare-Bombardament based at Craiova and with the 49th Airbase Ianca, and some, like No. 200 and No. 600, were used by CIZ for flight testing.

Even before the IAR-93 was grounded, its close air support role was partially assumed by a few standard IAR-99 combat jet trainers. A total of 17 aircraft was delivered to the Romanian AF, of which 15 are still in service at the 49th and 67th Airbases.

The most important close air support asset for the Romanian AF is now the MiG-21M/MF Lancer-A single-seater and MiG-21UM Lancer-B two-seater, which were upgraded to close air support configuration. Fitted with modern avionics, the Lancer can use a wide range of modern weapons, including laser- and IR-guided smart bombs. The Lancer-A and -B are in service at four airbases (the 95th AB at Bacãu, 86th AB at Fetesti/Borcea, 93rd AB at Timisoara Giarmata and 71st AB at Campia Turzii).

Intentions for upgrade

In 1996, the Romanian Ministry of Defence published a document relating to long-term procurement priorities, stating the intention to upgrade its IAR-93 fleet with an undisclosed foreign partner.

Yugoslav NJ-22 two-seater Orao 2D production amounted to 12 new-build aircraft and six conversions of earlier machines. Unlike their Romanian counterparts (IAR-93B), the Orao 2s retained ventral fins.

The upgrade of the weapons system would include the introduction of laser-guided weapons, together with the installation of specialised pods (such as ECM), as well as the use of different Western and Eastern weapons (A-91, K-13, R-60 air-to air missiles, UB-32 and LPR-122 with three 122-mm rocket launchers, SEBAV sub-munitions dispensers, etc.). Another proposal was to bring the existing engines to Viper 680 standard, increasing maximum thrust by around 20 per cent.

The Yugoslavs intended similar upgrades, but, like those of Romania, they never came to fruition. Some speculative proposals were published on the internet, proposing as power-plant either the RR Viper 680 or Russian RD-35, featuring the installation of a Kopyo radar, together with the use of advanced AA missiles (R-73, R-77) and ASM (H-31).

Service in former Yugoslavia

After the break-up of the former Yugoslavia in the early 1990s, Orao aircraft were withdrawn with the rest of the JNA (Yugoslav People's Army) units and equipment. After 1992, the Yugoslav air force became known as Ratno Vazduhoplovstvo i ProtivVazdusna Odbrana Vojske Jugoslavije (abbreviated RV i PVO, meaning Air Force and Air Defence of the Yugoslav Army). It operated several squadrons of Oraos, as follows:
■ 241.LBAE (Lovacko-Bombarderska Avijacijska Eskadrila – Fighter-Bomber Aviation Squadron) 'Tigrovi' (Tigers). The J-22 was used from 1986, based at Ladjevci AB.
■ 252.LBAE 'Kurjaci sa Usca' ('The Wolves From the Mouth of the River'), based at Batajnica AB near Belgrade – from 1996 to 1997

Left: A feature of the design since part way through the pre-production series are the LERXes (leading-edge root extensions), plainly visible on these IJ-22s of the 353.IAE, Yugoslav air force.

it used the J-22s received from the 242.LBAE in exchange for the G-4. The 242.LBAE used J-22s until 1997 when it exchanged them with 252.LBAE for G-4 trainers, based at Golubovci AB, Podgorica.

Both 241.LBAE and 252.LBAE are subordinated to 98. Lovacko-Bombarderski Avijacijski Puk (98th Fighter-Bomber Aviation Regiment).
■ 353.IAE (IAE – Izvidjacka Avijacijaska Eskadrila – Reconnaissance Aviation Squadron) 'Sokolovi' (Hawks) was the first unit to receive Oraos, in 1982. It uses IJ-22s and INJ-22s and is based at Ladjevci AB, Krajevo.

Bosnia-Herzegovina (Srspka Republic) has five to seven J-22s on strength, among them J-22 No. 25109; two NJ-22 two-seaters were lost in accidents in 1993 and 1995. The unit has been reported as the 238.LBAE/92.AB.

The Yugoslav Orao aircraft takes weapon loads similar to those of the IAR-93. All four wing stations are stressed for 500 kg (1,102 lb) and the fuselage station for 800 kg (1,763 lb), giving a maximum external stores capacity of 2800 kg (6,173 lb). Typical weapon loads, placed on single or multiple carriers, can include 50-kg, 100-kg, 250-kg or 500-kg bombs; four PLAB-350 napalm bombs (each 360 kg/794 lb); five BL755 bomblet dispensers; 16 BRZ-127 rockets; L-57-16MD (16 x 57-mm) or

L-128-04 (four x 128-mm) rocket pods; five 500-kg AM-500 sea mines; two launch rails for AGM-65B Maverick or Yugoslav-developed Grom air-to-surface missiles.

All J-22 versions in use with the Yugoslav AF have a standard camouflage consisting of green and grey on upper surfaces (as on Royal Air Force aircraft) with a light blue underside. Only aircraft No. 25101 was painted overall white with red stripes on both fuselage sides.

Orao in combat

The Oraos from the former Yugoslavia were heavily involved in different wars in the area, mainly on ground attack missions but also for the destruction of cruise missiles.

During the war in Croatia, only one Orao was acknowledged as being lost. On 19 September 1991 at 18.15, NJ-22 No. 25508 crashed near Ferkuševac, having been hit by a Strela 2M SAM over Dakovo. The pilot, Lieutenant Colonel Begić Muše, the commander of 172.LBAP, ejected and was taken prisoner. At least one other aircraft was destroyed on landing during the war in Bosnia-Herzegovina.

INJ-22M – maritime surveillance

Hitherto unknown in the West, the INJ-22M (25606) was a testbed for a maritime surveillance version of the Orao which was trialled around 1984. The most obvious feature externally was the cylindrical fairing under the fuselage which housed an Ericsson side-looking Doppler surveillance radar. The fate of the programme is unknown, although the aircraft itself was one of those 'donated' to the Aeronautical Museum as a result of the Dayton Peace Accord, albeit without the radar fairing.

Above: The rear cockpit of the INJ-22M featured a large screen for the Ericsson radar display and no instruments. A large removable box and rubber hood shrouded the display.

Romania's supersonic ambitions

In addition to developing a modern aviation industry in the late 1960s, Romania also established a strong research and design capability, concentrated within the ICPAS design institute (known as IMFCA from 1970, INCREST from 1977, and later renamed ICSIT-Av). Facilities for advanced research were created during the 1970s, and included a Mach 3-capable wind tunnel.

The policy of the Communist leadership of Ceausescu was to create a self-sufficient aviation industry. This encompassed the production in-country of most of the components for all categories of aircraft, ranging from gliders and light aircraft, to airliners and combat aircraft. The first important achievement of INCREST was the IAR-93, designed and built in co-operation with Yugoslavia. The later IAR-99 jet trainer was the first military aircraft of entirely Romanian design.

In the late 1970s, initial studies for a supersonic fighter were begun under the leadership of Dipl. Eng. Dumitru Badea. The **IAR-95**, a high-wing monoplane, was to be equipped with a single engine, lateral air intakes and an aft fuselage section similar to that of the F-16. One of the proposed designs featured two fins.

The proposed powerplant was the military version of the Rolls-Royce Spey. The intention was to obtain the engines from the People's Republic of China, to which a production licence was granted by Rolls-Royce in 1975, under the local designation WS-9. However, the intended production rate of WS-9s was not achieved (only four engines were completed between 1976 and 1980) due to technical problems encountered by the Chinese. Faced with this situation, the idea to use the Spey in the IAR-95 was abandoned.

The supersonic fighter programme was restarted in the early 1980s under the leadership of Colonel Eng. Constantin Rosca using the Tumanskii R-29-300 turbojet, which was available from the USSR. The first layout of the new design was designated **IAR-101** and had a general layout similar to that of its predecessor, but with a much thicker fuselage, and four hardpoints under the wings (instead of two on the IAR-95).

The next step was the **IAR-S**; following the request of the then-General Director of INCREST, Constantin Teodorescu, several models were built and tested in the wind tunnel. They featured a single engine

with a single fin, or two tails and two fins, or were single- and two-seaters. The two-seater was presented as a multi-role aircraft and had some similarities with the later Chinese Super 7 project. An attempt to establish a joint programme with Yugoslavia failed. That country began its own supersonic lightweight fighter project, the Novi Avion.

The supersonic programme was very ambitious and posed a real challenge for the Romanian aviation

This model shows the IAR-S in two-seat multi-role form. This layout formed the basis for the unbuilt IAR-95ME technology demonstrator.

industry. To test its ability to produce such an aircraft, the decision was taken to build a technology demonstrator known as the **IAR-95ME** (Model Experimental) with the layout of the two-seater IAR-S.

The demonstrator had to be built by IAv Bucharest in Baneasa and a special branch of INCREST moved to new facilities created near the factory. The aircraft reached the detailed design stage and a full-scale mock-up of the future aircraft was started, but in 1988, for financial reasons, the whole programme was definitively cancelled.

IAR-95ME technical data
Length: 16.0 m (52 ft 5.75 in)
Wing span: 9.3 m (30 ft 6 in)
Height: 5.45 m (17 ft 10.5 in)
Wing area: 27.9 m² (300 sq ft)
Empty weight: 7880 kg (17,372 lb)
Maximum take-off weight: 15200 kg (33,510 lb)
Maximum weapons load: 3200 kg (7,055 lb)
Powerplant: one Tumanskii R-29-300 turbojet rated at 122 kN (27,420 lb) with afterburner

Above: This IAR-S design showed great similarity to the earlier IAR-95 configuration.

One of the more ambitious IAR-S configurations had wedge intakes for the two engines, inward-canted twin fins and an area-ruled fuselage.

According to Lieutenant Colonel Sreto Malinovich, the commanding officer of 241.LBAE, during the war against Yugoslavia that started on 24 March 1999, the 98th Fighter-

In 1998 the Romanian IAR-93 force was grounded, its attack role having passed to the IAR-99 Soim and the Lancer-A (upgraded MiG-21). In July 2001 over 60 were in open storage at Craiova, this line-up numbering around 25. The aircraft nearest nearest the camera is the second pre-production IAR-93DC Preserie 1.

Bomber Regiment provided the bulk of close air support for units of the 3rd Army. Tasks were assigned to this unit in total secrecy, for earlier experience had indicated that breaks in communication were possible and that the enemy could discover Yugoslav intentions. Orders were passed only to those who would fulfil the tasks.

Knowing the strengths of the enemy's fighters and the abilities of the Yugoslav forces to

defend against them, the pilots used low-flying tactics and arrived at the target area from different directions. This proved wise, since on only one occasion did the coalition fighters succeed in being in a position to shoot the Yugoslav aircraft – too late, though, since they were in the zone controlled by Yugoslav air defence, and they left the area.

One J-22 was lost on the first night of the war upon return from a combat sortie. It

Three Yugoslav air force (RV i PVO) squadrons continued to fly Oraos at least until the Allied Force NATO operation commenced on 24 March 1999. Two operate J-22s on fighter-bomber duties while the third – the 353.IAE – uses the older IJ-22s (illustrated) for reconnaissance. An underfuselage camera pod is carried, with windows for downward- and forward-facing cameras.

crashed into a hillside, killing the pilot, Lieutenant Colonel Zirota Djuric. Another aircraft was damaged, but was considered to be repairable.

The number of Orao aircraft that survived the war is difficult to estimate – the figures released are eight IJ-22s and two INJ-22 two-seaters, and a number of J-22s and NJ-22s.

Epilogue

During the 1980s both countries made unsuccessful attempts to export the aircraft. The second J-22 (25102), wearing the air show registration number 407, was displayed at the Paris air show in 1985. The price of a Yugoslav J-22 was around $US4 million. In 1988, the Romanians proposed the IAR-93 to Iran. Iranian pilots, who praised the aircraft's performance, flew it at Craiova. A deal was not concluded, possibly due to events that transpired at the end of 1989.

Production was intended to comprise 165 aircraft for each of the two countries. This was divided into 12 lots, the first being eight aircraft for Yugoslavia and seven for Romania (including two two-seaters for each country); the following 10 lots were to have 14 aircraft each (including two to five two-seaters); and the last to have 17 aircraft each (including three two-seaters). Unfortunately, this was never accomplished.

Following the outbreak of the war in Yugoslavia and the UN embargo, the IAR-93 programme was put on hold in Romania, with several airframes at different stages of construction. The last aircraft delivered to the Romanian

AF were from the fourth and fifth lots. Unfinished Romanian airframes were kept in storage until 2000, when they were scrapped.

In the early 1990s the former INCREST was divided into several institutes. Design authority for various aircraft, including for IAR-93, went to INCAS (the National Institute for Aerospace Research 'Elie Carafoli'), which also holds the patent for the type.

Orao production ceased in 1992, when the plant at Mostar was dismantled. The last Yugoslav aircraft was delivered in February 1992. The UTVA factory at Pancevo subse-

quently assumed responsibility for the development and maintenance of Orao aircraft.

Three decades after its inception, the aircraft is in the twilight of its career. The IAR-93 is grounded and awaiting official retirement. The Orao is still in service, but in small numbers in countries that were heavily affected by the wars of the last decade. The aircraft represented an important step in the development of the aviation industries and of the air forces of Romania and Yugoslavia, and although it still had potential, it fell victim to political events in the area.

Danut Vlad

This J-22 is one of those probably converted from IJ-22 standard. It is surrounded by some of the weaponry available (including rocket pods, BL755 cluster bombs and indigenous FAB-100/-250 bombs) and carries an AGM-65 Maverick under the outer wing pylon. Other weapons associated with the Orao are the Durandal anti-runway munition and the Grom (AS-7 'Kerry' version).

Senior Bowl
From the Shadow of Black

Within Kelly Johnson's family of 'Blackbirds', the smallest and least known wonder was, and continues to be, the D-21. In both forms (the M/D-21 Tagboard programme and the D-21B/B-52H Senior Bowl operational programme), this unmanned 'Blackbird' has been carefully hidden behind a veil of secrecy for over 40 years.

Francis Gary Powers and his U-2 were lost over the central area of the former Soviet Union on 1 May 1960. The long history of manned overflights came to a screeching halt when Congress responded by mandating that all such missions (over the former Soviet Union and its allies during peacetime) cease immediately. Necessity thus demanded the development of technology to enable unmanned flights over hostile territories.

Many meetings with senior Central Intelligence Agency and key Air Force personnel were held to discuss the loss of the CIA's U-2 and to brainstorm possible alternatives. Kelly Johnson of Lockheed came up with the winning concept, which was an unmanned extension of the existing A-12 Oxcart programme. On 10 October 1962, Lockheed was authorised to make a study, which eventually spawned the Tagboard programme. Johnson was also given the go-ahead from the CIA to begin a formal study regarding the development of what culminated in the D-21. The initial meeting with Marquardt was held on 24 October 1962, at which Kelly Johnson, Ben Rich and Rus Daniel discussed engine requirements.

Lockheed had extensive experience with the ramjet-powered X-7A-1, X-7A-2 and X-7A-3 test vehicle series, and a close working relationship with Marquardt, a neighbouring company in the San Fernando Valley. Together, they determined that the unmanned drone could be powered by a highly-modified Marquardt RJ43-MA-11 ramjet engine, formerly used on the retired USAF/Boeing Bomarc IM-99B air defence weapon.

The D-21 engine is properly identified as an XRJ43-MA20S-4. The Bomarc A used Marquardt RJ43-MA-3 ramjet engines, and the Bomarc B used two externally-mounted RJ43-MA-11s. Each MA-11 engine had a fixed-geometry, Mach 2.35, isentropic spike inlet. The engine's integral combustion chambers/exit nozzles were designed for relatively low cruise altitudes and therefore did not require high-expansion-ratio nozzles. The ignition system in each engine consisted of two pyrotechnic flares. There was no re-ignition capability. The MA-11's fuel control and flame holder combustion limits would not allow operation at high altitudes.

The externally-mounted MA-11 engines on the Bomarc B used an all-pneumatic fuel control system that maintained a constant Mach number of two selectable speeds, as determined by pressure signals from the built-in inlet. These engines had the ability to function

as an independent external powerplant on any vehicle that could reach sufficient speed to allow efficient inlet operation. The MA-11 was developed in supersonic wind tunnels at Marquardt's Van Nuys, California, test facility; flight tested on the Lockheed X-7A-3 at Holloman AFB, Alamogordo, New Mexico; and deployed operationally on the Bomarc B.

Power for high-altitude cruise

The MA20S-4 engine employed in the D-21 used many MA-11 components but was modified to operate at lower pressures and higher temperatures. The S-4 was immersed in the body of the D-21 and had no inlet structures of its own, instead using the D-21's inlet system. The engine's centre body and main structure remained to house the fuel control, fuel pump, fuel injector nozzles and flame-holder assemblies. The flame-holder system was redesigned to allow stable combustion at extreme high-altitude, high-temperature and low-pressure situations. Ignition was by TEB (Tri Ethyl Boron) to enable re-ignition in the event of flame-out. The combustion chamber/exit nozzle was redesigned to provide for the much greater expansion ratio required for high-altitude cruising. The design also incorporated an ejector system for engine structure cooling. Of interest is that, until the advent of the D-21, no ramjet had ever powered any craft for more than a few minutes. The D-21's XRJ-MA20S-4 would be powered up during its entire flight of over 1.5 hours.

Area 51 at Groom Dry Lake, Nevada, was the principal flight test site for the Lockheed D-21 programme, as it had been for the U-2 and A-12, among others. This view is from the 1960s, at about the time the D-21s were under evaluation.

The pneumatic fuel control computer was modified to function at much lower pressures and higher temperatures. The input pressure sensors were redesigned to accept air pressures from the D-21 inlet and to provide continual, full-power operation, limited only by the D-21's inlet conditions and mission parameters. The fuel flow schedule, pumps, controls and injector nozzles were all updated to permit accurate flow control and injection at the much lower air flow requirements of extremely high altitudes.

By November 1962, the drone's design was beginning to take shape. Kelly Johnson outlined the basic requirements for the overall system. The design speed would be Mach 3.3 to 3.5 with an operational altitude over target between 87,000 and 95,000 ft (26517 and 28956 m). The D-21 would be designed with a very small radar cross-section and a photographic resolution capability of less than 6 in (15 cm). It would have a combat range of at least 3,000 nm (5556 km) and a recoverable payload bay (with camera) weighing approximately 425 lb (193 kg).

With these requirements laid down, Kelly Johnson's smallest Blackbird began development under the capable guidance of the Skunk Works chief of manufacturing, Bob Murphy.

By 7 December 1962, Lockheed had

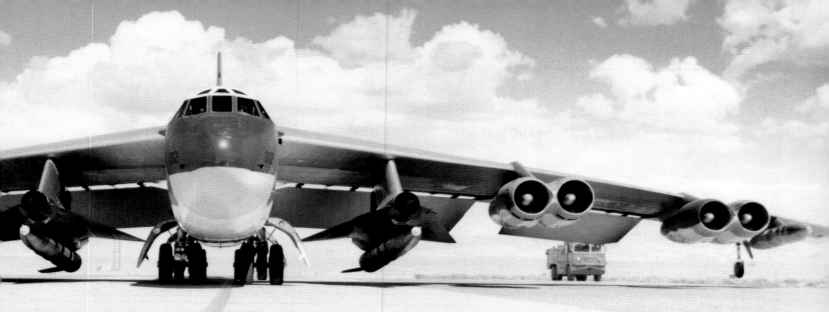

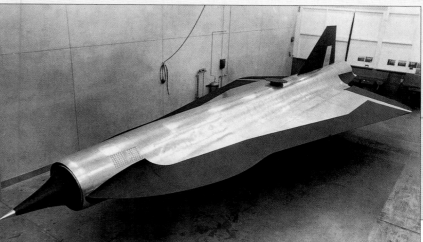

In its first guise (Tagboard), the D-21 drone was launched at Mach 3 from the back of a converted A-12 (below). The problems associated with such high-speed launches were considerable, leading to the Tagboard programme being terminated following the tragic loss of a mother-ship and the Launch Control Officer. A more pragmatic approach was adopted for Senior Bowl, involving subsonic launch from a B-52 and a rocket booster to propel the drone fast enough and high enough for the ramjet to be started and the drone sent on its way. In the main picture above, B-52H 61-0021 is seen prior to a captive-carry flight at Area 51 in September 1967, clutching its precious cargo of two D-21Bs and their rocket boosters beneath specially-developed wing pylons.

Above: On 10 October 1962 the CIA gave Lockheed Skunk Works the go-ahead for the drone programme. By 7 December this full-scale mock-up was ready to be shipped to Area 51 for radar cross-section evaluation. Note the angular fin/fuselage joint.

completed a full-scale mock-up including RCS (Radar Cross Section) simulation; the D-21 was then sent to the test site for further evaluation. Meanwhile, Marquardt had a very successful run of the Bomarc engine in its wind tunnel, simulating high-speed flight conditions. A large number of Skunk Works D-21 crew members, together with Marquardt staff, were in attendance at this event, and all were amazed that the engine could be shut off for as long as 45 seconds and still restart. This feat was possible because of the very hot engine parts.

On 20 March 1963, Lockheed was given an official CIA letter of contract for the D-21. (At this early date, the D-21 was still referred to as the Q-12; that designation was later changed.) The contract gave Lockheed responsibility for the navigation systems, the ramjet and the airframe.

The programme reached another milestone in September 1963, when Marquardt demonstrated a very good engine run to the highest

temperatures required. The company also appeared to be proceeding well in the development of the MA20S-4 variant.

Tagboard project

The D-21 was the heart of this programme and was designed as an extremely high-speed, high-altitude reconnaissance vehicle – in a sense, a much smaller, unmanned version of the A-12, with similar capabilities. It was considered to be a 'one-way aircraft', meaning that each D-21 would make one flight only and then self-destruct. While still in the design stages, two Lockheed A-12s were modified to carry the D-21 on a top-mounted dorsal pylon located on the rear centreline between the engines and the vertical stabilisers. A second cockpit was installed for the D-21 launch control officer (LCO) in the area of the A-12's 'Q' bay. The 'Q' bay was already pressurised and refrigerated, making the modification relatively easy.

The A-12 became known as the M-21, the letter M indicating that it was the Mother aircraft; the D in D-21 designated it as the Daughter aircraft. The 21 designation was an intentional reversal of the number 12, intended to reduce the possibility of Skunk Works personnel confusing the A-12 with the M-21 in documentation or security issues.

At this point, the Tagboard programme overall was progressing rather slowly. By mid-May 1965, the M/D-21 had achieved Mach 2.6, but not launch speeds. Problems had arisen from using the Hamilton Standard inlet control system in conjunction with Pratt & Whitney J58s. Between May and 21 October 1965, Kelly Johnson decided to put the newer 34,000-lb (151.21-kN) thrust J58 engines into M-21 number 135, and also converted from the Hamilton Standard inlet control system to one designed by Johnson's crew.

On 5 March 1966, a D-12 finally launched from the back of a Mother aircraft. The launch itself was a great success, but the D-21 was lost about 120 nm (222 km) from the launch point; nonetheless, the exercise demonstrated that Lockheed had developed a successful launch technique. Kelly Johnson was quoted as saying, "This was the most dangerous manoeuvre we have ever been involved in, in any airplane I have ever worked on." In this groundbreaking mission, Bill Park was at the helm and Keith Beswick was the LCO.

This overview shows a partially completed D-21 on the spine of an M-21. Noteworthy are the RAM wedges in the M-21's wing, and the outer wing panel/outer nacelle assembly which is partially cranked up fro access to the engines. The fixture on the D-21's spine allowed it to be lifted on and off the M-21 by an overhead gantry.

D-21 501 is about to be lifted on to the back of M-21 60-6940/134 in preparation for the first captive flight. Just visible on the right is the wingtip of the second M-21, 60-6941/135. The location is Hangar 1 at Area 51 and the date was 20 December 1964, two days prior to the first flight. Even at this top-secret location, security around the Tagboard programme was extremely tight, as evidenced by the security wall behind.

Following that very successful first launch, Kelly Johnson (accompanied by Dick Boehme) went to Point Mugu, California, to witness the second launch of a D-21, number 506. Once again, Johnson was delighted with the launch. The D-21 flew over 1,200 nm (2222 km) while holding course to within 0.5 mile (0.8 km) for the entire flight, reaching 90,000 ft (27432 m) and a speed of Mach 3.3. It came to an abrupt halt and fell out of the sky, however, when a hydraulic pump overheated and failed. The failure was due to running the pump unpressurised several times during checkout.

At this point in the programme, Johnson proposed substituting a B-52H as a new launch platform, with the D-21 being propelled to speed and altitude by a solid rocket booster. Johnson's goal was to get the greatest benefit from the programme at the lowest cost.

On 16 June 1966, Lockheed staged the third and most successful D-21 launch from an M-21. It flew almost 1,600 nm (2963 km), making eight programmed turns (in order to stay within a line of sight from the tracking ship). Everything went as planned except the ejection of the package due to an electronic failure. To quote Johnson, "It was a very successful go."

On 30 July 1966, on the fourth and final launch from the M-21, D-21 number 504 suffered an asymmetrical unstart and crashed back into the Mother aircraft. The collision resulted in the death of one of the crew

members aboard the M-21: Ray Torick, the LCO, survived the mid-air collision and successfully ejected from the stricken aircraft, but drowned in the Pacific Ocean. Bill Park, the Lockheed test pilot at the controls of the M-21, survived and went on to become the senior test pilot for Lockheed's Skunk Works.

This was the Blackbird programme's first fatality and it proved to be the demise of the Tagboard programme. The follow-on programme relied on a more conventional launch platform – the tried and proven Boeing B-52H Stratofortress.

Overview of the B-52H/D-21B

In conjunction with the CIA and senior Air Force staffers (under the direction of Kelly Johnson), plans were advanced for Lockheed to modify the D-21 to be launched from an Air Force/Boeing B-52H Stratofortress. The B-52 had already proved its success with NASA, launching hundreds of craft up to and including the North American X-15A-2, so it was accepted as being potentially safer than the previous Tagboard scheme. This programme eventually evolved into Project Senior Bowl (initially designated as 'A' Flight and later as the 4200th Support Squadron at Beale AFB, California). The 4200th, although designated as a squadron, was actually a wing-level unit with direct and primary responsibility to Strategic Air Command (SAC) headquarters. Administrative

functions were through the 14th Air Division at Beale, while operational functions were handled through SAC and other still-classified hierarchy.

Configuring the drop of the drone was the easier part of the transition, as similar operations had already met with success. Of greater difficulty were the challenges of it achieving a speed of Mach 3 at 80,000 ft (24384 m), and ensuring a safe separation of the booster without damage to the 'Tag', as it was called throughout the entire programme. Much work also needed to be done on fine-tuning the remote engine start-up, and on all aspects of the D-21's navigational system.

On 12 December 1966, the Air Force delivered the programme's first Boeing B-52H (assigned Air Force serial number 61-0021) to the Lockheed Palmdale facility at Air Force Plant 42, Site 2. A few months later, it was joined by number 60-0036. Both B-52H aircraft had undergone extensive modifications to enable them to carry and launch the D-21B.

In its proposed configuration, the Senior Bowl B-52H/D-21B combination, with the D-21's combat radius of over 3,000 nm (5556 km), could conceivably cover any location, anywhere in the world, with its global reach capabilities. Its operational altitude rendered it relatively safe from interception.

The Lockheed D-21B and modified Boeing B-52H combination formed the nucleus of Senior Bowl operations from January 1968 until 23 July 1971, when the project was terminated.

Senior Bowl aircraft modifications

Senior Bowl called for the modified D-21 to be carried on an underwing pylon, similar to

The first M/D-21 nestles between Hangars 1 and 2 at Groom Lake, just prior to its first flight on 22 December 1964. M-21 '940 was powered by early YJ58 engines and had Hamilton Standard inlet control systems. This combination prevented the M-21 achieving the necessary Mach 3 for D-21 launch. The second M-21, '941, had the later 'K'-model J58s and Lockheed-designed inlet systems, which produced the desired performance. Consequently, it was '941 that was used for the four D-21 launches.

The aerodynamic fairings originally designed for the D-21's inlet were to be jettisoned explosively. This view after a captive-carry flight graphically shows the result.

that used for launching the X-15 from the NASA/Boeing NB-52B. Due to the change in launch aircraft and the subsequent modifications to the D-21, the programme warranted a new designation. In the absence of mock-ups, models or working drawings of the D-21A (although some casual sketches may well have been made), the programme's progression officially went straight from D-21 to D-21B.

The major modifications to the two B-52H Senior Bowl aircraft encompassed the elimination of the electronic countermeasures operator and tail gunner's panels at the upper-rear crew station, and the installation of identical launch control panels for the D-21Bs on the right and/or left pylons. Two camera-mounting stations were installed in the B-52H's left and right forward wheel wells, holding a set of 35-mm very-high-speed cameras used to record the launch of the D-21B from the B-52H. The cameras were aimed at the D-21B from different angles and with a variety of lenses to capture the D-21B as it dropped from the pylon. The cameras' film magazines held 1,000 ft (305 m) of colour film and ran at a speed of about 100 in (254 cm) per second. In addition to the fuselage-mounted cameras, a wide-angle, downward-looking, high-speed camera was mounted inside each pylon to film the D-21B as it dropped away from the aircraft. The cameras would run for about 10 seconds, though the reality, of course, was a virtually instantaneous action with only a few seconds passing until the drone was out of sight of the camera's eye. When played back on a normal projector at 16 in (40 cm) per second, the film provided an exceptional slow-motion picture of the launch. This documentation, viewed millisecond by millisecond, was exceedingly useful in diagnosing any problems that might have occurred during the launch. The addition of special pylons, telemetry gear and communications systems, together with the associated wiring and instrumentation, completed the modification of the aircraft.

All D-21B vehicles launched by 'A' Flight/4200th Support Squadron B-52Hs were from the starboard pylon only, and the port pylon station was never used during operational launches. A number of publications have shown pictures of the D-21B hanging from both pylons; most likely, these photographs were of sorties flown by the Skunk Works.

The Marquardt RJ43-MA20S-4 ramjet engine powered both the D-21 and the B-52-launched D-21B. When released from the pylon of the subsonic B-52H, the D-21B needed a rocket booster capable of propelling it to above Mach 1.5, at which speed the ramjet would light. The nosecone of the booster was fitted with a Marquardt B-4 supersonic ram air turbine to provide the electrical and hydraulic power necessary during the drop and boost phase. Lockheed's Missile and Space Division in Sunnyvale, California, developed this unique propulsion system.

Once the D-21B was installed on the B-52H starboard pylon, the rocket booster was mounted to the underside of the D-21B using the original connecting points where the D-21 had formerly been attached to the back of the M-21.

The B-52H, with its D-21B and booster mounted on the right pylon, was then ready to take off for a sortie. At a precise, pre-planned time and geographic location, the LCO onboard the B-52H would start the sequence of operations by first dropping the D-21B from the pylon. Following separation from the pylon, the booster would ignite and then propel the D-21B to a speed in excess of Mach 3.0, at or above 75,000 ft (22860 m). After a burn time of about 90 seconds, the booster would separate from the D-21B via explosive bolts, and the D-21B would begin its programmed solo sortie.

'A' Flight and the 4200th

In the summer and early autumn of 1967, Strategic Air Command began assembling the nucleus of the Air Force unit that would prepare, launch, fly, recover and maintain the D-21Bs being carried by the modified B-52H aircraft. Assignments were levied throughout SAC for approximately 180 officers and airmen with the following skills:

■ Those personnel who would fly or work on the B-52H only
■ Those personnel who would work on the D-21B only
■ Those few personnel who would be involved in both the B-52H and D-21B programmes
■ A small, specially trained component of Security Police that initially would be responsible only to 'A' Flight (later, it would support the 4200th Support Squadron)
■ Supply, administrative and other support personnel who would not be directly involved with either the B-52H or D-21B programmes,

Two views from the first captive flight on 22 December 1964 show '940 and D-21 501 over the Nevada ranges. The photograph below was the first to be released, and was cropped at the bottom to avoid showing Area 51. The D-21 is fitted with aerodynamic fairings over the intake and nozzle to reduce drag, but the problems with jettisoning these safely prior to launch proved insurmountable, and they were discarded for the four launches. The D-21 was not forcibly ejected, but was released to float free. The first three launches were undertaken with the M-21 in a shallow bunt to aid this process: the fourth was made in straight and level flight, with tragic consequences.

The first of the M-21s had only the cockpit area and composite panels painted black, the titanium structure being left unpainted. The second M-21 was painted black all over with the exception of its rudders.

but who would make important contributions to these projects.

In addition to the Air Force personnel who would comprise the bulk of the staff, many Lockheed and vendor-support and advisory personnel became part of the team.

The requirements for all personnel were extremely stringent. The Air Force was, in effect, handpicking these individuals in order to put together the very best support for Senior Bowl. In November 1967, for example, Glenn Chapman, a staff sergeant avionics specialist (and former U-2 sensor specialist) then stationed at K.I. Sawyer AFB, Michigan, received a new assignment. When Chapman asked about where he was being sent and the nature of his next job, he was informed only that the assignment was for 'A' Flight at Beale AFB, California. When Chapman further inquired about the numerical designation of his new outfit, he was again very simply told only that it was 'A' Flight, 14th Strategic Aerospace Division (SAC) at Beale AFB, California – and nothing else!

When Chapman arrived at Beale for in-processing on 3 January 1968, he was amazed to find that the term 'A' Flight was a rather mysterious designation. The staff in the personnel, finance and other permanent party support operations at Beale had indeed heard of this new unit, but they had absolutely no idea what it represented. The general consensus was that it was a new addition to the very prestigious 9th Strategic Wing that flew the SR-71 aircraft. In reality, 'A' Flight never played even an indirect role with the 9th or the SR-71 programme. As an 'A' Flight designee, Chapman was moved to the head of the line of

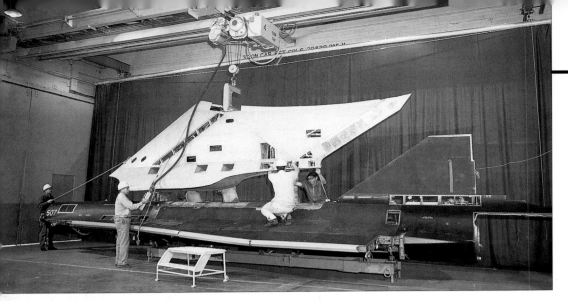

On 1 June 1967 Lockheed engineers performed the first D-21B/pylon mating. The drone, 507, was used as the 'pathfinder' airframe throughout the programme.

all personnel in-processing at that time, passing a lieutenant colonel who became quite indignant that a staff sergeant had been served before him. Evidently, all base services had been informed that anyone processing into 'A' Flight was to be given precedence in all administrative procedures.

A few days later, Chapman gleaned that 'A' Flight appeared to consist of nothing more than a single-storey wooden building directly across the street from the 9th Strategic Reconnaissance Wing headquarters. When Chapman entered

Technicians fit the nose fairing to a D-21B booster during final assembly. The rear fairing has yet to be fitted. Noteworthy are the three flared collars which attached the booster 'cigar' to the support beam, which in turn was attached to the D-21. The trolley was purpose-built.

the building for the first time, he was struck by the loud noise of many voices and found himself literally armpit-to-armpit with about 100 other men like himself, all wondering what was going on. No one seemed to know anything except the acting first sergeant and chief clerk, and he was not talking.

False start

A scenario soon developed wherein everyone in 'A' Flight would report to this building at 08.00 each morning to drink coffee and "swap a few lies" for about half an hour. They would then be dismissed, told to go home, and directed simply to call in once in a while. For about six weeks, this was the ongoing routine. Never in Chapman's Air Force career had he experienced so much authorised time off without being on official leave. In one respect, the unanticipated freedom was wonderful, yet in

another sense it was emotionally agonising: some project members felt abandoned, useless or worse. However, outside their knowledge, this time was being used for the project to achieve final operational status and obtain all of the clearances needed – all critical steps that had to take place before anyone could be told the nature of their assignments.

Around the middle of February 1968, Chapman was called in for his first meeting with squadron commander Colonel Arden B. Curfman (who, behind his back, became fondly known as 'ABC'). Curfman's number two man was Lieutenant Colonel Baldwin, 'A' Flight's 'chief spook' and the Air Force's liaison at the Skunk Works for the Senior Bowl project. This day was the only time anyone on base saw the lieutenant colonel in uniform; all personnel were instructed to refer to him simply as 'Mr Baldwin' from that point.

Intense security

Once Chapman was cleared for Senior Bowl, Curfman and Baldwin subjected him to the most intense security briefing he had ever received. The encounter lasted about three hours, with no one except Curfman, Baldwin, Chapman and, occasionally, the chief clerk in attendance. When something highly classified needed to be communicated, it was not done orally; instead, Baldwin or Curfman would write the critical information on a piece of paper and hand it to Chapman. After reading it, Chapman would be asked if he understood the material. With his affirmative answer, the paper would be set afire in an ashtray, immediately destroying it. At the conclusion of the briefing, the chief clerk gathered the ashes from the ashtray for further disposition. Chapman's impression was that he read more than he heard that day, because virtually everything they told him was highly top-secret material. Most important was the information they gave him concerning where they would be testing the D-21B; proper conduct whenever he or anyone else had to visit the Skunk Works or the test site; and the location where it was anticipated the programme would be put into operational use.

Later that week, along with three other men in his career field, Chapman began attending 'night school' in the same briefing room. This training was conducted by a vendor's technical representative and lasted about a week, with focus on the 'payload' system and on the D-21B itself. The first night, before they were too far into the session, someone jokingly asked the trainer if they were going to be working on something like the X-15. With a very stoic look, the trainer informed the group that they were "not too far off track on that". Chapman would later learn that this trainer never joked. The trainer's personality proved to be a challenge, but he was regarded as a very knowledgeable, intelligent, top-notch teacher. Following that one week of schooling, the team members never saw him again.

Chapman was within the first 50 members of the new group to receive full clearance. A few individuals failed to pass clearance and were immediately assigned to other bases or units. They left having received no information other than the project name – Senior Bowl – and the knowledge that they had been temporarily assigned to something called 'A' Flight.

Testing the 'Cigar'

The booster was tested at Lockheed's Rye Canyon facility, just north of Los Angeles (below). The booster was first cold-soaked in liquid nitrogen to simulate the -70°F conditions which would be experienced after a 10-hour flight from Beale to the operational launch point and altitude (40,000 ft/ 12192 m). The first test was conducted on 16 August 1967 (right).

The story of another sergeant serves as an indication of how difficult it was to get full clearance. A skilled technical sergeant in Chapman's crew had been one of the original Air Force personnel in the 4080th Strategic Reconnaissance Wing with the U-2 aircraft. The sergeant had already visited the test site (location of the D-21B) in 1957 when he was introduced to the U-2. Although the U-2 security clearance was akin to that for Senior Bowl, the sergeant's experience was that he had received his U-2 clearance relatively easily compared with what it took for him to pass the second time around. As it turned out, as a teenager in the early 1950s, he and some other kids had got drunk one night and had to 'sleep it off' in the local jail of their home town (Eldorado, Arkansas). Although this incident had not held him back from obtaining the top secret and project clearance for the U-2, it was of sufficient significance to delay his participation in the Senior Bowl programme for nearly six months, until the 1950s incident was finally dismissed.

Area 51 shuttle

During much of 1968, most of the cleared 'A' Flight personnel were sent to the test site each week, where they learned the ins and outs of the D-21B, the modified B-52H, specifics about the specialised equipment, and the plan of how everyone fitted into the programme. The team would meet at Beale AFB Base Operations every Monday morning at about 06.00 and climb onboard a civilian Fairchild F-27 turbo-prop aircraft for the flight to 'the area' (now better known as Area 51), where the men were housed in mobile homes. They were not allowed to leave the test site, but were free to wander within the boundaries of 'the area'. At 17.30 each Friday, the team would again board the F-27 for the flight back to Beale. Their weekends were free, but come Monday morning, the work week away from home began all over again.

Jerry Miller, of Marquardt, trained a number of the 'A' Flight personnel on the testing, operation and maintenance of the ramjet, Ramjet Test Set Trailer, APU and RAT. When 'graduation day' came, a number of the Beale men expressed their gratitude in a teasing way by chasing down the civilians with a stencil and a can of spray paint. Miller proudly wore his decorated shirt later at both 'the area' and at Beale. It still hangs in his closet.

High over the Nellis Range Complex, a 'Tag'-carrying B-52 refuels from a KC-135. Visible on the B-52's fuselage is the triangular fairing which covered the outward-facing camera system

In late 1968, the unit gained operational status and the 'A' Flight designation was changed to the 4200th Support Squadron. With the change in designation, programme members lost some of the priority treatment they had been enjoying but they retained enough status (far more than those associated with the SR-71) to know that they were in quite an elite outfit. While the team had been stationed at the test site, civilian contractors had been busy remodelling the nose dock at Beale (located near the current site of the fuel cell and phase hangars) as the home for the new 4200th Support Squadron. In December 1969, the unit moved permanently to the remodelled quarters at Beale. The two Senior Bowl B-52Hs (serial numbers 61-0021 and 60-0036) were parked at the farthest point of the northern end of the ramp, near the alert facility.

The 4200th had its own cadre of Security Police staff who, like the rest of the squadron, had been fully cleared for Senior Bowl. All team members (from E-2s to colonels) were

Inside the D-21B

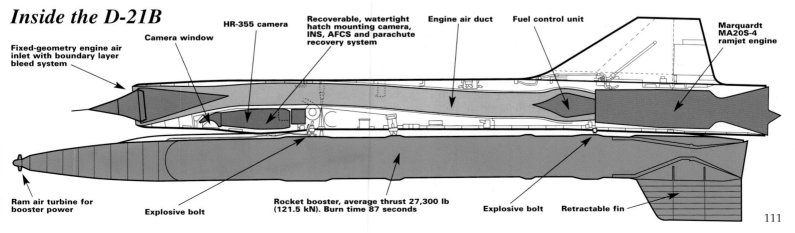

Fixed-geometry engine air inlet with boundary layer bleed system

Camera window

HR-355 camera

Recoverable, watertight hatch mounting camera, INS, AFCS and parachute recovery system

Engine air duct

Fuel control unit

Marquardt MA20S-4 ramjet engine

Ram air turbine for booster power

Explosive bolt

Rocket booster, average thrust 27,300 lb (121.5 kN). Burn time 87 seconds

Explosive bolt

Retractable fin

Removing the lower tail section fairing reveals the nozzle of the XRJ43-MA20S-4 ramjet. The device supporting the side of the fin is used for correct alignment of the vertical fin during assembly. The elevon alignment tool is also visible.

allowed exemption from the usual inspections, Maintenance Standardization and Evaluation Program (MSEP) inspections, base details and other irritants with which everyone else at Beale had to contend. The 180 or so people who comprised the 4200th Support Squadron became a very close-knit group.

Operations

The ground troops had no clue when a mission would be levied. From their perspective, the missions appeared to be called spontaneously. They could go weeks (and sometimes even months) with no specific duties other than extensive training. In addition to military staff, 10 to 20 per cent of the 4200th's support comprised Skunk Works personnel and vendors' technicians (otherwise known as

'technical representatives'). These team members assisted in training and helped prepare for each levied sortie. They also provided all parts and hardware for the D-21B, plus other equipment.

The D-21B was constructed primarily of titanium, stainless steel fasteners and composite structures. Composites were in their infancy at that time. All wiring in the vehicle, especially in the equipment hatch, was Teflon-coated and gold-alloyed. It required a whole new set of skills to work with this wiring which, because of its makeup, was extremely brittle and easily broken. A special type of solder was developed for use with this wiring, as were unique new soldering techniques. A tool often used was an item developed by Lockheed, called a solder sleeve – basically an in-line, 'stakon-type' wire splice, together with a shrinkable, sheathed plastic sleeve equipped with special solder encircling the inside of the sleeve. The technicians would strip the wire insulation using high-temperature heat strippers and then put the stripped wire ends inside the solder sleeve. Next they would subject the sleeve to high temperature using a heat gun (something like a blow dryer, except much hotter) until the solder melted and the plastic sheathing shrank, creating a perfectly spliced connection.

The stainless steel screws used with the titanium parts were very unusual. They were mostly flat and resembled a Phillips head, but the slots in the head were offset and looked vaguely like the old Nazi symbol, so they became known as swastika heads. The concept behind this configuration was to provide higher torque for tightening or loosening. Special swastika-shaped apex drivers were developed, and an apex holder welded to a piece of 3/8-in (0.95-cm) square stock about 24 in (61 cm) long became standard equipment.

When these screws were tightened, the apex tended to dig into the screw rather than slip out of the head (as a Phillips-type head might do); it was the same when taking them out. Due to the extremely high stresses encountered during flight, the screws in the hatch covers became even tighter. The swastika drivers made it a little easier to get them out because they would again tend to dig into the head rather than slip out, but it took great strength in the technician's arms and shoulders to accomplish this procedure. Chapman was in great shape and was one of only two or three in the shop who could break these screws loose easily. Of interest is that each screw was used only once; if it had to

be removed, it was thrown away and replaced by a new one. This happened to tens of thousands of screws during the life of the programme.

If screws were lost or damaged, staff members had to request additional screws in person from the Lockheed parts person. The first time Chapman did this, he was asked how many screws he needed. Chapman asked for "a handful" but was directed to go back and count the exact number required. Chapman returned with the figure of 30 or so, and the parts man counted out exactly that many and made Chapman sign for them. It was later learned that each of these swastika head screws (about 0.5 in/1.27 cm long) cost more than $5.00 – undoubtedly a hefty profit for Lockheed.

Ground-breaking technology

Lockheed was covering new ground with both the D-21 and its support systems. Every item, including all the test fixtures, had to be designed from scratch. As an example, one very innovative and talented Lockheed engineer designed a test rig that looked like something out of *Star Wars*, with a myriad of buttons, dials and switches. There wasn't a piece of solid state electronics in the entire fixture; it was all relays. It was about four times the size of a standard office desk and he had to stay with it all the time just to keep it running.

On numerous times, Lockheed Missiles and Space personnel would visit to audit the Skunk Works' activities, and the result often seemed like a semi-disaster. The auditors' area of expertise was missile technologies, so they were very sceptical that the Skunk Works' products would work at all.

On one occasion, Skunk Works engineers had to get a D-21B out the door immediately. They had already been working around the clock for several days in a small building behind Lockheed's main production building, 309/310. The lead engineer felt that the inspection team was interfering with the work, so he ordered them out of the facility and locked the door behind them. The D-21B successfully completed its checkout and was shipped. Later, Kelly Johnson asked the lead engineer why he had taken such action, and the reply was, "Because they were in my way. They weren't adding to anything. They were just pi**ing me off." Johnson's response was simply "Oh, okay", and that was the end of it.

Once a mission was levied, the first task was to determine who would go TDY to the Advance Party (ADVON) locations. This usually meant that at least 30 per cent of the D-21B staff and some of the B-52H people would be away from Beale while preparation for the mission took place. There were three land-based locations where the team would most likely be sent TDY: Andersen AFB, Guam; Kadena AFB, Okinawa (as a backup to Andersen); or Hickam AFB, Hawaii. An assortment of Navy ships also served as destination points.

The first location, Andersen AFB, Guam, would receive and deploy the B-52H/D-21B aircraft as scheduled, and from there the B-52H/D-21B would depart on its mission. On a few occasions, however, the missions commenced directly from Beale, in which case Andersen AFB personnel would recover the B-52 following launch of the D-21B. If weather

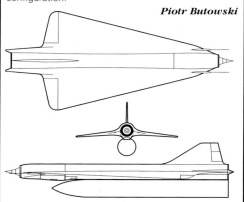

conditions prevented missions from Andersen, then Kadena AFB, Okinawa, would be considered the alternative launch site.

Once the D-21B had completed its mission, the hatch would be brought to location number two, Hickam AFB, Hawaii, for equipment recovery operations.

The third location, a 'floating TDY' (usually a Liberty Ship or Navy destroyer), could perform secondary recovery operations of the hatch in the event the 'Cat's Whiskers' (a JC-130B Hercules equipped with a nose-mounted fork) was unable to snag the hatch in flight.

No site-permanent personnel or personnel aboard the ships were cleared for Senior Bowl. The captain of the vessel would have been briefed by the ranking individual (usually an officer or high-ranking NCO) regarding only what he needed to know to get the ship where it needed to be. The ranking individual at the ground-based site would be briefed in the same fashion.

Mission preparation

In the hangar, technicians would start built-in testing (BIT) and inflight checkout (IFCO) procedures on the D-21B with special test equipment. The hatch would be removed from the D-21B and taken to the Payload Shop. Inside the hatch were the main avionics packages made by Honeywell, including the Inertial Navigation System (INS), the Automatic Flight Control System (AFCS) and the Air Data Computer (ADC). They were packaged within the hatch so they could take advantage of the same cooling system used for the payload, as well as be recovered with the hatch at the end of the mission. After the hatch was sealed, these systems were also tested via IFCO checks.

The autopilot was a combination of digital and analog technology, all housed in a 1-cu ft (0.028-m³) box with three line replaceable units (LRUs). One controlled the roll and yaw, one controlled the pitch axis, and the other was a power supply for the inflight checkout equipment. Due to the extreme lack of space and high vibration on the aircraft, new construction techniques were developed. The autopilot utilised 'welded cordwood construction', in which the resistors, capacitors and other pieces

of equipment stood on end, resembling cordwood. The ends of these units were welded together and to the motherboard with a technique similar to a spot weld but without using solder. Maintenance proved to be exceptionally difficult because units to be worked on had to be drilled out, the Mylar separators that held the devices in place had to be patched, and then the units being replaced had to be rewelded into position.

The inflight checkout equipment was unusual for its time, using an A-to-D converter plus much control circuitry. It had to exercise the entire aircraft before each mission, both on the ground and while airborne. Final checkout in Burbank, California, involved taking the aircraft into a small hanger and firing it up using an MA-1 air source. The air needed to be cooled in order to run the turbines and the procedure took many hours. When the Burbank team was finished, the unit would be packed into a covered system that looked like just a box and trucked to Palmdale, going from there to either Area 51 or Beale AFB.

Transfer troubles

One checkout task was to simulate an actual mission using the test set to ensure that the D-21B was operating properly. This same testing procedure would already have been run at

the Skunk Works facility, and the vehicle would not have been shipped had it not been in perfect operating order. The great puzzle was that in transit between the Skunk Works and Beale, 'gremlins' seemed to creep in and misalign the D-21B. Sometimes the readjustment needed at Beale was minor, but at other times it was a significant problem. Not once did a D-21B arrive at Beale in working order. (No fault could be levied against the Skunk Works, because it shipped them in perfect condition.) Following the on-site tune-up, all would appear to be well until the D-21B commenced its take-off roll on the B-52H for an upcoming sortie. Again, problems seemed to pop out of nowhere. Following a launch, it was not unknown for the whole thing to deteriorate. The D-21B was reputed to be a very fragile and temperamental aircraft.

Kelly Johnson himself dispatched a D-21 Tiger Team to discover why the D-21 was having so many problems and failures. The Tiger Team's conclusion was that, although the D-21 had a cutting-edge airframe and propul-

Antenna locations

After launch, the LCO on board the B-52 was in contact with the D-21B for about 10 minutes. Telemetry data was received back from the drone, allowing its boost phase and initial course-setting to be monitored. The LCO had some control available in this period, including the ability to command destruct.

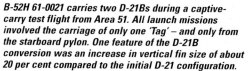

113

D-21B mission profile

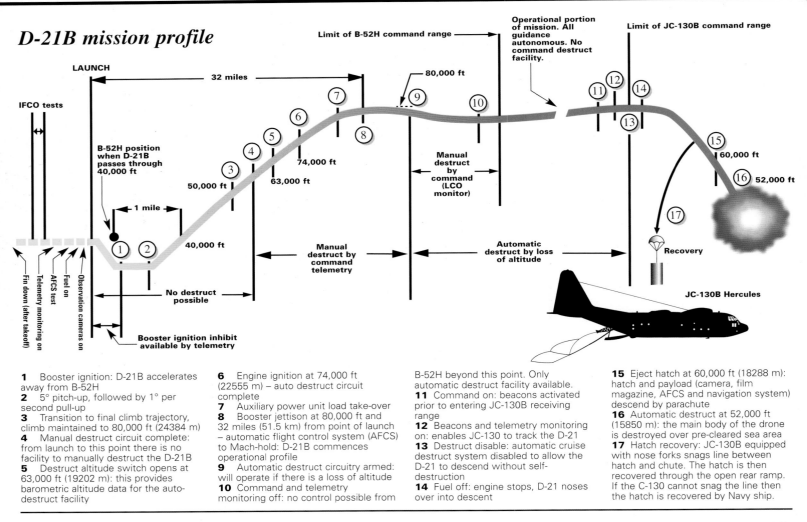

1 Booster ignition: D-21B accelerates away from B-52H
2 5° pitch-up, followed by 1° per second pull-up
3 Transition to final climb trajectory, climb maintained to 80,000 ft (24384 m)
4 Manual destruct circuit complete: from launch to this point there is no facility to manually destruct the D-21B
5 Destruct altitude switch opens at 63,000 ft (19202 m): this provides barometric altitude data for the auto-destruct facility

6 Engine ignition at 74,000 ft (22555 m) – auto destruct circuit complete
7 Auxiliary power unit load take-over
8 Booster jettison at 80,000 ft and 32 miles (51.5 km) from point of launch – automatic flight control system (AFCS) to Mach-hold: D-21B commences operational profile
9 Automatic destruct circuitry armed: will operate if there is a loss of altitude
10 Command and telemetry monitoring off: no control possible from

B-52H beyond this point. Only automatic destruct facility available.
11 Command on: beacons activated prior to entering JC-130B receiving range
12 Beacons and telemetry monitoring on: enables JC-130 to track the D-21
13 Destruct disable: automatic cruise destruct system disabled to allow the D-21 to descend without self-destruction
14 Fuel off: engine stops, D-21 noses over into descent

15 Eject hatch at 60,000 ft (18288 m): hatch and payload (camera, film magazine, AFCS and navigation system) descend by parachute
16 Automatic destruct at 52,000 ft (15850 m): the main body of the drone is destroyed over pre-cleared sea area
17 Hatch recovery: JC-130B equipped with nose forks snags line between hatch and chute. The hatch is then recovered through the open rear ramp. If the C-130 cannot snag the line then the hatch is recovered by Navy ship.

---

sion system, it utilised outdated 1940s-era electro-mechanical relays, technology and hardware that were not compatible with speeds in excess of Mach 3.3 at or above 90,000 ft (27432 m).

While the skilled technicians were working their magic, the Senior Bowl team would begin its own system checks and prepare the payload for installation into the hatch. Once installation was complete, the team performed its BIT and IFCO checks.

When the BITs and IFCOs had been completed, the hatch would be delivered back to the D-21B, where its BITs and IFCOs were still in progress and tests would be rerun. After

all the connections had been made, the hatch would be installed in the equipment bay on the forward underside of the vehicle.

Fragile electrics

Connectors, pins and broken wires caused innumerable problems. Very stiff, Kapton-coated wire was used because it was more compact and saved space. Kapton was new technology and the awkward wires tended to break while the connectors were seated, or the pins would move. For example, one of the primary connectors was a square Cannon plug with 100 pins, which had to mate perfectly with the matching connector inside the equipment

bay. This joining proved to be extremely difficult because the pins on the connector were easily damaged and there was minimal room in which to work. On one occasion, a connector was found to have been damaged during preparation for a mission. It took more than a week for the new harness and connector to be received from Lockheed. The hatch had to be taken apart again, the harness replaced, more BITs and IFCOs performed, the hatch resealed, and the component finally re-installed on the D-21B. To make matters worse, work on the BITs and IFCOs on the D-21B had to be resumed from the point where they had previously been suspended.

B-52 modifications

Externally, the Senior Bowl B-52Hs could be distinguished by additional antennas, and by side- and downward-facing cameras on either side of the forward fuselage (below). A large fairing was added to protect these cameras in flight.

Separate and identical stations for the Launch Control Officers were installed in the two aft upper stations (normally occupied by the EWO and gunner). Above is a view looking aft of a partially modified aircraft (note the removed ejection seat hatches) while at left is detail of the starboard LCO's side panels.

Prior to putting on the waterproof cover, workers would apply RTV sealant (the old, red, flaky-when-dry stuff) on and around any areas of the hatch that were not secured. Some 200 screws then had to be installed to hold down the cover. The screw holes in the hatch had been accurately drilled and tapped at Lockheed, yet as the crew worked to attach the cover, it often seemed as though some of the holes had miraculously moved. With the RTV sealant now blocking their visibility, it was very difficult for the crew to tighten the cover properly. They persevered, however, and the men using the swastika screwdrivers usually ended up with red hands from the RTV sealant, due to

D-21B 501 is suspended from B-52H 61-0021 for test at Area 51. On the ground the booster fin was folded to the side for ground clearance. After take-off, it was folded to the vertical position at the same time as the B-52's undercarriage was retracted.

the extreme physical effort.

When the D-21B and the hatch had passed all of their BITs and IFCOs, they would be taken to the B-52H under a canvas shroud, usually very early in the morning. The completed D-21B, minus its booster, was then uploaded onto the right inboard pylon. Once the D-21B hung securely from the pylon, the booster (or 'cigar', as it was casually called due to its shape) would then be brought out to be installed on the underside of the D-21B.

Defeating static

It was at this point that the situation could get very tense. The solid rocket booster was extremely volatile and very sensitive to static electricity, which could ignite the booster. This, of course, was never allowed to occur, as it would have wrought total havoc.

To prevent static electricity causing prob-

Modifications to both Senior Bowl B-52Hs were undertaken at Lockheed's SR-71/U-2 overhaul facility at Air Force Plant 42, Palmdale, California. Here '21 is about to have the special D-21B pylon attached under its wing. The vertical plates on the pylon itself were strain gauges used for pre-flight testing.

lems, everyone within 25 ft (7.62 m) of the booster had to wear 'leg stats': a pad beneath their shoes connecting to a strap worn around the upper part of the lower leg (looking somewhat like a garter). This contraption allowed the crew members to maintain conductivity to the ground at all times – as long as everyone remembered to keep one foot fully flat on the ground when kneeling around the booster. Had any static been released while in close contact with the D-21B and/or the booster, it could have caused a low-amperage, high-voltage arc of direct current (something like lightning) that in turn could have ignited the booster and sent

it on its way. Obviously, this would have resulted in the loss of the D-21B, probably also the B-52H, and possibly aircraft, buildings, the lives of many people, and destruction of whatever else might have been in the line of fire. Each member of the 'A' Flight/4200th crew made sure that the leg stats were religiously used. Most of the ground crew even wore them when the D-21B was being installed and the 'cigar' had yet to arrive.

Launching the mission

When it came time to launch Senior Bowl, nearly all personnel were busy at the squadron or at specific duty stations, taking care of any last-minute problems to ensure that the scheduled take-off time could be met. Timing was everything. If the bomber was not in the air on time, the mission would have to be aborted and rescheduled. Although this did happen on a

few occasions, most take-off times were met successfully.

Before and during each test flight of Senior Bowl, the D-21B's electronics were monitored closely via telemetry to the radio shack in the base hangar. One day, while the B-52's engines were spooling up, Frank Brink, the Honeywell technician responsible for the state of the AFCS and ADC, noticed a problem on the telemetry readout. He marched out to the nearby flight line, held up his hands in front of the B-52, and

announced, "You're not going." When the crew chief argued, "Yes, we are," Frank retorted, "No, you're not!" Frank won the argument, possibly preventing the loss of the mission in flight.

Once the B-52H was airborne, it was beyond the ground crew's control. It was the inflight crew's job to get the D-21B to its drop point accurately and exactly on time. The LCOs were able to perform IFCO checks and, additionally, had some manual control of the D-21B, if needed.

Any velocity or position errors would grow over time during the long flight prior to launch, and had to be corrected. En route to the operational launch point in the northern part of the Sea of Japan, a complex set of procedures was followed to update the D-21's inertial set in order for it to go its full mission distance. The velocity input was taken from the B-52H. The 'BUFF' would go through a series of U-type

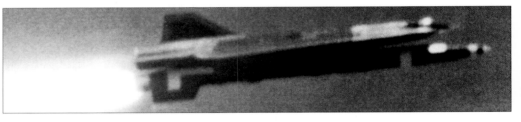

The downward-facing camera in the B-52's pylon recorded this view (left) of a D-21B dropping away from its carrier. The drone fell some way beneath the bomber before the booster ignited to avoid the risk of collision. With the rocket ignited (above), the D-21B climbed to 80,000 ft (24384 m) and Mach 3.2, where the ramjet engine was started and the booster rocket jettisoned.

manoeuvres, making three orthogonal (right-angle) turns in order to update the velocity and position parameters. The stellar systems were crude by today's standards. The computer in the navigational system comprised magnetic drums programmed in their own Assembly language. It was a 24-bit machine, limited in memory, and yet it had to store the entire sequence of tests for inflight checkout because it was the only computer on board.

After the final IFCO checks had been performed by the LCO, and if everything was in order and the operation had not been recalled (which happened occasionally), the LCO would initiate the launch sequence and drop the D-21B/booster. Once the D-21B was released from the pylon, very little control of it (other than some telemetry signals from the LCO) was possible.

Drone away

As the D-21B/booster dropped, automatic sequencing within the D-21B kicked in instantaneously. Approximately one to three seconds following the drop, the booster would ignite and the AFCS, INS, ADC and other systems inside the D-21B would follow their sequencing to start up the ramjet and propel the D-21B into proper trajectory. The AFCS had a very simple pitch programme, putting the D-21B into a steep climb and levelling off at the end of booster burn. At the end of the 90-second burn, the booster would be jettisoned, the programmed operations from the onboard computer would commence, and the D-21B would be on its way. Now all that could be done (other than a few actions remaining under control of the LCO) was to wait and hope. The most vital command the LCO could order was a signal for the destruction of the D-21B, sent if conditions demanded instant destruction of the drone for safety and/or security reasons.

Sensor hatch

A vital component of the D-21 system was the recoverable sensor hatch, which mounted the camera and its film magazines, and the inertial navigation system. The hatch occupied a very cramped compartment (right) under the engine air intake trunk, the lack of space for vital components being blamed for many system failures during the D-21 programme. The camera peered through a three-pane window, visible in the first hatch shown on the production line (below right). The hatch carried by D-21B 501 (below) was modified with an additional cut-out window for a camera which recorded the booster's separation after burn-out.

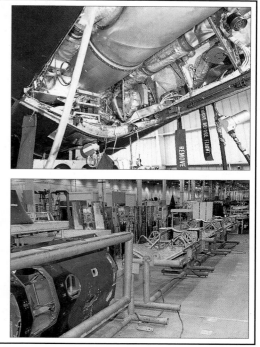

The mission track was programmed into the INS, which provided steering commands to the roll channel of the AFCS. The ADC was pre-set to keep the D-21B flying at a fixed Mach number.

Once en route and over target, the payload/camera equipment would begin operating and would continue functioning until the computer shut it down. The D-21B would then be vectored on to its final return leg. At an exact spot determined by the INS, the Marquardt engine would shut down and the vehicle would decelerate and enter a controlled descent to a lower altitude of about 60,000 ft (18288 m). At a pre-determined point, explosive bolts would fire and the hatch would be ejected. The hatch-less vehicle would then tumble on its way until an explosive charge went off, destroying the entire D-21B and leaving behind only a meaningless residue of ashes and debris.

After ejection, the hatch would drop to an altitude of about 15,000 ft (4572 m), when the drogue and main chute (attached to the inside

Below: The two Senior Bowl B-52s launched 16 drones intentionally, with one inadvertent launch. On only six flights did the D-21B function successfully, but on the one successful operational mission, the hatch was lost.

Tagboard and Senior Bowl launches – D-21 flight log summary

Serial number	Launch date	Launch vehicle	Distance flown (nm/km)
Functional fit/captive flights			
501	**19 June 1964**	M-21/134	**0**
First fit check in building 309/310; no launch			
501	**22 December 1964**	M-21/134	**0**
First mated flight of M/D-21; no launch			
Tagboard launches			
502	**5 March 1966**	M-21/135	**150/278**
Crew – Park/Beswick			
506	**27 April 1966**	M-21/135	**1,120/2074**
Crew – Park/Torick			
505	**16 June 1966**	M-21/135	**1,550/2870**
Crew – Park/Beswick			
504	**30 July 1966**	M-21/135	**0**
Crew – Park/Torick. M-21/D-21 mid-air collision; Ray Torick lost his life; aircraft/drone lost; Tagboard programme cancelled			
Senior Bowl launches			
501	**28 September 1967**	B-52H	**0**
Drone fell off the B-52H pylon en route from the test site because of poor workmanship in trying to retap a stripped nut in the right forward attachment to the pylon; the booster fired			
507	**6 November 1967**	B-52H	**134/248**
The booster took the drone to altitude but the drone nosed over and dived in after a relatively short flight			
509	**2 December 1967**	B-52H	**500/926**
Drone flew only 500 nm, at a too-low altitude and too-slow speed; quit flying when it ran out of hydraulic fluid			
508	**19 January 1968**	B-52H	**280/518**
After a few minutes, number 508 went out of control and was lost			
511	**10 April 1968**	B-52H	**0**
An unsuccessful launch; the engine did not light			
512	**16 June 1968**	B-52H	**2,850/5278**
Very good launch; reached an altitude of over 90,000 ft (27432 m) and the hatch and camera were recovered; the engine blew out in turns but re-ignited in climb-back			
514	**1 July 1968**	B-52H	**80/148**
Engine did not light; nosed over and was lost			
516	**28 August 1968**	B-52H	**78/144**
Carried two drones from 'the area' to Kauai, HI; D-21 number 516 was put into a perfect launch position, but the Marquardt MA20S-4 did not light and it was lost			
515	**15 December 1968**	B-52H	**2,953/5469**
Hatch and camera recovered; photos okay			
518	**11 February 1969**	B-52H	**751/1389**
Loss thought to have been caused by water contamination in the autopilot			
519	**10 May 1969**	B-52H	**2,753/5098**
Hatch and camera recovered; photos fair			
520	**10 July 1969**	B-52H	**2,937/5439**
Drone flew the Captain Hook route extremely well; hatch and camera recovered; photos good (The programme had now met all of the design requirements and objectives to the point where the Air Force deemed the programme successful and completed up to the operational phase.)			
517	**9 November 1969**	B-52H	**unknown**
First operational mission; crashed in the former USSR; subsequently, Lockheed changed the navigation system programming to enable the drone to miss one destination checkpoint but still continue to the following one			
521	**20 February 1970**	B-52H	**2,909/5387**
Ran another Captain Hook mission with the new navigation programming; the D-21 performed superbly, reaching an altitude of over 95,000 ft (28956 m) and meeting all of its checkpoints within 2-3 nm (3.7-5.5 km); hatch and camera recovered; photos good			
523	**16 December 1970**	B-52H	**2,648/4904**
Second operational mission; hatch lost due to parachute failure			
526	**4 March 1971**	B-52H	**2,935/5435**
Third operational mission; drone returned after a fine flight. The parachute was damaged during descent with the hatch, however, and it fell slowly into the water. The hatch floated and the Navy arrived with the recovery ship. During the recovery operation, the hatch was run over by the Navy recovery ship and damaged to the point where it sank. Another Navy ship found the D-21 afloat but was unable to get cables around it before it also sank			
527	**20 March 1971**	B-52H	**unknown**
Fourth operational mission; aircraft shot down three-quarters of the way through its mission to overfly the Chinese nuclear test facility near Lop Nor			

During conversion to D-21B, the drone was mounted in a fixture which could be rotated, allowing easy access to all parts of the airframe. The spine structure was removed so that new attachments could be added for compatibility with the B-52 pylon.

of the hatch) would engage, trailing the hatch via cable a few hundred feet below the chute. There were calculated markings on the cable that the JC-130B would hopefully engage. The hatch would then be taken into the aircraft and delivered to location number two for recovery operations by 'A' Flight/4200th Support Squadron personnel.

If the JC-130B missed its target, the ship (location number three) would attempt recovery operations, performed by 'A' Flight/4200th Support Squadron staff members already on board. In the case of a successful recovery, the ship would return to port and the camera pallet would be sent to the photo analysis centre at Hickam AFB, Hawaii. Not once did the Navy successfully recover a hatch; it was always either recovered by the JC-130B or lost completely.

Operational launches

It is believed that all four operational launches targeted the People's Republic of China nuclear weapons test facility in remote west-central China, near Lop Nor.

The first operational launch (D-21B number 517, launched on 9 November 1969) did not successfully institute the return manoeuvre to take it back to the recovery area. Instead, the D-21B continued on a straight course and crashed somewhere in the wilderness of the former Soviet Union. The cause for this loss was later determined by Honeywell to have been an error build-up in the computation of sine/cosine routines in the nav system.

After the fall of the Soviet Union, Ben R. Rich (then retired president of Lockheed's Skunk Works) finally had an opportunity to tour Russia. While in Moscow, the KGB presented Rich with a gift of what it thought was the remains of a stealth fighter that had crashed in their territory. As it turned out, the wreckage was actually pieces of the lost D-21B.

The second operational mission was launched on 16 December 1970, flown by D-21B number 523. It completed its 2,648-nm (4904-km) trip only to lose its payload at sea, this time due to a partially failed parachute.

The third operational launch of a Senior Bowl D-21B occurred on 4 March 1971. D-21B number 526 flew the complete mission profile of 2,935 nm (5436 km), the JC-130B missed the aerial recovery due to damaged parachute lines, and the payload landed safely in the Pacific. Once in the water, it was the Navy's task to recover the package.

The Navy recovery ship failed to pick up the package on the first pass, so a Navy SEAL team was put into the water. The SEALs could not cut through the parachute cables, which had been reinforced with stainless steel wire. In standard

Above: D-21s 507 to 511 are ready for conversion, having been stripped of all necessary components and, in the case of 510, its 'iron ball' radar-absorbent paint.

Right: The completed D-21Bs were thoroughly checked out in the Skunk Works. Here 501's twin pitot probes are aligned in a special fixture to ensure that they give the correct air data for engine inlet control.

Navy fashion, the recovery manoeuvre procedure was to approach the pallet from the windward side and drift towards the package. The problem was that the parachute (still attached) acted like a sea anchor, and when the recovery ship came beside the pallet, it drifted right over it. The result was that the only recoverable camera images from an operational mission were sunk at sea.

(Months before the first launch, the Air Force colonel responsible for payload recovery was tasked to Pearl to brief the Commander of the Pacific Fleet about their responsibilities in the event the camera pallet were to land in the Pacific. The Navy admiral's response to the colonel's visit was, "Just what could the Air Force tell the Navy that it doesn't already know?" With that, the colonel went on his way.)

D-21B number 527 was launched on 20 March 1971 as the fourth and final mission. Experts at the 4200th Support Squadron and the Skunk Works concluded that number 527 must have malfunctioned; it was thought to have been shot down near Lop Nor.

For each D-21B delivered from the Skunk Works to the 4200th, the initial programme cost (from mission through destruction) was estimated at $US5.5 million (1970 dollars). This price included the rocket, mission evaluation, operation of the B-52H, and all other programme-incurred per-mission expenses.

Conclusion

Senior Bowl and the 'A' Flight/4200th programme lasted only three years. It was a very difficult operation, utilising state-of-the-art technology of the day. A single problem would jeopardise the entire mission, and one problem tended to lead to others. The operation was extremely expensive, and that aspect alone undermined the project over time.

Overall, the successes were overwhelmed by less-than-stellar or totally unacceptable outcomes. Kelly Johnson and his Skunk Works geniuses did everything possible to make the programme a success, as did the men of 'A' Flight/4200th. The entire team was expertly trained and highly motivated, and each member of the squadron was fully capable of performing his duties successfully. 'A' Flight/4200th was a close-knit, highly-effective team that happened to be assigned an extremely challenging project with obstacles that proved to be insurmountable, for various reasons.

Some time after the end of the Senior Bowl programme surviving D-21 drones appeared in open storage at Davis-Monthan AFB. In 1994 four were delivered to NASA Dryden, potentially to be used for ramjet research, but they were not used.

Three months prior to the termination of the project, many of the troops (especially those with overseas-imbalance skills or critical skills) received orders for Vietnam. Senior Bowl lasted from January 1968 until its abrupt termination on 23 July 1971.

Lockheed's challenge has been described as "an overhead mission with airborne technology that just didn't run long enough to make it". With greater financing and more time to work through the problems, the outcome of the project could have been markedly different. The Skunk Works had technology for air-breathing vehicles but was trying to do a satellite-type mission, and the implementation was flawed. It overcame many difficult hurdles (fuel sealants, aerodynamics, matching engines to nacelles, etc.), but had insufficient experience with electrical or electronic issues. Even though Kelly Johnson stressed the importance of the reliability of electronics, Lockheed's success in that arena was lacking.

One story goes that Kelly Johnson had long mistrusted anything electrical. Jim Eastham, Lockheed's chief pilot on the YF-12, once said, "If Kelly could have invented a hydraulic radio, he would have." Early in the development of the Tagboard programme, Kelly met with Honeywell's D-21/Tagboard engineering team in his Burbank office. He had some questions about the reliability of the autopilot and navigation system, which the Honeywell group had presented to him in a box. He shocked every-one by suddenly throwing it on the floor, demanding "Okay, can it take that? It has to take that!" His point was that it might meet its specs, but it also had to be invulnerable to abuse.

During its operational lifetime, Senior Bowl was one of the best-kept secrets in the military. 'A' Flight and the 4200th Support Squadron launched 16 D-21B vehicles from the B-52H, in both training and operational sorties. Only a very few select personnel were cleared for the project, each person being cleared first to top secret and then also requiring a Special Access Required (SAR) clearance. This unique level of clearance was (and still is) classified information. All Senior Bowl personnel had to be cleared to the same level, regardless of rank or grade. When the programme began, everyone involved had to sign security paperwork (jokingly referred to as 'burn before reading' material) promising, in effect, that they would never mention the term D-21B nor discuss the Senior Bowl programme with anyone not equally cleared.

Like the U-2, SR-71, F-117 and other formerly 'black' operations, many more details about Senior Bowl may be made available to the public. Until that time, this article summarises most of the information available about this unique operation at the Skunk Works – a programme it sometimes fondly refers to as its "twice-unsuccessful success".

James C. Goodall and Nora D. Goodall

Fw 190
Tank's 'Cavalry Horse'

When it first went into action in the summer of 1941, the Fw 190, dubbed *Dienstpferd* (cavalry horse) by the company's Technical Director Kurt Tank, came as a nasty shock to Germany's enemies. The Fw 190 demonstrated a clear margin of superiority over the Spitfire Mk V, the most potent fighter type then available to RAF Fighter Command. For the remainder of World War II the Fw 190 was a major element of the German fighter and Reich Air Defence forces and, from the end of 1943, the type also formed the backbone of the ground attack force.

In the spring of 1938 the Luftwaffe Technical Office invited the Focke-Wulf company at Bremen to submit design proposals for a new fighter to supplement the Messerschmitt Bf 109. By that time the Bf 109B was serving with several fighter gruppen, and had seen combat in Spain. Although its maximum speed was only 289 mph (465 km/h) at 13,000 ft (3962 m), the Bf 109B had a clear edge in performance over the Soviet-built fighters it had encountered.

This was a time of rapid advances in aviation, however, and other nations were also developing high performance fighter types. In Great Britain the Supermarine Spitfire, in production for the Royal Air Force, was a good deal faster than the Bf 109B. Willi Messerschmitt had several ideas of his own for improving the performance of his little fighter plane. Rather than stake everything on their success, however, the Luftwaffe sought a new high performance fighter to supplement the Bf 109 in production.

Focke-Wulf's Technical Director, Kurt Tank, acknowledged there was a place for what he termed 'racehorse' fighter designs like the Bf 109 and the Spitfire. Their designers had subordinated almost everything else in their quest for high rates of climb and high maximum speeds. How well these 'racehorses' would fare in the rough-and-tumble of combat flying was not clear. Kurt Tank saw the need for a rather different type of fighter aircraft. He told this writer:

"During the First World War, I served in the cavalry and in the infantry. I had seen the harsh conditions under which military equipment has to work in wartime. I felt sure that a quite different breed of fighter would also have a place in any future conflict: one that could operate from ill-prepared front-line airfields; one that could be flown and maintained by men who had received only a short training; and one that could absorb a reasonable amount of battle

Far left: With several of the aircraft displaying the famous Mickey Mouse emblem of II. Gruppe, Schlactgeschwader 2 'Immelmann', this line-up of Fw 190Gs is seen in the Eastern Front theatre during the latter half of 1943. Note the lack of cowling-mounted cannon – a feature of the 'G' series.

Left: With their weapons racks empty, a pair of Schlachtgeschwader 1 Fw 190Fs returns from an attack on the Soviet front line. In addition to their bombing duties, the Schlacht 190s were also heavily involved in the role for which the aircraft was originally devised – fighter interceptor – with many of their pilot's becoming high-scoring aces.

Below: The Fw 190 largely took over the Ju 87's close-support dive-bombing role in the final two years of the war. Here an SC 500 500-kg (1,100 lb) bomb is about to be released during a demonstration of the aircraft's capabilities.

damage and still get back'. This was the background thinking behind the Focke-Wulf 190; it was to be not a 'racehorse' but a *Dienstpferd*, a cavalry horse.

"Obviously, if it was fitted with an engine developing the same power, a 'racehorse' fighter with a lighter structure would always out-run and out-climb the *Dienstpferd* fighter we had in mind; yet we could not allow this difference to become too great. The design problem centred around building a stronger airframe and one able to carry heavier weapons, without sacrificing too much in the way of flying performance."

Concept to fruition

By careful design, Tank hoped to achieve for his new fighter a combination of high performance, simplicity of operation, high structural integrity and ease of maintenance under combat conditions. Willi Kaether, Tank's assistant, co-ordinated the work on the fighter. Rudi Blaser in the drawing office oversaw the detailed design. He had the difficult task of achieving the necessary strength factors, without allowing the structure to accumulate too much weight.

To achieve the performance he needed, Tank chose the most powerful German air-cooled radial engine then available. In contrast to British and other German high-speed fighters of the period which used in-line engines, Tank chose an air-cooled engine because these were far more rugged and less vulnerable to battle damage than their in-line equivalents. He selected the 18-cylinder BMW 139 radial engine which developed 1,550 hp (1156 kW) during bench tests. To smooth the airflow around the radial engine and reduce cooling drag to a minimum, Tank designed a novel type of ducted spinner that would fit around the nose of the aircraft.

Apart from the use of the radial engine and the unusual ducted spinner arrangement, the layout of Tank's new

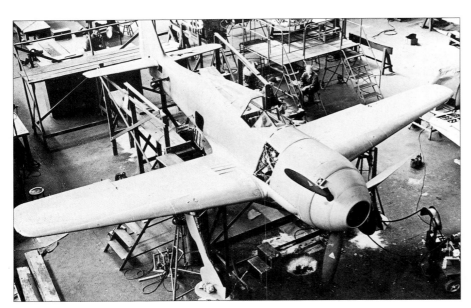

Two of the most important figures in the Fw 190's genesis were Technical Director Dipl.-Ing Kurt Tank (above) and chief test pilot Dipl.-Ing Hans Sander (below). Sander conducted the first flight and much of the test flying phase, while Tank, and his design team headed by Oberingenieur R. Blaser, overcame the design hurdles encountered in turning the concept into a formidable fighter. Tank himself flew a number of test flights, helping him to gauge the exact nature of the problems encountered.

Above: The prototype, designated Fw 190 V1, nears completion in Focke-Wulf's experimental shop in April 1939. V1 and V2 were both powered by the ill-fated BMW 139 engine, before it was replaced by the BMW 801, transforming what could have been a troublesome and mediocre fighter into one of the finest warplanes of World War II.

Below right: By January 1940, Fw 190 V1 had been refitted with an orthodox spinner in an attempt to alleviate the ongoing engine cooling problems. Despite tests proving little difference between the two systems, the decision was taken to ditch the ducted spinner in favour of the more simple design.

Below: Seen here in an unpainted state conducting the first taxiing trials during May 1939, the Fw 190 V1 incorporated the unusual ducted spinner, but lacked the 10-bladed cooling fan which was designed to rotate inside the cowling at approximately three-times the speed of the airscrew. Note the distinctive hinged door covers fitted to the 'short-wing' early prototypes.

fighter was entirely conventional. It was a low-winged monoplane with the nose-mounted engine driving a tractor airscrew. At the time this was considered the optimum layout for a high-performance fighter aircraft. The low wing provided a convenient housing for the retractable undercarriage, allowing the undercarriage legs to be kept short, and not restricting the pilot's vision in the upper hemisphere. From his own flying experience, Tank knew the importance of a good all-round view and he designed a frameless bubble canopy to fit over the cockpit. In later years these clear-view canopies became fashionable for fighters, but in 1938 the idea was novel.

Control surfaces

If the new fighter was to be successful it would have to handle well in the air. The key to achieving this was to make the control surfaces large enough to provide the necessary forces, and balance them with great care both statistically and dynamically. Tank and his design team did a lot of work to achieve a crisp control response from the aircraft's elevators and ailerons. The rudder forces were less critical, because a pilot can exert a far greater force through the legs than through the arms. The flying controls in most aircraft at that time employed a system of wires, pulleys and bell cranks. With use, the wires stretched and introduced 'play' into the system. Tank opted for a novel system using rigid rods instead of wires to connect the control stick to the control surfaces, thus overcoming that problem.

In another far-sighted decision, Tank stressed the undercarriage and other areas to take greater loads than the aircraft's initial all-up weight warranted. He believed that once the aircraft entered service, the need to improve performance and military effectiveness would inevitably lead to it putting on more weight. The structure had to be strong enough to accommodate these changes.

In the summer of 1938 the Luftwaffe Technical Office accepted Tank's proposals for the new fighter and placed an order for the construction of three prototypes. With that order the aircraft received its official designation: from now on it was known as the Focke-Wulf Fw 190.

In the workshops at Bremen the construction of the first two prototypes moved ahead rapidly. In the spring of 1939 the company received an order for an additional, fourth, prototype to speed development. Before the first prototype had flown the company received instructions to set up an assembly line to build 40 pre-production aircraft.

By April 1939 the Fw 190 V1, the first prototype, was in the final assembly stage and work on the V2 was well advanced. In the meantime, however, the BMW 139 had run into difficulties with overheating when running at full power. By then the company was in a position to offer a better engine, its new BMW 801 14-cylinder radial. This had the same diameter as the BMW 139, and in its developed form it was expected to offer an additional 150 hp (112 kW). The BMW 801 was somewhat heavier than the BMW 139, however, and to install it in the Fw 190 required

Left: Wearing the quasi-civilian registration D-OPZE, Hans Sander made the Fw 190s maiden flight on 1 June 1939. Initial test flights revealed the aircraft to possess excellent handling and impressive performance, however, the engine and cockpit cooling problems, which were to plague the aircraft's development, were also readily apparent.

a redesign of the forward fuselage and the restressing of the airframe. Officials at the Technical Officer felt that the improvement in performance justified these changes and agreed to fund them.

Following that decision, the Fw 190 development programme was revised. The V1 and V2 initial prototypes would be completed and flown with the BMW 139 engine as originally planned. The V3 and V4 prototypes, then in the early stages of construction, were cancelled. Work had yet to begin on the V5 prototype and this would have the revised airframe, becoming the first Fw 190 fitted with the BMW 801.

Maiden flight

During May 1939 the Fw 190 V1 commenced its taxiing trials. By the end of the month these had been completed and the fighter was ready to fly. On 1 June test pilot Hans Sander took the prototype into the air for the first time. Throughout the flight he kept close to the airfield, taking the new fighter in a spiral to about 6,500 ft (2000 m) to get the feel of the controls. Sander described that important flight to this writer:

"I made a couple of high-speed runs to see how she handled close to her maximum speed, then turns at different speeds and noted the stick forces that were necessary. Aerodynamically, she handled beautifully. The controls were light, positive and well balanced and throughout the initial flight I never once had to make use of the tailplane trim. I suppose most test pilots would have made at least a roll in the new aircraft, but I did no aerobatics during the maiden flight of the Fw 190; I was quite happy to leave such fancy flying until later in the test programme, when I knew a little more about her. At this stage my task was merely to 'taste' the handling characteristics of the new fighter."

During that initial flight the BMW 139 engine demonstrated its propensity to overheat. It had been intended to fit a 10-bladed engine-driven cooling fan on the front of the engine to assist with cooling, but this was not ready in time and the V1 made its first flight without it. Soon after take-off Sander became uncomfortably hot and he began to sweat profusely.

"The rear of the engine was hard up against the front wall of the cockpit, and my feet on the rudder pedals were on either side of the engine accessories. The temperature in the cockpit rose to 55° C. I felt as though I was sitting with my feet in a fire! The heat was bearable, but very uncomfortable."

One disadvantage of the bubble canopy was that it could not be opened in flight to cool the cockpit, because that would have caused excessive turbulence to the airflow over the tail. Potentially lethal carbon monoxide exhaust fumes started to seep into the cockpit. Sander clamped on his mask and for the remainder of flight he breathed pure oxygen.

Another, smaller, problem was that the undercarriage up-locks failed to engage properly. When Sander pulled *g* the main wheels sagged a little way below the wings and the red 'undercarriage unlocked' lights illuminated in the cockpit.

In November 1939, V1 was joined in the test flight programme by the second prototype (V2). This aircraft was totally destroyed in a crash after just 50 hours flying, leaving V1 as the sole trials aircraft, before the first BMW 801-powered example (V5) flew in April 1940. Here, V1 is seen having had the ducted spinner replaced by a radial cowl. The civil registration had also been discarded, replaced successively by the codes FO+LY and RM+CA.

Above: V7 was the first BMW 801-powered Fw 190 to be fitted with armament, comprising two 7.9-mm MG 17 machine-guns mounted above the engine and two similar weapons in the wing roots. The aircraft has boxes in position to collect the belt links and cartridge cases, in preparation for firing at the stop butts.

Right: The Fw 190 V5 (top) was built with the original 'small wing' but, after suffering damage in a collision with a tractor during take-off, it was decided to rebuild the aircraft with a new large wing intended for one of the Fw 190A-0 pre-production prototypes. Thus, the aircraft received the restrospective designations V5k (kleiner Flügel; small wing) and V5g (grosser Flügel; large wing). Despite the success of the new wing, construction of the first seven Fw 190A-0s was too far advanced, and these were finished with the smaller wing, the first example (right) was allocated the Versuchs number V6.

A trio of early Fw 190As on the Focke-Wulf flight-test line in early 1941. Note the undercarriage attachment to the underside of the wing on the nearest aircraft is closer to the leading-edge – indicating that it is a small wing Fw 190A-0. The other two aircraft have two MG FF 20-mm cannon mounted immediately outboard of the undercarriage attachment points. This trial arrangement was introduced on the Fw 190A-1 before becoming a standard fit on the A-2.

Commenting on that first flight of the prototype Fw 190 many years later Hans Sander said:

"Reading about aircraft which have proved successful, one often hears how the test pilot got out after the maiden flight and proclaimed that here was a world-beating flying machine. Such statements might make nice copy for the firm's publicity people, but in my experience the reality of initial test flying is less theatrical. For the record, I never said any such thing after the maiden flight of the Focke-Wulf 190. I am an engineer and during my training I had been taught to be cautious. After the first flight I told the members of the design team what I had learned about the new fighter, which was not a great deal, since the flight had lasted only half an hour. I said that so far as I had tried them the controls were light, positive and well-balanced, the trim was excellent and the aircraft had not demonstrated any vices; but about the heat coming into the cockpit, and that undercarriage up-lock . . ."

Ejection seat trials

With no doubt one eye on his own well-being, Hans Sander was involved in the development of an experimental ejection seat for possible incorporation into the Fw 190. In the summer of 1943, Fw 190A-0 (WNr 0022) was converted as a test bed for the trials, which were conducted at the Focke-Wulf test centre at Langenhagen. A wooden structure was built around the fuselage to protect it from the falling dummy and/or seat. However, results of these tests showed that there were several problems which were insurmountable given the resources available to the project, and further development was abandoned a few months later.

For test firing of the seat, the dummy was lowered into the cockpit using a pulley system attached to the hangar roof (above). Once in position the aircraft was moved outside to the dedicated test area and the protective wooden structure was moved into place. The firing sequence could then be initiated (right), seen here with a brave observer present by the nose of the aircraft.

The problem with the undercarriage up-lock was soon cured and the application of additional sealant around the cockpit prevented the ingress of exhaust fumes. The overheating troubles with the BMW 139 would, however, plague the engine even after the cooling fan was fitted. In an attempt to improve matters, the aircraft's ducted spinner was replaced with a normal-type spinner. Although this failed to solve the problem of engine overheating, it was noted that the reduction in performance was negligible. The extra weight and complication of the ducted spinner was unjustified and it was not fitted to subsequent aircraft.

During speed trials conducted at the Luftwaffe test establishment at Rechlin, the new fighter clocked a maximum speed of 369 mph (594 km/h) in level flight. Service test pilots praised its handling characteristics, which were significantly better than those of the Bf 109.

Further prototypes

In October 1939 the V2 made its first flight. This aircraft was the first to carry armament, comprising a Rheinmetall Borsig MG 17 7.9-mm machine-gun in each wing root. The V2 joined the V1 in the test programme, and Hans Sander and his colleagues systematically explored the aircraft's flight envelope.

In April 1940 the V5, the first prototype with a BMW 801 engine, joined the Fw 190 test programme. With the additional weight of the new engine and the strengthened structure necessary to take it, the V5 weighed about 1,400 lb (635 kg) more than V1. Hans Sander recalled:

"The 18-cylinder BMW 801 was heavier than the BMW 139, which meant that a stronger mounting was necessary to support it. To compensate for this increased weight in the nose the fuselage had to be redesigned, with the cockpit moved back a little to keep the centre of gravity in the right place. This caused a deterioration in the pilot's field of vision forwards and downwards, but it did confer one

great bonus: since the engine and the cockpit were now further apart, at last one could fly in the new fighter without having one's feet gently roasted!"

With that extra weight, the wing loading rose significantly and the Fw 190 V5 handled less well than earlier prototypes. To restore the fighter's previous handling it was fitted with a new wing 20 per cent greater in area, and with the span increased to 34 ft 5.5 in (10.51 m). To maintain the correct dimensional relationship between the wing and tailplane, the span of the latter was increased too.

Fitted with new wing and tailplane surfaces, the V5 resumed test flying in the summer of 1940. With the extra engine power and the larger wing Sander found that the fighter's rate of climb and its general handling were greatly improved. Officials at the Technical Office now asked that

all Fw 190s not yet in an advanced stage of construction be fitted with the larger wing.

During the autumn of 1940 the first aircraft in the pre-production batch of 40 Fw 190A-0s started to emerge from the factory at Bremen. The first seven pre-production aircraft had the smaller wing and tailplane, the eighth and subsequent aircraft carried the enlarged surfaces. By now the Focke-Wulf factory at Marienburg, the Arado factory at Warnemunde and the AGO factory at Oschersleben were tooling up to build the new fighter in quantity.

Entry into service

In March 1941 Oberleutnant Otto Behrens assumed command of Erprobungsstaffel 190 based at Rechlin-Roggenthin. The unit received six pre-production Fw 190A-0s and its brief was to test the new fighter under service conditions. The pilots and ground crews assigned to the Erprobungsstaffel were drawn from II. Gruppe of Jagdgeschwader 26, and the latter unit was earmarked to receive the first production Fw 190s when these became available.

During early service trials the Fw 190A-0 exhibited a number of serious shortcomings. The new BMW 801C engine suffered from overheating, although not to the same extent as the BMW 139. The engine's automatic fuel control system also gave trouble. For a given throttle setting, set by the pilot, this automatic system should have established the optimum relationship between aircraft altitude, fuel flow, fuel mixture, engine revolutions, super-charger gear selection, propeller pitch setting and ignition timing. The system did not work reliably at first, but a string of modifications over a long period reduced the problems to an acceptable level.

In June 1941 the first four production Fw 190A-1s emerged from the Marienburg factory. By August, monthly

Above: Wearing the WNr 0025, this aircraft was the 11th 'large-wing' Fw 190A-0 to be built. It was used for testing the BMW 801D engine, which was intended to solve many of the problems associated with the engine overheating. This engine was later incorporated, in a developed form, into the Fw 190A-3.

Above left: The kleiner Flügel Fw 190A-0s were worked hard, despite the constant engine problems. With Focke-Wulf and BMW both blaming each other, the project was placed in jeopardy. During operational trials conducted by II./JG 26 personnel at le Bourget, a visiting RLM commission actually recommended the cancellation of the entire project. However, the decision was delayed and, after some 50 modifications, the Fw 190A was accepted for service.

Left: Based at Moorseele in Belgium, 6. Staffel of Jagdgeschwader 26 was the first operational unit to receive the Fw 190A-1, replacing the unit's Bf 109E-7s from late July 1941. By late September the rest of II.Gruppe/JG 26 had completed their conversion to the type.

Below: Operational Fw 190A-1s, A-2s, and A-3s were characterised by the lack of the tail fin-mounted aerial mast, which was a feature of the A-4 series onwards.

Above: An Fw 190A-2 from the Geschwaderstab of JG 26 runs-up at St Omer in the spring of 1942, possibly to join the mêlée of aircraft scribing contrail cirles in the sky overhead. It is not known if this was actual combat with the RAF, or the pilot's compatriots practising their combat tactics in a staged dogfight.

Front-line Fw 190 units – 27 July 1942

On this date a total of 486 Fw 190s of all versions was serving with combat units, of which 454 were assigned to 11 fighter gruppen, 30 to the two fighter-bomber staffeln, and two aircraft to reconnaissance units. During July 1942 the factories delivered 194 new Fw 190s to the Luftwaffe.

Significantly, the two geschwader causing so much grief to the RAF, Nos 2 and 26 based in France and Belgium, possessed only 235 Fw 190s. Of those just under 200 were serviceable.

Jagdgeschwader 1, based in Germany for Reich defence duties, saw action only occasionally, when its fighters scrambled to engage the small-scale daylight attacks mounted from time to time by unescorted RAF bombers.

Unit	Total	Serviceable
Luftflotte 3 (France/Belgium)		
Jagdgeschwader 2		
Stab	4	3
I. Gruppe	36	29
II. Gruppe	37	34
III. Gruppe	39	31
10. Staffel	15	11[1]
Jagdgeschwader 26		
Stab	4	4
I. Gruppe	38	28
II. Gruppe	41	36
III. Gruppe	36	33
10. Staffel	15	12[1]
Aufklärungsgruppe 33		
1. Staffel	1	0[2]
Aufklärungsgruppe 123		
1. Staffel	1	0[2]
Luftflotte 5 (Arctic sector, Eastern Front)		
Jagdgeschwader 5		
I. Gruppe	35	28
IV. Gruppe	26	20
Luftwaffenbefehlshaber Mitte (Reich Air Defence)		
Jagdgeschwader 1		
Stab	4	4
I. Gruppe	37	34
II. Gruppe	38	28
III. Gruppe	40	33
IV. Gruppe	39	28

[1] Fighter-bomber unit
[2] Reconnaissance unit (also operated Bf 109s and Ju 88s)

JG 2 was the second geschwader to re-equip with the Fw 190, beginning the process in the spring of 1942. Completing paperwork by the tail of his aircraft in August of that year is Oblt Egon Mayer, Staffelkapitän of 7./JG 2. At this time Mayer had achieved some 50 of his eventual total of 102 victories, all of which were achieved in the Western Front theatre.

production reached 30 aircraft. The first two aircraft off the Arado/Warnemunde production line were delivered in August, and the first two from the AGO/Oschersleben plant followed in October. The initial production version carried an armament of four MG 17 7.9-mm machine-guns, two on top of the forward fuselage and two in the wing roots, with all four synchronised to fire through the airscrew.

By the end of September 1941 the Luftwaffe had accepted a total of 82 Fw 190A-1s. One Gruppe, II./JG 26 based at Moorseele in Belgium, had re-equipped with the new fighter and deliveries had started to III./JG 26 based at Liegescourt in northern France.

British intelligence

By this time the British Air Ministry had received vague and contradictory evidence as to the existence of the new German fighter. The Air Ministry Weekly Intelligence Summary dated 13 August 1941, a secret document issued to all RAF units and made available to all officers and aircrew, carried the following report:

"A certain number of these new fighters have been produced, but information is very scanty. The general design is said to be based on American practice and the aircraft is probably a low-wing monoplane with a fairly short fuselage and a span of about 30 feet. This new aircraft is fitted with a two-bank radial, an engine of the same type as that in the Dornier 217. It is definitely known that this particular machine had to be fitted with an auxiliary mechanically-driven fan to keep the engine temperatures within reasonable limits. It is also reported that it is equipped with a very large airscrew and that the undercarriage is extraordinarily high in order to give the necessary ground clearance. Rough estimates show that the speed of the Fw 190 is somewhere between 370 and 380 mph at 18-20,000 ft."

Although brief, the report was accurate except in two respects. The propeller fitted to the Fw 190 was not particularly large. Also, and more importantly, the report underestimated the maximum speed of the Fw 190 by about 30 mph (48 km/h).

Soon after II./JG 26 commenced combat patrols in September, the RAF pilot's reports began to mention encounters with a new German fighter type. Following action on 18 September, a combat report noted the destruction of "a Curtiss Hawk (or Fw 190)". Almost certainly the aircraft was the Fw 190 flown by the commander of II./JG 26, Hauptmann Walter Adolph, who was shot down and killed on that day.

Three days later, while escorting Blenheim bombers attacking the power station at Gusnay near Bethune, the

First into combat – JG 26 and JG 2

Fw 190A-2, II./JG 26
Following the loss of II./JG 26's Gruppenkommandeur, Hauptmann Walter Adolph, in September 1941, the leader of 7./JG 26 Joachim Münchenberg was promoted to succeed him. His aircraft is depicted here at Coquelles in December 1941 with 62 'kills' displayed on the rudder, of which the final six had been achieved on the Fw 190 that autumn.

Fw 190A-3, III./JG 2
Hauptmann Hans 'Assi' Hahn's III. Gruppe was the first of JG 2's gruppen to re-equip with the Fw 190, becoming operational on the A-2 version in March 1942. Wearing the 'cockerel's head' motif favoured by Hahn (whose surname means cockerel in German), this A-3 had become his regular mount by September 1942.

In a staged photograph, an Fw 190A-2 closes in on an 'RAF bomber' over warships in the English Channel on 6 July 1942. By this time the true danger posed by the 190 to the RAF had manifested itself in combat, and the two geschwaders' 'kills' against Fighter Command's Spitfire Mk V-equipped squadrons were rapidly mounting.

Below: In an all-too familiar scene during the Fw 190's early career, a BMW 801 is covered with foam by members of the base fire section after overheating and catching fire. Such was the unreliability of the engine during early trials that pilots were loathed to leave the vicinity of the airfield in case the engine failed or caught fire.

Polish No. 315 Squadron reported that its Spitfires had destroyed "one unknown enemy aircraft with a radial engine". Almost certainly this was the Fw 190 of Lieutenant Ulrich Dzialas, who was lost at that time.

The evidence mounted slowly, and more months elapsed before the RAF Intelligence Sevice committed itself to a positive identification of the new German fighter. In the issue dated 29 October 1941 the Weekly Intelligence Summary stated: "In recent weeks a radial-engined type of fighter has been reported as a French aircraft, the Bloch 151, and as a new type of German fighter, the Fw 190. There is as yet insufficient evidence to say with certainty what the new aircraft is".

By the beginning of 1942 RAF Intelligence had at last established beyond doubt that the aircraft was indeed the Fw 190. Also, from the reports of disgruntled fighter pilots who encountered it in combat, it became clear that the radial-engined Fw 190 was a formidable opponent. It had a clear margin in performance over the Spitfire Mk V, the best aircraft RAF Fighter Command then had available.

Even after it began flying combat missions the Fw 190 continued to suffer from engine overheating. Sometimes this led to fires in flight and, following losses to this cause, an edict was issued forbidding pilots to fly over the sea beyond gliding range from the coast. Despite that difficulty, the Fw 190 proved a formidable adversary. In the months that followed the RAF learned to its discomfort that the new German fighter had the edge in performance over any of its operational types.

New variants

During the autumn of 1941 the Fw 190A-2 replaced the A-1 on the production lines. Powered by the improved BMW 801C-2 engine, this version was fitted with two Mauser MG 151 20-mm cannon in place of the MG 17 machine-guns in each wing root. Yet, even with the new armament, the Fw 190 was considered inadequately armed to attack enemy bombers. As a result, several A-2s were retrofitted with two additional Oerlikon MG/FF 20-mm cannon in the wings, firing outside the propeller disc.

By the end of the 1941 more than 200 Fw 190s had been delivered to the Luftwaffe. Early in 1942 the A-3 replaced the A-2 in production, powered by the BMW 801D-2 engine giving 1,700 hp (1268 kW) at take-off. The fighter's armament was standardised with the four cannon and two machine-guns, as carried by the retrofitted A-2s. Soon after this variant entered production the FuG 7 HF radio was

Below: A Stab JG 26 Fw 190A-2 is pushed back into its camouflaged individual revetment in the early spring of 1942. The aircraft is believed to be the mount of Geschwader-Adjutant Wilfred Sieling, who was killed in combat with RAF fighters on 30 April 1942.

Above: JG 2 'Richthofen's' area of operations spread westwards from the Somme to the Atlantic seaboard. Here, 6./JG 2 is seen during conversion from Bf 109Fs (background) in the spring of 1942. 'Yellow 2', in the centre, was lost over the Channel in a fierce dogfight during the abortive Dieppe landings on 19 August 1942.

Right: This ex-II./JG 26 A-1, used to train pilots of II./JG 1 on temporary detachment to Abbeville-Drucat in March 1942, reveals its ferocious 'shark's mouth' paint scheme. Only training aircraft wore such flamboyant markings.

Each of JG 2's staffeln had their own badge, which their aircraft proudly wore. The 'thumb pressing a top hat' emblem belonged to 7./JG 2, a schwarm of Fw 190A-2s here being readied for one of the first combat missions.

Operation Airthief – the plan to hijack an Fw 190A

By the spring of 1942 the Fw 190 had become an uncomfortably sharp thorn in the side of RAF Fighter Command. Obviously, if an airworthy example of the Fw 190 could be captured and its secrets probed, that would be of inestimable value. Capt. Philip Pinckney, a British commando officer, hatched a daring plan to gain that end.

In an operation of this type, two men might succeed where more might fail. Pinckney suggested that his good friend Jeffrey Quill, chief test pilot at the Supermarine company, should accompany him on the enterprise.

The essentials of the plan were as follows. On Night 1 a Royal Navy motor gunboat, equipped with direction-finding radio, was to carry the pair to a point within about two miles of a selected beach on the French coast, where they would disembark into a folding canoe. The pair would paddle ashore, hide their boat in sand dunes and lie up during the following day. On Night 2 the pair would move inland to within observation range of the selected Fw 190 airfield, and hide up before dawn. During the daylight hours the pair would keep the airfield under observation and plan their attack. On Night 3 the pair would penetrate the airfield defences by stealth, and conceal themselves as near as possible to one or more Fw 190s at their dispersal points. The pair would then wait until the next day, when the ground crew arrived to run the engine of one of the fighters.

The pair would then break cover, shoot or drive away the ground crewmen, and Jeffrey Quill would jump into the cockpit and taxi the machine to the runway. As he did so, Pinckney would be outside the plane warding off any attempt to interfere with the operation. Once Quill was safely airborne, Pinckney would withdraw to a previously prepared hide. On Night 4 he would return to the hidden canoe. Just before dawn he would launch the craft and paddle out to sea, making radio transmissions so that the motor gunboat could home on the craft and pick him up.

Yet in a remarkable coincidence, on the very day Pinckney submitted his proposal, the need for this risky operation disappeared. On the afternoon of 23 June an Fw 190 pilot had become disorientated in a dogfight with Spitfires over southern England. He mistook the Bristol Channel for the English Channel and made a wheels-down landing at Pembrey airfield, south Wales (below). Thus, the RAF gained the coveted example of an Fw 190, without having to resort to the risky 'Airthief' operation.

replaced with the more effective FuG 16 VHF set.

By the late spring of 1942 Jagdgeschwader 2 and Jagdgeschwader 26 had re-equipped with the Fw 190. Between them these units mustered about 260 of these formidable fighters. The engine troubles that had plagued the Fw 190 earlier had largely been cured. With the embargo on overwater flights lifted, German pilots were able to exploit the fighter's capabilities to the full and engage the enemy with greater confidence.

The Fw 190 pilots' more aggressive mood manifested itself on 1 June 1942, when the RAF mounted operation Circus No. 178. Eight bomb-carrying Hurricanes attacked a target near Bruges in Belgium. Seven squadrons of Spitfire Mk Vs from the Hornchurch and Biggin Hill Wings provided close escort, while four squadrons from the Debden Wing provided target support. Positioned by radar, some 40 Fw 190s of I. and III. Gruppen of Jagdgeschwader 26 attacked the raiding force from out of the sun during its withdrawal. The Debden Wing took the force of the attack and lost eight Spitfires in rapid succession, including that flown by its commander. Five Spitfires limped home with battle damage. No Focke-Wulf suffered serious damage during the encounter.

Ascendancy over the Spitfire

The following day proved equally disastrous for a Fighter Command unit, when several squadrons of Spitfires flew a sweep through the St Omer area. Usually the German fighter controllers ignored such incursions, but not this one. I. and II. Gruppen of JG 26 delivered a co-ordinated attack on No. 403 (Canadian) Squadron, led by the redoubtable Squadron Leader Alan Deere. In the desperate seven-minute brawl that followed, seven Spitfires were shot down. Two more returned with serious damage. Again, no Focke-Wulf suffered serious damage.

A few weeks later the Commander-in-Chief Fighter Command, Air Chief Marshal Sir Sholto Douglas, wrote a strongly worded letter to the Under Secretary of State for Air, Lord Sherwood. Douglas complained that his force had lost the technical edge it had once had over the Luftwaffe and went on to say:

"There is ... no doubt in my mind, nor in the minds of my fighter pilots, that the Fw 190 is the best all-round fighter in the world today."

As mentioned elsewhere in this account, near the end of June 1942 a German pilot became disorientated during a combat with Spitfires over western England and mistakenly landed his Fw 190A-3 at Pembrey in south Wales. So the RAF secured an intact example of this important fighter. At the time of the capture, however, that version of the Fw 190 had been superseded in production by the A-4. The latter's BMW 801D-2 engine carried the MW 50 water methanol injection system which boosted power for short periods at low and medium altitudes.

During this period there were experiments using Fw 190s in the fighter-bomber role, to mount tip-and-run

After some nine hours of test flying at RAE Farnborough as MP499, the Fw 190 was transferred to the AFDU at Duxford on 13 July 1942. After six months of evaluation flying the aircraft was grounded and later relegated to engine bench tests.

Testing the Fw 190

On 23 June 1942 Leutnant Arnim Faber of III./JG 2 became disorientated during a dogfight with Spitfires over southwest England, and landed in error at the RAF airfield at Pembrey, south Wales. After undergoing trials at the Royal Aircraft Establishment at Farnborough, the captured fighter went to the Air Fighting Development Unit (AFDU) at Duxford for tactical trials against each of the British and US fighter types that was likely to meet the German aircraft in combat. An abridged version of the resultant report, issued in August 1942 and reproduced below, shows how the German fighter compared with its contemporaries. It should be remembered that the words were not those of Focke-Wulf salesmen trying to boost their company's product, but came from those forced to give grudging admiration to a product of their foe.

Fw 190 vs Spitfire Mk VB

The Fw 190 was compared with an operational Spitfire Mk VB for speed and all-round manoeuvrability at heights up to 25,000 ft. The Fw 190 is superior in speed at all heights, and the approximate differences are as follows:-

At 2,000 ft (610 m) the Fw 190 is 25-30 mph (40-48 km/h) faster than the Spitfire Mk VB
At 3,000 ft (915 m) the Fw 190 is 30-35 mph (48-56 km/h) faster than the Spitfire Mk VB
At 5,000 ft (1525 m) the Fw 190 is 25 mph (40 km/h) faster than the Spitfire Mk VB
At 9,000 ft (2744 m) the Fw 190 is 25-30 mph (40-48 km/h) faster than the Spitfire Mk VB
At 15,000 ft (4573 m) the Fw 190 is 20 mph (32 km/h) faster than the Spitfire Mk VB
At 18,000 ft (5488 m) the Fw 190 is 20 mph (32 km/h) faster than the Spitfire Mk VB
At 21,000 ft (6400 m) the Fw 190 is 20-25 mph (32-40 km/h) faster than the Spitfire Mk VB

Climb: The climb of the Fw 190 is superior to that of the Spitfire Mk VB at all heights. The best speeds for climbing are approximately the same, but the angle of the Fw 190 is considerably steeper. Under maximum continuous climbing conditions the climb of the Fw 190 is about 450 ft/min better up to 25,000 feet (7620 m). With both aircraft flying at high cruising speed and then pulling up into a climb, the superior climb of the Fw 190 is even more marked.
Dive: Comparative dives have shown that the Fw 190 can leave the Spitfire with ease, particularly during the initial stages.
Manoeuvrability: The manoeuvrability of the Fw 190 is better than that of the Spitfire VB except in turning circles, when the Spitfire can quite easily out-turn it. The Fw 190 has better acceleration under all conditions of flight and this must obviously be useful during combat.

When the Fw 190 was in a turn and was attacked by the Spitfire, the superior rate of roll enabled it to flick into a diving turn in the opposite direction. The pilot of the Spitfire found great difficulty in following this manoeuvre and even when prepared for it was seldom able to allow the correct deflection. It was found that if the Spitfire was cruising at low speed and was 'bounced' by the Fw 190, it was easily caught even if the Fw 190 was sighted when well out of range.

A number of other Fw 190s were tested by the AFDU, including PM679, an ex-I./SKG 10 Fw 190A-5/U8 (seen here with a P-47D) that mistakenly landed at Manston on 20 June 1943.

Fw 190 vs Spitfire Mk IX

The Focke Wulf 190 was compared with a fully operational Spitfire Mk IX for speed and manoeuvrability at heights up to 25,000 ft. The Mk IX, at most heights, is slightly superior in speed, and the approximate differences in speeds at various heights are as follows:-

At 2,000 ft (610 m) the Fw 190 is 7-8 mph (11-13 km/h) faster than the Spitfire Mk IX
At 5,000 ft (1524 m) the Fw 190 and the Spitfire Mk IX are approximately the same
At 8,000 ft (2440 m) the Spitfire Mk IX is 8 mph (13 km/h) faster than the Fw 190
At 15,000 ft (4573 m) the Spitfire Mk IX is 5 mph (8 km/h) faster than the Fw 190
At 18,000 ft (5488 m) the Fw 190 is 3 mph (5 km/h) faster than the Spitfire Mk IX
At 21,000 ft (6400 m) the Fw 190 and the Spitfire Mk IX are approximately the same
At 25,000 ft (7620 m) the Spitfire Mk IX is 5-7 mph (8-11 km/h) faster than the Fw 190

Climb: During comparative climbs at various heights up to 23,000 ft, with both aircraft flying under maximum continuous climbing conditions, little difference was found between the two aircraft although on the whole the Spitfire Mk IX was slightly better. Above 22,000 ft the climb of the Fw 190 falls off rapidly, whereas the climb of the Spitfire Mk IX is increasing. When both aircraft were flying a high cruising speed and were pulled up into a climb from level flight, the Fw 190 had a slight advantage in the initial stages of the climb due to its better acceleration. This superiority was slightly increased when both aircraft were pulled up into the climb from the dive.
Dive: The Fw 190 is faster in a dive than the Mk IX, particularly during the initial stage. The superiority is not so marked as with the Mk VB.
Manoeuvrability: The Fw 190 is more manoeuvrable than the Mk IX except in turning circle, when it is out-turned without difficulty.

The superior rate of roll of the Fw 190 enabled it to avoid the Spitfire Mk IX if attacked when in a turn by flicking over into a diving turn in the opposite direction and, as with the Spitfire Mk VB, the Mk IX had great difficulty in following this manoeuvre. The initial acceleration of the Fw 190 is better than the Spitfire Mk IX under all conditions of flight, except in level flight at such altitudes where the Spitfire has a speed advantage and then, providing the Spitfire is cruising at high speed, there is little to choose between the two aircraft.

Fw 190 vs Mustang Mk 1A

The Fw 190 was compared with a fully operational Mustang Mk 1A for speed and all-round performance up to 23,000 ft. There was little to choose between the aircraft in speed at all heights except between 10,000 and 15,000 ft, where the Mustang was appreciably faster. Approximate differences were as follows:

At 2,000 ft [610 m] the Fw 190 is 2 mph (3 km/h) faster than the Mustang
At 5,000 ft (1525 m) the Mustang is 5 mph (8 km/h) faster than the Fw 190
At 10,000 ft (3050 m) the Mustang is 15 mph (24 km/h) faster than the Fw 190
At 20,000 ft (6100 m) the Fw 190 is 5 mph (8 km/h) faster than the Mustang
At 23,000 ft (7010 m) the Fw 190 is 5 mph (8 km/h) faster than the Mustang

Climb: The climb of the Fw 190 is superior to that of the Mustang Mk 1A at all heights. The best climbing speed for the Mustang is approximately 10 mph (16 km/h) slower than that for the Fw 190; the angle is not nearly so steep and the rate of climb is considerably inferior. When both aircraft are pulled up into a climb after a fast dive, the inferiority in the initial stage of the climb is not so marked, but if the climb is continued the Fw 190 draws away rapidly.
Dive: Comparative dives have shown that there is little to choose between the two aircraft and, if anything, the Mustang is slightly faster in a prolonged dive.
Manoeuvrability: The manoeuvrability of the Fw 190 is better than of the Mustang except in turning circles where the Mustang is superior. In the rolling plane at high speed the Mustang compares more favourably with the Fw 190 than does the Spitfire.

The acceleration of the Fw 190 under all conditions of flight is slightly better than that of the Mustang and this becomes more marked when both aircraft are cruising at low speed. When the Fw 190 was attacked by the Mustang in a turn, the usual manoeuvre of flicking into a diving turn in the opposite direction was not so effective against the Mustang as against the Spitfire, particularly if the aircraft were flying at high speed. The fact that the engine of the Mustang does not cut during the application of negative '*g*' proved a great asset, and gave the Mustang a reasonable chance of following the Fw 190 and shooting it down.

Fw 190 vs P-38F Lightning

The Fw 190 was compared with an operational P-38F flown by an experienced US Army Air Force pilot. The two aircraft were compared for speed and all-round manoeuvrability at heights up to 23,000 ft. The Fw 190 was superior in speed at all heights up to 22,000 ft, where the two aircraft were approximately the same. The approximate differences in speeds are as follows:

At 2,000 ft [610 m] the Fw 190 is 15 mph (24 km/h) faster than the P-38F
At 8,000 ft (2440 m) the Fw 190 is 15 mph (24 km/h) faster than the P-38F
At 15,000 ft (4573 m) the Fw 190 is 5-8 mph (8-13 km/h) faster than the P-38F
At 23,000 ft (7010 m) the P-38F is 6-8 mph (9-13 km/h) faster than the Fw 190

Climb: The climb of the P-38F is not as good as that of the Fw 190 up to 15,000 ft. Above this height the climb of the P-38F improves rapidly until at 20,000 ft [6010 m] it becomes superior. The best climbing speed for the P-38F is about 20 mph (32 km/h) less than that of the Fw 190 and the angle approximately the same. The initial rate of climb of the Fw 190, either from level flight or a dive, is superior to that of the P-38F at all heights below 20,000 ft and above this height the climb of the P-38F becomes increasingly better.
Dive: Comparative dives proved the Fw 190 to be better, particularly in the initial stage. During prolonged dives the P-38F, on occasion, was slowly gaining on the Fw 190, but in combat it is unlikely that the P-38F would have time to catch up, before having to break off the attack.
Manoeuvrability: The Fw 190 is superior to that of the P-38F, particularly in the rolling plane. Although at high speed the Fw 190 is superior in turning circles, it can be out-turned if the P-38F reduces its speed to about 140 mph (225 km/h), at which speed it can carry out a very tight turn, which the Fw 190 cannot follow.

The acceleration of the two aircraft was compared and the Fw 190 was found to be better in all respects. When the Fw 190 'bounced' the P-38F and was seen when over 1,000 yards away, the pilot's best manoeuvre was to go into a diving turn and, if it found the Fw 190 was catching it up, to pull up into a spiral climb, flying at its lowest possible speed.

Conclusions

The Fw 190 is undoubtedly a formidable low- and medium-altitude fighter. Its designer has obviously given much thought to the pilot. The cockpit is well laid out and the absence of large levers and unnecessary gadgets most noticeable. The pilot is given a comfortable seating position, and is well protected by armour. The simplicity of the aircraft as a whole is an excellent feature, and enables new pilots to be thoroughly conversant with all controls in a very brief period. The all-round search view is the best that has yet been seen from any aircraft flown by this unit.

The rough running of the engine is much disliked and must be a great disadvantage, as lack of confidence in an engine makes flying over bad country or water most unpleasant.

The armament is good and well positioned, and the ammunition capacity should be sufficient for any normal fighter operation. The sighting view is approximately half a ring (of deflection) better than that from the Spitfire.

The flying characteristics are exceptional, and a pilot new to the type feels at home immediately. The controls are light and well harmonised and all manoeuvres can be carried out without difficulty at all speeds. The fact that the Fw 190 does not require re-trimming under all conditions of flight is a particularly good point. The initial acceleration is very good and is particularly noticeable in the initial stages of a climb or dive. Perhaps one of the most outstanding qualities of this aircraft is the remarkable aileron control. It is possible to change from a turn in one direction to a turn in the opposite direction with incredible speed.

The main conclusion gained from the tactical trials of the Fw 190 is that our fighter aircraft must fly at high speed when in an area where the Fw 190 is likely to be met. This will give our pilots the chance of 'bouncing' and catching the Fw 190 and, if 'bounced' themselves, the best chance of avoiding being shot down.

Right: The design of tropical air filters stemmed from the Fw 190A-3/U7 (above). Three examples of this special high-altitude fighter were fitted with open-faced intakes on the cowling blister locations, allowing greater airflow to the engine supercharger and rear cylinder banks. These were adapted on Fw 190A-3/U3 trials aircraft WNr 130511 (below) to incorporate sand filters. The refined tropical filters were later used operationally, particularly by Fw 190Fs in Italy.

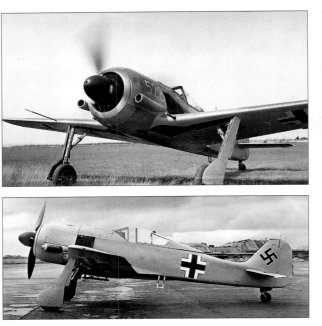

In late 1942 a new phase of the battle on the Western Front began as the growing numbers of USAAF four-engined heavy bombers began to mount ever larger daylight raids. These were at first concentrated on coastal targets, but soon proceeded further inland and eventually over Germany itself. For the next two years the Fw 190s of JGs 1, 2 and 26 (later joined by JGs 6 and 11) were tasked with repelling the bombers, facing increasingly insurmountable odds. Attacks from the rear were soon dropped in favour of head on attacks. JG 6 painted a full-size head-on view of a B-17 on its hangar doors as an aid to judging range (bottom left). Once an enemy bomber had been damaged and forced to leave the defensive formation, it was invariably a victim of the endgültige Vernichtung (final destruction), seen below being administered by Fw 190 during a 11 January 1944 raid on Focke-Wulf's Oschersleben factory (right). The USAAF bombers, particularly the B-17, could however, take a great deal of damage, as evidenced by this 457th BG aircraft, which survived two hits by an Fw 190's 30-mm cannon (below right).

Above: Although never fitted with tropical filters, II./JG 2's Fw 190s were detached to North Africa from November 1942. Although only present in the theatre for four months, the gruppe was in daily action against both USAAF and RAF fighters and bombers, racking up an amazing 150 victories for the loss of just 18 Fw 190s (of these, eight were lost in accidents and two to 'friendly fire'). Here, a II./JG 2 aircraft hides under rudimentary camouflage at Tindja-South, Tunisia, in December 1942.

attacks on targets along the south coast of England. The two Jagdgeschwader in the west each operated a Staffel with specially modified Fw 190A-3s and A-4s. These aircraft had the MG/FF cannon removed from the outer wing positions, and had a rack to carry an SC 250 250-kg (550-lb) or SC 500 500-kg (1,100-lb) bomb under the fuselage.

An end to the easy times

By the late summer of 1942 the German armed forces were almost at the limits of their territorial gains, following deep thrusts eastwards into the Soviet Union and along the coast of North Africa. This period also marked the apogee of the Fw 190's service career, when the units equipped with the type enjoyed an easy-going qualitative superiority over almost every enemy type that they met in combat.

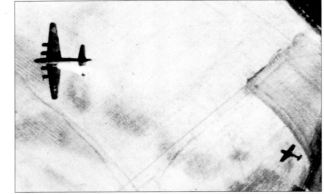

In war nothing stands still. From the summer of 1942 the Spitfire Mk IX, powered by the new Merlin 61 engine with two-stage supercharging, appeared in action with a performance remarkably close to that of the German fighter. The type was in full production and it was becoming available in useful numbers. In combat a German pilot could not to tell the difference between the Spitfire Mk IX and the earlier Mk V. From now on they had to treat every Spitfire they encountered as a Mk IX.

Eighth Air Force arrives

At the same time, the US Eighth Air Force in Britain began sending formations of B-17 and B-24 heavy bombers by day to attack targets in occupied Europe. Thier appearance came as a shock to the German fighter pilots. Not only could these aircraft put up a powerful defensive crossfire with their batteries of 0.5-in (12.7-mm) machine-guns, but they were able to absorb more battle damage than any of the types previously encountered. Put simply, the German single-seat fighters lacked the fire power to deal with these resilient targets. Both the Fw 190A-3 and A-4 carried four 20-mm cannon and two 0.31-in (7.9-mm) machine-guns. In a three-second burst it loosed off 130 rounds of 20-mm ammunition (the machine-guns were almost useless in such an engagement).

On average, it took 20 cannon hits to destroy a bomber during an engagement from the rear quarter. Combat films revealed that the pilots of average ability scored hits with only 2 per cent of the carefully-aimed rounds they fired. Using these figures, to obtain the necessary 20 hits on a heavy bomber, 1,000 20-mm rounds would have to be fired.

Front-line Fw 190 units – 17 May 1943

On this day 914 Fw 190s were serving with combat units. Of those, 602 were assigned to 16 fighter gruppen. Eight gruppen served on the Eastern Front, five gruppen on the Western Front and three gruppen were assigned to Reich air defence. There were 279 Fw 190s assigned to eight ground attack or fighter-bomber gruppen and three independent staffeln, and 33 Fw 190s assigned to two reconnaissance gruppen.

During May 1943 the factories delivered 275 Fw 190s of all variants to the Luftwaffe.

With the US daylight bombing attacks now hitting targets in Germany itself, there were moves to strengthen the fighter defences of the homeland. As part of that process III./JG 1 had been renumbered I./JG 11, and formed the nucleus of the new Reich defence geschwader then in the process of forming.

Unit	Total	Serviceable
Luftflotte 1 (Northern sector, Eastern Front)		
Jagdgeschwader 54		
Stab	4	4
I. Gruppe	36	30
10. Staffel	9	3 [1, 2]
Luftflotte 2 (Italy)		
Schlachtgeschwader 2		
II. Gruppe	22	4 [3]
Schnellkampfgeschwader 10		
III. Gruppe	20	2
Luftflotte 3 (France/Belgium)		
Jagdgeschwader 2		
Stab	4	4
I. Gruppe	40	40
II. Gruppe	24	18
III. Gruppe	40	37
Jagdgeschwader 26		
Stab	4	4
II. Gruppe	40	40
III. Gruppe	40	35
Jagdgeschwader 54		
11. Staffel	16	9 [1]
Schnellkampfgeschwader 10		
Stab	6	6
I. Gruppe	42	42
II. Gruppe	40	38
IV. Gruppe	30	23
Aufklärungsgruppe 123		
4. Staffel	2	2 [4]
Nahaufklärungsgruppe 13		
	31	25
Luftflotte 4 (Southern sector, Eastern Front)		
Schlachtgeschwader 1		
Stab	6	6
I. Gruppe	41	32 [3]
II. Gruppe	25	17 [5]
Schlachtgeschwader 2		
Stab	3	1
I. Gruppe	8	4
II. Gruppe	25	17 [5]
Luftflotte 5 (Arctic sector, Eastern Front)		
Jagdgeschwader 5		
Stab	2	2
I. Gruppe	35	23 [6]
II. Gruppe	23	20
IV. Gruppe	40	31 [6]
14. Staffel	11	7 [3]
Luftflotte 6 (Central sector, Eastern Front)		
Jagdgeschwader 26		
I. Gruppe	36	30
Jagdgeschwader 51		
Stab	14	11
I. Gruppe	39	20
III. Gruppe	40	21
IV. Gruppe	28	20
Luftwaffenbefehlshaber Mitte (Reich Air Defence)		
Jagdgeschwader 1		
Stab	3	1
I. Gruppe	31	27 [6]
II. Gruppe	39	31
Jagdgeschwader 11		
I. Gruppe	40	27

[1] Fighter-bomber unit
[2] Unit forming
[3] Unit also flew Henschel Hs 129s
[4] Reconnaissance unit, also flew Bf 109s
[5] Unit also flew Henschel Hs 123 and 129s
[6] Unit also flew Bf 109s

But the aircraft's magazines carried only 500 rounds of cannon ammunition. In other words, the destruction of a heavy bomber required sustained attacks from two or more Fw 190s. It is stressed that these are average figures; ace German pilots scored a much higher proportion of hits, while those below-average pilots scored even less.

On 9 October a force of 108 B-17s and B-24s, with fighter escort, attacked the Fives-Lille steel works in Belgium. Oberleutnant Otto Stamberger of III./JG 26, an Fw 190 pilot who went into action that day, later wrote:

"We attacked the enemy bombers in pairs, going in with great bravado: closing in fast from behind with throttles wide open, then letting fly. But at first the attacks were broken off much too early – as those great 'barns' grew larger and larger our people were afraid of colliding with them. I wondered why I had scored no hits but then I considered the size of the things: 40 metres span! The next time I went in I thought: get in much closer, keep going, keep going. Then I opened fire, starting with his motors on the port wing. By the third such firing run the two port engines were burning well, and I had shot the starboard outer engine to smithereens. The enemy 'kite' went down in wide spiralling left-hand turns, and crashed just east of Vendeville; four or five of the crew bailed out."

Right: This remarkable gun-camera sequence came from Flt Sgt A. Robson's Spitfire Mk VB during combat north of Boulogne on 4 May 1942. As he closed in on what was probably a JG 26 Fw 190A-2 and opened fire, first the port undercarriage leg involuntarily lowered, then the pilot jettisoned the canopy and lept from the cockpit, missing the trailing edge of the starboard wing. Amazingly, Robson, of No. 485 (New Zealand) Squadron, failed to notice the pilot leaving the aircraft, and claimed it as 'probably destroyed'.

Below: An Fw 190A-5/U3 fighter-bomber of 10.(Jabo)/JG 54 taxies out at St Omer-Wizernes in early 1943, with an SC 500 500-kg (1,100-lb) bomb on its ventral bomb rack. Formerly 10.(Jabo)/JG 26, this specialised cross-Channel 'tip and run' fighter-bomber staffel was again redesignated, as 14./SKG 10, in April of that year. The SC 500 was most accurately delivered using dive-bombing techniques, which were regularly practised by the staffel.

Mediterranean theatre

Fw 190A-5, Jagdergänzungsgruppe Ost
Non-operational units were allowed much greater freedom in the schemes adopted by their aircraft. No-one exploited this more than Major Hermann Graf, Gruppenkommandeur of Jagdergänzungsgruppe Ost (Operational Fighter Training Wing East) based at Bussac, southern France, in the summer of 1943.

Fw 190A-4, II./JG 2
Gruppenkommandeur of II./JG 2 at the start of their successful deployment to North Africa was Oberleutnant Adolf Dickfeld. His aircraft is finished in the desert tan scheme applied during the unit's stay in Tunisia. The most succesful pilots of the campaign were Kurt Bühligen and Erich Rudorffer – a combined score of 67 'kills' in under four months.

Stamberger's narrative highlights the difficulty of engaging these bombers, and the severe punishment they could take. The B-17 he attacked had become separated from the formation, and he made three deliberate attacks without having to worry about any concentrated return fire. Attacking the US bombers in formation was a much more difficult business, and even battle-hardened pilots were unnerved by the defensive cross-fire. That day defending fighters shot down four heavy bombers, for a loss of two of their number.

Head-on Attacks

After examining shot down US heavy bombers, the commander of III./JG 2, Major Egon Mayer, noted that their armour gave little protection against attacks from head-on. He saw that if an attack came from that direction it would be possible to inflict fatal damage with far fewer hits than was necessary in an attack from the rear. Moreover, a bomber formation could bring far fewer guns to bear against an attack from the forward hemisphere, and the fighter spent far less time within range of the enemy cross-fire.

On 23 November 1942 a force of 36 B-17s and B-24s, without fighter escort, attacked the U-boat base at St Nazaire on the west coast of France. Egon Mayer led his gruppe in a head-on attack on the heavy bombers and the unit shot down three B-17s and seriously damaged one more, for the loss of one fighter. Fired from head-on, four or five hits with 20-mm rounds were sufficient to knock down a heavy bomber. It was the most successful defensive effort so far by German fighters against the US bombers and, as the news spread, other German units copied these tactics.

There were problems with the head-on attack, however. The fighter closed on the bomber at around 500 mph (800 km/h), or 200 yards per second. That left time for only a brief half-second burst from 500 yards, before the German pilot had to break away sharply to avoid colliding with his victim. It took considerable skill to press home such an attack, and inexperienced pilots often failed to get their gunsight on the target in the short time available. Using head-on attacks a few ace pilots amassed impressive scores against the heavy bombers, but pilots of average ability achieved little.

During the spring of 1943 the Fw 190A-5 entered production. This had the engine mounting lengthened by 15 cm

'Wilde Sau' night fighters

In the spring of 1943 Major Hajo Hermann proposed the use of single-engined fighters, Fw 190s and Bf 109s, in the target defence role to engage RAF night bombers. He argued that over a city under attack the massed searchlights, the fires on the ground and the Pathfinders' marker flares would, from time to time, illuminate the bombers long enough for the fighter pilots to press home a visual attack. Hermann received permission to conduct small-scale experiments with these so-called 'Wilde Sau' (Wild Boar) tactics, and achieved some success.

Then, in July 1943, RAF bombers began dropping 'Window', metal foil strips, to counter the ground control and airborne interception radars used by the twin-engined night fighter force. The effect of 'Window' on the radars was devastating, and bomber losses fell dramatically.

Since the 'Wilde Sau' tactics made no use of radar, they were impervious to the British radar jamming. On orders from Göring, Hermann hastily expanded the 'Wilde Sau' force into a full geschwader, JG 300. In the months that followed, two further 'Wilde Sau' units were formed, JG 301 and JG 302, and all three units played an important role in the night air defence of Germany in the autumn of 1943.

The Luftwaffe twin-engined night fighter force quickly came to terms with the new situation. Following the introduction of a new type of radar that was less vulnerable to 'Window', it was able to regain its effectiveness. In February 1944, the three 'Wilde Sau' geschwader were redesignated as 'day and night fighter' units; for the remainder of the war they flew most of their intercept missions by day.

During 1944, a few of the Fw 190s were fitted with the Neptun airborne interception radar for night defence missions. These aircraft achieved little, however, and the concept was soon dropped.

The night-fighter detachment of IV./JG 3 was one of the first operators in the role. Above, one of the unit's pilots egresses the cockpit after a sortie in mid-1943. A few Wilde Sau aircraft were fitted with the FuG 217 Neptun radar, to enable them to seek out bombers on their own (above right). This aircraft belonged to the operational trials unit Nachtjagdgeschwader 10, based at Werneuchen, near Berlin. It carried the transmitter aerials above the rear fuselage, the azimuth receiver aerials above each wing and the elevation receiver aerials in front of the cockpit and under the starboard wing. The cathode-ray tube display for the radar (right) was mounted above the main instrument panel.

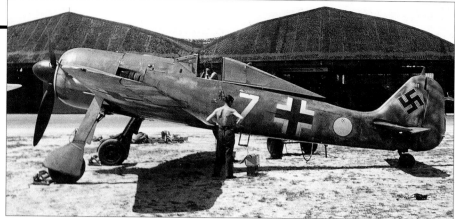

Left: A mixed pair (one Fw 190A-3 and one A-4) from an operational training unit based in the south of France in late 1943. The aircraft lack outboard cannon armament.

Above: Another training aircraft – this time an A-4 fighter-bomber of IV. Ergänzungsgruppe, Schnellkampfgeschwader 10, a training and replenishment unit based at Cognac, south France.

(just under 6 in) to give improved handling. A few months later, this version was superseded by the A-6, with heavier armour and fast-firing MG 151 20-mm weapons in place of the MG/FF cannon in the outer wing positions. Towards the end of the year the Fw 190A-7 entered production, with a pair of 13-mm Rheinmetall MG 131 heavy machine-guns replacing the 7.9-mm weapons mounted above the engine. The Fw 190A-8, produced in greater numbers than any other version, had several detailed improvements over the A-7, and was designed to accept a larger range of field modifications than its predecessors.

Fw 190 fighter-bomber variants

The first Fw 190s to serve in the fighter-bomber role had been fighter versions modified to carry a rack for a single bomb under the fuselage. During attacks on lightly defended targets these aircraft suffered few losses. For the battlefield support role there was a clear requirement for an armoured version of the Fw 190, however, and this duly appeared.

The first two specialised ground attack variants of the fighter, the Fw 190F-1 and the F-2, were based respectively from the A-4 and A-5. These had the outer wing cannon removed. They were fitted with conformal armour plate mounted externally on the underside of the fuselage to protect the engine, the cockpit and the internal fuel tanks from rounds fired from below. These new variants also had strengthened undercarriages, and provision to carry a range of different attack loads. The Fw 190G was similar to the F variant, but featured a number of refinements including an autopilot.

In the autumn of 1943 the Luftwaffe army support units underwent large-scale re-organisation, with Fw 190F and G variants replacing the obsolete Junkers Ju 87 dive-bombers. At the same time the Sturzkampfgeschwader (dive-bomber geschwader) were renamed Schlachtgeschwader (ground attack geschwader).

New weapons, new tactics

In September 1943 the four factories building Fw 190s – the Focke-Wulf plant at Marienburg, Ago at Oschersleben, Arado at Warnemunde and Fieseler at Kasel – delivered 317 aircraft to the Luftwaffe. The newest versions of the Fw 190 had provision to carry a heavier armament if their operational role required it. Attempts at air-to-air bombing of enemy formations, using 250-kg (550-lb) high-explosive bombs, achieved little, due to the difficulties of aiming the weapons and getting them to detonate sufficiently close to the bombers (the Germans failed to develop an effective proximity fuse during the war).

In the case of the Fw 190, the most important of the new weapons were the WGr 21 rocket launcher and the MK 108 heavy cannon.

The WGr 21 was a 21-cm calibre, tube-launched, spin-stabilised rocket. The Fw 190 carried a maximum of two, mounted under the wings outboard of the undercarriage legs. A time fuse detonated the 88-lb (40-kg) explosive charge at a preset distance, usually about 1,000 yards, from the launch point. The intention was to bring down enemy bombers if possible, or cause sufficient damage to force them to leave the formation and be picked off as stragglers. Occasionally, the WGr 21 was successful in damaging or destroying bombers, but lacking a proximity fuse, the weapon failed to yield consistent results. In the heat of combat, pilots found it extremely difficult to judge the

Fw 190s were heavily involved in the defence of Italy in 1943. Particularly hard-worked were the Fw 190A-4 fighter-bombers of SKG 10 in the latter half of the year. A normal load comprised a single SC 250 or SC 500 (pictured on the aircraft below left) bomb mounted on the fuselage rack. Below, a group of five SKG 10 A-4s form up, prior to setting out for their target.

When the US daylight bombing campaign began in earnest in January 1943, Jagdgeschwader 1 was the only day-fighter geschwader defending the homeland. Led by Oberstleutnant Hans Philipp, the Staff flight emblem (right) symbolised the German word for chain – Kette – which was also the term for a formation of three aircraft. It was therefore probably only worn by Philipp's aircraft and that of his two wingmen. To aid recognition and regrouping during attacks on USAAF bombers, from the spring of 1943 JG 1 Fw 190s began to appear with black and white geometric patterns on their cowlings. These materialised in the form of thick bands or checkerboard patterns (far right). Note the I. Gruppe insignia first worn by the Bf 109s of IV./JG 1.

Below: The Fw 190A-4/U4 was a factory-converted photo reconnaissance variant equipped with up to two internal, downward-facing cameras with ventral ports (visible here beneath the fuselage cross) protruding from the underside. Typical of early A-4s, this aircraft has cooling slots behind the cowling rather than the later adjustable cooling gills.

firing range to the necessary fine limits. As a result, most of the rockets were launched either too soon or too late and, as a result, exploded harmlessly away from the target.

More effective was the MK 108 cannon, which fired 30-mm high explosive/incendiary rounds at a rate of 600 per minute. Three hits from any direction were usually sufficient to bring down a heavy bomber. The weapon had a relatively low muzzle velocity of 1,750 ft (540 m) per second, which made it unsuitable for long-range engagements. To score hits, the fighter had to close to within 200 yards of the target, and that meant flying into the teeth of the bombers' defensive fire.

To overcome this problem, Luftwaffe engineers modified the Fw 190 as a specialised bomber-destroyer, the Fw 190A-8/R8 nicknamed the 'Sturmbock' (battering ram). This aircraft carried an MK 108 cannon in each outer wing position, and extra armour protection around the pilot and other vital parts of the aircraft. The extra armour and heavier armament added about 400 lb (180 kg) to the weight of this variant, limiting its performance and manoeuvrability. The role of the 'Sturmbock' was to brave the return fire and close from behind to within 100 yards of the enemy formation. Then it would engage the selected heavy bomber from short range with its heavy cannon. In the spring of 1944 a small unit, Sturmstaffel 1, tested the 'Sturmbock' in action, and found it to be highly effective.

Meanwhile, the nature of the daylight air actions over western Europe was about to undergo a profound change.

In the spring of 1944 the US Eighth Air Force in Britain took delivery of large numbers of P-51B Mustang fighters. Now it had a high performance escort fighter that could provide full-route cover for bombers penetrating to any point in Germany.

The appearance by Mustangs deep inside their homeland placed the Reich air defence fighter units in a difficult situation. If the defending fighters carried sufficient fire power to give a good chance of destroying the American heavy bombers, they were too heavy and unwieldy to dogfight with the escorts. And if the defending fighters were nimble enough to dogfight with the escorts, they were too lightly armed to engage the bombers effectively.

Enter the Sturmgruppen

During the spring of 1944 the 'white hope' of the German fighter force was the Messerschmitt Me 262 jet fighter, which had the speed to outrun the US escort fighters and the firepower – four MK 108 cannon – to knock down the heavy bombers. As a stop-gap measure until the jet fighter became available in sufficient numbers, the Luftwaffe developed the Sturmgruppe tactic. One gruppe, IV.(Sturm)/JG 3 was formed to operate the 'Sturmbock' Fw 190s. Manned by pilots who had volunteered for this hazardous role, this unit began training to deliver massed attacks on enemy bomber formations from short range and from behind. The weight of the extra armament and armour made this variant vulnerable if it was engaged by American escort fighters, so the Sturmgruppe was itself to be escorted by two gruppen of lightly armed Messerschmitt Bf 109 fighters fitted with up-rated engines.

The American heavy bombers flew in columns up to 100 miles (161 km) long, so their escorts could not be present at every point in strength. Once the German battle formation had assembled, its ground fighter controllers were to

Right: A trio of Fw 190A-4/U4s of Fernaufklärungsgruppe 123 prepares to leave its Le Luc base, near Toulon, southern France, for an operational sortie in the summer of 1944. For improved camouflage, the aircraft have received non-standard dark grey mottling paint on the rudders and lower fuselage. To reduce weight the outboard wing cannon were removed.

Above: RB 12.5 cameras, mounted as a vertical split pair in the rear fuselage of an Fw 190-A4/U4. These short focal length cameras were suitable only for low-altitude missions, longer focal length cameras being fitted for high altitude photography. For activating the cameras, a control box was mounted beneath the instrument panel.

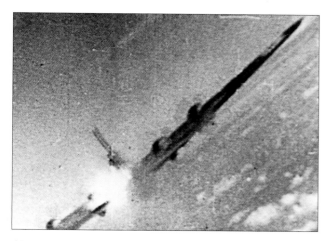

Above: This still image was taken from the camera flim of Unteroffizier 'Willi' Maximowitz, one of the original members of the original Sturm unit Sturmstaffel 1, during an attack from short range on a B-17 of the 457th BG in April 1944. At this time Maximowitz was flying an Fw 190A-8/R8 with IV.(Sturm)/JG 3 and, as the newly imposed tactical doctrine urged, closed to within 50 m of the aircraft during the attack.

Right: Feldwebel Hans Schäfer of IV.(Sturm)/JG 3 was credited with 27 victories, including eight four-engined bombers. Note the 'Whites of the Eyes' insignia proudly worn by Sturmgruppe pilots on their flying jackets, denoting the fact that they engaged the enemy bombers from ultra-short range.

vector the force to hit the bomber stream about mid-way along its length where the escort would be weak. The Messerschmitts were to hold off the American escorts, while the 'Sturmbock' Fw 190s closed on the bomber formation and delivered their deadly massed attack.

The Sturmgruppe tactics were first tried out on a large scale on 7 July 1944 against a raiding force comprising 1,129 Fortresses and Liberators with an escort of about 700 fighters, heading for a spread of targets in the Leipzig area. Near the targets Major Walther Dahl led his battle formation into position. With the two escorting gruppen of Bf 109s giving top cover and ready to beat off the enemy escorts, Dahl led IV.(Sturm)/JG 3 into action. The three Sturmstaffeln ran in to attack the bomber formation comprising Liberators of the 492nd Bomb Group.

Each Sturmstaffel moved into position about 1,000 yards behind a squadron of B-24s then, maintaining close formation in line abreast, the Fw 190s advanced on their prey. Each of the fighters carried only 55 rounds for each of its 30-mm cannon, sufficient for about five seconds' firing, so their pilots couls not afford to engage in wild shooting from long range. The Fw 190s held their fire until they were close to the bombers, as Leutnant Walther Hagenah, one of

Above: Hauptmann Wilhelm Moritz, commander of IV.(Sturm) JG 3, leads his men on an interception mission in the summer of 1944. On most A-8/R8s, the fuselage machine-gun armament was removed in favour of 30-mm wing-mounted cannon.

the pilots involved, explained:

"We were to advance like Frederick the Great's infantrymen, holding our fire until we could see 'the whites of the enemies' eyes.' During the advance each man picked a bomber and closed in on it. As our formation moved forwards, the American bombers would, of course, let fly at us with everything they had. I can remember the sky being almost alive with tracer. With strict orders to withhold our fire until the leader gave the order, we could only grit our teeth and press on ahead. In fact, with the extra armour, surprisingly few of our aircraft were knocked down by the return fire. Like the armoured knights in the middle ages, we were well protected. A staffel might lose one or two aircraft during the advance, but the rest continued relentlessly on."

Powerful armament

When the surviving 'Sturmbock' fighters finally reached a firing position about 100 yards behind the bombers, they could retaliate. They did so with awesome effect. From that range the German pilots could hardly miss, and their 30-mm explosive rounds tore great holes in the bombers. Within a space of about a minute all 11 B-24s of the 492nd Bomb Group's Low Squadron had been shot down. The US 2nd Air Division lost 28 Liberators that day, the majority of

Typical of many of the 'sturmbock' aircraft, this Fw 190A-8/R8 features the additional armoured glass side canopy and armoured plate panel around the cockpit area. In addition, the outboard MK 108 cannon and their ammunition bins were protected with 4-mm internal wing armour plating. This aircraft belonged to IV.(Sturm)/JG 3 and is seen at Salzwedel circa May 1944.

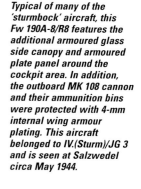

Left: The improved armour in the Fw 190A-8 necessitated moving the ETC 501 centreline store rack forward by 20 cm (7.9 in) to ensure the centre-of-gravity remained within limits. Here, a II.(Sturm)/JG 300 (the second Sturmgruppe unit to form) example lands at Loebnitz in late 1944, with a 300-litre (66-Imp gal) fuel tank on the centreline rack.

'Sturmbocks' of JG 300

Fw 190A-8/R8, JG 300
One of the most formidable of the 'Sturmbock' aces was Major Walter Dahl, who destroyed more USAAF four-engined bombers than any other pilot. Fitted with the armour-plated cockpit, and carrying a standard under-fuselage fuel tank, Dahl's aircraft featured here was the example he flew when first appointed Geschwaderkommodore of JG 300 in spring 1944. His total score eventually reached 51 in the west – this including 36 heavy bombers.

Following the Allies' D-Day invasion, a number of ground-attack geschwader were rushed to the area to try and prevent the Allies breaking out from their bridgehead. For longer range missions, Fw 190A-8s, Fs and Gs could be fitted with two underwing 300-litre (66-Imp gal) fuel tanks, which could be jettisoned if necessary. As demonstrated by this Fw 190G on the Normandy front, a groundcrewman was often carried on the wing during taxiing to guide the pilot. The forward view from the cockpit on the ground was notoriously poor.

them to the Sturmgruppe attack. During the action IV./JG 3 lost nine fighters shot down and three damaged. Five German pilots were killed. By Luftwaffe standards it had been a highly successful air defence operation, and it was decided to form further Sturmgruppen in JG 4 and JG 300.

Much of the success of the Sturmgruppe stemmed from the surprise effect when the new tactics were first used. Once the American planners became aware of the threat they sent large forces of fighters to sweep the sky ahead of the bombers, The aim was catch the unwieldy German battle formation as early as possible, and break it up before they got near the bombers. Once an attack formation was broken up it could not reform in the presence of the enemy, and that particular air defence operation had to be abandoned. Although the Sturmgruppen would have a few more successes, these became increasingly few and far between.

The Battle of France

When Allied troops landed on the coast of Normandy on 6 June 1944, the Luftwaffe was taken completely by surprise and its reaction was weak. The troops coming ashore enjoyed the protection of more than 3,000 fighters and fighter-bombers patrolling the beachhead, flying in relays from airfields in southern England.

In the face of this powerful aerial umbrella, Luftflotte 3 was able to mount only pin-prick attacks during the critical period following the initial landings. The first Luftwaffe aircraft to reach the landing area were two Fw 190s from

JG 26, piloted by the Geschwader commander Oberst 'Pips' Priller and his wing man Unteroffizier Heinz Wodarczyk. That morning, after receiving a telephone call that the invasion had begun, the pair took off from Lille-Nord airfield and flew at low altitude along the Normandy coast from east to west. Near Ouistreham they came upon Sword Beach, the most easterly landing beach, where British troops were streaming ashore. Despite heavy fire from warships off the coast, the Focke-Wulfs made a brief strafing run, then pulled up into cloud and headed for home.

The total Luftwaffe effort during the daylight hours of D-Day amounted to about 100 sorties, mostly by fighters and fighter-reconnaissance aircraft. The long-planned influx of German combat air units to airfields in France to combat the invasion came too late to effect the initial landings. III. Gruppe, Schlachtegeschwader 4, a ground-attack unit with some 50 Focke-Wulf Fw 190Fs based at Clastres, near St Quentin, and at Le Luc and Frieres in the south of France, was one of the units now pitchforked into battle. Its problems were typical of those experienced by the units moving forwards. The first reports of the invasion reached the gruppe at 3 am on 6 June, but not until 9.35 am did it receive the executive order to move to its designated forward operating bases at Laval and Tours. As was normal during rapid deployments of this type, each Focke-Wulf flew with a mechanic in the rear fuselage. On the way to their new bases the Fw 190s were intercepted by Mustangs and Thunderbolts, which shot down five of them. Eight out of the 10 men on board were killed. The mechanics had no

Above: Both cockpits of the Fw 190A-8/U1 featured sideways-opening canopies, hinged on the starboard side. The A-8 variant could be differentiated from the A-5 conversion by its retention of the bulged fuselage armament panel, although all armament had been removed to reduce weight. Duel controls and flight instruments were standard, with the instructor usually seated in the rear cockpit.

Right: To address the extremely poor forward view for the instructor, particularly during take-off and landing when the attitude of the aircraft was nose-high, a number of S-8s were fitted with four triangular flat transparencies on both sides of the rearmost part of the canopy. Creating a 'bulge', this modification allowed the instructor a modicum of forward vision, looking down either the port of starboard sides of the fuselage.

Two-seat trainers

By 1943, the importance of developing a two-seat training version of the Fw 190 had become more apparent. With a number of the Ju 87 units now converting to to the type, a quick and easy way of retraining the pilots was needed. After a number of conversions using 190A-5 airframes (provisionally designated A-5/U1), the main production variant was based on the Fw 190A-8 and assigned the factory designation Fw 190A-8/U1. Unarmed, the aircraft featured a rearward extension of the cockpit using flat transparency plates. Later, the two versions became more commonly known as the Fw 190S-5 and S-8, respectively. Some Fw 190F-8 airframes were also converted.

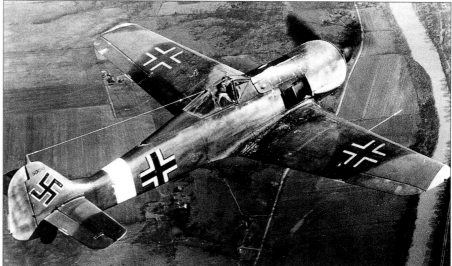

way of abandoning the aircraft in flight, and when aircraft were hit, their pilots refused to bail out and leave them to certain death.

Late that afternoon 9. Staffel mounted three attacks against the landing area near the mouth of the River Orne, with a total of 13 aircraft. Allied fighters prevented one raiding force from reaching its target, and the other two made fleeting attacks, during which their pilots were unable to assess the damage caused.

On the following day, 7 June, III./SG 4 was again in action. Early that morning the unit sent 24 Fw 190s to attack British troops coming ashore near the mouth of the Orne River. Allied fighter patrols forced most of the German aircraft to jettison their bombs before they could reach their target. Also that morning, Mustangs attacked the airfield at Laval, shooting down one Focke-Wulf and destroying four on the ground. That evening, Mustangs shot down another Fw 190 near the airfield.

Meanwhile, several Luftflotte Reich single-seat fighter units had arrived in France from Germany. For these units the new theatre of operations was quite unlike the one they had left. Previously, these units had the advantage of operating from well-stocked permanent airfields, with an established fighter control system to direct their activities. In France, many fighter units had to operate from field landing grounds with minimal facilities, and the system of fighter control functioned poorly.

Desperate defence

Representative of the home defence units sent to France was II. Gruppe of Jagdgeschwader 1. On the afternoon of 6 June the unit's 25 Fw 190s flew from their home base at Rheine, western Germany, to Le Mans. On the following day, the gruppe flew a fighter sweep to cover the roads to the south-east of the beachhead, along which German reinforcements were passing. The gruppe flew three such patrols that day, without encountering enemy aircraft.

On the next day, the 8th, almost all serviceable aircraft were loaded with 250-kg (550-lb) bombs for an attack on shipping off the coast. None of the pilots had previous experience of fighter-bomber operations, and over the invasion area they ran into flak they described as 'terrific'. The pilots released their bombs and sped home at low alti-

tude. All the Fw 190s returned, some with minor damage. From Allied records it appears that no ship was hit. A repeat operation on the following day was similarly unsuccessful, but again the luck of the gruppe held and there were no losses.

On 10 June, Le Mans airfield came under attack from more than 100 Lancasters and Halifaxes of the Royal Air Force. The operations room, three hangars and several buildings were demolished, and several hundred craters pockmarked the landing ground. In anticipation of such an attack the unit's aircraft had been dispersed and camouflaged in the surrounding fields, however, and none was damaged. Due to the absence of earth-moving equipment and the ever-present risk of attack from Allied fighter-bombers, it took six days to fill in the more troublesome bomb craters so the unit could resume flying.

On 16 June the unit moved to Essay and flew fighting patrols over the battle area during each of the next four days. Then it transferred to the field landing ground at Semalle, south-east of Alencon. As the gruppe was establishing itself at the new base, its charmed existence in France came to an abrupt end. A force of Mustangs carried out coordinated strafing runs on the airfield and, within a few minutes, 15 Fw 190s had been destroyed. II./JG 1 was out of the battle and its personnel were withdrawn to Germany where the unit reformed.

Early in August, American troops broke out of the beachhead area and rapidly advanced south then eastwards. In the week that followed the German armies in Normandy suffered defeat then rout. By now Luftflotte 3 was down to about 75 serviceable single-engined fighters. A German army catch phrase of that time ran: "If the aircraft above us were camouflaged, we knew that they were British. If they were silver, we knew that they were American. And if they weren't there at all, we knew that they were German!"

Above left: The success of the Fw 190A in the ground attack role led directly to the development of the dedicated close-support series, designated Fw 190F. The outboard cannon were removed, along with their associated bulged underwing armament panels, and additional armour plating was added around the engine, lower fuselage and fuel tanks. This example is one of the Fw 190A-5/U3s which were used as prototypes for the F series. Note the tropical filter, which was a factory-fitted option on early Fw 190Fs.

Above: Based on the Fw 190A-4/U8 conversion, the Fw 190G was a high-performance, long-range fighter-bomber with a fuselage-mounted ETC 501 bomb rack fitted as standard. The only armament was the two wing root MG 151 cannon, with the fuselage-mounted machine-guns having been faired-over. This example is a captured Fw 190G-3 tested by the USAAF.

Fw 190Fs were active on both the Eastern and Western Fronts. These examples are from Schnellkampfgeschwader 10, at the Deblin-Irena airfield, near Warsaw. Eastern Front attack gruppen regularly used this airfield to conduct training missions, utilising the nearby range for live ordnance drops.

Fw 190A-8/F-8 armour protection

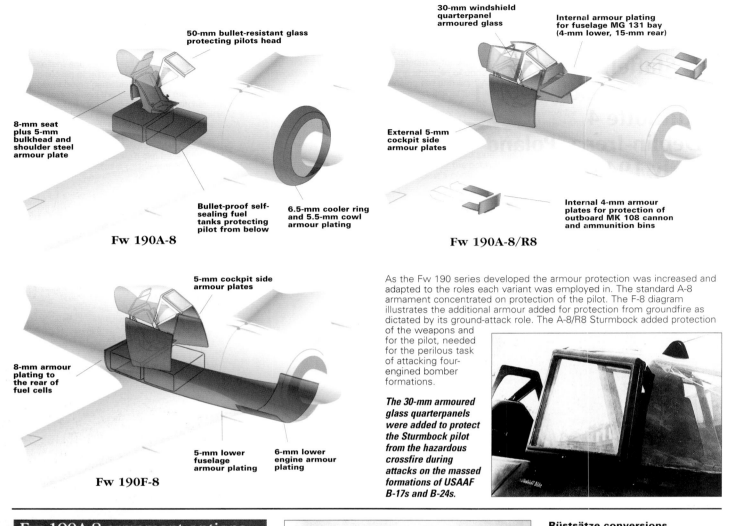

50-mm bullet-resistant glass protecting pilots head

8-mm seat plus 5-mm bulkhead and shoulder steel armour plate

Bullet-proof self-sealing fuel tanks protecting pilot from below

6.5-mm cooler ring and 5.5-mm cowl armour plating

Fw 190A-8

30-mm windshield quarterpanel armoured glass

Internal armour plating for fuselage MG 131 bay (4-mm lower, 15-mm rear)

External 5-mm cockpit side armour plates

Internal 4-mm armour plates for protection of outboard MK 108 cannon and ammunition bins

Fw 190A-8/R8

5-mm cockpit side armour plates

8-mm armour plating to the rear of fuel cells

5-mm lower fuselage armour plating

6-mm lower engine armour plating

Fw 190F-8

As the Fw 190 series developed the armour protection was increased and adapted to the roles each variant was employed in. The standard A-8 armament concentrated on protection of the pilot. The F-8 diagram illustrates the additional armour added for protection from groundfire as dictated by its ground-attack role. The A-8/R8 Sturmbock added protection of the weapons and for the pilot, needed for the perilous task of attacking four-engined bomber formations.

The 30-mm armoured glass quarterpanels were added to protect the Sturmbock pilot from the hazardous crossfire during attacks on the massed formations of USAAF B-17s and B-24s.

Fw 190A-8 armament options

A wide range of cannon and machine-gun arrangements was incorporated into the Fw 190A-8. A number were only fitted for experimental purposes, however many reached operational status, with each arrangement being given its own Rüstsätze designation.

Rüstsätze conversions

The Fw 190A-8's versatility came through the large number of Rüstsätze (field conversion sets) offering a host of additional equipment and, most importantly, various weapons fits:

R1 Addition of a WB 151 weapons container under each wing housing a pair of MG 151/20E cannon with 125 rpg
R2 Outboard wing armament comprising two 30-mm MK 108 cannon with 55 rpg
R3 Two MK 103 30-mm cannon mounted in pods (gondolas) beneath each wing
R4 Two MG 151/20E 20-mm cannon installed in the wings
R6 Incorporated the rocket-launching system for WGr 21 anti-bomber rockets
R7 Additional external and internal armour for Sturm units
R8 Combination of R2 weapons and R7 armour with additional wing ammunition armour plates
R11 All-weather fighter with auto-pilot, blind flying equipment, heated windscreen and BMW 801 TU engine
R12 R11 equipment with R2 weapons and powerplant

Above left: Mounted in underwing gondolas, the A-8/R3 carried two MK 103 30-mm cannon.

Above: The Fw 190A-5/U12 tested the weapons trays housing twin MG 151/20E 20-mm cannon, later incorporated in the Fw 190A-8/R1.

Left: Used as a weapons testbed for the A-8, the A-5/U9 had fuselage-mounted 13-mm MG 131 machine-guns and four wing-mounted MG 151 20-mm cannon.

Focke-Wulf Fw 190A-8

1 Pitot head
2 Starboard navigation light
3 Detachable wingtip
4 Pitot tube heater line
5 Wing lower shell 'floating rib'
6 Aileron hinge points
7 Wing lower shell stringers
8 Leading-edge ribs
9 Front spar
10 Outboardmost 'solid rib'
11 Wing upper shell stringers
12 Aileron trim tab
13 Aileron structure
14 Aileron activation/control linkage
15 Ammunition box (125 rpg)
16 Starboard 20-mm MG 151/20E wing cannon
17 Ammunition box rear suspension arm
18 Flap structure
19 Wing flap upper skinning
20 Flap setting indicator peep-hole
21 Rear spar
22 Inboard wing construction
23 Undercarriage indicator
24 Wing rib strengthening
25 Ammunition feed chute
26 Static and dynamic air pressure lines
27 Cannon barrel
28 Launch tube bracing struts
29 Launch tube carrier strut
30 Mortar launch tube
31 Launch tube internal guide rails
32 21-cm (WfrGr 21) spin-stabilised Type 42 mortar shell
33 VDM three-bladed adjustable-pitch constant-speed propeller
34 Propeller boss
35 Propeller hub
36 Starboard undercarriage fairing
37 Starboard mainwheel
38 Oil warming chamber
39 Thermostat
40 Cooler armoured ring
41 Oil tank drain valve
42 Annular oil tank (12.1-Imp gal; 55-litre)
43 Oil cooler
44 Twelve-bladed engine cooling fan
45 Hydraulic-electric pitch control unit
46 Primer fuel line
47 Bosch magneto
48 Oil tank armour (5.5-mm)
49 Supercharger air pressure pipes
50 BMW 801D-2 14-cylinder radial engine
51 Cowling support ring
52 Cowling quick-release fasteners
53 Oil pump
54 Fuel pump
55 Starboard oil filter
56 Wingroot cannon synchronisation gear
57 Gun troughs/cowling upper panel attachment
58 Engine mounting ring
59 Cockpit heating pipe
60 Exhaust pipes (cylinders 11-14)
61 MG 131 link and casing discard chute
62 Engine bearer assembly
63 MG 131 ammunition boxes (400 rpg)
64 Fuel filter recess housing
65 MG 131 ammunition cooling pipes
66 MG 131 synchronisation gear
67 Ammunition feed chute
68 Twin 13-mm MG 131 machine-guns
69 Windscreen mounting frame
70 Emergency power fuse and distributor box
71 Rear hinged gun access panel
72 Engine bearer/bulkhead attachment
73 Control column
74 Transformer
75 Aileron control torsion bar
76 Rudder pedals
77 Fuselage/wing spar attachment
78 Rudder push rod
79 Fuel filter head
80 Cockpit floor support frame
81 Throttle lever
82 Seat back plate armour
83 Seat guide rails
84 Side-section back armour
85 Shoulder armour
86 Oxygen supply valve
87 Steel frame turnover pylon
88 Windscreen spray pipes
89 Instrument panel shroud
90 30-mm armoured glass quarterlights
91 50-mm armoured glass windscreen
92 Revi 16B reflector gunsight
93 Canopy
94 Aerial attachment
95 Headrest
96 Head armour (12-mm)
97 Head armour support strut
98 Explosive charge canopy emergency jettison unit
99 Canopy channel slide
100 Auxiliary fuel tank
101 FuG 16ZY transmitter-receiver unit
102 Handhold cover
103 Primer fuel filler cap
104 Battery
105 FuG 16ZY power transformer
106 Entry step cover plate
107 Two tri-spherical oxygen bottles
108 Auxiliary fuel tank filler point
109 FuG 25a transponder unit
110 Autopilot position integration unit
111 FuG 16ZY homer bearing converter
112 Elevator control cables
113 Rudder control DUZ-flexible rods
114 Fabric panel (bulkhead 12)
115 Rudder differential unit
116 Aerial lead-in
117 Rear fuselage lift tube
118 Triangular stress frame
119 Tailplane trim unit
120 Tailplane attachment fitting
121 Tailwheel retraction guide tube
122 Retraction cable lower pulley
123 Starboard tailplane
124 Aerial
125 Starboard elevator
126 Elevator trim tab
127 Tailwheel shock strut guide
128 Fin construction
129 Retraction cable upper pulley
130 Aerial attachment stub
131 Rudder upper hinge
132 Rudder structure
133 Rudder trim tab

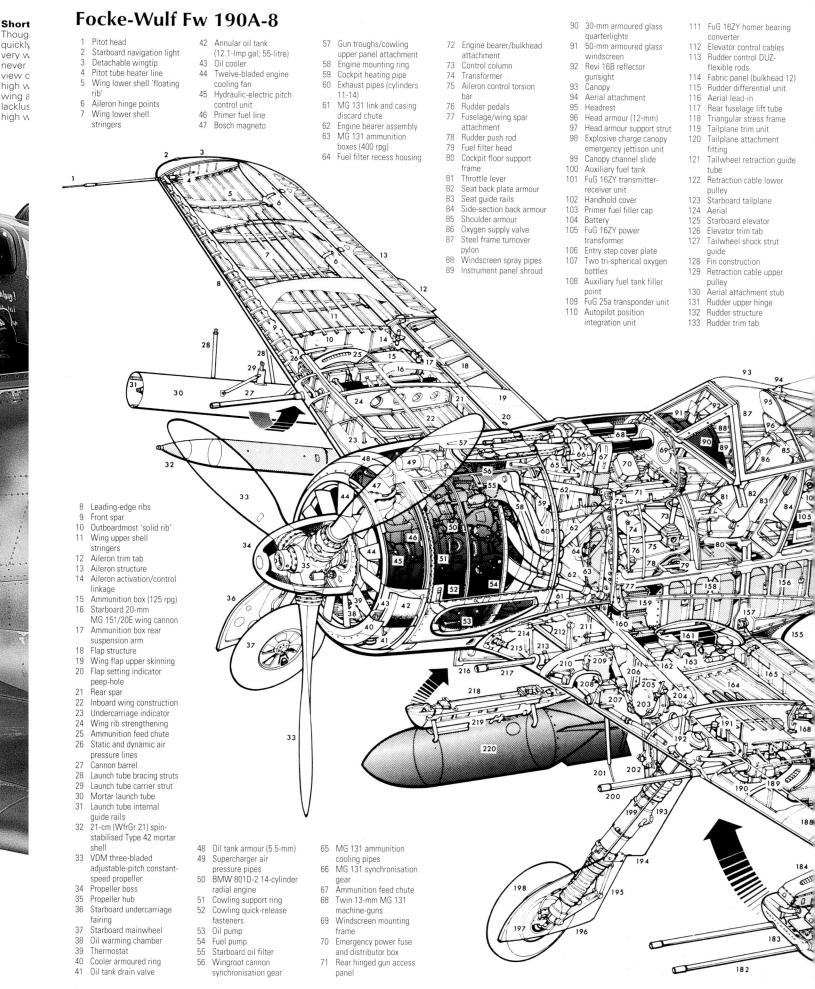

The cowlings on either side of the engine hinged downward to provide access to the BMW 801D engine. Note the exhaust pipes leading rearwards from the engine cylinders, which expelled the gases past the cooling gills, seen here in the closed position.

134 Tailwheel retraction mechanism access panel
135 Rudder attachment/actuation fittings
136 Rear navigation light
137 Extension spring
138 Elevator trim tab
139 Port elevator structure
140 Tailplane construction
141 Semi-retracting tailwheel
142 Forked wheel housing

153 Single tri-spherical oxygen bottle
154 Retractable entry step
155 Wingroot fairing
156 Fuselage rear fuel tank
157 Fuselage/rear spar attachment
158 Fuselage forward fuel tank
159 Port wing root cannon ammunition box (250 rpg)
160 Ammunition feed chute

180 A-8/R1 variant underwing gun pack (in place of outboard wing cannon)
181 Link and casing discard chute
182 Twin unsynchronised 20-mm MG 151/20E cannon
183 Light metal fairing (gondola)
184 Ammunition feed chutes
185 Ammunition boxes (125 rpg)
186 Carrier frame restraining cord

143 Drag yoke
144 Tailwheel shock strut
145 Tailwheel locking linkage
146 Elevator actuation lever linkage
147 Angled frame spar
148 Elevator differential bellcrank
149 FuG 25a ventral antenna
150 Master compass sensing unit
151 FuG 16ZY fixed loop homing antenna
152 Radio compartment access hatch

161 Port wing root MG 151/20E cannon
162 Link and casing discard chute
163 Cannon rear mount support bracket
164 Upper and lower wing shell stringers
165 Rear spar
166 Spar construction
167 Flap actuating electric motor
168 Flap position indicator scale and peep-hole
169 Port 20-mm MG 151/20E wing cannon
170 Aileron transverse linkage
171 Ammunition box (125 rpg)
172 Aileron control linkage
173 Ammunition box rear suspension arm
174 Aileron control unit
175 Aileron trim tab
176 Port aileron structure
177 Port navigation light
178 Outboard wing stringers
179 Detachable wingtip

187 Ammunition box rear suspension arms
188 Leading-edge skinning
189 Ammunition feed chute
190 Ammunition warming pipe
191 Aileron bellcrank
192 Mainwheel strut mounting assembly
193 EC-oleo shock strut
194 Mainwheel leg fairing
195 Scissors unit
196 Mainwheel fairing
197 Axle housing
198 Port mainwheel
199 Brake lines
200 Cannon barrel
201 FuG 16ZY Morane antenna
202 Radius rods
203 Rotating drive unit
204 Mainwheel retraction
205 Undercarriage indicator
206 Sealed air-jack
207 BSK 16 gun camera
208 Retraction locking hooks
209 Undercarriage locking unit
210 Armament collimation tube
211 Camera wiring conduits
212 Wheel well
213 Cannon barrel blast tube
214 Wheel cover actuation strut
215 Ammunition hot air
216 Port inboard wheel cover
217 Wingroot cannon barrel
218 ETC 501 carrier unit
219 ETC 501 bomb rack
220 SC 500 500-kg (550-lb) bomb

Smaller bombs: This Fw 190A-5/U3 shows the configuration for a full SC 50 50-kg (110-lb) bomb load, comprising four on an ETC 500 ventral rack and one each on four wing-mounted ETC 50 racks.

Larger bombs: Used as a prototype for the Fw 190G, the same aircraft is seen here with an SC 500 500-kg (1,100-lb) bomb on the ventral rack and two wing-mounted SC 250 250-kg (550-lb) bombs.

Outsize bombs: The Fw 190G could carry the SB 1000 (seen here) and SC 1000 1000-kg (2,205-lb) bombs, however, the largest bomb used operationally was the 3,968-lb SC 1800 'bridge-buster'.

Air-to-air rockets: The Fw 190A-8/R6 was configured to carry the 21-cm WGr 21 air-to-air rocket. Launched from a tube under each wing, the weapon was designed to destroy heavy bombers.

Torpedo: The Fw 190A-5/U14 and versions of the F-8 could carry an LTF 5b torpedo on an adapted ETC 502 fuselage rack. It also featured an enlarged fin and a lengthened tailwheel leg.

BV 246 glide-bomb: Intended for use on a modified version of the Fw 190F-8, the BV 246 Hagelkorn (hailstone) glide-bomb was tested, but never used operationally.

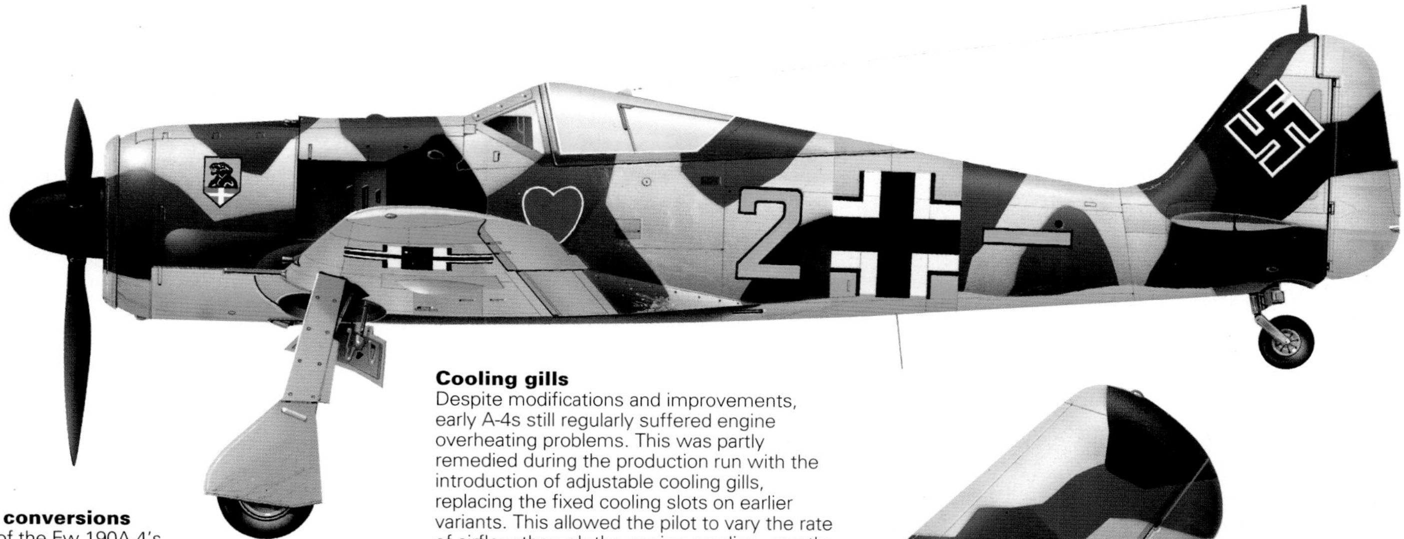

Multi-role conversions

At the time of the Fw 190A-4's introduction, Focke-Wulf was in the process of transforming the aircraft from an out-and-out interceptor into a multi-role combat aircraft. To meet these aims, factory conversion (Umrüst-Bausätze, or U-series) and field conversion sets (Rüstsatze, or R-series) began to be made available. The more important of these were:

U1 Conversion for high-speed bomber role with fuselage and wing root armament removed and ventral bomb rack fitted. Exhaust shields and a landing light for night operations

U3 Close-support variant with outboard cannon and undercarriage doors removed and ventral ETC 501 weapons rack fitted.

U4 Photo-reconnaissance version with outboard cannon removed and two internal cameras protruding through a ventral fuselage hatch

U8 High-speed fighter bomber with outboard cannon removed, a ventral bomb rack and faired 300-litre underwing fuel tanks

R1 Installation of improved FuG 16ZE radio

R6 Incorporation of rocket-launching tubes for WGr 21 air-to-air anti-bomber rocket

Cooling gills

Despite modifications and improvements, early A-4s still regularly suffered engine overheating problems. This was partly remedied during the production run with the introduction of adjustable cooling gills, replacing the fixed cooling slots on earlier variants. This allowed the pilot to vary the rate of airflow through the engine cowling, greatly reducing the tendency to overheat.

Camouflage

During the spring thaw periods, a number of Eastern Front gruppen removed part of the winter whitewash covering to reveal a two-tone green camouflage beneath. This helped break-up the aircraft's outline, especially when viewed from above. On some aircraft batches of very dark grey or black paint was added to break up the outline further. This 6./JG 54 aircraft was flown by Oberfeldwebel Heinrich Sterr in the spring of 1943.

Focke-Wulf Fw 190A-4
6. Staffel, Jagdgeschwader 54 Ryelbitzi, Russia circa March 1943

Powerplant

Intended to be capable of serving in tropical climates, the Fw 190A-4 was powered by the BMW 801D-2 engine, driving a 3.3-m (10-ft 10-in) diameter VDM three-bladed propeller. A limited number of A-4s were fitted with the MW 50 methanol-water engine boosting system, increasing available output for short periods to 2,100 hp (1566 kW).

...ament

...w 190A-4's armament comprised two ...m fuselage-mounted MG 17 machine-guns ...1,000 rpg, two 20-mm MG 151 cannon ...nted in the wing roots with 200 rpg and two ...FF cannon in the outer wings with 55 rpg. ...outboard cannon were sometimes removed ...duce weight and increase performance.

External differences

The Fw 190A-4 was essentially the same as the A-3, with the most noticeable external difference being the incorporation of a vertical fin-top antenna mast. This was necessitated by the incorporation of the much improved FuG 16 radio, replacing the FuG 7 of the A-3.

The Eastern Front was the ultimate testing ground for both the Fw 190 and its pilots. Often operating from ill-equipped forward bases, in temperatures which could range from 90°F in summer to -30°F in winter, serviceability rates were naturally lower than experienced by Western Front units. The problems are illustrated here by the first Eastern Front unit, I./JG 51, coping with frozen ground in the spring of 1943 (below), and a 'Jabo' taking off in dusty conditions on the Russian steppes six months later (right).

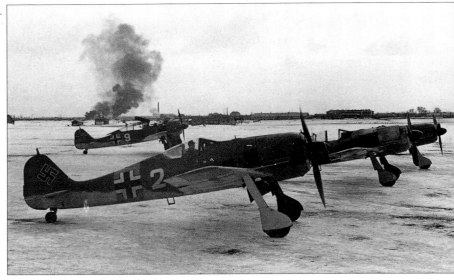

In a desperate move, four recently formed fighter gruppen were rushed to France to provide air cover for the badly mauled German ground forces in their retreat. One of the new units to reach France was II./JG 6, an Fw 190 Gruppe formed recently with pilots from Messerschmitt Me 410 bomber-destroyer units that had disbanded. The gruppe arrived at its designated field landing ground at Herpy, near Reims on 23 August. Feldwebel Fritz Bucholz, one of the pilots, commented:

"Our airstrip at Herpy was nothing more than a piece of flat cow pasture surrounded by trees in which our aircraft could be hidden; nearby was our tented accommodation. The Allied fighter-bombers seemed to be everywhere and our survival depended on the strictest attention to camouflage. As part of this we even had a herd of cows which were moved on to the airfield when no flying was in progress; as well as giving the place a rustic look, these performed the valuable task of obliterating the tracks made on the grass by the aircraft. Such attention to detail paid off and there were no attacks on Herpy while I was there."

II./JG 6 fought its first major action on 25 August, when Hauptmann Elstermann led the gruppe, with some 40 fighters, on an offensive patrol towards the battle area. Near St Quentin the German force surprised a dozen P-38 Lightnings of the 394th Fighter Squadron, which were strafing the airfield at Clastres. The Fw 190s shot down six American fighters in quick succession. Then the American pilots' distress calls summoned the P-38s of the other two squadrons of the 367th Fighter Group. When these joined the fight, they quickly turned the tables. In the mêlée that followed II./JG 6 lost 16 aircraft destroyed and several more damaged, and accounted for only one more Lightning.

Although it had lost nearly half of its strength, II./JG 6 was allowed no time to mourn its losses. On the following day its surviving aircraft and pilots were ordered to mount a fighting patrol to provide cover for German forces pulling back over the River Seine. Fritz Bucholz recalled:

JG 51 and JG 54 were the first, longest serving and most famous of the Fw 190 Eastern Front geschwader. The first gruppe into combat was I./JG 51, which re-equipped with the A-3 in September 1942. By the time this photograph was taken, the gruppe had re-equipped with the Fw 190A-4 and was operating from the central sector of the front in the vicinity of Orel.

Front-line Fw 190 units – 31 May 1944

On this day, 881 Fw 190s served with combat units, of which 265 were assigned to 13 fighter gruppen, 387 to 14 ground-attack gruppen and 11 to the single reconnaissance staffel operating the type.

One fighter gruppe, IV.(Sturm)/JG 3, was in the process of forming with the 'Sturmbock' version of the Fw 190, and a further five ground-attack gruppen were in the process of converting to Fw 190Gs from Ju 87s.

During May 1944, 841 new Fw 190s of all variants were delivered to the Luftwaffe. This total was more than three-times as many as in May 1943, and the largest number in any month since production of the Fw 190 began.

Unit	Total	Serviceable
Luftflotte 1 (Northern sector, Eastern Front)		
Jagdgeschwader 54		
Stab	4	4
I. Gruppe	44	36
II. Gruppe	52	48
Luftflotte 2 (Italy)		
Schlachtgeschwader 4		
Stab	3	2
I. Gruppe	14	4
II. Gruppe	27	9
Luftflotte 3 (France/Belgium)		
Jagdgeschwader 2		
Stab	3	0
I. Gruppe	19	14
III. Gruppe	29	19
Jagdgeschwader 26		
Stab	2	2
I. Gruppe	33	23
II. Gruppe	32	25
Schlachtgeschwader 4		
III. Gruppe	40	36
Schnellkampfgeschwader 10		
I. Gruppe	33	19

Unit	Total	Serviceable
Aufklärungsgruppe 123		
5. Staffel	4	2 [1]
Luftflotte 4 (Southern sector, Eastern Front)		
Schlachtgeschwader 2		
II. Gruppe	42	20
Schlachtgeschwader 10		
Stab	5	2
I. Gruppe	32	16
II. Gruppe	31	15
III. Gruppe	40	24
Schlachtgeschwader 77		
I. Gruppe	34	32 [1]
II. Gruppe	33	21
Luftflotte 5 (Arctic sector, Eastern Front)		
Schlachtgeschwader 5		
I. Gruppe	15	12 [2]
Luftflotte 6 (Central sector, Eastern Front)		
Jagdgeschwader 51		
Stab	16	16
Schlachtgeschwader 1		
II. Gruppe	12	2 [2]
III. Gruppe	42	33

Unit	Total	Serviceable
Luftflotte Reich		
Jagdgeschwader 1		
Stab	2	2
I. Gruppe	43	15
II. Gruppe	42	20
Jagdgeschwader 3		
IV.(Sturm) Gruppe	54	1 [4]
Jagdgeschwader 11		
I. Gruppe	28	20
III. Gruppe	28	11
10. Staffel	10	7 [1]
Jagdgeschwader 54		
III. Gruppe	23	8
Jagdgeschwader 300		
Stab	2	1
II. Gruppe	32	23
Nachtjagdgruppe 10		
	4	2 [3]
Schlachtgeschwader 3		
III. Gruppe	34	31 [4]

[1] Unit also operated Bf 109s
[2] Unit also operated Ju 87s
[3] Night-fighter trials unit, also operated a number of other types
[4] Unit forming/reforming

"Again I led my Schwarm [four aircraft flight] and we made for our briefed patrol area near Rouen. Soon after our arrival in the battle area, however, we were 'bounced' out of the sun by Mustangs. I never even saw the aircraft that hit me. All I heard was a loud bang and the next thing I knew my aircraft was tumbling out of the sky with part of the tail shot away."

Bucholz jettisoned his canopy and struggled to get out of the cockpit. As he fell from the fighter one foot struck the tailplane, causing a painful injury. He came down to the west of the River Seine, near Duclair, and was picked up by an army rearguard unit whose doctor treated his wound.

II./JG 6 suffered grievous losses during its time in France. After his spell in hospital, Fritz Bucholz returned to the unit early in October. He arrived to find only four pilots left, from about 40 that had left for France in August. The rest were dead, wounded or languishing in prisoner of war camps.

Eastern Front fighter-bombers

Although one or two Fw 190 ground-attack gruppen appeared in the west and on the Mediterranean fronts, the majority of these units operated on the Eastern Front. In the summer of 1944, Soviet forces launched a succession of massive ground offensives. In meeting these thrusts the main task of the Luftwaffe was to impose delays on the Soviet advances, to allow German troops time to improvise defensive positions ahead of them. During this period Leutnant Werner Gail served with III./Schlachtgeschwader 3 operating Fw 190Fs. He remembered:

"Wherever there was a hole in the front, it was our job to try to plug it. During this period the ground situation was so fluid that we had to start each day with an armed reconnaissance: two or three Schwärme were sent to patrol different parts of the area assigned to our gruppe, to see if the enemy had moved, and if so where. Since we soon came to know our area well and we knew where the enemy had been the night before, we had a good idea where to start looking for him the following morning. Also, whenever enemy armoured units had broken through, they would advance through open country which made the task of finding them much easier."

Once the latest enemy positions were known, each gruppe was allocated its targets for the day. The Fw 190F carried an internal armament of two 13-mm machine-guns

A detachment of I./JG 51 aircraft is dispersed on the frozen surface of Lake Ivan, west of Moscow, during the winter of 1942/43. Conditions at the airfield were extremely primitive; note the aircraft in the top left is in the process of having an engine change in the open.

The first Russian winter of 1942/43 was a true test of the Fw 190's durability. A whitewash finish was applied to the aircraft as an aid to camouflage although, on this II. Gruppe/JG 54 aircraft (above), the whitewash is already beginning to weather after only a few weeks of service. At this time the unit was transitioning to the type staffel by staffel (note the Bf 109G in the foreground). For much of the late winter, JG 54 was stationed at Krasnogvardeisk, near Leningrad. A I. Gruppe Fw 190A-4 is seen landing at this airfield (top) proudly displaying the geschwader's 'Green Hearts' badge.

Fw 190s on the Eastern Front

Fw 190A-3, 3./JG 51
Fw 190A-3s were only active in the east for a short period. From January 1943, JG 51 began to re-equip with A-4s and A-5s, while JG 54 converted straight to the A-4. Wearing temporary whitewash, this A-3 was the mount of Hauptmann Heinz Lange in December 1942. During nearly four years of service, Lange scored 69 Eastern Front 'kills'.

Fw 190F-2, Schl.G 1
In January 1943, the first Schlachtgeschwader (ground-attack wing) to re-equip with the Fw 190 entered the combat arena. In mid-1943, Schl.G 1 was heavily involved in the Battle of the Kursk. This aircraft was flown by the unit's C.O., Alfred Druschel, and is seen with an AB 250 250-kg (550-lb) bomb beneath the fuselage. This weapon was particularly effective against against soft-skinned vehicles and troop concentrations.

Above: A number of different methods were employed during the harsh winter months to ensure that maintenance could be conducted, and the engine kept at a sufficiently high temperature to start; this Fw 190F has its forward fuselage in a heated tent. If such luxuries were not available small fires were lit under the aircraft's engines.

Top: The Zwerg (dwarf) petrol-fired hot air heater was an important item of equipment during the cold Russian winters. These examples are not operational aircraft however, but are two Fw 190A-2s sent to the Eastern Front for cold weather service evaluation in early 1942.

Schlacht Fw 190Fs were active in the southern sector of the Eastern Front, particularly in Romania during 1944, where this I./SG 10 Fw 190F-8 rests on the grass as a formation of five Bf 110s 'beats-up' the airfield. Like a number of Fw 190 units operating from these dusty airfields in the summer of 1944, this example is fitted with a tropical filter, helping to prolong the life of the engine.

and two 20-mm cannon, which were used in strafing attacks. The main external weapons carried by the fighter-bombers were SC 250 250-kg (550-lb) and SC 500 500-kg (1,100-lb) general-purpose bombs, and containers which held SD-2, SD-4 or SD-10 bomblets.

When Gail's unit found an enemy unit moving forwards unopposed, the fighter-bombers concentrated their attacks on the soft-skinned supply vehicles. The latter were relatively easy to knock out with machine-gun and cannon fire and, without frequent replenishments of fuel, the tanks spearheading the advance would not get far. If the enemy force was in contact with German ground forces, however, the priority changed. Then Soviet tanks were the main targets for attack.

During these operations the normal attack force was the four-plane Schwarm, although against a large enemy force several such Schwärme might be used. The Fw 190Fs usually flew to the target area at altitudes around 6,000 ft (1830 m),

above the effective reach of light flak. Shortly before reaching the target area the fighter-bombers descended to low altitude to deliver their attacks. A usual tactic against tanks or armoured vehicles was to run in at speeds of around 300 mph (483 km/h), about 30 ft (9 m) above the ground, and release the bomb as the vehicle disappeared from view beneath the engine cowling. Dropped in this way a 250-kg (550-lb) bomb would either smash straight into the tank, or ricochet off the ground and then hit the tank. The bombs were fused to detonate one second after impact to give the aircraft time to get clear of the fragments. The Fw 190 pilots found that method effective against the tanks they caught in open country. After releasing their bombs the Fw 190F pilots would use their cannon and machine-guns against soft-skinned vehicles, if they found these in the area. When the Soviet offensives began, the unit was heavily committed, with pilots sometimes flying as many as eight sorties per day. On average these sorties lasted about half an hour, with the aircraft returning to base each time to re-arm. Werner Gail continued:

"The enemy was never very far away. Sometimes we caught Russian units that had outrun their flak cover and then we could do a lot of damage and suffer hardly any losses ourselves. But if the enemy units did have proper flak cover our losses were sometimes heavy. Only rarely did we come into contact with Russian fighters. I personally saw them on only two occasions and on neither did we lose an aircraft."

The superb 'Dora'

The next major fighter version, the Fw 190D, entered service in the autumn of 1944. This was fitted with a Junkers Jumo 213 engine which, with water-methanol injection, developed 2,240 hp (1670 kW) for take-off and 2,000 hp (1491 kW) at 11,150 ft (3400 m). At first glance, the Fw 190D looked as if it was powered by an air-cooled radial engine like its predecessors, but in fact the Jumo 213 was a liquid-cooled in-line engine. That misleading appearance was caused by the annular radiator mounted in front of the engine. With the additional power, the Fw 190D had

Fw 190F-9s of SG 2 taxi out to bomb an enemy supply column from their base at Sopoc/Puszta, Hungary, in January 1945. The aircraft have received a mottled white/grey winterised camouflage, which was particularly important by this time as airfield attacks by enemy aircraft were increasing in frequency. This particular aircraft was flown by the II./SG 2 Kommandeur, Major Karl Kennel.

Fw 190 Panzerjäger

Two Fw 190s were fitted with an experimental installation for the SG 113 Förstersonde anti-tank weapon. The streamlined fairing fitted in each wing housed the barrels for two of these weapons, mounted vertically. The method of operation was as follows. As the pilot began his attack run he armed the system, and selected to fire a single barrel, a pair or all four barrels in rapid succession. As he passed low over the enemy vehicle, a magnetic sensor detected the latter's presence and triggered the weapon.

The vertically-mounted barrels, 7.7 cm (3.03 in) in diameter, fired 45-mm armour-piercing rounds fitted with discarding sabots. This arrangement gave the 1.9-kg (4.2-lb) round a velocity of 650 m (2,100 ft) per second, sufficient to defeat the relatively thin top armour of Allied tanks. To balance the recoil forces, as the round was fired downwards a 12-kg (26-lb) counterweight was simultaneously fired upwards from the opposite end of the barrel at 125 m (410 ft) per second.

Of the anti-tank weapons developed for use by aircraft during World War II, the Förstersonde was likely to have been the most effective in terms of tank 'kills' per sortie. The aircraft had only to make a high-speed run over the tank, and the automatic system fired the rounds at the optimum time to score hits. SG 113 performed successfully during test firings against tanks on the Völkenrode firing range in January 1945, but so far as is known, the weapon was never used in action.

The experimental SG 113 installation was tested on this trials Fw 190. Despite showing promise, further development was abandoned.

Production
Always considered by Kurt Tank as an 'emergency solution' pending the production of the Ta 152, the Fw 190D-9 was built at Focke-Wulf's Cottbus factory and by Fieseler at Kassel. It had been intended that the D-9 have a pressurised cabin, but development problems led to this feature being deleted. Some aircraft were completed with the MW 50 water-methanol injection system installed, this allowing the Jumo 213 to produce 2,240 hp (1670 kW) at sea level for short periods.

Powerplant
The 'Dora' was an attempt to address the Fw 190's mediocre performance at altitudes above 20,000 ft (6096 m). Having rejected an Fw 190 variant powered by a turbocharged version of the BMW 801 engine, another fitted with the GM-1 nitrous-oxide boost system and the Fw 190C powered by the massive DB603 powerplant, the RLM was attracted to the simple expedient of fitting a Junkers Jumo inline engine to a suitably modifed Fw 190A. Developing 1,776 hp (1324 kW) for take-off and 1,600 hp (1193 kW) at 18,000 ft (8165 m), the Junkers Jumo 213A-1 was an inverted 12-cylinder Vee design based on that of the Jumo 211 – a bomber engine widely employed in such types as the He 111 and Ju 88. Neatly cowled, with an annular radiator and cooling gills it drove a three-bladed, paddle-bladed propeller.

Fw 190D series
Six other D-series variants were under development at war's end; none saw service:

D-10	fighter; Jumo 213C-1, engine-mounted MK 108 30-mm cannon and single MG 151/20 in port wing root
D-11	fighter/fighter-bomber; Jumo 213F with three-stage supercharger and MW50 boost, two MG 151/20 and two MK 108 cannon
D-12	fighter/fighter-bomber; Jumo 213F, engine-mounted MK 108 and two MG 151/20 cannon in wing roots
D-13	fighter/fighter-bomber as D-12, with MG 151/20 replacing MK 108
D-14	DB 603E or LA-powered variant
D-15	DB 603EB or G-powered variant

Though its markings indicate assignment to a Major posted to the Geschwaderstab of JG 2, this 'Dora-9' was flown by Feldwebel Werner Hohenberg of 4./JG 2 'Richthofen' on the first day of 1945. Stab./JG 2 was based at Merzhausen in December 1944 for the defence of Reich airspace and took part in the 1 January massed attacks on Allied airfields. Hit by US Army groundfire, the aircraft crashed near Liège, Belgium and Hohenberg was captured.

Focke-Wulf Fw 190D-9
4. Staffel, Jagdgeschwader 2 Operation Bodenplatte 1 January 1945

Structural changes
Few changes to the Fw 190A's airframe were necessary to produce the Jumo-powered D-9. To restore the aircraft's centre-of-gravity with the Jumo engine installed, a plug was inserted in its rear fuselage, just ahead of the tail fin. A broader tail fin was also fitted. As the Jumo used an annular radiator, there was no need to incorporate new airframe-mounted cooling equipment.

Armament
The D-9's basic armament comprised two MG 131 13-mm machine-guns mounted over the engine (each supplied with 475 rounds) and a pair of MG 151/20 20-mm cannon in the wing roots. All were synchronised to fire through the propeller arc. Early production aircraft also had an ETC 501 rack under the fuselage for a 500-kg (1,100-lb) bomb or 300-litre (66-Imp gal) drop tank.

Fuel
Internal fuel capacity totalled 635 litres (140-Imp gal); the D-9 employed the same fuselage tank arrangement as the Fw 190A-9 – a proposed high-altitude vesion of the A-8. In addition the D-9 had an aft-fuselage 115-litre (25.3-Imp gal) tank (as fitted to the F-8). This was able to carry either the water-methanol mixture for the aircraft's MW 50 system (if fitted) or extra fuel.

Above: Intended initially as an interim development, pending the arrival of the definitive Ta 152, the Fw 190D (or 'Dora') emerged as an extremely effective fighter in it own right. Fw 190 V53 was the first engine testbed for the Jumo 213A-1 engine, which was to be fitted to the main production aircraft – the Fw 190D-9. Converted from an Fw 190A-8, the V53 first flew in late 1943, before being lost in an accident on 5 June 1944.

Above: A pair of Fw 190D-9s from Stab IV./JG 3 waits at readiness at its Prenzlau base, near Berlin, in March 1945. The parachutes waiting for the pilots on the tailplanes had taken on added importance, as Allied air superiority by this time was overwhelming.

Right: Captured on film at the completion of a diving stern quarter attack on a formation of USAAF 9th AF B-26 Marauders in December 1944, this 'Dora' has to contend with the added hazard of bombs falling from the bombers as they attacked German positions on the Western Front.

Above: This works photo portrays an Fw 190D-9 from the first production batch of 300 aircraft built at Focke-Wulf's Cottbus plant between August-December 1944. The early-type canopy seen here was replaced by a clear-vision blown hood on late production D-9s.

a performance comparable with that of the Spitfire Mk XIV and the P-51D Mustang, the best fighter types then in service with the RAF and the USAAF.

Oberleutnant Oskar-Walter Romm flew with IV./JG 3 (by then no longer a Sturmgruppe unit) when it re-equipped with the new Fw 190 variant early in 1945. Romm's unit was operating on the Eastern Front, and the new fighter was superior to any of those opposing it. He recalled:

"As an air superiority fighter and interceptor the Fw 190D-9 handled better than the Fw 190A; it was faster and had a superior rate of climb. During dogfights at altitudes of between about 10,000 and 24,000 ft [3048-7315 m], usual when engaging the Russians, I found that I could pull the Fw 190D into a tight turn and still retain my speed advantage. In the descent the Dora-9 picked up speed much more rapidly than the A type; in the dive it could leave the Russian Yak-3 and Yak-9 fighters standing."

The armament of the new variant was optimised for fighter-versus-fighter combat and comprised two MG 131 13-mm machine-guns mounted on top of the engine, and an MG 151 20-mm cannon in each wing root. All four weapons were synchronised to fire through the airscrew.

Although the Fw 190D had a fine performance, the company and the Luftwaffe regarded it as an interim type

Matching the fate of many Fw 190D-9s, this Stab./JG 4 aircraft was shot down by Allied fighters in the final weeks of the war. On the rear fuselage, Defence of the Reich bands are prominently visible. Indicating that the engine was still running at the time of the forced-landing, the three-bladed wooden propeller has splintered back to the hub.

pending production of the definitive Fw 190 derivative: the Ta 152. The 'Ta' prefix was in belated recognition of Kurt Tank, for the pivotal role he had played in designing and developing this line of fighters.

Focke-Wulf Ta 152H

Like the Fw 190D, the initial production version of the Ta 152H was powered by the Jumo 213 engine. To give optimum performance and manoeuvrability at high altitude the Ta 152 featured a lengthened wing with a span of 47 ft 4.5 in (14.44 m). With a maximum speed of 472 mph (760 km/h) at 41,000 ft (12497 m), the Ta 152H had a performance that matched that of the Spitfire Mk 21 and the P-51H Mustang. The Ta 152 carried an armament of one MK 108 30-mm cannon firing through the propeller hub and two MG 151 20-mm weapons in the wings.

Deliveries of Ta 152s to the Luftwaffe began early in 1945. After about 160 examples had been built, however, advancing Soviet ground forces neared the factory at Cottbus that produced the fighter and German army engineers blew up the plant to prevent its capture. Stab and III./JG 301 re-equipped with the Ta 152H during the closing weeks of the war, but due to shortages of fuel the new variant saw little action.

Night ground-attack aircraft

During the final six months of the war the scale of Allied air superiority in the Western and the Mediterranean Fronts meant that Luftwaffe fighter-bomber units were unable to operate effectively by day. They could exert a pressure on enemy ground forces only at night, and a number of Nachtschlachtgruppen (night ground-attack gruppen) were formed.

The ultimate development of the Fw 190 series was the Ta 152 (the 'Ta' prefix being allocated in honour of Kurt Tank's influence and prestige). Various prototypes were built, including the Daimler-Benz DB 603L-engined Ta 152C (far left), intended primarily as a Zerstörer and fitted with short-span wings. The longer-span wings fitted to the Ta 152H high-altitude fighter version are clearly visible (above left) on the fifth pre-production prototype, seen on compass swinging trials at Cottbus. Only a handful of Ta 152s reached frontline units before the war's end, including these of III./JG 301 (left), seen at Alteno in April 1945.

In January 1945 Fähnenjunker Feldwebel Franz Züger joined the training course for pilots flying the Fw 190 in the night ground attack role. He described the tactics employed during this difficult operation:

"By the end of the course we were able to navigate at night to the target area at altitudes below 300 metres [1,000 ft]. At a previously designated pull-up point we would start our climb to an attack altitude of around 2400 metres [8,000 ft], at the same time warning the ground liaison officer that we were coming. The aim was to be over the target at the correct altitude with our speed well down. We then called the ground liaison officer again, and he would mark the target with flares. Once the flares were in view we would head towards them; as they disappeared under the leading edge of the wing close to the engine we would count 1 - 2 - 3 - 4, then roll the aircraft upside down. By putting one's head right back against the armour one could see the illuminated target. Then one had to pull back on the stick until the target was in front of the Revi [reflector] sight.

"During the dive, made at an angle of about 40°, the propeller blades were set to fine pitch so that they acted as an airbrake to prevent speed building up too rapidly. As soon as the target was in the centre of the Revi one held it there for a few seconds, then eased back slightly on the stick so the bomb would clear the propeller, and pressed the release button. For safety reasons the minimum release altitude was round 1000 metres [3,300 ft] and by the time we got there our speed was around 615 km/h [380 mph]; after the release we pulled out of the dive, then descended below 300 metres for the return flight."

In February 1945 Franz Züger was posted to Italy to join the newly-formed 3. Staffel of Nachtschlachtgruppe 9 with Fw 190Fs. The other two staffeln in the gruppe operated Junkers Ju 87s in the night ground-attack role. Züger's unit frequently changed its base. Typical of the airfields used was that at Villa Franca near Verona. By day the aircraft were dispersed in the surrounding fields, sitting carefully camouflaged in small individual revetments made from piled stones.

"The attacks we made against Allied positions in Italy differed somewhat from those on the bombing range at

Carrying twin 300-litre (66-Imp gal) underwing fuel tanks, this Fw 190A-5 was one of a number modified as a Nacht Jabo-Rei (night long-range fighter-bomber) under the designation Fw 190A-5/U2. On either side of the fuselage aft of the engine were elliptical shields to protect the pilot's eyes from the glare of the exhaust flames. Additionally, a powerful landing light and a gun-camera installation were mounted on the port wing.

Front-line Fw 190 units – 9 April 1945

This was one of the last dates for which a reasonably reliable order of battle for the Luftwaffe can be given. In the chaos of impending defeat there were breakdowns in communications. Where no official figure is available, an approximate figure is given. No figures are available for Fw 190 deliveries to the Luftwaffe in April 1945.

On this day, 1,612 Fw 190s and three Ta 152s were serving with combat units, double the number available 11 months earlier. Of these, about 732 were assigned to 18 fighter gruppen, about 809 to 21 ground attack gruppen and one ground-attack staffel, and about 74 to the four reconnaissance gruppen operating the type.

Two factors contributed to the maintenance of Luftwaffe strength at this stage of the war. Firstly, following the huge surge in production during the previous year, there were plenty of aircraft available in the holding units to make good losses. Secondly, with the critical shortage of high grade aviation fuel for Luftwaffe use at this stage of the war, units equipped with piston-engined aircraft flew low sortie rates. As a result, their loss rates were low. Many of the Fw 190s listed below would sit out the remainder of the war in relative satety, hidden in camouflaged dispersals some distance from their airfields.

Luftflotten 4 and 6, and Luftflotte Reich, were the only major fighting formations remaining. These had been squeezed back into Germany itself and the dwindling neighbouring territories still under German occupation. In the final weeks of the war they no longer confined their operations to defined geographical areas, and because of that, their combat zones are not included in the table below.

Unit	Total	Serviceable
Luftflotte 4		
Schlachtgeschwader 2		
I. Gruppe	33	21
Schlachtgeschwader 10		
Stab	6	4
I. Gruppe	23	21
II. Gruppe	24	15
III. Gruppe	30	17
Luftflotte 6		
Jagdgeschwader 3		
Stab	4	4
IV. Gruppe	61	56
Jagdgeschwader 6		
Stab	4	4 [2]
I. Gruppe	72	59
II. Gruppe	48	45
Jagdgeschwader 11		
Stab	4	4
I. Gruppe	55	53
III. Gruppe	54	51
Schlachtgeschwader 1		
Stab	3	2
I. Gruppe	40	39
II. Gruppe	44	38
III. Gruppe	42	36
Schlachtgeschwader 2		
Stab	6	6
II. Gruppe	44	38
Schlachtgeschwader 3		
Stab	8	4
II. Gruppe	47	43
Schlachtgeschwader 4		
I. Gruppe	30	24
II. Gruppe	39	39
III. Gruppe	24	20
Schlachtgeschwader 9		
I. Gruppe	59	54
Schlachtgeschwader 77		
Stab	8	8
I. Gruppe	34	34
II. Gruppe	34	27
III. Gruppe	47	46
Schlachtgeschwader 151		
13. Staffel	18	17
Nahaufklärungsgruppe 31		
	15	12 [3]
Luftflotte Reich		
Jagdgeschwader 2		
I. Gruppe	5	3
II. Gruppe	8	4
III. Gruppe	12	9
Jagdgeschwader 4		
Stab	6	4
II. Gruppe	50	34
Jagdgeschwader 26		
Stab	4	3
I. Gruppe	44	16
II. Gruppe	57	29
III. Gruppe	35	15
Jagdgeschwader 301		
Stab (Ta 152)	3	2
I. Gruppe	35	24
II. Gruppe	32	15
Jagdgruppe 10		
	15	9
Nachtschlachtgruppe 20		
	27	11
Kampfgeschwader 200		
III. Gruppe	31	21 [4]
Luftflottenkommando East Prussia		
Jagdgeschwader 51		
Stab	20	11
Schlachtgeschwader 3		
I. Gruppe	27	24
Luftwaffe General Norway		
Jagdgeschwader 5		
IV. Gruppe	20	15 [5]
Aufklärungsgruppe 32		
	10	5 [5]
Luftwaffenkommando Courland		
Jagdgeschwader 54		
Stab	5	5
I. Gruppe	38	33
II. Gruppe	41	38
Schlachtgeschwader 3		
III. Gruppe	43	41
Nahaufklärungsgruppe 5		
	25	18 [5]
I. Gruppe	38	33
II. Gruppe	41	38
Luftwaffe General Italy		
Nachtschlachtgruppe 9		
	38	35 [1]
Nahaufklärungsgruppe 11		
	24	14 [5]

[1] Unit also operated Ju 87s
[2] Unit also operated Bf 109s
[3] Unit also operated Siebel Si 204s
[4] Fighter-bomber unit
[5] Due to the mounting chaos the figure given is approximate

Long-nosed Focke-Wulfs

Fw 190D-9, 13./JG 51
The 'Dora' was active on both fronts during the final six months of the war. One of the final units to receive the Fw 190D-9 was IV. Gruppe/JG 51, which operated the type alongside Fw 190A-8s from late March 1945. This example was flown by Leutnant Kurt Tanzer, who scored 126 of his 143 victories on the Eastern Front.

Ta 152H-1, Stab JG 301
The only Luftwaffe front-line unit to operate the Ta 152 was the Geschwaderstab JG 301. This particular aircraft was flown by the only pilot to achieve ace status on the type – Josef Keil – who achieved five 'kills' during the last few weeks of the war. The aircraft carries JG 301's brightly coloured red and yellow Defence of the Reich fuselage bands.

Guided-missile trials

Three Fw 190s were fitted with a trials installation of the Ruhrstahl X-4, the world's first practical air-to-air guided missile. The X-4 weighed 60 kg (132 lb) at launch and had a maximum range of around 5000 m (16,400 ft). Powered by a liquid fuel rocket motor, the X-4 attained a maximum speed of some 700 mph (1127 km/h). The weapon was steered in flight by command signals transmitted down thin wires that unreeled from the weapon as it sped towards the target. The 20-kg (44-lb) high-explosive warhead was fitted with acoustic proximity, impact and self-destroying fuses. The acoustic proximity fuse, of doubtful effectiveness and never tested under operational conditions, was to be triggered by engine noises from a heavy bomber. On 11 August 1944 an Fw 190 carried out the first airborne firing of an X-4 on the Karlshagen range.

The X-4 entered production in January 1945 and more than 1,000 missile bodies were built. However, production of the all-important rocket motors ceased when the BMW works at Stargrad were destroyed in a bombing raid, and there was no time to repair or relocate the production line before Soviet troops entered the area in February 1945.

Had the war continued a little longer, the X-4 would probably have become the first air-to-air guided missile used in action. In the light of what is now known about guided weapons, however, the X-4's effectiveness is questionable. It could not be used at night or in cloud, nor could it engage a manoeuvring target. The X-4's flight time was between 15 and 22 seconds, during which the pilot of the launch aircraft had to maintain straight and level flight to keep himself, the glow from the missile's rocket motor and the target in line. If an enemy escort fighter approached and the pilot of the launch aircraft had to evade, he would have had to leave the X-4 to its own devices in an unguided state. Given these tactical limitations, attacks with the X-4 are unlikely to have been more effective than those with standard 30-mm cannon armament.

The X-4 Ruhrstahl missile system was tested on three Fw 190F-8s, mounted on specially-designed wing pylons outboard of the undercarriage attachment (top/left). Flight trials were conducted between 7 January and 6 February 1945. To control the wire-guided X-4, a joy-stick control unit was fitted into the right side of the control panel (above), allowing the pilot to input rudimentary up-down/left-right commands.

Juterbog. For one thing the targets were usually far beyond the front line, so there was no ground liaison officer to do the marking for us. In practice this meant that to achieve any sort of bombing accuracy, we could attack only on clear moonlight nights. A further change was that instead of the half-roll and pull-through type of attack used during training, we used the simpler method of approaching to one side of the target. As it disappeared under the wing, we banked into the dive. That enabled us to keep the unmarked target in view almost the whole time, and our speed did not build up so rapidly when we entered the dive."

During these operations the Fw 190s flew singly. Once they had released their bombs, the pilots had orders to make strafing attacks on any enemy road vehicles they saw.

"Sometimes the lorry drivers got a bit careless and drove with their lights on, which provided us with a bit of sport. But usually at night there was little to be seen over the other side of the lines. Nevertheless, it was frowned upon if we came back with a full ammunition load. So we would fire a few bursts into the 'enemy darkness', to keep everyone happy."

Typical of the larger-scale attacks Züger's unit made were those to support German paratroops cut off in Bologna, flown on the nights of 22, 23 and 24 April. For these missions the Focke-Wulfs flew from Villa Franca.

"Since the target was only about 110 km [70 miles] from the airfield, less than twenty minutes flying, we did not bother with a low-altitude approach. Instead we climbed straight ahead and flew an almost direct route to the target at altitudes around 4000 m [13,000 ft], jinking from time to time in case there were night fighters about. The nights were clear, and with a battle raging in the city we could see the burning buildings from some distance away. We were briefed to hit a group of buildings on the northern side, so the paratroops could get out. On each night we operated in full staffel strength, making standard dive attacks with 550-kg [1100-lb] bombs; the buildings were flattened."

A few days later NSGr 9 withdrew to Innsbruck in Austria, and arrived just before the ceasefire for German forces on the southern front, which came into effect on 2 May. The unit set fire to its aircraft, then disbanded itself. The officers and men were left to their own devices. For his part, Franz Züger began the 450-mile (724-km) walk to Bremen where his wife lived.

Evacuation aircraft

During the chaos of the closing weeks of the war, Fw 190s were used in ways nobody had previously considered. As Soviet troops thrust deep into Germany's eastern provinces, panic evacuations of aircraft from the mainte-

As Germany's situation worsened more and more desperate measures were introduced to slow the Allied advance. The Mistel (mistletoe) composite weapon comprised a bomb-laden unmanned Ju 88 linked to a controlling fighter aircraft. Both Bf 109s and Fw 190s (designated Fw 190A-8/U3) were used for the task. This example was captured intact by the US Army at Merseburg airport in April 1944.

nance parks ensued. Adolf Dilg was one such pilot involved in these operations. "In the middle of March 1945 we received orders to evacuate all aircraft from Kolberg (now Kolobrzeg in Poland), just before it fell. I flew out an Fw 190 with the armour plate behind the seat removed. In its place there crouched a 12-year-old girl. The radio had been removed from the rear fuselage and there huddled her mother, who had first to remove all metal objects from her clothing so as not to interfere with the master compass beside her. Another ferry pilot, Gefreiter Herzmann, flew an Fw 190 out of Kolberg with a young child on each knee and their mother in the rear fuslage."

A month later Leutnant Werner Gail of II./SG 3 was one of those cut off in the Courland pocket in Latvia, bypassed by the Soviet advance westwards. When the ceasefire was declared on the Eastern Front, on 8 May 1945, those aircraft able to, took off and headed for Germany. Werner Gail made one such flight in an Fw 190F: "My Gruppe stayed in the Courland pocket until the very end. Only on the day of the armistice, did we receive permission to fly our aircraft out. That afternoon I took off from Nikas with four ground-crew squeezed into [the rear fuselage of] my Focke Wulf. For my passengers the flight of almost 600 miles (966 km) to Schleswig-Holstein was long and uncomfortable; but it was neither as long or as uncomfortable as the captivity in Russia for those we left behind."

Altogether about 19,500 Fw 190 and Ta 152s were built. The aircraft saw action on all the main battle fronts, and was one of the truly outstanding fighter planes of World War II. However, use as an evacuation transport aircraft must have been the role furthest from Kurt Tank's mind, when he had conceived his *Dienstpherd* fighter seven years earlier.

Dr Alfred Price

The bitter end for Schlachtgeschwader 1

Lieutenant Helmut Wenk flew Fw 190F-9 fighter bombers with III. Gruppe of Schlachtgeschwader 1, during the final week of the war. These translated excerpts from his flying logbook describe the desperate actions during the losing battle north of Berlin. In those hectic seven days, Wenk's unit was forced to move base four times.

Date	Time	Route	Enemy Activity	Results of Flight
27/4	14.40-15.40	Neubrandenburg – west of Prenzlau – Neubrandenburg	Light flak, fighters	1 x 250 kg container with SD-4 hollow-charge bombs released in the dive from 1500 m, on the road through the wood near Gollmitz. Precise result not observed, but the bombs fell in the target area. Attacked a self-propelled gun from low altitude, results not observed. Air combat with four La-5s; one fired at, disappeared into a layer of cloud.
27/4	18.50-19.45	Neubrandenburg – near Boizen – Neubrandenburg	Light and medium flak, fighters	1 x 250 kg container and 4 x 50 kg bombs released in the dive from 2275 m, on the briefed target at the corner of the wood near Zervelin. Due to poor light, results not observed. Ten La-5s tried to intercept and fired at the second Rotte (pair).
28/4	16.35	Neubrandenburg – east of Neubrandenburg – Neubrandenburg	Light flak	Reconnaissance flight at between 1000 m and ground level. Enemy armour and troops to the east and south-east of Neubrandenburg, seen advancing. Bad weather and rain showers, cloud base in places 200 m.
28/4	18.05-19.00	Neubrandenburg – east of Burgstargrad – Barth	Light flak	1 x 500 kg armour-piercing bomb dropped from 400 m on the road through the wood on the outskirts of Burgstargrad. Target hit. Unit then withdrew to Barth.
29/4	15.40-16.25	Barth – Treptow – Barth	Light flak, fighters	1 x 500 kg armour-piercing bomb dropped on the road where enemy columns were passing, east of Treptow. Low-altitude attack, hit observed. Air combat with Yak-3, no results observed.
29/4	18.00-18.50	Barth – Treptow – Barth	Light flak	1 x 250 kg container and 4 x 50 kg bombs released on the column. Due to thick smoke, results not observed. Oblt Lehn [Wenk's wing man] crashed on take-off and killed.
30/4	10.30-11.40	Barth – Neubrandenburg – Barth	Nil	Schwarm leader became disorientated in cloud and began to run short of fuel. 1 x 500 kg bomb jettisoned.
30/4	17.00-17.45	Barth – east of Griesfwald – Barth	Nil	The roads in the target area were found to be in our hands and the roads in the enemy occupied area were all packed with refugees. 1 x 500 kg bomb jettisoned.
30/4	19.30-20.15	Barth – east of Griesfwald –	Light flak	1 x 500 kg and 4 x 50 kg bombs dropped on a column of enemy vehicles heading for the outskirts of the town. Bombs laid accurately. Tanker vehicle hit, thick smoke clearly seen. Withdrew to Wismar.
2/5	14.00-15.00	Wismar – Barth – Flensburg	Fighters (P-47s). Hit twice by own flak	Russians and English almost at the airfield. Transfer to Flensburg.

Ceasefire on 3/5 at 08.00 hours, on the orders of Grossadmiral Doenitz.

Following a parade with a solemn address by the commander and the singing of the national anthem, Schlachtgeschwader 1 (with a strength of one gruppe of about 30 aircraft), undefeated by the enemy, disbanded itself into small groups to make their way home, and pledged to continue to do their duty and build a new, better Germany.

Above left: *A relieved crewman exits from the fuselage hatch of an Fw 190, following one of the many emergency evacuation flights in the final days of the war. Groundcrewman, doctors and nurses from base hospitals and even small children were saved from Soviet captivity.*

Left: *Typical of the Allied collection point/dumps for captured German aircraft, a range of Fw 190 variants along with Bf 109s and Ju 88s are scattered around the airfiled. The nearest aircraft is from the first production batch of Fw 190A-8s, whereas, by contrast, 'White 8' to the right is an early Fw 190A-3. Note the aircraft have had their rear fuselages sawn-through to prevent use/escape.*

Left: The only remaining example of a two-seat Fw 190, WNr 584219 was captured in Denmark in 1945. An exhibit at the RAF Museum, Hendon since 1990, the Fw 190F-8/U1 is known to have served with Jagdfliegerschule 103.

Below: In the early hours of 17 April 1943 this Fw 190A-4/U8 was among a number of SKG 10 aircraft despatched on an experimental moonlit fighter-bomber raid on targets in southern England. Having dropped a 250-kg (550-lb) bomb on his allotted target near the River Thames in London's East End, the pilot headed back towards France. However, he became disorientated en route and, running low on fuel, landed at RAF West Malling in Kent. Test flown by the RAE, the aircraft was serialled PE882. After a year it was passed to No. 1426 (EAC) Flight at Collyweston, but crashed fatally in October.

Captured 'butcher birds'

In the years that followed the arrival of Oberleutnant Faber's Fw 190A-3 at RAF Pembrey in June 1942, a number of other airframes were acquired by the Allies on various fronts. Around 16 different examples are known to have been examined and evaluated in the UK; others were shipped to the US for similar testing. A number have survived in museums, while many others were scrapped.

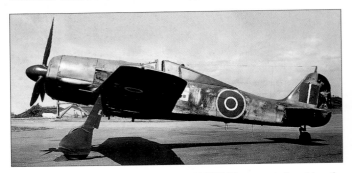

Above: Fw 190A-5/U8 WNr 2596 'White 6' of I./SKG 10 was part of a raid on the London area on 20 June 1943 when its pilot became lost in cloud. His radio unserviceable, he landed at RAF Manston by mistake. Serialled PM679, the aircraft was test flown by RAE and the Air Fighting Development Unit.

Right: Believed to have been assigned at one point to special operations unit III./KG 200, this Fw 190F-8/R15 (with an extended tailwheel leg and an ETC 502 rack for the carriage of torpedo-bombs) was flown to the UK in July 1945. Identified as Air Ministry 111, the aircraft is known to have remained extant at the College of Aeronautics, Cranfield, until at least 1948.

Below: An Fw 190F-8 extensively test flown in the US, T2-116 sports a winter camouflage pattern of a type applied to aircraft on the Eastern Front. 'Air Technical Service Command FE' codes (for 'Foreign, Evaluation' or 'Foreign Equipment') were replaced by 'T2' codes in late 1945, when organisational changes placed the aircraft under Air Technical Intelligence control. Although T2-116 did not survive, another Fw 190F-8 (T2-117) resides with the NASM.

Below: Three Fw 190D-9s and a single D-13 were acquired by the Allies for shipment to the US. A single D-9 (FE-120) survived and was donated to the National Air & Space Museum in 1960 (currently on loan to the USAF Museum). FE-121 (WNr 401392) was test flown extensively and eventually scrapped.

Below: Only one Ta 152 has survived; FE-112 (later T2-112) is a pre-production Ta 152H-0 (WNr 150020) that is believed to have served with JG 301 from early 1945. Captured by the British, the aircraft was turned over to the Americans and shipped to the US for evaluation. Later stored, it was passed to the NASM in 1960 and was fully restored for display in the late 1990s.

Fw 190 Operators

LUFTWAFFE FRONT-LINE UNITS

The Fw 190 equipped a wide-range of fighter, fighter-bomber, ground-attack, night-fighter and reconnaissance units on both Eastern, Mediterranean and Western Fronts. The table below is inclusive only of front-line geschwaders and gruppen which operated the type in numbers and/or for a significant period. Training, replenishment and support units which operated the Fw 190, along with mixed-type gruppen and trials and development units, are not included:

Jagdgeschwader (fighter wing): JG 1, 2, 3, 4, 5 ,6, 11, 26, 27, 51, 52, 54, 300, 301, 302
Jagdgruppe (fighter group): JGr 10, 200
Schlachtgeschwader (ground-attack wing): Schl.G or SG 1, 2, 3, 4, 5, 9, 10, 77, 151
Schnellkampfgeschwader (high-speed bomber wing): SKG 10
Kampfgeschwader (bomber wing): KG 200
Nachtjagdgruppe (night-fighter group): NJGr 10
Nachtschlachtgruppe (night ground-attack group): NSGr 9, 20
Aufklärungsgruppe (reconnaissance group): AGr 32, 33, 123
Nahaufklärungsgruppe (short-range recce group): NAGr 5, 11, 13, 31

HUNGARY

Hungary received several small batches of ground-attack-configured Fw 190As in early 1944 which were immediately allocated to front-line fighter-bomber units carrying codes in the Z-100 series (Z standing for *zuhanó-bombázó* or dive-bomber). Despite ongoing problems with the powerplant, Hungary's Fw 190 force received a boost between October 1944 and January 1945, with the delivery of 36 Fw 190F-8s. Coded in the W-500 series, the aircraft were allocated to 1 'Pavian' and 2 'Puli' Squadrons of 102 Fighter-Bomber Group. Some 36 additional Fw 190F-8s were received from January 1945, these retaining German markings, with white serial numbers on the cowlings being the only identifying features.

JAPAN

A small batch of Fw 190As (including this Fw 190A-5) was supplied to Japan for evaluation and possible licence-production. After ground and air tests, Japan decided not to acquire the type for operational use. The existence of the Fw 190 in Japan was, however, apparent to the Allies, and it was allocated the codename 'Fred'.

ROMANIA

At the time an ally of Germany, a small number of Fw 190As were supplied to the Romanian air force between 1943 and early 1944. The aircraft saw combat against Allied bombers, but all Fw 190 operations ended with the anti-Axis *coup* in the summer of 1944.

SOVIET UNION

Captured Fw 190s of many variants were extensively tested by Soviet air force trials units from 1943. However, by mid-1944 the rapid Soviet advance allowed the capture of factories and aircraft depots intact. A significant number of Fw 190Ds were allocated to various units, including at least one operational squadron of the Baltic Fleet (above), which operated the type in the immediate post-war period. The aircraft received large Soviet red stars on the fuselage and tail, as on this Fw 190D-9 photographed at a Baltic Fleet airfield in August 1945.

Pilots of II.(Sturm)/JG 300 wait at readiness beside their aircraft in the autumn of 1944. The Gruppe's identification marking is the solid line to the right of the fuselage cross, with the individual aircraft number appearing to the left.

FRANCE

The only unit with which the NC 900 served operationally was GC III/5 Normandie-Niemen, the French volunteer unit which had fought alongside the Soviet air force on the Eastern Front.

By early 1944 the demand for the Fw 190 was such that Kurt Tank helped establish a 'shadow factory', under the Focke-Wulf umbrella, operated by the SNCA du Centre (SNCAC) at Cravant, near Auxerre. In the event, the first Fw 190A-5 did not fly until 16 March 1945, and only a handful reached Germany. After the German surrender, production of this model, and subsequently the Fw 190A-8, continued for Armée de l'Air use under the designation NC 900. Production ceased in early 1946 after only 64 examples had been completed, and operational service life lasted little longer, their withdrawal hastened by continual trouble with the BMW 801D-2 engines.

The NC 900 was not a success in French air force service and was quickly replaced from 1946 by British and American types. This line-up shows at least seven NC 900s awaiting their final disposal.

TURKEY

From 1943 Turkey operated both Axis and Allied types as illustrated by this formation of a tropicalised Spitfire Mk V and an Fw 190A-3.

Having signed a non-aggression pact with Germany in 1942, Turkey was the first foreign air arm to operate the type. A total of 60 (some sources state 75) Fw 190A-3s was built in Germany for export to Turkey between October 1942 and March 1943. Along with the aircraft (at a unit cost of 510,000 Reichsmarks), Turkey also acquired a wide range of weaponry for the Fw 190s and 60 replacement BMW 801 engines. The fact that Germany went against normal policy restrictions on modern military equipment sales to complete the deal proved a mistake when Turkey rescinded the treaty and declared war on Germany in 1945.

Twin Mustang in Korea

North American's F-82 was the last of the piston-engined night-fighters – an expedient concoction of two lightweight P-51F fuselages mated by a common centre-section which carried radar. It flew the first combat missions and scored the first kills of the Korean War.

The jet age had dawned by the time World War II entered its final 18 months. Just a short time after the war ended, even though no operational US jet squadrons had seen combat, numerous squadrons were flying the aircraft. This meant that many of the conventional types that had done a commendable job in the war became outdated and were sent to 'the boneyard'. The highly specialised night-fighter/all-weather operators were no exception, but they stuck to their propeller-driven aircraft much longer than other fighter types. The ageing Northrop P-61 Black Widow was forced to shoulder the all-weather tasking

until the North American F-82 was ready to enter operational service.

The original Twin Mustang configuration called for two cockpits with a pilot in each. The purpose of the aircraft was to provide a long-range fighter escort for B-29s on their lengthy bombing missions to Japan. At the time the contract was awarded to North American, it was not feasible for P-51 Mustangs to reach Japan and return. When the war in the Pacific ended abruptly, as a result of the dropping of atomic bombs on Japan, there was no further need for the mission that had been reserved for the F-82. It was, however, obvious that a stop-

A newly arrived F-82G Twin Mustang shares the ramp at Johnson AB, Japan, with two P-61 Black Widows in September 1949. The ageing P-61s had all seen combat in World War II, and by this time had become a maintenance nightmare. Spare parts were cannibalised from as far afield as Clark AB in the Philippines.

gap aircraft would have to be in position to cover the all-weather mission until the jets became operational, and the Black Widow would not be able to bridge that gap.

The duties of all-weather/hours of darkness coverage in the Far East were split between three squadrons, all of which were attached to front-line fighter groups. The 35th FG, flying

Left: Under the command of Lt Col John Sharp, the 4th Fighter (All Weather) Squadron was a very proficient unit whose task was the protection of Naha and Kadena Air Bases. Squadron-strength formation sorties around Okinawa were routine training exercises, six aircraft being seen here in the spring of 1950.

Above: One might be forgiven for thinking this photograph depicted an F-82 on a strafing mission in the war zone, but closer examination reveals B-29s parked in their dispersals. The location was Kadena AB, Okinawa and the 4th F(AW)S F-82G was on a training sortie in early 1950. The smoke remains unexplained.

F-80s from Johnson AB, was responsible for the defence of the greater Tokyo area; the 339th Fighter (All Weather) Squadron was attached to this group. Some distance away at Itazuke AB, the 8th Fighter Group controlled the 68th Fighter (All Weather Squadron). The third and final squadron of F-82s to operate in the Far East was the 4th Fighter (All Weather Squadron), located on the island of Okinawa, at Naha AB. It was under the direct control of the 51st Fighter Group. All three of the parent groups were operators of the F-80, which, at the time, was the USAF's front-line jet fighter.

The late 1940s was a period in which the USAF was trying to keep a very high profile with the American public. In order to obtain maximum funding from Congress, the USAF pushed the image of an all-jet air force – and it was well accepted by those who counted, i.e., the voters. This meant that conventional fighter aircraft types were on their way out. The F-94 all-weather interceptor was to fulfil the mission for which the F-82 had been slated, but it was still a couple of years from entering service. In the meantime, the F-82 was brought into the force, but the type did not provide the glamour demanded by the force's new image.

F-82G in service

By mid-summer 1949, the F-82G began filtering into the three Far East squadrons and, although it was not a sleek jet, it was well received by all personnel in the all-weather units. The potential of this twin-fuselage fighter was recognised only by those who flew it and those who serviced it. It gave the F-80 pilots much trouble on their practice intercepts. The only time the Twin Mustang was exposed to the public in Japan and on Okinawa was during Armed Forces Day displays and flyovers.

The F-82 and its aircrew were in their element during the hours of darkness and inclement weather. They honed their skills in this realm, and if the balloon ever went up, they were ready to scramble into the blackness and take on anything that might be intruding into friendly airspace.

Left: Lt Morris Washatka poses at Naha in the cockpit of his F-82G Wee Pea II. Within weeks he and his R/O. Lt D.T. Aldred, would be at war, flying combat missions from Itazuke.

Below: This scene from Naha in early June 1950 shows 4th F(AW)S F-82Gs preparing for a daylight mission. At the time the training schedule primarily consisted of formation flights and nocturnal scrambles. In-service rates of the 4th's Twin Mustangs were extremely good.

Above: Lt H.W. 'Rocky' Jones is at the helm of F-82G 46-390 The Sexy Doo-Ver during a pre-war training hop, while Lt Cecil W. Wills works the radar system. Pilot and Radar Observer usually remained together as a 'hard' crew.

Left: Double Trouble was from the 4th F(AW)S, and is seen over Naha in early 1950. The proximity of the squadron's parking ramp to the sea made saltwater corrosion a major factor in maintenance.

4th Squadron pilot Lieutenant John Redrup recalled some of his early experiences in the F-82 prior to the beginning of the Korean War. "I started flying the Twin Mustang in December 1949. I found it to be very manoeuvrable, fast, with a vast amount of power. On one test hop I flew, I had feathered the right prop and was checking engine performance when I was jumped by an F-80 (51st Fighter Group) that was also based on Okinawa. I immediately turned into him and we went around for several minutes before I realised that I had one engine shut down! By the time I got it unfeath-

13 All Around *is seen on a maintenance test flight in early 1950. The aircraft was assigned to the 68th F(AW)S at Itazuke. The period before the war was peaceful, and many of the crews were accompanied by their families.*

ered, he was long gone. He had the speed, but I sure could turn inside him. The aircraft was a superb single-engine performer.

"I can recall another memorable experience before the war. We usually flew a squadron formation when it was possible to get all of our aircraft in commission. So, one fine morning, we briefed for a mass gaggle… 12 aircraft! We took off for a fly-by of all the island's airfields. After the show, we broke off and assumed the line astern position and proceeded to follow the leader through rolls, loops and various other weird manoeuvres. We ended up at about 1,000 ft [305 m] headed for Naha AB. I was somewhere in the rear of the gaggle when I noticed our fearless leader, Lieutenant Colonel John Sharp, feather his right prop and then

each of us followed suit. I did not remember this particular manoeuvre being mentioned in the briefing or on the radio, but I went ahead and feathered mine and we all roared across the field on one engine! Needless to say, there was some discussion about this at our debriefing!"

First combat mission

The net worth of this rugged warrior was about to overshadow that of the F-80, thanks to North Korean aggression against South Korea in June 1950. The Twin Mustang's moment of glory began on the night of 24/25 June, at about 4:00 a.m. The closest Japanese air base to the Korean Peninsula was Itazuke, which meant that the 68th Fighter (All Weather) Squadron received the first call.

First Lieutenant George D. Deans and his radar observer, Lieutenant Marvin R. Olsen, were one of the F-82 aircrews on alert. Lieutenant Olsen recalled, "We were scrambled with orders to contact 'Moonshine Control' (the radar-controlled area for southern Japan). Soon

4th F(AW)S deployment

The following aircraft and crew members from the 4th Fighter (All Weather) Squadron were directed to proceed to Itazuke Air Base, Japan on 26 June 1950 per Flight orders # 175 issued by 20th Air Force:

Capt. Ross C. Ford/Lt Keith H. Morehouse	46-400
Lt H.W. Jones/Lt C.W. Wills	46-390
Capt. R.E. Gillingham/MSgt G.L. Umbarger	46-366
Lt C.C. Sherman/Lt R.L. Greer	46-403
Capt. E.C. Fiebelkorn/Lt J.J. Higgins	46-359
Capt. W.M. Foley/Lt T.E. Symonds	46-358
Lt M.J. Washatka/Lt D.T. Allred	46-402
Lt J.L. Redrup/SSgt P.B. Brown	46-394

The 4th Squadron CO, Lt Col John Sharp, had been on leave in the US, and had just returned to Japan to visit friends before going on to Okinawa when the war started. He arranged for immediate transportation to Itazuke to join his troops. This was the reason that he was not listed as one of the crew members on the flight to Itazuke AB.

Li'l Bambi was the personal mount of Lt George Deans of the 68th F(AW)S. With Radar Observer Lt Marvin Olsen, Deans flew the first combat mission of the Korean War on 25 June 1950, a reconnaissance mission to the Seoul area to assess the scale of the North Korean invasion.

after beginning our climb-out, we were given a vector to Seoul, South Korea! The instructions told us to fly up to the 38th Parallel and report back on any activity seen on the main roads and/or railroads. It seemed that FEAF had received a report that North Korea had crossed the 38th and was moving to the south, towards Seoul.

"When we arrived in the area, it was overcast with tops at about 8,000 ft [2438 m]. Deans flew us out over the water for letdown, using our airborne search radar (mounted on the central wing between the two fuselages). We broke out at about 2,000 ft [610 m] just west of Inchon and proceeded to Kimpo Airfield before heading north towards the 38th. About 10 miles [16 km] south of the line, we saw a huge convoy of vehicles, close to 60 tanks, trucks and assorted vehicles, moving on the road, and that's all we could count before passing over. We immediately climbed up to 8,000 ft, so we could report back what we had observed. HQ ordered us to return to Itazuke where we were debriefed by an Army colonel from General MacArthur's staff. This was later recorded as the first combat mission flown in the Korean War."

Evacuation from Seoul

It did not take a rocket scientist to realise that the Communist north had indeed invaded South Korea. There was an urgent need to evacuate American civilians and key South Korean government personnel from the Seoul area. This rapidly developed into a highly volatile situation when the NKPAF began making appearances over the area on Day 2. Their aircraft included a variety of Soviet-built conventional fighter types, which posed a serious threat to any cargo aircraft caught on the ground at Kimpo.

4th F(AW)S F-82Gs prepare to take off during a mass scramble from Naha in late June 1950. The eight aircraft sent to Itazuke returned to Naha in July, continuing to fly on night/all-weather air defence missions until replaced by Lockheed F-94s in early 1952.

Right: One of the luckiest escapes for the F-82 community occurred just before the war, in late May 1950. As an armourer checked the guns on the flightline, one gun inadvertently fired into the top of a fuel bowser. Mercifully, the bowser was full to the brim: if there had been an air pocket the tank would surely have exploded, taking several crew and aircraft with it.

At this point, a weakness of the F-80 became apparent. A large number of these aircraft were available from the three groups based in Japan. The 8th Fighter-Bomber Group's Shooting Stars initially were called into the crisis, primarily because they were based at Itazuke and that was the closest Japanese air base to the Korean Peninsula. As the 'kill' reports show, the conventional aircraft of the North Korean AF were no match for the jets, but the jets proved to be ineffective against ground targets because they had a very short loiter time over the fluid front. No sooner would they begin their rocket attacks against the advancing armour columns than they would become low on fuel and have to return to Itazuke. At the time, there were no bases in South Korea capable of sustaining F-80 operations.

In contrast, the F-82s were very capable of taking on any aircraft type in the NKPAF's inventory, they could carry an enormous load of ordnance, and their loiter time over the front was well over an hour. These traits quickly moved them to the top of FEAF's priority list. There was only one nagging problem: very few of these aircraft were available in the Far East. Two squadrons were based in Japan and one on Okinawa. An emergency call went out to all three to bring everything they could spare to Itazuke AB, resulting in the formation of the 347th All Weather Fighter Group (Provisional). The commanding officer was Lieutenant Colonel John F. Sharp, who was the 4th All Weather Squadron's CO.

Left: Photographed at Itazuke in 1950, 46-383 Bucket of Bolts was the 68th F(AW)S F-82G used by Lt William G. 'Skeeter' Hudson (pilot) and Lt Carl Fraser (R/O) to score the first aerial kill of the Korean War on 27 June 1950. Their victim was a Yak-11.

Right: 46-383 can be seen again, over North Korea in early 1951. By this time the nose art had gone, but a red star beneath the windscreen commemorated Hudson's kill. The aircraft remained with the 68th until the unit converted to the F-94B, before serving with the 449th Fighter (All Weather) Squadron in Alaska.

In mid-June 1950, there was a grand total of 34 operational F-82Gs in the Far East, of which 27 converged on Itazuke AB. The 339th All Weather Squadron (attached to the 35th Fighter Group at Johnson AB) sent seven aircraft, and the 4th All Weather Squadron at Naha AB rounded up eight. The remainder came from the 68th All Weather Squadron at Itazuke. All of these big Twins, parked on the ramp, presented an impressive sight. They represented a tremendous amount of firepower that could be delivered against the North Korean forces moving south on the main roads.

As the evacuation process continued into its second day, the close proximity of the North Korean and American aircraft meant it was just a matter of hours before the two met. 26 June proved to be nerve-wracking, as one of the F-82s was fired on by a North Korean fighter, but the integrity of the formation was steadfast and it maintained its established umbrella over the activities below. The sporadic appearances of the NKPAF in the area proved to be ineffective in penetrating the protective fighter cover.

On 27 June, the inevitable happened. The remaining civilian types to be removed from the Seoul area had to be gone on this day, due to the rapid advances of the North Korean People's Army. The C-54s were used to bring out the evacuees while the F-82s and F-80s were layered above in a defensive pattern. The F-80s were at the higher altitudes, which meant that the F-82s had to intercept anything coming in fast and low. A flight of four Twin Mustangs from the 68th All Weather Squadron orbited right above the airport at Kimpo. There had been relays of both aircraft types, on station, all morning, ensuring no gaps in the coverage.

Orders must have come down from Pyongyang to do whatever was necessary to disrupt the evacuation process, and the North Korean pilots involved did just that. As noon approached (11:50 a.m.), five North Korean aircraft (Soviet-built Yaks and La-7s) suddenly dropped from a low cloud cover and attacked the trailing F-82 in the flight. Before the crew could respond, one of the Yaks scored several hits on the vertical stabiliser of Lieutenant Charlie Moran's fighter; quick reflexes kept the damage to a minimum.

First kill

At the very moment this took place, Lieutenant William G. 'Skeeter' Hudson made a high-g turn in the direction of the attacking fighters. According to his radar observer, Lieutenant Carl Fraser, "We turned quickly, and before the Yak pilot realised it, we were locked onto his 6 o'clock position. He tried everything he could to shake us, and when he realised he couldn't, he pulled his nose straight up into the cloud layer. By this time, it was too late for him because we were so close. As we pursued him through the clouds, we were close enough to keep a constant visual. As we broke out, Lieutenant Hudson fired a short burst, and at the impact of all six guns hitting the fragile fighter, pieces of the Yak's tail and fuselage came flying back past us. At that time, the enemy pilot racked his aircraft over into a steep turn to the right, with us following closely. A second burst showered all over his right wing, setting one of his fuel tanks on fire. At the same time, his right flap and aileron flew off and we were so close that we almost collided. I could clearly see the pilot turn around in his seat and say something to the rear seat observer. He then pushed his canopy back, stepped out on the wing and again said something to his back-seater. It was at this time that I figured he was either unconscious or dead, because he never showed any movement to exit the stricken aircraft. The pilot then pulled his ripcord and the chute dragged him off the wing as it opened. The shooting had been at very close range and at altitudes below 1,000 ft [305 m].

Shortly after Hudson's kill, Lt Charlie Moran of the 68th F(AW)S shot down a Lavochkin La-7 over Kimpo airfield to notch up the second kill of the war, after his F-82 had taken some hits in the tail. His mount was 46-357, seen above at Itazuke just before the North Korean invasion. Moran (photographed by his R/O, right) was killed on 7 August 1950, along with Lt Francis Meyer, when their Twin Mustang hit a cable stretched across a valley to catch low-flying UN aircraft. At the time the F-82 force was heavily involved in ground attack missions to stem the advance of the North Koreans as they pushed back the 'Pusan Perimeter'.

The Radar Observer occupied the right-hand cockpit. The equipment was rudimentary, with two small oscilloscope screens. Considerable skill was required to interpret the displays and direct the pilot to a successful intercept.

'Skeeter' Hudson, who had scored the first kill of the war, poses in full flight gear by a Twin Mustang being readied with 5-in (12.7-cm) HVARs and bombs for an air-to-ground mission in November 1950. The ground attack role had all but evaporated by that time, apart from some missions where only the Twin Mustang had the required range for the job.

"We made a fast turn to come back around to see where the pilot had landed. There were a large number of RoK troops standing around the pilot. I thought he had surrendered, but later found out from one of their majors that the downed pilot had started shooting at his men, at which time they returned the fire and killed him. Just about the time we were watching our 'kill' plunge into the ground, Lieutenant Charlie Moran was shooting down a North Korean La-7 right over Kimpo airport."

Three kills for the Twin

The records show that the F-82s scored three confirmed kills within minutes of each other. Although the F-80s were credited with more kills on that day, the big Twins held their own against the new 'all-jet' force.

The third kill was made by Major James Little, commanding officer of the 339th All Weather Squadron. His encounter occurred beyond sight of Kimpo airport, so confirmation of his kill did not come as quickly.

Also included in this dogfight was an element of the 339th F(AW)S that included Captain David Trexler and his wingman, Lieutenant Walter Hayhurst. They mixed it up with several Yaks farther from Kimpo airfield. Captain Trexler recalled what took place in that very brief encounter. "My wingman and I attacked one of the Yaks, which immediately broke hard to the left, directly into my line of flight! As I closed to about 3,000 ft [914 m], I fired a short burst and the enemy fighter then started a hard turn to the right and down. I tracked him perfectly and fired a second burst, causing him to reverse his turn again. I fired a

For a three-week period in late June/early July 1950 ground crews at Itazuke worked double shifts to keep the 27 Twin Mustangs of the hastily assembled 347th All Weather Fighter Group (Provisional) in the air. Their work was vital: the North Koreans were rushing headlong through the south of the country, and the need to deliver as much ordnance as possible to hold up the advance was paramount.

third burst from less than 1,000 ft [305 m] as he went into a slow roll left to an inverted position as he dropped down into the overcast, nose low, at about 425 mph [684 km/h] indicated. I immediately pulled up because there were mountains jutting through the clouds. We never saw him hit the ground, so we were both credited with a probable."

A number of pilots indicated that they knew they had scored hits on several attacking aircraft, but only three were confirmed kills. The North Korean pilots who returned safely to their Pyongyang airfield probably had a lot to talk about that night!

The next day (28 June) was extremely tough on the F-82 ground crews at Itazuke AB. The big Twin Mustangs were normally considered high-maintenance aircraft, and this was their first exposure to such rigorous flights since their arrival in the Far East. At this time, there were no options or relief aircraft to back them up. The Twin Mustangs and B-26 Invaders were the first line of defence for stopping the North Korean advance, because they could carry heavy loads of ordnance effectively. The newly

formed 347th AWFGp (P) was taxed beyond its ability to deliver.

Lieutenant Colonel John Sharp recalled one of their first top-priority assignments. "On 28 June, I received word through 5th Air Force HQ that a classified mission would need fighter escort the next day and it would have to be provided by my group. I alerted the necessary aircrews to set it up. The following morning we assembled in a guarded ready room and were briefed by one of the generals. I sat in on the session because, as 347th commander, I had to know the schedule, to keep other fighter sweeps clear. The mission was classified as 'need to know', with no further details given. A C-54 would be flying from Tokyo and the escort would rendezvous with it over Pusan, South Korea and escort it to its destination and

Mid Night Sinner *was one of the most photographed Twin Mustangs in the Far East. It was on the strength of the 4th F(AW)S, attached to the 51st Fighter Group.*

Miss Tippi *was the mount of Lt George Boughton of the 68th F(AW)S. He was killed on 12 February 1951 during a maintenance test flight, although his R/O, 2nd Lt Frederick Reberg, bailed out safely. Boughton remained in the aircraft to steer it away from a populated area.*

return. The callsign of the mystery aircraft was 'Tony'. The F-82 escort flight took off at precisely the briefed time and its callsign was 'Cleopatra'. I followed with another flight of four on a fighter sweep north to Seoul about 20 minutes later.

"The weather at Itazuke was usually bad during this time of year, but on this day it was lousy, with about a 200-ft [61-m] ceiling and light rain. I did not get my flight formed up until we crossed the coast of South Korea. From this point, we took a heading toward Seoul. About 10 minutes later I heard 'Tony' trying to contact his fighter escort. He was out of the clouds over Pusan and there was no escort in sight. After his second call, I radioed 'Tony' and told him a flight of F-82s was supposed to meet him there. 'Tony' replied that no escorts had showed up. I told him I was on a fighter sweep (I cannot remember the 4th callsign), but would turn around and find him. Shortly thereafter, I spotted the C-54, and Captain Ross Ford, my element leader, and I set up a scissor cover escort all the way to Suwon.

"After the C-54 had landed safely at Seoul, I resumed the fighter sweep north, but very shortly 'Tony' started calling for escort again. I started to explain that I was returning to my original mission when Captain Ford piped up and said, 'I think he wants company!' I radioed to the transport that we were on the way to escort him back. We covered him all the way to Pusan, where he went on his way back to Japan and we entered some heavy clouds. We stayed in IFR formation until I contacted the tower at Itazuke AB, at which time they broke us up and we made individual GCAs. The ceiling was still only 200 ft and the clouds were full of aircraft!

"After we landed, I learned that the escort flight had aborted and we obviously filled in. Then we found out that the mystery aircraft was General MacArthur's and 'Tony' was his personal pilot, Anthony Storey."

Switch to ground attack

The air superiority role did not last long for the F-82 (from 26 June until 30 June). The F-80s were more than able to counter anything the NKPAF had in inventory, and the F-82's services were needed badly in other areas: close air support and interdiction.

It was routine for these big fighters to load up with a combination of 5-in (12.7-cm) HVARs, 500-lb (227-kg) GP bombs, napalm and the normal rounds of 0.50-in (12.7-mm) ammunition. Of course, not all of this was carried at the same time. According to Lieutenant Colonel Sharp, they usually loaded five rockets under each wing or carried two

500-pounders and two napalm canisters (on the same load). Given this potential destruction and the aircraft's ability to spend over an hour roaming the front lines or the major supply routes, the F-82's real value became obvious. In a matter of days, these specialised all-weather fighters had transitioned into the day fighter-bomber role.

On 4 July, the F-82s were still trying to make a difference by slowing the southward movement of the North Korean armour columns, but the weather continued to hamper attempts to provide air support. Lieutenant Colonel John Sharp related the details of a midnight mission that resulted in the first loss of a USAF aircrew in the war. "Since 25 June, the North Koreans had been rolling practically unopposed, and low cloud cover had kept us guessing as to how many and how far. On this night I sent out two F-82s to watch for any breaks in the clouds so we could get down and report the ground activity.

"Captains Warren Foley and Ernest Fiebelkorn stayed on station for several hours without a break. (As a first lieutenant, Ernest Fiebelkorn had been the top-scoring ace with the 20th Fighter Group in World War II.) As a last resort, Captain Fiebelkorn told Foley that he was going to try and get below the clouds. Minutes later, radio contact was lost with him. Upon returning to Itazuke, Captain Foley stated that he thought the other F-82 had gone in, and as we later found out, that is exactly what had happened. The R/O of the downed aircraft was Lieutenant J.J. Higgins.

"The surviving aircrew stated that they believed the clouds were beginning to break up. With this information, I called Armament and told them to load one of the F-82s with eight rockets.

"I took off at midnight and, sure enough, the clouds were breaking up over South Korea. Soon, through the spotty clouds, I saw a lot of activity down on the roads! This was approximately 20 miles [32 km] south of the bomb line, so the enemy was moving very fast. I talked it over with my R/O, Sergeant Umbarger, and we

The 339th F(AW)S of the 35th Fighter Group sent seven aircraft to Itazuke to answer 5th AF's emergency call in late June 1950, but on 6 July the aircraft were recalled to their home base at Johnson AB, Japan, from where they provided night/all-weather defence for the Tokyo region. The squadron also undertook strip alert duties at Misawa, and was tasked with intercepting Soviet aircraft which made regular probing flights around northern Japan. Seen at Johnson in the summer of 1950 are Lover Boy *(below), which was lost in an accident in March 1951, and* Gruesome Twosome *(below right), which returned to war duty with the 68th FS, and then flew with the 449th FS in Alaska.*

Indicative of the kind of conditions facing all crews during the Far East winters, F-82Gs of the 339th F(AW)S are seen on an ice-covered ramp at Misawa, where the squadron maintained an air defence detachment. Behind is a B-29 and two Boeing SB-17Gs of the 3rd Rescue Squadron.

both decided that we could probably tell the good guys from the bad guys, but to defy the designated bomb line was asking for trouble. So we headed north. One of the targets that we hit caused a secondary explosion that lit up half of South Korea. A little farther north, I spotted a speeding car… lights on high beam and moving south. This could only be a staff car trying to catch up to the war. I deliberately took aim on the rocket ladder, cranked in a little 'Kentucky windage' to lead him, snapped my eyes closed and cut loose two 5-in rockets, then waited and watched… BLAM! Both rockets exploded right at the base of the car and the lights went out. This was the best shot I ever made!"

Throughout those first two rigorous weeks, the strain began to show on both the aircrews and the enlisted types working on the flight line

An F-82G of the 68th F(AW)S cruises high over North Korea at dawn, some time in early 1951. Weather reconnaissance missions deep into enemy territory were the primary role for the unit after the hectic air-to-ground work of July to November 1950.

at Itazuke. Humour, though, kept them on the 'sane' side of a thin line – as in this story related by Lieutenant George Deans, one of the first 68th Squadron pilots to fly an F-82 over South Korea. "My R/O, Lieutenant Marv Olsen, and I were on our way back from a long mission over Korea when he spotted a large radar return on his scope. We immediately knew what it was: a large aircraft-carrier positioned off the southern coast of Korea.

"It was evening and we were returning early due to very bad weather all over the peninsula. We had descended to a few hundred feet when we broke out of the clouds, with the carrier just a couple of miles away and off to our starboard side. We dropped our landing gear and flaps as we initiated a turn toward the stern of the ship. You never saw so many flashing red lights in all your life! I guess they thought we were going to land on the deck.

"At the time, we thought it was real funny, but when we returned back to Itazuke, the squadron CO and wing ops officer were waiting for us. They failed to see any humour in our antics!"

The Commander of 5th Air Force, Lieutenant General Earle E. Partridge, once stated that even though he had never flown the F-82, he wished he had more of them when the Korean War began. This statement was triggered by the fact that the aircraft could carry such a wide array of effective ordnance on their long missions from Itazuke. Under normal conditions, the Twin Mustang had a combat range of 1,945 nm (3602 km) at an average airspeed of 250 kt (463 km/h), and could carry an ordnance load of 4,000 lb (1814 kg). Aerial refuelling had not yet been perfected, so the versatile fighters relied on 576 US gal (2180 litres) of fuel carried internally and another 620 US gal (2347 litres)

5th Air Force F-82 unit badges: 4th Fighter (All Weather) Squadron (left), 68th Fighter (All Weather) Squadron (centre), 339th Fighter (All Weather) Squadron (right).

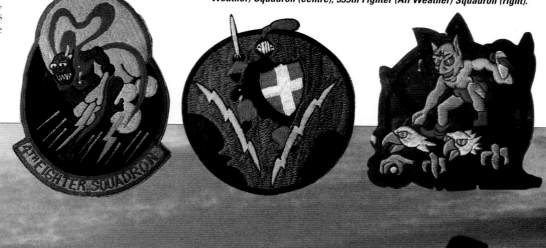

Enlisted personnel of the 68th Fighter Squadron take the rare opportunity for a formal group photograph at Itazuke in early 1951. The F-84 in the background is from the 27th Fighter Escort Wing, which operated from the base for a short while. The number of Twin Mustangs on strength dwindled throughout the year, although the 68th maintained night-fighter alert detachments at Kimpo and Suwon.

Left: The 68th F(AW)S/FIS planned its operation out of this building at Itazuke. Although the temporary huts at the base were relatively primitve, the conditions were better than those experienced by UN fliers based in Korea itself.

carried in external, droppable tanks. With a full load of fuel, the G version of the F-82 could handle two 1,000-lb (454-kg) bombs and up to 20 5-in (12.7-cm) rockets (suspended on removable mounts under the outer wing pylons).

Over the years, a gross misconception has arisen regarding the horsepower developed by the huge Allison engines in the F-82G models. In many periodicals, it has been stated that these 12-cylinder engines developed 1,600 hp (1194 kW), but this is incorrect. This figure was true of the early, lighter-weight models, but for the all-weather versions, laden with radar gear and added equipment, 1,600 hp would hardly be sufficient to get the aircraft off the ground.

Lieutenant Colonel John Sharp shed some light on the powerplants of his G models. "The 1,600-hp engines that are currently published

The Twin Mustang squadrons usually applied their unit badges to the outside of the vertical fins. This aircraft proudly wears the 68th's 'Lightning Lancers' badge, depicting a knight girding for battle while skiing on a pair of lightning bolts.

on the F-82 stats pertain only to the early day fighter models, which were significantly lighter. After World War II, the all-weather version was built and it was much heavier. These engines did not have enough power. Even the vaunted Rolls-Royce Merlin could not satisfy the power requirements. Finally, the giant 2,250-hp [1678-kW] Allisons, originally designed for the P-51H, were installed – and with the counter-rotating props, it was a dream to fly!"

Bombing profiles

During the first week of Korean War interdiction operations, a number of tactical procedures were developed based on experiences with various types of ordnance. On bombing missions, it was discovered that napalm tanks were not very accurate for night use. The drops were unpredictable due to the lack of fins on the tanks, so they had to be made at high airspeed (for safety from ground fire) and at very low level. The tanks would wobble off and could easily miss the target by several yards, rendering them ineffective. The M-76 incendiary bombs were preferable, as were the 500-lb (227-kg) or 1,000-lb (454-kg) general-purpose bombs, all of which had a very stable trajectory to the aiming point. It was determined that a 75° angle should be used, rather than gliding, with a maximum initial altitude of

8,000 ft (2438 m) and a release point of approximately 4,000 ft (1219 m). The latter was to lessen the chance of the F-82 being damaged by debris from the explosions.

The 339th Squadron was pulled back from Itazuke to Johnson AB on 6 July, to resume defensive duties. Squadron records for the month of August 1950 shed some light on just how thinly the squadron was spread over a wide area. Tactical operations performed by the 339th during the month of August included strip alert for the Kanto Plain and Misawa areas, and two crews being on standby for Soviet escort duty (the Soviets constantly tested the defensive posture of FEAF, making runs towards Japan from bases around the Vladivostok/Nakhodka area). According to 339th CO Major 'Poke' Little, the Soviets made frequent probes across the strait from Sakhalin into Hokkaido. This was probably the reason that the squadron was pulled from combat duties and returned to Johnson AB at such an early stage in the war. The normal requirements for the squadron in this area were for two aircrews and aircraft on 10-minute strip alert, and another two on 45-minute standby.

The commitment for the Misawa area called for two aircraft and crews on 10-minute strip alert and one crew on 45-minute standby alert, ensuring adequate coverage seven days a week, 24 hours a day. The F-80s from the 41st Fighter Squadron fulfilled the required daylight defensive commitment, except when the weather was bad enough to need the services of the F-82s. Although the Soviets were not involved directly in the war, they continued to test US air defences on Japan and in Alaska.

One 339th pilot, First Lieutenant David Trexler, related an incident of mistaken Soviet identity – funny to the aircrew, but not to the radar intercept people on the ground.

"One afternoon, my R/O, Lieutenant Larry Sander, and I were flying a maintenance hop in an F-82 from Misawa AB. It was a beautiful

By the start of the war at least seven of the 68th's F-82Gs were adorned with artwork in a similar vein to Hot to Go illustrated. By early 1951, when operations had fallen into routine strip alert and weather recon missions, most of the artwork had been removed.

clear day. We decided to see how high we could climb and I think we got up to around 45,000 ft [13716 m] or so. We were not making contrails at that altitude, we were not talking to GCI (ground controlled intercept) and we were not even monitoring the radio. In fact, it was simply an uncontrolled VFR flight. As our altitude peaked out, I rolled the aircraft over on its back and Split-S'd with full power. At some point in the dive, we started making contrails, which were spotted by a flight of F-80s from the 49th Fighter Group (at Misawa AB).

"As the dive progressed, the indicated air speed built up rapidly and soon passed the 500-mph [805-km/h] mark. I mentioned that to Lieutenant Sander, and he was impressed! Then he asked me why my head was bent down so low; I looked over at him, and his head was nearly up against the canopy, to get a great view. I mentioned that canopies had been known to blow off at high IAS, and if mine blew, I didn't want my head to go with it. At that time, his head disappeared from view!

"We turned the radio on after completing our dive and switched over to tower frequency to ask for landing instructions. The tower informed us to stand clear, fuel permitting, because the base was on alert and all available F-80s were scrambling!

"After all the F-80s had launched, we went ahead and landed. Then we heard the story. It seems that two F-80s spotted us in our dive when we were leaving contrails. From their vantage point, it did not appear that we were in a dive, but going straight and level. They radioed in that they had sighted a twin-engined, dark-coloured Russian bomber, and it was outrunning them! The base went on alert. When we stopped conning, but were still in the dive, the two F-80s lost sight of us and they thought we were still at altitude right below the contrail level. After a brief period, the base alert ended and the F-80s returned. I have no idea how far they ranged out, but Larry and I laughed quietly and never mentioned anything about it."

All major maintenance for the F-82 force was performed at Itazuke. Here an aircraft from the 4th F(AW)S undergoes a double propeller change. Twin Mustang maintenance personnel were rated among the best in the theatre, and in the last months of the type's combat career performed superbly to keep the few aircraft that were left in the air, despite a dwindling spares stock.

On 9 July, a flight of F-80s struck a string of road traffic trying to cross a bridge at Pyongtaek. Their 500-lb (227-kg) bombs destroyed the structure, resulting in a massive jam of North Korean armour and vehicles. The next day, a large number of F-80s, B-26s and F-82s were loaded and briefed on the target. The Twin Mustangs were mostly 68th Squadron aircraft, but there were a few 4th Squadron birds in the strike force. (All of the 339th detachment and most of the 4th's had already departed for their home bases.) The glut of road traffic was much greater than anticipated. Post-strike photos show that 117 trucks, 38 tanks and seven half-tracks were destroyed, and a large number of enemy troops killed. The most effective weapons utilised in this strike were napalm and 0.5-in (12.7-mm) rounds.

The 68th soldiers on

When the remaining 4th aircraft returned to Okinawa, the 68th Squadron assumed a heavy load of air defence at Itazuke and countless requests for interdiction missions. On one mission to the Chinju area, Lieutenant George Deans led several F-82s against a known transportation hub that was intermingled with the

village's houses and buildings. Orders were to level everything in order to shut down this operation. They were armed with 500-lb GP bombs, 5-in rockets and machine-guns. Satisfied that they had accomplished the mission, the F-82s proceeded farther north into the Sumchon/Chongjui area to reconnoitre the roads. Five miles (8 km) north of Kumchon, they met with intense ground fire: one of the rounds hit one of Dean's coolant radiators, forcing him to shut down that engine.

With the prop feathered, he climbed to the preferred cruising altitude and flew all the way back to Itazuke on one engine, with no difficulty. All the Twin Mustangs that had launched for the mission returned safely.

At this point in the war, the situation for the UN forces was dismal, and getting worse by the day. The infamous 'Pusan Perimeter' was shrinking and there was a distinct possibility that the first major test of the United Nations could end up being a disaster. At 03.00 on 7 August, Lieutenant Charlie Moran and

F-82Gs from the 68th F(AW)S 'Lightning Lancers' line the ramp at Itazuke in 1951. Just visible are two Lockheed F-94s, the radar-equipped jet fighter which replaced the F-82G in its night/all-weather role.

Left: Mechanical problems during a return from a mission are the most likely reason this 68th aircraft was at Pusan East (K-9, the 'Dogpatch') in May 1951. For most of 1951 and into the following year the squadron maintained night strip alerts at Suwon and Kimpo, and also flew missions from Taegu.

Below: At Kimpo (K-14) a bomb dump was as good a place as any to read the paper. Captain Rogers Littlejohn of the 68th FS enjoys the August sunshine in 1951, while the strip alert night-fighters in the background await darkness to fall. The bombs had been delivered to Kimpo for use by the 18th FBG's F-51Ds.

R/O Lieutenant Francis Meyer took off for a routine interdiction mission over Korea, flying in a/c number 46-355A rather than their regularly-assigned F-82. They disappeared without a trace or a radio transmission. Several weeks later, when the ground forces had regained much of the Korean Peninsula (thanks to the successful Inchon invasion), the wreckage of this aircraft was found in a valley: the F-82 had hit a cable deliberately strung between two mountains. At such a low altitude, the crew probably had no chance to recover. The loss had a significant impact on the entire squadron.

A few weeks later (29 September), another tragedy struck the 68th. This time it was on friendly turf but, nevertheless, it was felt by every member of this small, specialised squadron. According to official records, Lieutenant Billy Stanton and R/O Captain Robert MacDonald had taken an F-82G (a/c number 46-373) for a test hop. During a series of manoeuvres, they had a mid-air collision with an F-80. Witnesses stated that immediately after the hit, the Twin Mustang wobbled for a few seconds and then plunged to the ground, killing both crew members. The F-80, although seriously damaged, was able to make a safe landing at Itazuke, with its pilot uninjured.

No more replacement F-82s were coming into the Far East, so this was an attrition rate that the squadrons could ill afford.

Weather reconnaissance

During the final two months of 1950, the role of the 68th had been limited to weather reconnaissance over North Korea. There were a few exceptions, however, when the Twins were summoned in marginal weather conditions to assist UN troops hitting pockets of resistance.

The F-82 could range from Itazuke all the way to the Yalu River, drop its ordnance and get back easily to Japan. A good example of its enormous range is related by a 68th pilot, Lieutenant R.K. Bobo. "The weather recces we flew were, in most cases, a bore! Sometime we were ordered to look at a specific target or a series of targets, but most of the time it was just general conditions over a wide area that the fighter-bombers were going to hit later that day. On this type of mission, we usually carried a full load of 0.50-in ammunition and drop tanks.

"On one flight, we took off from Kimpo AB and headed north. Our job was to fly up to the Yalu and then head east, flying parallel to the river. All of North Korea was under a heavy cloud cover and the Yalu was frozen over, so that made the radar almost useless since we depended on it to show the difference between open water and land. The high winds were also a factor on this day. As we turned to the east, my R/O, Ray Ruscoe, established an ETA for hitting the Sea of Japan on the radar, but we flew for a long time and still no sign of the sea. We just kept flying in that direction, thinking the headwinds could have thrown us off. It seemed like we had flown forever when Ruscoe finally told me he could see water ahead.

"When we were out over the sea, we turned south, following the coastline. We had a DF station at Wonson and I started calling them for a fix. It took a while to get them on the radio and when we did, they told us we were still far to their northeast! We finally passed over the station and went back to Kimpo AB. We recomputed our time, speed and headings and came to the conclusion that we had been given the reciprocal direction for the wind, and figuring the time we flew and replotting where we must have flown, it had us practically right over Vladivostok! Certainly, we spent a lot of time over their territory. I've often wondered why they didn't come up to intercept us, but figured they must have decided we were no threat. I'm sure they had us on their radar from the time we took off from Kimpo! It could have been a very hazardous mission for us!"

Over a two-year period, several F-82 aircrews and aircraft were lost. On 12 February 1951, one of these tragic accidents occurred close to Itazuke AB. During a routine test hop, the pilot, Lieutenant George Boughton, was killed; R/O Lieutenant Frederick Reberg managed to bail out successfully, and remembers that ill-fated

A pair of war-weary 68th F-82Gs flies in formation over the Sea of Japan while returning from an early 1951 weather recon mission. As well as these and strip alert duties, F-82s were occasionally called upon to perform visual recce missions, and to provide long-endurance night combat air patrols.

Twin Mustang in Korea

Left: Two Twin Mustangs head into North Korean airspace at first light. Having transited from Japan as a pair, the aircraft would have individual weather recon assignments to be performed, before they joined up again for the flight home.

Below: On 6 November 1951 this 68th F-82G came to grief while landing at Suwon (K-13) in poor visibility shortly before sunset. The mainwheels struck the ground hard, and sheared off. Luckily, the aircraft slid along on its belly, discarding propellers and other accoutrements as it proceeded. It came to a gentle stop in soft mud, allowing its uninjured occupants an unimpeded, if rather hasty, egress.

flight. "The day before the accident, George and I had flown a mission over North Korea that lasted over six hours. Most of the missions at that time in the war followed the same pattern: after standing alert at Taegu AB, we would fly a CAP over Pyongyang and then fly east just below the Chinese border, over to the coast. From there we would head back to our base in Japan. On 12 February we were assigned to fly a test hop to check out an F-82 that had reported elevator problems.

"About 20 minutes into the flight, we experienced a jammed elevator. After 10 minutes of trying to free it up, George decided that we should bail out. For some reason, the hydraulic boost failed, leaving George to fight the problem with just his strength. He held the aircraft in a bank while I bailed out. There were a couple of F-86s in the vicinity, so one followed my descent to the ground while the other stayed with the stricken F-82. George was not able to get out of the aircraft because he was just too physically exhausted. This was a real tragedy for all of us."

Transition to the F-94

By the end of August 1951, only eight F-82Gs remained operational in the 68th Squadron. With the huge numbers of fighter-bomber types and the presence of two full wings of Sabres in-theatre, the importance of the Twin Mustangs lessened. The new F-94Bs began arriving at Itazuke on 10 October and by the end of that

Both carrying the 68th FIS badge, an F-82G and Lockheed F-94B share the pierced steel matting at Suwon. During the long transition period between the two types, which lasted from October 1951 to March 1952, the 68th was tasked with supplying three Twin Mustangs and two of the new jets for the Suwon strip alert detachment, which provided night-fighter protection for the Seoul region. Maintaining F-94s on alert at Suwon, as well as other alert commitments at Johnson and Misawa in Japan, was deemed to be too much of a burden for the 68th. As a consequence, the Suwon detachment was replaced by the full strength of the 319th FIS and its F-94s, moved forward to the war zone from McChord AFB, Washington.

month there were 11, although during October they were flown only in a training role within the squadron. From the USAF's point of view, this left only two vintage prop types involved in combat missions, with the F-51 still carrying a heavy commitment to the fighter-bomber mission in Korea.

Historical documents from the 68th state that in October the new Starfires were flown a total of 84 hours, while the F-82 logged 498 hours. Probably the most significant event, to the veteran personnel of the 68th, was the milestone of an F-82 (a/c number 46-383) reaching the 100-combat flight hour mark. It was the first squadron aircraft to achieve this. This F-82 had made the first kill of the Korean War and was a high-timer in the fighter-bomber role many months later.

Of the first seven pilots and five R/Os who became combat-ready in the F-94B, none had F-82 experience. All were assigned to the Misawa detachment for alert duties. Officially, the first operational test of the F-94 began on Thanksgiving Day 1951. During that month, 68th figures show that the F-94s logged 223 hours of flight time, while the F-82s dropped to 299. Of this, the latter spent 219 hours in a hostile environment, performing weather

reconnaissance, interdiction, armed reconnaissance, etc. After losing one of its Twins in November in a landing accident, the squadron was down to a total of 10 – and with the lack of spare parts, there was no way to get all 10 airborne.

For some reason, in October the 68th was called to Suwon (K-13), where it weighed in heavily in the armed reconnaissance role. Most of these missions were launched with at least two 500-lb (227-kg) bombs on each F-82. All loading, servicing and recovering was undertaken at Suwon, meaning the rotation of pilots and R/Os from Itazuke lasted 30 to 60 days.

March 1952 proved to be the final effective month for the Twin Mustang in the Far East. By then, the F-94s had come on line with all three squadrons and had completely taken over the all-weather/nocturnal responsibilities. The Suwon commitment was discontinued officially on 23 March. Squadron records show that the F-82s were ferried to Kisarazu, Japan, during that month, the last one flying out on 28 March. Quite a few of these aircraft were shipped to Alaska for all-weather duty. From there, they disappeared into oblivion, remembered only by the crews who flew and serviced them.

Warren E. Thompson

Canadair CP-107 Argus

'Hundred-eyed all-seeing Beast'

Still ranked as one of the most outstanding Canadian design achievements, Canadair's Argus was the world's most advanced anti-submarine warfare aircraft at the time of its introduction in 1959. Based on Bristol's Britannia airliner, the Argus spent its entire 23-year front-line career countering the biggest Cold War threat to western security – the Soviet submarine force.

In late 1949, Canadair began to formulate a proposal to the Royal Canadian Air Force for a new long-range maritime patrol aircraft to replace its Lancasters. The proposal that it submitted to the Department of National Defence was for a stretched version of the North Star (which Canadair was producing as a licence-built derivative of the C-54 and DC-4) powered by either Wright R-3350, Bristol Hercules 763, or Bristol Centaurus 661 radial engines.

The RCAF began looking for a replacement for its Avro Lancaster MR.Mk 10s (built in Canada by Victory Aircraft) in 1952, when it issued its requirements for a long-range patrol aircraft equipped with sophisticated detection and weapons systems. Bristol proposed a version of its Britannia 100 turboprop airliner, and Lockheed submitted a proposal based on its Super Constellation. Canadair was asked to evaluate the requirements and prepare several design studies to meet them, at least one of which was for a completely new aircraft.

The RCAF's interest in the Bristol Type 175 (later named Britannia), which had made its first flight on 16 August 1952, led to it awarding a contract to study a derivative of the British

aircraft. The Lockheed design was ruled out due to its inability to manoeuvre safely at low altitudes and low speeds. Canadair then proposed its Model CL-33 as a low-cost alternative. It was basically a large, unpressurised Lancaster that weighed about 9000 kg (19,840 lb) less than the Britannia and was powered by R-3350s. (The CL-29 and CL-31 were other maritime patrol aircraft design proposals and the CL-32 was an Americanised Britannia.)

Britannia basis

However, Air Marshal Wilf Curtis preferred the Britannia because it could be adapted as both a patrol aircraft and a transport to replace the North Star. Also, by using the Britannia as a starting point, considerable time and money were saved when compared with developing a completely new design. It was eventually decided to proceed in this way and Canadair began negotiations with Bristol. As an interim measure, 25 Lockheed Model 826-45-14 P2V-7 Neptunes were ordered in 1953.

In mid-1953, a combined Canadair/RCAF team visited Bristol to evaluate the Britannia as the basis for a long-range maritime patrol and

anti-submarine warfare aircraft. Initial concerns that its tab-operated ailerons would not provide sufficient manoeuvrability at low speeds were countered by the addition of spoilers to augment roll control.

By the end of 1953, the Royal Canadian Air Force had decided on a Britannia Type 175 derivative. On 23 February 1954, the government announced that Canadair would build the new aircraft under licence. On 16 March 1954, a licence agreement was signed with the Bristol Aeroplane Company that allowed the development and manufacture of both a maritime reconnaissance version, which became the CP-107 Argus, and a transport version, which became the CC-106 Yukon. On 27 May 1954, Ottawa awarded Canadair an initial contract.

The go-ahead order was received by Canadair in April 1954 under Model Specification RD-28-103, Issue 2. Contract Demand CD 362007 was raised in the amount of \$C85,876,670 and covered one pre-production and 12 production aircraft, 52 installed engines, an unknown number of spare engines, other spares, and publications. It is unknown if this contract also included the Operational Flight Tactical Trainer or if a separate, later contract was issued. The contract was subsequently reduced by \$C12,725,000 when it was realised that the engines were to be supplied by Canadair as part of the aircraft, rather than provided by the government to Canadair as government-furnished aircraft equipment.

The Model CL-28 (as it was known to Canadair) was considered to be a development